CORE
MATHEMATICS PRINCIPLES
WITH OVER
500
WORKED PROBLEMS

SKILLS FOR SENIOR HIGH SCHOOL STUDENTS

ALOYSIUS ASEERVATHAM

Inquiries and Book Orders should be addressed to:

Great Writers Media
Email: info@greatwritersmedia.com
Phone: 877-600-5469

ISBN: 978-1-959493-52-5 (sc)
ISBN: 978-1-959493-53-2 (ebk)

PREFACE

Almost 50 years of teaching mathematics in Australia, Asia, Europe and Africa has confirmed one of my firmest beliefs. For students to excel in mathematics, they must practice their skills. They must solve problems. The problems must be varied, with different parameters, knowns, unknowns and constraints, for students to flexibly exercise their foundational knowledge and build confidence in applying mathematical techniques.

While many textbooks offer the variety of problems needed and the answers to the problems, students often remark that they cannot find enough worked solutions to guide their study. Without worked solutions, a student's ability to self-teach problem-solving is limited. The purpose of this book is to put the considerable power of self-study back into students' hands.

The pedagogical features of this book follow a deliberate pattern aimed at guiding students comprehensively through problem-solving. Basic mathematical concepts are presented with an explanation of the principles involved. Simple examples help convey the application of these concepts, and they are followed by a set of problems with detailed answers to each problem. Some practical application questions, with answers, are provided to illustrate how real-life mathematical problems are approached. Finally, a set of problems, the "Practice set", is provided with answers. Students should try and reach the answers themselves before referring to the detailed working.

This book includes, among other topics, fractions, factorisation, matrices, linear equations, non-linear equations, geometry and statistics.

I hope this approach to confident mathematical problem-solving provides students with an easier way to gain mastery of the subject.

AA

August 2019

1

TABLE OF CONTENTS

1. FRACTIONS, PERCENTAGES, RATIO & PROPORTION

A **fraction** is simply a part of a whole. If we draw a circle and then draw a diameter (a line through the centre of the circle), it divides the circle into two equal parts. Each equal part is called a **half** of the whole circle.

 The word 'half' is written '$\frac{1}{2}$'. **Two halves make one whole.**

If we draw another diameter perpendicular to the first one, we divide the circle into four equal parts. Each equal part is called a **quarter**.

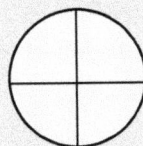 The word quarter is written '$\frac{1}{4}$'. **Four quarters make one whole.**

A circle could be divided into any number of equal parts and a certain number of the equal parts expressed as a "fraction" of the total of all equal parts e.g. $\frac{5}{16}$, $\frac{7}{12}$ and so on.

A fraction thus expressed is called the **common fraction**. A common fraction has a number above a horizontal line called the **numerator** and a number below the horizontal line called the **denominator**. A **proper fraction** is one with the numerator less than the denominator.

- If the numerator is greater than the denominator, it is referred to as an **improper fraction** e.g. $\frac{4}{3}$, $\frac{7}{6}$, $\frac{9}{4}$ and so on.

- An improper fraction may be written as a **mixed number** (i.e. a whole number and a proper fraction). For example, $\frac{4}{3}$ as a mixed number is $1\frac{1}{3}$.

An ability to work out the biggest number (**Highest Common Factor, HCF**) that can divide each of a given set of numbers and a smallest number that could be divided by each of these numbers (**Lowest Common Multiple, LCM**) is important when working with fractions.

Consider the set of numbers: 15, 30 and 45.
Formal method of determining the HCF and LCM of these numbers is shown below:

15 = **3 × 5**	3 and 5 are called prime factors
30 = **2 × 3 × 5**	2, 3 and 5 are called prime factors
45 = **3 × 3 × 5**	3 and 5 are called prime factors

Find the factor common to the three numbers (if more than one as in this case, multiply them) to get the HCF. The answer is 3 × 5 = **15**. 15 is therefore the highest number that can divide all three numbers 15, 30 and 45. In order to find the LCM, just multiply the HCF by the remaining numbers 2 and 3. The LCM is therefore 15 × 2 × 3 = **90**. That is, 90 is the smallest number which each of 15, 30 and 45 can divide (without a remainder).

Consider a more general case with numbers 18, 48 and 96. We express each of the three numbers again as a product of its prime factors.

$$18 = \mathbf{2} \times \mathbf{3} \times 3$$

$$48 = \mathbf{2} \times 2 \times 2 \times 2 \times \mathbf{3}$$

$$96 = \mathbf{2} \times 2 \times 2 \times 2 \times 2 \times \mathbf{3}$$

HCF = 2 × 3 = 6

In this case, we even take the factor that is common for only two numbers and multiply the HCF with it.

LCM = 6 × 2 × 2 × 2 × 2 × 3 = 288

Note that three pairs of 2 are common to two numbers only and they multiply the HCF together with the other isolated 2 and 3.

The numerator and denominator of a fraction can be multiplied by a given number without affecting the fraction. The resulting fraction is called its **equivalent fraction.**

- One equivalent fraction of $\frac{1}{2}$ is $\frac{2}{4}$. Here the numerator and denominator are multiplied by 2

- The equivalent fraction of $\frac{1}{2}$ is $\frac{3}{6}, \frac{4}{8}, \frac{5}{10}$ etc. when the number used as the multiplier is 3, 4, 5 and so on

A COMMON FRACTION EXPRESSED AS A DECIMAL FRACTION

The simplest case is when the denominator of an equivalent fraction of a given common fraction is able to be expressed as a power of 10 (i.e. 10, 100, 1000, 10000 etc.) For example, the fraction $\frac{1}{2}$ can be expressed as its equivalent fraction $\frac{5}{10}$ with 10 in the denominator.

$\frac{1}{2} = \frac{5}{10} = \mathbf{0.5}$. The decimal fraction **0.5** is obtained by counting the number of zeros in the denominator and then counting to the left that many places from the numerator and placing a dot (or a decimal point). If there are not enough digits in the numerator, then a zero (or zeros) will have to be inserted as shown in the examples below:

- The decimal fraction equivalent of $\frac{1}{4}$ (i.e. $\frac{25}{100}$) is 0.25

- The decimal fraction equivalent of $\frac{1}{20}$ (i.e. $\frac{5}{100}$) is 0.05

- The decimal fraction equivalent of $\frac{3}{8}$ (i.e. $\frac{375}{1000}$) is 0.375

- The decimal fraction equivalent of $\frac{18}{5}$ (i.e. $\frac{360}{100}$) is 3.60

Notice that if there is no non-zero digit before the decimal point, a zero is inserted.

As a general rule, any common fraction (proper or improper) can be expressed as a decimal fraction by dividing the numerator by the denominator. A calculator helps here. A decimal fraction could be a **terminating** one, **recurring** or a **non-recurring**.

- 0.225, 0.875 are terminating decimal fractions.

- 0.33333........., 0.128128......... are recurring decimal fractions.

- 0.0434782......., 0.977528......... are non-recurring decimal fractions.

Decimal fractions could be rounded to the nearest whole number or corrected to a required number of decimal places. (usually the **rounding up** is followed when the digit to the right of the required number of place is 5 or more)

- 23.6754 to the nearest whole number is 24

- 23.6754 corrected to two places of decimals is 23.68

- 23.6754 corrected to one decimal place is 23.7

- 23.6754 corrected to three decimal places is 23.675

When rounding is done to a stated number of **significant digits,** the following rules are followed.

Non-zero digits are always significant for a decimal fraction. When there are zeros in the fraction, the following rules apply:

1. Zeros placed before other digits but immediately after the decimal point are not significant (0.092 has two significant digits).

2. Zeros placed between other digits are always significant (0.3004 has four significant digits).

3. Zeros placed after other digits but behind a decimal point are significant (1.20 has three significant digits).

Example 1:

Arrange the following fractions in the ascending order:

(a) $\dfrac{7}{8}, \dfrac{3}{4}, \dfrac{5}{6}, \dfrac{11}{12}, \dfrac{15}{16}$

(b) $\dfrac{3}{17}, \dfrac{4}{19}, \dfrac{5}{26}, \dfrac{6}{29}$

Solution:

(a) The LCM of the denominators of the given fractions is 96

$$\dfrac{7}{8}, \quad \dfrac{3}{4}, \quad \dfrac{5}{6}, \quad \dfrac{11}{12}, \quad \dfrac{15}{16}$$

$$= \dfrac{84}{96}, \quad \dfrac{72}{96}, \quad \dfrac{80}{96}, \quad \dfrac{88}{96}, \quad \dfrac{90}{96}$$

Therefore, the required ascending order is: $= \dfrac{3}{4}, \dfrac{5}{6}, \dfrac{7}{8}, \dfrac{11}{12}, \dfrac{15}{16}$

Example 1 (continued):

(b) $\dfrac{3}{17}, \quad \dfrac{4}{19}, \quad \dfrac{5}{26}, \quad \dfrac{6}{29}$

= 0.176, 0.211, 0.192, 0.207

Therefore, the required ascending order is: $\dfrac{3}{17}, \dfrac{5}{26}, \dfrac{6}{29}, \dfrac{4}{19}$

Example 2:

Find the difference between the largest and the smallest of the following:

(a) $\dfrac{1}{3}, \dfrac{2}{5}, \dfrac{3}{8}, \dfrac{4}{7}, \dfrac{5}{11}$

(b) $\dfrac{5}{12}, \dfrac{5}{6}, 0.16, \dfrac{2}{5}, 0.25, 0.1$

Solution:

(a) $\dfrac{1}{3}, \quad \dfrac{2}{5}, \quad \dfrac{3}{8}, \quad \dfrac{4}{7}, \quad \dfrac{5}{11}$

= 0.33, 0.40, 0.375, 0.57, 0.45

The largest number is $\dfrac{4}{7}$ and the smallest number is $\dfrac{1}{3}$.

The difference is: $\dfrac{5}{21}$ or 0.24

(b) $\dfrac{5}{12}, \quad \dfrac{5}{6}, \quad 0.16, \quad \dfrac{2}{5}, \quad 0.25, 0.1$

= 0.42, 0.83, 0.16, 0.4, 0.25, 0.1

The largest number is $\dfrac{5}{6}$ and the smallest number is 0.1

The difference is 0.73

ADDING FRACTIONS

Example 1:

Simplify: $\dfrac{4}{7} + \dfrac{3}{8}$

LCM of 7 and 8 = 56

$\dfrac{4}{7} + \dfrac{3}{8} = \dfrac{32}{56} + \dfrac{21}{56} = \dfrac{53}{56}$

Notice the equivalent fractions and the same denominator of the two fractions.

Example 2:

Simplify: $2\frac{2}{9} + 3\frac{5}{6}$

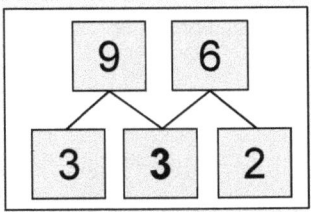

$= 2 + \frac{2}{9} + 3 + \frac{5}{6} = 5 + \frac{2}{9} + \frac{5}{6}$

LCM of 9 and 6 is $3 \times 3 \times 2 = 18$

Therefore: $2\frac{2}{9} + 3\frac{5}{6} = 5 + \frac{4}{18} + \frac{15}{18} = 5 + \frac{19}{18} = 5 + 1 + \frac{1}{18} = 6\frac{1}{18}$

Example 3:

Simplify: $\frac{29}{11} + \frac{13}{8} + 1\frac{5}{6}$

Here, firstly we can either change the mixed number to improper fraction or change the improper fractions to mixed numbers. Working with mixed numbers:

$\frac{29}{11} + \frac{13}{8} + 1\frac{5}{6} = \frac{29}{11} + \frac{13}{8} + \frac{11}{6}$

The LCM of 11, 8 and 6 is: $11 \times 4 \times 2 \times 3 = 264$

$= \frac{696}{264} + \frac{429}{264} + \frac{484}{264} = \frac{1609}{264} = 6\frac{25}{264}$

Example 4:

Simplify: $3.34 + 0.078 + 7$

Line the decimals up:
```
    3.34
    0.078
  + 7.
```

"Pad" with zeros:
```
    3.340
    0.078
Add:  + 7.000
    10.418
```

SUBTRACTING FRACTIONS

Example 1:

Simplify: $\frac{7}{10} - \frac{8}{15}$ | The LCM of 10 and 15 is 30 |

Therefore: $\frac{7}{10} - \frac{8}{15} = \frac{21}{30} - \frac{16}{30} = \frac{5}{30} = \frac{1}{6}$

Example 2:

Simplify: $2\frac{14}{19} - \frac{8}{7}$

Change the mixed number to an improper fraction and then subtract:

$$2\frac{14}{19} - \frac{8}{7} = \frac{52}{19} - \frac{8}{7} = \frac{364}{133} - \frac{152}{133} = \frac{212}{133} = 1\frac{79}{133}$$

Example 3:

Simplify: $4\frac{1}{3} - 1\frac{5}{7} - \frac{13}{6}$

$$= 4 + \frac{1}{3} - 1 - \frac{5}{7} - 2 - \frac{1}{6} = 1 + \frac{1}{3} - \frac{5}{7} - \frac{1}{6}$$

$$= 1 + \frac{14}{42} - \frac{30}{42} - \frac{7}{42} = 1 - \frac{23}{42} = \frac{42}{42} - \frac{23}{42} = \frac{19}{42}$$

Example 4:

Simplify: $2.874 - 0.078 - 1.332$

There are two methods of doing this:

Method 1: Subtract 0.078 from 2.874 and from the result subtract 1.332:

$$
\begin{array}{r} 2.874 \\ -\ 0.078 \\ \hline 2.796 \end{array}
\qquad
\begin{array}{r} 2.796 \\ -\ 1.332 \\ \hline 1.464 \end{array}
$$

Method 2: Add 0.078 and 1.332 and subtract the result from 2.874:

$$
\begin{array}{r} 0.078 \\ +\ 1.332 \\ \hline 1.410 \end{array}
\qquad
\begin{array}{r} 2.874 \\ -\ 1.410 \\ \hline 1.464 \end{array}
$$

MULTIPLICATION OF FRACTIONS

A fraction can be multiplied by a whole number or by another fraction. It is necessary to first express all fractions as improper fractions. It is usual to look for all possible common factors that can divide a number on the "top" and a number at the "bottom". The resulting fraction that is obtained by multiplying the remaining numbers on top and bottom will be in the lowest possible term. Answer in improper fraction has to be converted to a mixed number. The examples that follow will make this clear.

Example 1:

Simplify: $\frac{15}{28} \times 1\frac{2}{5} \times \frac{3}{1}$

$$= \frac{\overset{3}{\cancel{15}}}{\underset{4}{\cancel{28}}} \times \frac{\cancel{7}}{\cancel{5}} \times \frac{3}{1} = \frac{9}{4} = 2\frac{1}{4}$$

Example 2:

Simplify: $\frac{3}{5}$ of $(\frac{1}{3} \times 2\frac{1}{2})^3$

Here we have to simplify what is within the parenthesis first and then raise the result to the power 3 (i.e. multiply the result 3 times by itself). The operation "of" has the same meaning as multiplication.

$$\frac{3}{5} \text{ of } (\frac{1}{3} \times 2\frac{1}{2})^3 = \frac{3}{5} \times (\frac{5}{6})^3 = \frac{\cancel{3}}{\cancel{5}} \times \frac{5}{6^2} \times \frac{5}{6} \times \frac{5}{6} = \frac{25}{72}$$

DIVIDING A FRACTION BY A FRACTION

The rule for dividing a number or a fraction (**dividend**) by another fraction (**divisor**) is to **invert the divisor and multiply the dividend**.

Dividing 1 by $\frac{1}{2}$ can be written as $\dfrac{1}{\frac{1}{2}}$

The answer is $1 \times \frac{2}{1} = 2$ | There are two halves in a whole |

Example 1:

Simplify: $\dfrac{\frac{9}{28} \times \frac{1}{6}}{\frac{4}{3} \times 1\frac{3}{14}}$

$$= \dfrac{\frac{9}{28} \times \frac{1}{6}}{\frac{4}{3} \times 1\frac{3}{14}} = \frac{9}{28^2} \times \frac{1}{6^2} \times \frac{3^1}{4} \times \frac{14^1}{17} = \frac{9}{272}$$

COMBINED OPERATIONS

The four arithmetic operations — addition, subtraction, multiplication and division when combined in a question together with parenthesis could produce the wrong answer if **BOMDAS** rule is not followed.

The BOMDAS (or BODMAS) rule

Brackets (parentheses) first i.e. simplify the numbers within the brackets and remove them. Three types of brackets namely simple, curly and square are used with fractions and have to be removed in that order.

Orders (of, Powers and Square Roots, Cube Roots, etc.) next

MD (or DM) → Multiplication and Division (start from left to right) thirdly.

AS → Addition and Subtraction (start from left to right) fourthly.

Example 1:

Simplify: $20\frac{5}{8} \div 3\frac{3}{4} - \frac{5}{8} \times 4\frac{4}{5} + 2\frac{2}{3} \div 1\frac{3}{4}$

$$= \frac{165}{8} \times \frac{4}{15} - \frac{5}{8} \times \frac{24}{5} + \frac{8}{3} \times \frac{4}{7} = \frac{11}{2} - 3 + \frac{32}{21}$$

LCM $= 2 \times 21 = 42$

$$= \frac{231}{42} - \frac{126}{42} + \frac{64}{42} = \frac{169}{42} = 4\frac{1}{42}$$

Example 2:

Simplify: $\dfrac{1\frac{7}{8} - \frac{1}{2} - \frac{1}{4}}{2\frac{1}{5} \div 3\frac{3}{5} \text{ of } 1\frac{2}{9}}$

$$= \frac{\frac{15}{8} - \frac{1}{2} - \frac{1}{4}}{2\frac{1}{5} \div 3\frac{3}{5} \text{ of } 1\frac{2}{9}} = \frac{\frac{15}{8} - \frac{4}{8} - \frac{2}{8}}{2\frac{1}{5} \div \frac{18}{5} \times \frac{11}{9}} = \frac{\frac{9}{8}}{2\frac{1}{5} \div \frac{22}{5}} = \frac{\frac{9}{8}}{\frac{11}{5} \times \frac{5}{22}} = \frac{\frac{9}{8}}{\frac{1}{2}} = \frac{9}{8^4} \times \frac{2^1}{1} = \frac{9}{4} = 2\frac{1}{4}$$

Example 3:

Simplify: $\dfrac{1.21 - 0.2025}{2.015} \times 4.03$

$$= \frac{1.21 - 0.2025}{2.015} \times 4.03 = \frac{1.0075}{2.015} \times 4.03 = \frac{10075 \times 403}{2015000} = \frac{10075}{5000} = 2.015$$

Example 4:

Simplify: $[\{\frac{1}{2} \times (\frac{3}{4} \div \frac{3}{2}) + 3(\frac{1}{3} + \frac{5}{3})\} \times 4] \div 5$

$$= [\{\frac{1}{2} \times \frac{3}{4} \times \frac{2}{3} + 3 \times 2\} \times 4] \div 5 = [\{\frac{1}{4} + 3 \times 2\} \times 4] \div 5$$

$$= [6\frac{1}{4} \times 4] \div 5 = 25 \div 5 = 5$$

Example 5:

Simplify: $\dfrac{4\frac{2}{5} - 2\frac{1}{4} + 1\frac{2}{3} - \frac{1}{4}}{(4\frac{1}{5} - 3\frac{1}{4}) \div 1\frac{2}{3} \text{ of } \frac{1}{4}} \div \dfrac{\frac{3}{4} - \frac{2}{3}}{\frac{3}{4} + \frac{2}{3}}$

$$= \frac{\frac{22}{5} - \frac{9}{4} + \frac{5}{3} - \frac{1}{4}}{(\frac{21}{5} - \frac{13}{4}) \div \frac{5}{3} \text{ of } \frac{1}{4}} \div \frac{\frac{3}{4} - \frac{2}{3}}{\frac{3}{4} + \frac{2}{3}} = \frac{\frac{264}{60} - \frac{135}{60} + \frac{100}{60} - \frac{15}{60}}{(\frac{84}{20} - \frac{65}{20}) \div \frac{5}{3} \times \frac{1}{4}} \div \frac{\frac{9}{12} - \frac{8}{12}}{\frac{9}{12} + \frac{8}{12}} = \frac{\frac{214}{60}}{\frac{19}{20} \times \frac{12}{5}} \div \frac{\frac{9}{12} - \frac{8}{12}}{\frac{9}{12} + \frac{8}{12}}$$

$$= \frac{\frac{214}{60}}{\frac{57}{25}} \div \frac{1}{17} = \frac{214}{60} \times \frac{25}{57} \times 17 = \frac{107}{6} \times \frac{5}{57} \times 17 = \frac{9095}{342} = 26\frac{203}{342}$$

10

EXPRESSING COMMON & DECIMAL FRACTIONS AS PERCENTAGES

A common or decimal fraction when multiplied by 100 gives a result which is termed **percentage**. For example, the common fractions $\frac{1}{2}$ and $\frac{1}{4}$ when multiplied by 100 becomes 50 percent and 25 percent respectively.

The symbol for percentage is '%'

A percentage could be changed to a fraction by dividing by 100 and expressing the result in its simplest form. For example, 80% expressed as a fraction would be 80/100 $= \frac{4}{5}$ or 0.8, 125% is $\frac{125}{100} = 1\frac{1}{4}$ or 1.25. Some fractions expressed in the three forms are given. These should be memorised.

Common fraction	Decimal Fraction	Percentage (%)
$\frac{1}{4}$	0.25	25
$\frac{1}{2}$	0.5	50
$\frac{3}{4}$	0.75	75
$\frac{1}{8}$	0.125	$12\frac{1}{2}$ (12.5)
$\frac{3}{8}$	0.375	$37\frac{1}{2}$ (37.5)
$\frac{5}{8}$	0.625	$62\frac{1}{2}$ (62.5)
$\frac{7}{8}$	0.875	$87\frac{1}{2}$ (87.5)

CALCULATING INCREASED AND DECREASED VALUES

A given number can be increased or decreased by a stated percentage.

$$\text{Percentage increase (decrease)} = \frac{\text{Increase (or decrease)}}{\text{Original value}} \times 100$$

- Increased value = Original value + Percentage increase applied to the original value
- Decreased value = Original value − Percentage decrease applied to the original value

Example 1:

   If $80 is increased to $96, what is the percentage increase?

Solution:

Increase = $96 − $80 = $16

Percentage increase $= \frac{16}{80} \times 100 = 20$

Example 2:

If \$80 is decreased to \$60, what is the percentage decrease?

Solution:

Decrease = \$80 − \$60 = \$20

Percentage decrease = $\dfrac{20}{80} \times 100 = 25$

Example 3:

If the number 50 is increased by 10%, what is the increased value?

Solution:

Increased value = 50 + 10% of 50 = 50 + 5 = 55 or 50 × 1.1 = 55

Example 4:

If the number 120 is decreased by 30%, what is the decreased value?

Solution:

Decreased value = 120 − 30% of 120 = 120 − 36 = 84 or 120 × 0.7 = 84

The following table gives additional examples of increased and decreased value.

Original Number	Percentage increase or decrease	Increased value	Decreased value
60	10	60 × 1.1 = 66	60 × 0.9 = 54
90	20	90 × 1.2 = 108	90 × 0.8 = 72
80	25	80 × 1.25 = 100	80 × 0.75 = 60
112	40	112 × 1.4 = 156.8	112 × 0.6 = 67.2
130	50	130 × 1.5 = 195	130 × 0.5 = 65

FINDING THE "WHOLE" FROM A PERCENTAGE OF WHOLE

Percentage of whole	Value	Whole
26%	52	(52/26) × 100 = 200
10%	80	(80/10) × 100 = 800
90%	810	(810/90) × 100 = 900
120%	240	(240/120) × 100 = 200

Percentages are widely used in real life. In business, we calculate percentage profit or percentage loss, the interest payable or receivable using a percentage rate of interest, apply percentage tax rates to calculate tax payable on incomes and profits.   Increases and decreases in the items such as sales, expenses, population etc. when expressed as a percentage increase or decrease are easy to understand.

PERCENTAGE PROFIT OR LOSS

Businesses buy and sell or manufacture and sell goods. The amount of money they spend on getting the goods for sale is called **Cost Price** (CP). The actual price for which they sell the goods to the customers is called the **Selling Price** (SP). Profit (or loss) refers to the difference in the selling price and the cost price. The percentage profit or loss is calculated as follows:

$$\text{Percentage profit/loss} = \frac{\text{Profit (or Loss)}}{\text{Cost Price}} \times 100$$

In practice, the businesses put a percentage mark up on cost to get the marked price and then give a reduction on the marked price called percentage discount and call the result the selling price.

$$\text{Percentage mark-up} = \frac{\text{Mark-up}}{\text{Cost Price}} \times 100$$

$$\text{Percentage discount} = \frac{\text{Discount}}{\text{Marked Price}} \times 100$$

Example:

An item which cost $80 is marked as $120 and sold at a discount of 20%. What is:
(i) the percentage mark-up
(ii) the discount amount
(ii) the final selling price
(iv) the percentage profit?

Solution:

Mark-up = $120 − $80 = $40

(i) Percentage mark-up = $\dfrac{40}{80} \times 100 = 50$

(ii) Discount = 20% of 120 = $\dfrac{1}{5} \times 120 = \$24$

(iii) Selling price = $120 − $24 = $96

(iv) Percentage profit = $\dfrac{96 - 80}{80} \times 100 = 20$

INTEREST

Interest is a reward to the lender paid by the borrower. It is usually expressed as a percentage of the money lent payable for a year e.g. 9% per annum (for a year). If money is borrowed for a period other than a year, the interest is pro-rated.

Example:

> Amount borrowed = $1,000, Interest per annum = 8%

Calculate the interest payable for:
(i) one year
(ii) 6 months
(iii) 3 months
(iv) 73 days

Solution:

(i) Interest payable for one year = $1,000 \times \dfrac{8}{100}$ = $80

(ii) Interest payable for 6 months = $\dfrac{1}{2} \times 80$ = $40

(iii) Interest payable for 3 months = $\dfrac{1}{2} \times 40$ = $20

(iv) Interest payable for 73 days = $\dfrac{73}{365} \times 80$ = $16

COMMISSION

A **Commission** is a reward paid to sales people to motivate them. It is a form of variable-pay remuneration for services rendered or products sold. It is usually paid as a percentage of the sales value.

Example 1:

> A sales person is paid a salary of $1,200 per week plus a commission of 7% on all sales. If the sales for a week is $6,200, What would be earnings for the week?

Solution:

Commission earned = $6,200 \times \dfrac{8}{100}$ = $496

Earnings for the week = $1,200 + $496 = $1,696

Example 2:

> A car salesperson received a commission of $4 800 for the month of January. If the commission is 6% of all sales value, what was the value of sales for January?

Solution

6% of sales = $4,800

Sales value = $\dfrac{4800}{6} \times 100$ = $80,000

TAX

Taxing salaries and wages incomes of individuals and sales incomes and profits of businesses is a means by which governments finance their expenditure. The purpose of taxation is to accumulate funds for the functioning of the government machineries. Taxes are levied as a percentage according to the various Taxation laws.

In a progressive tax system, tax payable increases as an individual's income grows: Low incomes fall into tax brackets with relatively low income tax rates, while higher earnings fall into brackets with higher rates.

Example 1:

Calculate the sales tax that is included in receipts of $2,200 from items subject to sales tax of 10%.

Solution:

110% represents $2,200

Therefore $10\% = 2200 \times \dfrac{10}{110} = \$200$

Example 2:

Calculate the tax payable by an individual with a taxable income of $100,000 if the following tax rates are applicable.

0 – $18,200	Nil
$18,201 – $37,000	19c for each $1 over $18,200
$37,001 – $90,000	$3,572 plus 32.5c for each $1 over $37,000
$90,001 – $180,000	$20,797 plus 37c for each $1 over $90,000

Solution:

Tax payable $= \$20,797 + \dfrac{37}{100} \times 10\,000 = \$20,797 + \$3,700 = \$24,497$

FRACTION VS RATIO

A fraction compares a part to a whole. A ratio on the other hand is a relationship between two quantities. For example, if in a class of 24 students, there are 8 boys and 16 girls, the ratio of boy to girl is 1 to 2. It is customary to write this as:

Boy:Girl :: 1:2 | Read, Boy to Girl is as 1 to 2

Another way to describe the class situation is, one third (1/3) are boys and two thirds (2/3) are girls. A ratio when multiplied by any number will remain the same.

- The ratio 1:2 is the same as 2:4 = 3:6 = 4:8 etc.

They are all equivalent ratios. 1:2 is the simplest of the equivalent forms.

RATIOS OF FRACTIONS

Ratios of two fractions are usually expressed as ratios of two numbers.

Example 1:

Find the ratio of $\frac{2}{9}$ to $\frac{1}{6}$

The LCM of 9 and 6 = 18. Multiplying the two fractions by 18:

We state: $\frac{2}{9} : \frac{1}{6} = 4:3$

Example 2:

Find the ratio of $1\frac{1}{2}$ to $2\frac{1}{4}$

This is the same as $\frac{3}{2}$ to $\frac{9}{4}$

LCM of 2 and 4 is 4. Multiplying the two fractions by 4:

We state: $\frac{3}{2} : \frac{9}{4} = 6:9 = 2:3$

Example 3:

Find the ratio of 1.25:0.75

Multiplying each number by 100:

1.25:0.75 = 125:75 = 5:3 | Dividing by 25 |

RATIO vs PROPORTION

A ratio compares a part to another part. Proportion compares a part to the whole just like the common fraction.

Example:

I have $500 to give to my two sons, John and Peter. I give $300 to my older son John and $200 to my younger son Peter.
(i) In what ratio did I give the $500 to my two sons?
(ii) What proportion of $500 did each receive?

Solution:

(i) The ratio of my gift is: John:Peter = 300:200 = 3:2

(i) Proportion of $500 John received = $\frac{300}{500} = \frac{3}{5}$

Proportion Peter received = $\frac{200}{500} = \frac{3}{5}$

DIRECT AND INDIRECT PROPORTION

If two quantities are related in such a way that when one increases the other also increases and when one decreases the other also decreases, they are said to be in **direct proportion**.

If X and Y are in direct proportion, then the ratio $\dfrac{X}{Y}$ will remain the same (i.e. a constant).

Example:

When buying 6 apples, amount paid = $3

When buying 12 apples, amount paid = $6

When buying 3 apples, amount paid is $1.50.

That is, $\dfrac{3}{6} = \dfrac{6}{12} = \dfrac{1.5}{3}$ $\boxed{\text{constant } \dfrac{1}{2}}$

If two quantities are related in such a way that when one increases the other decreases and when one decreases the other increases, they are said to be in **indirect proportion**. If X and Y are in indirect proportion, then the product **XY** will remain the same (i.e. a constant).

Example:

When speed is 60km per hour, time taken to travel from A to B = 60 minutes = 1 hr

When speed is 90km per hour, time taken to travel from A to B = 40 minutes = $\dfrac{2}{3}$ hr

When speed is 40km per hour, time taken to travel from A to B = 90 minutes = 1.5 hr

That is, $60 \times 1 = 90 \times \dfrac{2}{3} = 40 \times 1.5$ $\boxed{\text{constant } 60}$

ALGEBRAIC FRACTIONS

Algebraic fractions are similar to common fractions but they have algebraic expressions in both the denominator and numerator or denominator only. The approach to simplifying them is also similar to common fractions. That is, firstly we need to find the lowest common multiple of the expressions in the denominators of the fractions concerned. The same rules for simplification (i.e. BODMAS) apply to algebraic fractions as well.

Example 1:

Simplify: $\dfrac{1}{x} + \dfrac{2}{y}$

LCM = xy

Therefore: $\dfrac{1}{x} + \dfrac{2}{y} = \dfrac{y + 2x}{xy}$

Example 2:

Simplify: $\dfrac{2}{x+3} - \dfrac{3}{2x+1}$

LCM $= (x+3)(2x+1)$

Therefore: $\dfrac{2}{x+3} - \dfrac{3}{2x+1} = \dfrac{2(2x+1) - 3(x+3)}{(x+3)(2x+1)} = \dfrac{4x+2-3x-9}{(x+3)(2x+1)} = \dfrac{x-7}{(x+3)(2x+1)}$

Example 3:

Simplify: $\dfrac{4}{x-1} + \dfrac{3}{x^2+1}$

LCM $= (x-1)(x^2+1)$

Therefore: $\dfrac{4}{x-1} + \dfrac{3}{x^2+1} = \dfrac{4(x^2+1) + 3(x-1)}{(x-1)(x^2+1)} = \dfrac{4x^2+4+3x-3}{(x-1)(x^2+1)} = \dfrac{4x^2+3x+1}{(x-1)(x^2+1)}$

Example 4:

Simplify: $\dfrac{3}{(x+1)(x+2)} - \dfrac{5}{(x+2)(x+3)}$

LCM $= (x+1)(x+2)(x+3)$

Therefore: $\dfrac{3}{(x+1)(x+2)} - \dfrac{5}{(x+2)(x+3)} = \dfrac{3(x+3) - 5(x+1)}{(x+1)(x+2)(x+3)}$

$= \dfrac{3x+9-5x-5}{(x+1)(x+2)(x+3)} = \dfrac{4-2x}{(x+1)(x+2)(x+3)}$

Example 5:

Simplify: $\dfrac{3}{2x} \times \dfrac{4}{x+1}$

Here, we simply multiply the numerators and denominators separately. The final answer is expressed in its simplest form.

$\dfrac{3}{2x} \times \dfrac{4}{x+1} = \dfrac{12}{2x(x+1)} = \dfrac{6}{x(x+1)}$ 2 goes into 12, 6 times

---

Example 6:

Simplify: $\dfrac{3x}{y} \div \dfrac{9}{x+1}$

Here, we follow the rule that when dividing, invert the divisor, and multiply. The final answer is expressed in its simplest form.

Therefore: $\dfrac{3x}{y} \div \dfrac{9}{x+1} = \dfrac{3x}{y} \times \dfrac{x+1}{9} = \dfrac{x(x+1)}{3y}$ 3 goes into 9, 3 times

The following problems require knowledge of factorisation. Refer to Chapter 2.

Example 7:

Simplify: $\dfrac{x^2 + 5x + 6}{x + 2}$

$$\dfrac{x^2 + 5x + 6}{x + 2} = \dfrac{(x + 3)(x + 2)}{x + 2} = x + 3$$

Example 8:

Simplify: $\dfrac{a^2 - 4a - 5}{a^2 - 25}$

$$\dfrac{a^2 - 4a - 5}{a^2 - 25} = \dfrac{(a + 1)(a - 5)}{(a + 5)(a - 5)} = \dfrac{(a + 1)}{(a + 5)}$$

Example 9:

Simplify: $\dfrac{m^2 + m - 6}{m^2 + 5m - 14} \times \dfrac{m^2 + 9m + 14}{m^2 - m - 12}$

$$\dfrac{m^2 + m - 6}{m^2 + 5m - 14} \times \dfrac{m^2 + 9m + 14}{m^2 - m - 12} = \dfrac{(m + 3)(m - 2)}{(m + 7)(m - 2)} \times \dfrac{(m + 7)(m + 2)}{(m + 3)(m - 4)} = \dfrac{(m + 2)}{(m - 4)}$$

MISCELLANEOUS PROBLEMS

1.(a) Simplify: $\dfrac{2\frac{1}{3} + 5\frac{2}{3} \div 2\frac{3}{7}}{7\frac{2}{9} + \frac{3}{4} \text{ of } 3\frac{2}{5}}$

(b) Simplify giving the answer corrected to three places of decimals: $\dfrac{5.894 \times 0.3869}{0.497}$

2.. Simplify: $\dfrac{2\frac{3}{7} + \frac{13}{4} \div 6\frac{1}{2}}{\left(3\frac{1}{8} \div 3\frac{1}{11}\right) \text{ of } 1\frac{2}{9}}$

3. Evaluate: (a) $1\frac{3}{8} - \dfrac{2\frac{1}{6} + \frac{2}{5}}{5\frac{1}{2} - 2\frac{17}{30}}$ (b) $\dfrac{0.086 \times \sqrt{0.057}}{0.00258}$

4. Last year a man's net income was \$48,000 and he spent $\dfrac{11}{15}$ of it. This year, his income increased by 20% and he spent $\dfrac{13}{16}$ of it. How much more did he save last year compared to this year?

5.(a) The population of a town this year is 10% more than it was 10 year's ago. The population in another 10 years is expected to increase again by 10% to 21,780,000. What was the population 10 years' ago?

(b) A rectangular plot is 40m long and 28m wide. If each side is increased by 2m, what would be the percentage increase in area of the plot?

6.(a) Two numbers are in the ratio 3:8 and their sum is 44. What are the two numbers?

(b) The ratio of the ages of three brothers is 4:3:2. If the oldest is 44 years, how old are the other two?

7.(a) If $\dfrac{a}{b} = \dfrac{c}{d}$, prove that $\dfrac{a-b}{a+b} = \dfrac{c-d}{c+d}$

(b) In a Parliament, the government party members and the opposition were in the ratio 7:4. This ratio changed to 3:2 by the crossing over of 4 government party members to the opposition party. What is the total number of members in the Parliament?

8. Simplify the following:

(a) $\dfrac{3}{x+5} - \dfrac{4}{3x+1}$ (b) $\dfrac{2}{x-2} - \dfrac{3x}{2x^2+1}$

(c) $\dfrac{7}{(x-1)(x+5)} - \dfrac{5}{(x+2)(x+5)}$ (d) $\dfrac{x^2-2x-8}{x^2-16}$

PRACTICAL APPLICATIONS

1. A man sold one-third of his property. He gave half of the remaining property to his wife and divided the remainder equally among his four children. If each child received $145,000, estimate the value of the property sold.

Property sold $= \dfrac{1}{3}$,   Remaining property $= \dfrac{2}{3}$

Property to wife $= \dfrac{1}{2} \times \dfrac{2}{3} = \dfrac{1}{3}$

Each child's share $= \dfrac{1}{4} \times (1 - \dfrac{1}{3} - \dfrac{1}{3}) = \dfrac{1}{4} \times \dfrac{1}{3} = \dfrac{1}{12}$

$\dfrac{1}{12}$th of the sale value of the property $= \$145,000$

Value of property $= \$145,000 \times 12 = \$1,740,000$

Value of property sold $= \dfrac{1}{3} \times 1,740,000 = \$580,000$

2. A retailer marks his goods 20% above their cost price. He gives 10% reduction for cash payment and 5% reduction for credit. If one fourth of his goods are sold for cash and the rest on credit, what percentage profit does he make on his total cost price?

Cost of goods sold for cash $= \$\dfrac{1}{4}x = \$0.25x$ | Let the total cost be $x |

Cost of goods sold on credit $= \$\dfrac{3}{4}x = \$0.75x$

Sale value of goods sold for cash $= \dfrac{1}{4}x \times \dfrac{120}{100} \times \dfrac{90}{100} = \$0.27x$

Sale value of goods sold on credit $= \dfrac{3}{4}x \times \dfrac{120}{100} \times \dfrac{95}{100} = \$0.855x$

Profit made on cash sale $= 0.27x - 0.25x = \$0.02x$

Profit made on credit sale $= 0.855x - 0.75x = \$0.105x$

Total profit $= \$0.125x$

Percentage profit $= \dfrac{0.125x}{x} \times 100 = 12.5$

3. Three partners A, B and C start a business contributing an initial capital of $60,000, $80,000 and $100,000 respectively. One tenth of the profit is paid to A as manager. The remainder of the profit is divided among the three in proportion to their capitals. If the amount paid to A is $ 45,500. What was the total profit?

Ratio of Capitals $= 60,000:80,000:100,000 = 3:4:5$

A's share of the profit shared $= \dfrac{3}{12} = \dfrac{1}{4}$

Profit shared $= 1 - \dfrac{1}{10} = \dfrac{9}{10}$

Total share of profit to A $= \dfrac{1}{10} + \dfrac{1}{4} \times \dfrac{9}{10} = \dfrac{13}{40}$

$\dfrac{13}{40}$th of the total profit $= \$45,500$

Total profit $= \dfrac{\$45,500}{\dfrac{13}{40}} = \$140,000$

ANSWERS TO MISCELLANEOUS PROBLEMS

1.(a) $\dfrac{2\frac{1}{3} + 5\frac{2}{3} \div 2\frac{3}{7}}{7\frac{2}{9} + \frac{3}{4} \text{ of } 3\frac{2}{5}} = \dfrac{2\frac{1}{3} + \frac{17}{3} \times \frac{7}{17}}{7\frac{2}{9} + \frac{3}{4} \times \frac{17}{5}} = \dfrac{2\frac{1}{3} + \frac{7}{3}}{7\frac{2}{9} + \frac{51}{20}} = \dfrac{\frac{7}{3} + \frac{7}{3}}{\frac{65}{9} + \frac{51}{20}}$

$= \dfrac{\frac{14}{3}}{\frac{1300+459}{180}} = \dfrac{14 \times 60}{1759} = \dfrac{840}{1759}$

(b) $\dfrac{5.894 \times 0.3869}{0.497} = \dfrac{2.2803886}{0.497} = 4.588307 = 4.588$ (corrected to 3 places of decimals)

---

2. $\dfrac{2\frac{3}{7} + \frac{13}{4} \div 6\frac{1}{2}}{\left(3\frac{1}{8} \div 3\frac{1}{11}\right) \text{ of } 1\frac{2}{9}} = \dfrac{2\frac{3}{7} + \frac{13}{4} \times \frac{2}{13}}{\left(\frac{25}{8} \times \frac{11}{34}\right) \text{ of } 1\frac{2}{9}} = \dfrac{2\frac{3}{7} + \frac{1}{2}}{\left(\frac{25}{8} \times \frac{11}{34}\right) \times 1\frac{2}{9}} = \dfrac{2\frac{13}{14}}{\frac{25}{8} \times \frac{11}{34} \times \frac{11}{9}}$

$= \dfrac{\frac{41}{14} \times 8 \times 34 \times 9}{25 \times 11 \times 11} = \dfrac{41 \times 4 \times 34 \times 9}{7 \times 25 \times 11 \times 11} = \dfrac{50184}{21175} = 2\dfrac{7834}{21175}$

3.(a) $1\frac{3}{8} - \dfrac{2\frac{1}{6} + \frac{2}{5}}{5\frac{1}{2} - 2\frac{17}{30}} = 1\frac{3}{8} - \dfrac{2\frac{17}{30}}{5\frac{1}{2} - 2\frac{17}{30}} = 1\frac{3}{8} - \dfrac{2\frac{17}{30}}{3 - \frac{2}{30}}$

$= 1\frac{3}{8} - \dfrac{2\frac{17}{30}}{3 - \frac{2}{30}} = 1\frac{3}{8} - \dfrac{\frac{77}{30}}{\frac{88}{30}} = 1\frac{3}{8} - \frac{7}{8} = \frac{4}{8} = \frac{1}{2}$

(b) $\dfrac{0.086 \times \sqrt{0.057}}{0.00258} = \dfrac{0.086 \times 0.23875}{0.00258} = 7.958$ (corrected to 3 decimal places)

---

4. Last year's income = $48 000

Last year's savings = $48,000 $\times \frac{4}{15}$ = $12,800

This year's income = $48,000 $\times$ 1.2 = $57,600

This year's savings = $57,600 $\times \frac{3}{16}$ = $10,800

More savings made last year = $12,800 − $10,800 = $2,000

5.(a) Population 10 years' ago = $\dfrac{21,780,000}{1.1 \times 1.1}$ = 18,000,000

(b) Original area of the plot = 40 × 28 = 1,120m^2

New area of the plot = 42 × 30 = 1,260m^2

Increase in area = 1,260 − 1,120 = 140m^2

Percentage increase in area = $\dfrac{140}{1,120} \times 100$ = 12.5

6.(a) The ratio of the two numbers is 3:8

Therefore, one number is $\dfrac{3}{11}$th and the other is $\dfrac{8}{11}$th of the sum

The numbers are $\dfrac{3}{11} \times 44$ and $\dfrac{8}{11} \times 44 = 12$ and 32

(b) The ratio of the ages of the brothers $= 4:3:2$

4 represents 44 years   1 represents 11 years

Therefore: 3 represents $3 \times 11 = 33$ years

2 represents $2 \times 11 = 22$ years

Therefore, the ages of the other brothers are 33 years and 22 years

---

7.(a) $\dfrac{a}{b} = \dfrac{c}{d}$ .... (1)

Add 1 to both sides of (i): $\dfrac{a}{b} + 1 = \dfrac{c}{d} + 1$

That is: $\dfrac{a + b}{b} = \dfrac{c + d}{d}$ .... (2)

Similarly, subtract 1 from both sides of (i): $\dfrac{a - b}{b} = \dfrac{c - d}{d}$ .... (3)

Divide (3) by (2): $\dfrac{a - b}{a + b} = \dfrac{c - d}{c + d}$

(b) Old proportion of Government party members $= \dfrac{7}{11}$

New proportion of Government party members $= \dfrac{3}{5}$

Difference $= \dfrac{7}{11} - \dfrac{3}{5} = \dfrac{35 - 33}{55} = \dfrac{2}{55}$

$\dfrac{2}{55}$ represents 4 members.

Therefore, number of members in the Parliament $= \dfrac{4}{\frac{2}{55}} = 110$

8.(a) $\dfrac{3}{x+5} - \dfrac{4}{3x+1} = \dfrac{3(3x+1) - 4(x+5)}{(x+5)(3x+1)} = \dfrac{9x+3-4x-20}{(x+5)(3x+1)} = \dfrac{5x-17}{(x+5)(3x+1)}$

(b) $\dfrac{2}{x-2} - \dfrac{3x}{2x^2+1} = \dfrac{2\left(2x^2+1\right) - 3x(x-2)}{(x-2)(2x^2+1)} = \dfrac{4x^2+2-3x^2+6}{(x-2)(2x^2+1)} = \dfrac{x^2+8}{(x-2)(2x^2+1)}$

(c) $\dfrac{7}{(x-1)(x+5)} - \dfrac{5}{(x+2)(x+5)} = \dfrac{7(x+2) - 5(x-1)}{(x-1)(x+5)(x+2)}$

$= \dfrac{7x+14-5x+5}{(x-1)(x+5)(x+2)} = \dfrac{2x+19}{(x-1)(x+5)(x+2)}$

(d) $\dfrac{x^2-2x-8}{x^2-16} = \dfrac{(x-4)(x+2)}{(x+4)(x-4)} = \dfrac{x+2}{x+4}$

1. Simplify: $\dfrac{2\frac{2}{3} \times 1\frac{1}{8} \div \frac{1}{6}}{1\frac{1}{8} \text{ of } 2\frac{2}{3} - \frac{1}{6}} \times \dfrac{17}{113} \div \dfrac{1}{2}$

2. Simplify: $\dfrac{110.6 + 0.018 \div 0.08}{1.5 \times 0.08 + 0.09}$

Use a calculator and give an answer corrected to two decimal places.

3. (a) Using the rule that the difference between the squares of two numbers is the same as the product of their sum and difference, simplify the following to 3 decimal places:

$$\dfrac{(8.72)^2 - (1.28)^2}{9.3 \times 96}$$

(b) If $87.54 \times 0.654 = 57.25116$, write down the values of the following:

(i) 8.754×0.654

(ii) 0.8754×0.0654

4. Evaluate: (a) $\dfrac{1}{2 + \dfrac{1}{2 + \dfrac{1}{2 + \frac{1}{2}}}}$ (b) $\dfrac{0.1 + 0.01 - 0.001}{0.41} \div \dfrac{1}{0.037}$

Give the answer correct to three places of decimals and also to two significant digits.

5.(a) A car dealer, in selling two motor cars for $63,000 each, gains 12.5% on one and loses 12.5% on the other. What percent does he gain or lose on the sale of the two cars?

(b) A retailer marks an article 35% more than its cost price and sells it at a discount. If he gains 8%, what percentage discount did he give?

6 (a) Sam bought a new pair of shoes that cost him $187 getting a 15% discount and paying 10% tax. What was the marked price of the shoes?

(b) Tim is paid a wage of $720 per week plus a 12% commission on the sales value of the items he sold. If in one week he was paid $3,120, what was the value of the sales?

7.(a) x varies directly as y. When $x = 5$, y is 9. What is the relationship between x and y?

(b) Pressure varies inversely as Volume. When the pressure is 80 atmospheres, the Volume is 10 litres. What is the value of Volume when the pressure decreases to 25 atmospheres?

8 Simplify the following:

(a) $\dfrac{7}{4y} - \dfrac{2}{y + 5}$ (b) $\dfrac{10}{(x + 1)(x + 3)} - \dfrac{4}{(x + 1)(x - 6)}$ (c) $\dfrac{3x}{(x + 5)(x + 2)} + \dfrac{5}{(x + 5)(x - 6)}$

1. $\dfrac{2\frac{2}{3} \times 1\frac{1}{8} \div \frac{1}{6}}{1\frac{1}{8} \text{ of } 2\frac{2}{3} - \frac{1}{6}} \times \dfrac{17}{113} \div \dfrac{1}{2} = \dfrac{\frac{8}{3} \times \frac{9}{8} \times \frac{6}{1}}{\frac{9}{8} \times \frac{8}{3} - \frac{1}{6}} \times \dfrac{17}{113} \div \dfrac{1}{2} = \dfrac{18}{3 - \frac{1}{6}} \times \dfrac{17}{113} \div \dfrac{1}{2}$

$= \dfrac{18}{\frac{17}{6}} \times \dfrac{17}{113} \div \dfrac{1}{2} = \dfrac{108}{113} \div \dfrac{1}{2} = \dfrac{216}{113} = 1\dfrac{103}{113}$

2. $\dfrac{110.6 + 0.018 \div 0.08}{1.5 \times 0.08 + 0.09} = \dfrac{110.6 + 0.225}{0.12 + 0.09} = \dfrac{110.825}{0.21} = 527.74$

3. (a) $\dfrac{(8.72)^2 - (1.28)^2}{9.3 \times 96} = \dfrac{(8.72 + 1.28)(8.72 - 1.28)}{9.3 \times 96} = \dfrac{(10 \times 7.44)}{9.3 \times 96} = \dfrac{74.4}{892.8} = 0.083$

(b) If $87.54 \times 0.654 = 57.25116$

(i) $8.754 \times 0.654 = 5.725116$

(ii) $0.8754 \times 0.0654 = 0.05725116$

4.(a) $\dfrac{1}{2 + \dfrac{1}{2 + \dfrac{1}{2 + \frac{1}{2}}}} = \dfrac{1}{2 + \dfrac{1}{2 + \dfrac{1}{\frac{5}{2}}}} = \dfrac{1}{2 + \dfrac{1}{2 + \frac{2}{5}}} = \dfrac{1}{2 + \dfrac{1}{\frac{12}{5}}} = \dfrac{1}{2 + \frac{5}{12}}$

$= \dfrac{1}{\frac{29}{12}} = \dfrac{12}{29} = 0.414 \text{ or } 0.41 \text{ (correct to 3 and 2 significant digits)}$

(b) $\dfrac{0.1 + 0.01 - 0.001}{0.41} = \dfrac{1}{0.037} = \dfrac{0.109}{0.41} \times 0.037$

$= 0.0098365 = 0.010 \text{ or } 0.01 \text{ (correct to 3 and 2 significant digits)}$

5.(a) Cost price of the first car $= \dfrac{63000}{112.5} \times 100 = \$56,000$

Cost price of the second car $= \dfrac{63000}{87.5} \times 100 = \$72,000$

Total cost $= \$128,000$

Total Sales $= \$126,000$

Loss $= \$2,000$

Percentage loss $= \dfrac{2000}{128000} \times 100 = 1\dfrac{9}{16}$

(b) CP $= 1000$

SP $= 108$

MP $= 135$

Discount $= 27$

Percentage discount $= \dfrac{27}{135} \times 100 = 20$

6.(a) Let the Marked Price = 100

Discounted price = 85

Tax = 8.50

Price paid = 85 + 8.50 = 93.50

Marked price $= \dfrac{100}{93.50} \times 187 = \$200$

(b) Total payment = $3,120

Wages = $720

Commission = $2,400

Sales Value $= \dfrac{2400}{12} \times 100 = \$20,000$

7 (a) $x \alpha y$

That is: $x = Ky$

When $x = 5$, $y = 9$

Therefore: $5 = 9K$

$K = \dfrac{5}{9}$

The relationship between x and y is: $x = \dfrac{5}{9}y$

(b) $P \alpha \dfrac{1}{V}$

That is: $P = K\dfrac{1}{V}$

When $P = 80$ atmospheres, $V = 10$ litres

$80 = K\dfrac{1}{10}$

Therefore: $K = 800$

That is: $P = 800\dfrac{1}{V}$

When $P = 25$:

$25 = 800\dfrac{1}{V}$

$V = \dfrac{800}{25} = 32$ litres

8.(a) $\dfrac{7}{4y} - \dfrac{2}{y+5} = \dfrac{7(y+5) - 2(4y)}{4y(y+5)} = \dfrac{7y + 35 - 8y}{4y(y+5)} = \dfrac{-y+35}{4y(y+5)}$

(b) $\dfrac{10}{(x+1)(x+3)} - \dfrac{4}{(x+1)(x-6)} = \dfrac{10(x-6) - 4(x+3)}{(x+1)(x+3)(x-6)} = \dfrac{10x - 60 - 4x - 12}{(x+1)(x+3)(x-6)}$

$= \dfrac{6x - 72}{(x+1)(x+3)(x-6)} = \dfrac{6(x-12)}{(x+1)(x+3)(x-6)}$

(c) $\dfrac{3x}{(x+5)(x+2)} + \dfrac{5}{(x+5)(x-6)} = \dfrac{3x(x-6) + 5(x+2)}{(x+5)(x+2)(x-6)} = \dfrac{3x^2 - 18x + 5x + 10}{(x+5)(x+2)(x-6)}$

$= \dfrac{3x^2 - 13x + 10}{(x+5)(x+2)(x-6)} = \dfrac{(3x-10)(x-1)}{(x+5)(x+2)(x-6)} = \dfrac{3x}{(x+5)(x+2)} + \dfrac{5}{(x+5)(x-6)}$

2. FACTORISATION

FACTORISATION BY ISOLATING COMMON FACTOR

When an algebraic expression is a sum of variables and the variable terms have common factors, these factors are isolated as the following examples illustrate. This is called isolating the common factors.

Examples:

- $3x - 12y = 3(x - 4y)$
- $5c^4 + 10bc^2 = 5c^2(c^2 + 2b)$
- $7lm^3n^2 - 28lmn = 7lmn(m^2n - 4)$
- $3x^3y^2 - 6xy^2 + 9xy = 3xy(x^2y - 2y + 3)$
- $a(a + c) + b(a + c) = (a + c)(a + b)$
- $x^2(m - 3) - (3 - m) = x^2(m - 3) + (m - 3) = (m - 3)(x^2 + 1)$

Note that in order to make $(m - 3)$ common to both the terms of the given algebraic expression, $-(3 - m)$ is written as $(m - 3)$.

FACTORISATION BY GROUPING TERMS

With some algebraic expressions, it is necessary to group terms in pairs to facilitate taking out a common factor. The following examples illustrate this point.

Example 1:

Factorise: $ax + bx + ay + by$

$= \underline{ax + bx} + \underline{ay + by}$ | The terms grouped are underlined |

$= x(a + b) + y(a + b)$ | The common factor is a + b |

$= (a + b)(x + y)$

Example 2:

Factorise: $ab + 1 - b - a$

$= ab + 1 - b - a$

$= \underline{ab - a} - \underline{b + 1}$ | The terms grouped are underlined |

$= a(b - 1) - 1(b - 1)$ | The common factor is b − 1. Note the change in sign |

$= (b - 1)(a - 1)$

Example 3:

Factorise $3xy - 4y - 6x + 8$

$= \underline{3xy - 4y} - \underline{6x + 8}$

$= y(3x - 4) - 2(3x - 4)$ | Note the change in sign |

$= (3x - 4)(y - 2)$

Example 4:

Factorise: $m^3 - m^2 + m - 1$

$= \underline{m^3 - m^2} + \underline{m - 1}$

$= m^2(m - 1) + 1(m - 1)$

$= (m - 1)(m^2 + 1)$

Example 5:

Factorise: $(x + 3y)^2 - 2x - 6y$

$= (x + 3y)^2 - 2x - 6y$

$= (x + 3y)(x + 3y) - 2(x + 3y)$

$= (x + 3y)(x + 3y - 2)$

FACTORISATION OF QUADRATIC EXPRESSIONS

A **quadratic expression** is an algebraic expression with terms containing powers of the variable, the highest power being 2.

Example 1:

Factorise $2x^2 + 11x + 5$

- The middle term of this quadratic expression is $11x$. This is really $11x^1$

- The number 5 is actually $5x^0$, x^0 has a value of 1 and so $5x^0 = 5$

- The powers of x involved in this expression are thus: 2, 1 and 0

Observe that in the quadratic expression $2x^2 + 11x + 5$ the coefficient of x^2 is 2, the coefficient of x is 11 and the constant is 5. To factorise this quadratic expression, we follow the steps shown below.

Steps:

1. Multiply the coefficient of x^2, 2, by the constant to give 10.

2. Split 10 into two factors so that their product is 10 and their sum is 11.
   The answer is 10 and 1.

3. Rewrite the quadratic expression by replacing $11x$ with $10x$ and $1x$ as follows:
   $\underline{2x^2 + 10x} + \underline{1x + 5}$

4. Factorise the underlined grouped terms and write the results as follows:
   $2x(x + 5) + 1(x + 5)$

5. Decide that the factors are $(x + 5)$ and $(2x + 1)$.
   Therefore, $2x^2 + 11x + 5 = (x + 5)(2x + 1)$

Example 2:

> Factorise: $y^2 - 7y + 12$

Steps:

1. Multiply the coefficient of y^2, 1, by the constant 12 to give 12.

2. Split 12 into two factors so that their product is 12 and their sum is -7.
   The answer is -4 and -3.

3. Rewrite the quadratic expression by replacing -7y with -4y and -3y as follows:
   $\underline{y^2 - 4y} - \underline{3y + 12}$

4. Factorise the underlined grouped terms and write the results as follows:
   $y(y - 4) - 3(y - 4)$

5. Decide that the factors are $(y - 4)$ and $(y - 3)$.
   Therefore, $y^2 - 7y + 12 = (y - 4)(y - 3)$

Example 3:

> Factorise: $6a^2 + 13a - 28$

Steps:

1. Multiply the coefficient of a^2, 6, by the constant -28 to give -168.

2. Split -168 into two factors so that their product is -168 and their sum is 13.
   The answer is - 8 and 21.

3. Rewrite the quadratic expression by replacing 13a with -8a and 21a as follows:
   $\underline{6a^2 - 8a} + \underline{21a - 28}$

4. Factorise the underlined grouped terms and write the results as follows:
   $2a(3a - 4) + 7(3a - 4)$

5. Decide that the factors are $(3a - 4)$ and $(2a + 7)$.
   Therefore, $6a^2 + 13a - 28 = (3a - 4)(2a + 7)$.

FACTORISATION OF THE DIFFERENCE OF TWO SQUARES

The difference of the squares of two numbers is equal to the product of their sum and their difference.

Examples:

- $x^2 - y^2 = (x + y)(x - y)$

In some expressions that could be factorised using the difference of two squares method, a common factor needs to be taken out first.

- $3a^2 - 3b^2 = 3(a^2 - b^2) = 3(a + b)(a - b)$

In other expressions one or both terms in the expression may have to be put in a complete square form before factorising using the method of difference of two squares.

Examples:

- $16p^2 - q^2 = (4p)^2 - q^2 = (4p + q)(4p - q)$
- $25x^2y^2 - 9z^2 = (5xy)^2 - (3z)^2 = (5xy + 3z)(5xy - 3z)$
- $4(a + b)^2 - c^2 = (2a + 2b)^2 - c^2 = (2a + 2b + c)(2a + 2b - c)$
- $9a^2 - 16(b + c)^2 = (3a)^2 - (4b + 4c)^2 = (3a + 4b + 4c)(3a - 4b - 4c)$

ROOTS OF A POLYNOMIAL

An algebraic expression is called a **polynomial function** when it contains different powers of the same variable(s). An example of a polynomial in x, is $x^2 - 5x + 8$.

There are different types of **Polynomials**:

- A **Monomial** is a polynomial with **one term**
- A **Binomial** is a polynomial with **two unlike terms**
- A **Trinomial** is a polynomial with **three unlike terms**

The roots (or zeros) of a polynomial function of a given variable are the values of the variable that will make the function equal zero. A polynomial of degree 'n' has 'n' roots which may be real or complex. The largest number of real roots that an 'n' degree polynomial could have is n. The smallest number is 1, real or complex.

All roots of a polynomial function need not be integers; there can be decimal roots as well as complex roots. If a polynomial can be factorised into say three linear factors $(x - a)$, $(x - b)$ and $(x - c)$ we can write: $f(x) = (x - a)(x - b)(x - c)$. This means that a, b and c are the roots of f(x).

DIVISION OF POLYNOMIALS

When a polynomial is divided by a linear factor the quotient will be a polynomial of a lower degree and a remainder which may or may not be a constant. In some cases, there may not be any remainder. The same is true when a polynomial is divided by another polynomial with a lower degree.

Example 1:

Divide: $x^3 - 6x - 4$ by $x - 2$

$$
\begin{array}{r}
x^2 \quad +2x \quad -2 \\
x - 2 \,\overline{)\, x^3 \qquad\;\; -6x \;\; -4} \\
\underline{x^3 \;\; -2x^2} \\
+2x^2 \;\; -6x \\
\underline{+2x^2 \;\; -4x} \\
-2x \;\; -4 \\
\underline{-2x \;\; +4} \\
-8
\end{array}
$$

Example 2:

Divide: $p^3 - 12p - 16$ by $p^2 - 2p + 8$

```
                      p    + 2
p² - 2p + 8 | p³              -12p      -16
              p³   -2p²       +8p
              ───────────────────────
                    2p²       -20p      -16
                    2p²       -4p       +16
                    ─────────────────────────
                              -16p      -32
```

Example 3:

Divide: $m^4 + 3m^3 + 7m^2 + 12m + 12$ by $m^2 + 3m + 3$

```
                    m²              +4
m² + 3m +                          +12m   +12
        3 | m⁴    +3m³    +7m²
            m⁴    +3m³    +3m²
            ──────────────────────
                          +4m²    +12m    +12
                          +4m²    +12m    +12
```

REMAINDER THEOREM

The **Remainder Theorem** states that if a polynomial f(x) is divided by (x − a), the remainder is f(a). If we call the quotient P(x), then we can write:

f(x) = (x − a)P(x) + f(a)

Example 1:

Use the remainder theorem to find the remainder when $2x^2 + 5x - 9$ is divided by x − 2. Check the answer by long division.

$f(x) = 2x^2 + 5x - 9$

Remainder $= f(2) = 2(2)^2 + 5(2) - 9 = 8 + 10 - 9 = 9$

Long Division:

```
                  2x    +9
x - 2 | 2x²    +5x     -9
        2x²    -4x
        ──────────────
               9x      -9
               9x      -18
               ───────────
                       9
```

Therefore, the quotient is 2x + 9 and the remainder is 9.

Example 2:

Find the remainder when $3x^3 + 2x^2 - 5x + 7$ is divided by $(x + 3)$

Remainder $= f(-3) = 3(-3)^3 + 2(-3)^2 - 5(-3) + 7$

$= -81 + 18 + 15 + 7 = -41$

Long Division:

$$
\begin{array}{r}
3x^2 \quad -7x \quad +16 \\
x + 3 \overline{\smash{\big)}\, 3x^3 \quad +2x^2 \quad -5x \quad +7} \\
\underline{3x^3 \quad +9x^2} \\
-7x^2 \quad -5x \\
\underline{-7x^2 \quad -21x} \\
+16x \quad +7 \\
\underline{-16x \quad +48} \\
-41
\end{array}
$$

Therefore, the quotient is $3x^2 - 7x + 16$ and the remainder is -41.

FACTOR THEOREM

The **Factor Theorem** states that if a polynomial $f(x)$ is divided by $(x - a)$ and the remainder is zero, then $(x - a)$ is a factor of $f(x)$. That is, $f(x) = (x - a) \times P(x)$.

Example 1:

Use the factor theorem to factorise $f(x) = x^2 + x - 2$

The coefficient of x^2 is 1 and the constant term is -2. Their product is −2.
The integer factors of -2 are 1, -1, 2 and -2.

There may be fractional roots of $f(x)$. We shall find these, if any, by long division.
We try the integer factors of -2 in turn to find out which ones make $f(x) = 0$.

$f(1) = 1 + 1 - 2 = 0$

$f(-1) = 1 - 1 - 2 \neq 0$

$f(2) = 4 + 2 - 2 \neq 0$

$f(-2) = 4 - 2 - 2 = 0$

Therefore, $x = 1$ and $x = -2$ are roots. The factors are therefore $(x - 1)$ and $(x + 2)$

Hence, $f(x) = (x - 1)(x + 2)$

Example 2:

Use the factor theorem and long division to factorise: $f(x) = 3x^2 + 2x - 1$

The coefficient of x^2 is 3 and the constant term is -1. Their product is -3.
The factors of -3 are 1, -1, 3 and -3.

$f(1) = 3 + 2 - 1 \neq 0$

$f(-1) = 3 - 2 - 1 = 0$

$f(3) = 27 + 6 - 1 \neq 0$

$f(-3) = 27 - 6 - 1 \neq 0$

Therefore, $x = -1$ is a root and $x + 1$ is a factor of $f(x)$. A quadratic equation must have two roots. The other root can be found by long division as follows:

```
              3x    -1
        ┌─────────────────
x + 1   │ 3x²  +2x   -1
          3x²  +3x
        ─────────────────
                 -x   -1
                 -x   -1
                ─────────
                       0
```

The other factor of $f(x)$ is $3x - 1$.
Therefore, $f(x) = (x - 1)(3x - 1)$

Example 3:

Factorise: $f(x) = x^3 - 6x^2 + 7x + 6$

The coefficient of x^3 is 1 and the constant term is 6. Their product is 6.
The factors of 6 are 1, 2, 3 and 6. We try these in turn to find out which ones make $f(x) = 0$.

$f(1) = (1)^3 - 6(1)^2 + 7(1) + 6 \neq 0$

$f(2) = (2)^3 - 6(2)^2 + 7(2) + 6 \neq 0$

$f(3) = (3)^3 - 6(3)^2 + 7(3) + 6 = 0$

$f(6) = (6)^3 - 6(6)^2 + 7(6) + 6 \neq 0$

Therefore, $x = 3$ is one root and $x - 3$ is a factor. We now do the long division to find the other factor.

```
              x²    -3x    -2
        ┌──────────────────────
x - 3   │ x³   -6x²   +7x   +6
          x³   -3x²
        ──────────────────────
                -3x²   +7x
                -3x²   +9x
               ───────────────
                       -2x   +6
                       -2x   +6
                      ──────────
                              0
```

Hence, the factors of $f(x) = x^3 - 6x^2 + 7x + 6$ are: $(x - 3)$ and $(x^2 - 3x - 2)$
Note that one is a linear factor and the other is a quadratic factor.

MISCELLANEOUS PROBLEMS

1. Factorise by isolating the common factor(s):

(a) $2x + 6y$　　　　(b) $3a - 9b$　　　　(c) $ax - x$　　　　(d) $ab + a$

(e) $x^4 + 2x^3$　　　(f) $a^2 - 2a^2b$　　(g) $x^2y^2 - x^4y^4$　　(h) $4c^4 - 12c^2d$

2. Factorise by isolating the common factors:

(a) $6m^3n^4 + 12m^4n^3$ 　　　　　　(b) $3p^2q^2r^3 + 9pq^2r$

(c) $12ab^3c^2 - 18b^2c^2$ 　　　　　　(d) $6x^3y^2z + 24xyz$

(e) $21ax^2y^4 + 14ax^3y^3$ 　　　　　(f) $13lm^3n^2 - 26lm^2n^3$

(g) $9a^3b^2x^4 - 27a^2bx^3$ 　　　　　(h) $15p^4q^3r^3 + 5p^3q^2r^4$

3. Factorise by isolating the common factors:

(a) $(a + b)x + (a + b)y$ 　　　　　(b) $a(x + y) - (x + y)$

(c) $x^2(a - 2b) - 2(a - 2b)$ 　　　(d) $5(a - b) - (a - b)c$

(e) $(3x + y)a^2 + (3x + y)b^2$ 　　(f) $x^2(a - 2) - (2 - a)$

(g) $m^2(b - c) + 3(c - b)$ 　　　　(h) $p^2(l - m) - 3(m - l)$

4. Factorise by grouping terms:

(a) $ax + ay + bx + by$ 　　　　　(b) $x^2 + xy + xz + yz$

(c) $m^2 + mn + m + n$ 　　　　　(d) $a^2 + ab - a - b$

(e) $2ax + 2ay - 2bx - 2by$ 　　　(f) $m^2 + 2m + 2n + mn$

(g) $p^2 - px + pq - qx$ 　　　　　(h) $x^3 + x^2 - 3x - 3$

5. Factorise the following quadratic expressions by inspection:

(a) $a^2 + 3a + 2$ 　　　　　　　　(b) $x^2 + 5x + 4$

(c) $m^2 + 5m + 6$ 　　　　　　　(d) $a^2 + 10a + 9$

(e) $p^2 + 4p + 4$ 　　　　　　　(f) $y^2 + 6y + 9$

(g) $x^2 + 12x + 35$ 　　　　　　(h) $p^2 + 8p + 7$

6. Factorise the following quadratic expressions by splitting the middle term:

(a) $2x^2 + 3x + 1$

(b) $2x^2 + 9x + 4$

(c) $2m^2 + 7m + 3$

(d) $2a^2 + 5a + 2$

(e) $3p^2 + 5p + 2$

(f) $3x^2 - 11x + 6$

(g) $4x^2 + 11x - 3$

(h) $3a^2 - 5a - 2$

7. Factorise using difference of two squares:

(a) $2x^2 - 50$

(b) $2a^2 - 8b^2$

(c) $x^3 - 16x$

(d) $49a^2x^2 - a^2$

(e) $27a^2 - 12a^4$

(f) $2x^3 - 18xy^2$

(g) $4x^8 - x^6$

(h) $52x^2y^2z - 13a^2b^2z$

8. Find all the factors of each of the following:

(a) $x^2 - 2x - 3$

(b) $a^2 - 4a - 21$

(c) $p^3 + 4p^2 + p - 6$

(d) $m^3 + m^2 - 16m - 16$

(e) $x^4 - 4x^3 + 9x^2 - 24x + 18$

(f) $y^4 + y^3 - y - 1$

(g) $x^3 - y^3$

(h) $b^4 + 3b^3 - 3b^2 - 12b - 4$

1.

(a) $2x + 6y = 2(x + 3y)$

(b) $3a - 9b = 3(a - 3b)$

(c) $ax - x = x(a - 1)$

(d) $ab + a = a(b + 1)$

(e) $x^4 + 2x^3 = x^3(x + 2)$

(f) $a^2 - 2a^2b = a^2(1 - 2b)$

(g) $x^2y^2 - x^4y^4 = x^2y^2(1 - x^2y^2)$

(h) $4c^4 - 12c^2d = 4c^2(c^2 - 3d)$

2.

(a) $6m^3n^4 + 12m^4n^3 = 6m^3n^3(n + 2m)$

(b) $3p^2q^2r^3 + 9pq^2r = 3pq^2r(pr^2 + 3)$

(c) $12ab^3c^2 - 18b^2c^2 = 6b^2c^2(2ab - 3)$

(d) $6x^3y^2z + 24xyz = 6xyz(x^2y + 4)$

(e) $21ax^2y^4 + 14ax^3y^3 = 7ax^2y^3(3y + 2x)$

(f) $13lm^3n^2 - 26lm^2n^3 = 13lm^2n^2(m - 2n)$

(g) $9a^3b^2x^4 - 27a^2bx^3 = 9a^2bx^3(abx - 3)$

(h) $15p^4q^3r^3 + 5p^3q^2r^4 = 5p^3q^2r^3(3pq + r)$

3.

(a) $(a + b)x + (a + b)y = (a + b)(x + y)$

(b) $a(x + y) - (x + y) = (x + y)(a - 1)$

(c) $x^2(a - 2b) - 2(a - 2b) = (a - 2b)(x^2 - 2)$

(d) $5(a - b) - (a - b)c = (a - b)(5 - c)$

(e) $(3x + y)a^2 + (3x + y)b^2 = (3x + y)(a^2 + b^2)$

(f) $x^2(a - 2) - (2 - a) = (a - 2)(x^2 + 1)$

(g) $m^2(b - c) + 3(c - b) = (b - c)(m^2 - 3)$

(h) $p^2(l - m) - 3(m - l) = (l - m)(p^2 + 3)$

4.

(a) $ax + ay + bx + by = a(x + y) + b(x + y) = (x + y)(a + b)$

(b) $x^2 + my + xz + yz = x(x + y) + z(x + y) = (x + y)(x + z)$

(c) $m^2 + mn + m + n = m(m + n) + 1(m + n) = (m + n)(m + 1)$

(d) $a^2 + ab - a - b = a(a + b) - 1(a + b) = (a + b)(a - 1)$

(e) $2ax + 2ay - 2bx - 2by = 2a(x + y) - 2b(x + y) = 2(x + y)(a - b)$

(f) $m^2 + 2m + 2n + mn = m(m + 2) + n(2 + m) = (m + 2)(m + n)$

(g) $p^2 - px + pq - qx = p(p - x) + q(p - x) = (p - x)(p + q)$

(h) $x^3 + x^2 - 3x - 3 = x^2(x + 1) - 3(x + 1) = (x + 1)(x^2 - 3)$

5.

(a) $a^2 + 3a + 2 = (a + 1)(a + 2)$

(b) $x^2 + 5x + 4 = (x + 1)(x + 4)$

(c) $m^2 + 5m + 6 = (m + 2)(m + 3)$

(d) $a^2 + 10a + 9 = (a + 1)(a + 9)$

(e) $p^2 + 4p + 4 = (p + 2)(p + 2)$

(f) $y^2 + 6y + 9 = (y + 3)(y + 3)$

(g) $x^2 + 12x + 35 = (x + 5)(x + 7)$

(h) $p^2 + 8p + 7 = (p + 1)(p + 7)$

6.

(a) $2x^2 + 3x + 1 = 2x^2 + 2x + x + 1 = 2x(x + 1) + 1(x + 1) = (2x + 1)(x + 1)$

(b) $2x^2 + 9x + 4 = 2x^2 + 8x + x + 4 = 2x(x + 4) + 1(x + 4) = (2x + 1)(x + 4)$

(c) $2m^2 + 7m + 3 = 2m^2 + 6m + m + 3 = 2m(m + 3) + 1(m + 3) = (2m + 1)(m + 3)$

(d) $2a^2 + 5a + 2 = 2a^2 + 4a + a + 2 = 2a(a + 2) + 1(a + 2) = (2a + 1)(a + 2)$

(e) $3p^2 + 5p + 2 = 3p^2 + 3p + 2p + 2 = 3p(p + 1) + 2(p + 1) = (3p + 2)(p + 1)$

(f) $3x^2 - 11x + 6 = 3x^2 - 9x - 2x + 6 = 3x(x - 3) - 2(x - 3) = (3x - 2)(x - 3)$

(g) $4x^2 + 11x - 3 = 4x^2 + 12x - x - 3 = 4x(x + 3) - 1(x + 3) = 4(x - 1)(x + 3)$

(h) $3a^2 - 5a - 2 = 3a^2 - 6a + a - 2 = 3a(a - 2) + (a - 2) = (3a + 1)(a - 2)$

7.

(a) $2x^2 - 50 = 2(x^2 - 25) = 2(x + 5)(x - 5)$

(b) $2a^2 - 8b^2 = 2[a^2 - (2b)^2] = 2(a + 2b)(a - 2b)$

(c) $x^3 - 16x = x[x^2 - (4)^2] = x(x + 4)(x - 4)$

(d) $49a^2x^2 - a^2 = [(7ax)^2 - a^2] = a^2[(7x)^2 - 1] = a^2(7x + 1)(7x - 1)$

(e) $27a^2 - 12a^4 = 3a^2[9 - 4a^2] = 3a^2[3^2 - (2a)^2] = 3a^2(3 + 2a)(3 - 2a)$

(f) $2x^3 - 18xy^2 = 2x[x^2 - (3y)^2] = 2x(x + 3y)(x - 3y)$

(g) $4x^8 - x^6 = x^6[(2x)^2 - 1] = x^6(2x + 1)(2x - 1)$

(h) $52x^2y^2z - 13a^2b^2z = 13z[(2xy)^2 - (ab)^2] = 13z(2xy + ab)(2xy - ab)$

8.

(a) $x^2 - 2x - 3 = (x + 1)(x - 3)$

(b) $a^2 - 4a - 21 = (a + 3)(a - 7)$

(c) $f(p) = p^3 + 4p^2 + p - 6$

$f(1) = 1 + 4 + 1 - 6 = 0$

Therefore, $p - 1$ is a factor.

$f(-2) = -8 + 16 - 2 - 6 = 0$

Therefore, $p + 2$ is a factor.

Obtain the third factor by dividing $f(p)$ by $p^2 + p - 2$

$f(p) = (p - 1)(p + 2)(p + 3)$

(d) $m^3 + m^2 - 16m - 16 = m^2(m + 1) - 16(m + 1)$

$= (m^2 - 16)(m + 1) = (m + 4)(m - 4)(m + 1)$

(e) $f(x) = x^4 - 4x^3 + 9x^2 - 24x + 18$

$f(1) = 1 - 4 + 9 - 24 + 18 = 0$

Therefore, $x - 1$ is a factor.

$f(3) = 81 - 108 + 81 - 72 + 18 = 0$

Therefore, $x - 3$ is a factor.

Obtain the third factor by dividing $f(x)$ by $x^2 - 4x + 3$

$f(x) = (x - 1)(x - 3)(x^2 + 6)$

(f)
$y^4 + y^3 - y - 1 = y^3(y + 1) - 1(y + 1)$

$= (y^3 - 1)(y + 1) = (y - 1)(y^2 + y + 1)(y + 1)$

(g) $x^3 - y^3 = (x - y)(x^2 + xy + y^2)$

(h) $f(b) = b^4 + 3b^3 - 3b^2 - 12b - 4$

$f(2) = 16 + 24 - 12 - 24 - 4 = 0$

Therefore, $b - 2$ is a factor.

$f(-2) = 16 - 24 - 12 + 24 - 4 = 0$

Therefore, $b + 2$ is a factor.

Obtain the third factor by dividing $f(b)$ by $b^2 - 4$

$f(b) = (b + 2)(b - 2)(b^2 + 3b + 1)$

PRACTICAL APPLICATIONS

1. A tournament is organised between a number of soccer teams, each of which is to play against another team only once. The number of games played when there are x teams taking part in the tournament is given by the function: $f(x) = \dfrac{x^2 - x}{2}$.

If the number of games played is 36, how many teams took part in the tournament?

$$f(x) = \dfrac{x^2 - x}{2}$$

$$36 = \dfrac{x^2 - x}{2}$$

Cross multiplying, we get $x^2 - x = 72$

That is, $x^2 - x - 72 = 0$

Factors of $x^2 - x - 72$ are $(x - 9)$ and $(x + 8)$.

Therefore, $(x - 9)(x + 8) = 0$

The positive value of x that will satisfy the equation = 9

Hence, the number of teams that took part in the game = 9

---

2. A farmer wants to make a rectangular pen for his sheep. He has 48 metres of fencing material to cover three sides. A brick wall will serve as the fourth side. What should be the length and width of the pen to maximise the space for the sheep?

Let the width of the pen be x metres.

Therefore, the length of the pen will be 48 − 2x.

Area of the pen A, is given by:

A = x(48 − 2x)

That is, A = 2x(24 − x)

Let us create a grid with areas corresponding to different values of x.

x	2	4	6	8	12	16
A	88	160	216	256	288	256

It can be seen that the area is the largest at 288m^2 when x = 12 metres.

Therefore, the area of the pen is maximum when its width is 12 metres.

3. A playing field is to be constructed such that its area is to be 66 square metres. If the length of the field is to be greater than its width by 5 metres, what should be the dimensions of the field?

Let the width of the field $=$ x metres.

Therefore, the length of the field $=$ (x + 5) metres.

Area of the field $=$ x(x + 5) square metres.

Hence, x(x + 5) $=$ 66

That is, $x^2 + 5x - 66 = 0$

Factorising, (x + 11)(x − 6) $=$ 0

The positive value of x satisfying the above is 6.

Therefore, the dimensions of the field are:

Length $=$ 11 metres, Width $=$ 6 metres

1. Factorise by isolating common factor:

(a) $4x + 8y - 12$

(b) $7a + 14b + 21c$

(c) $2am - 6an + 4al$

(d) $a^2 - a^3 + a^4$

(e) $4p^3 + 8p^2 + 20p$

(f) $x^3 + x^2y - xy^2$

(g) $8x^2 + 20x + 4$

(h) $2xy^2 - 6x^2y - 2x^2$

2. Factorise by isolating common factors:

(a) $5x^2y^2 - 10xy^2 + 15xy$

(b) $2am^4 - 6a^2m^2 + 8am^2$

(c) $8x^4 - 8x^2y^2 + 16x^2y^2$

(d) $14a^3b^4 + 28a^4b^2 - 7a^3b^2$

(e) $18l^2m^3n + 27lm^2n^2 - 9l^3m^3n^3$

(f) $2x^2yz^3 - 8xy^2z^2 - 6yz^3$

(g) $3x^3y + 2x^2y^2 - 4x^2yz$

(h) $6a^4bc - 3a^2b^3c - 3a^2bc^3$

3. Factorise by grouping terms:

(a) $a^4 - a^3 - 2a + 2$

(b) $(x + 2)^2 - 5x - 10$

(c) $x^2 - (2 - 5y)x - 10y$

(d) $3x^2 - y(x + 1) + 3x$

(e) $2a^2b - 1 - a^2 + 2b$

(f) $x^2 - 1 + 3x^5 - 3x^3$

(g) $ax + bx - a^2 - ab + cx - ac$

(h) $ax + bx - a^2 - ab - x + a$

4. Factorise the following by inspection:

(a) $3 - 2a - a^2$

(b) $2 - x - x^2$

(c) $p^2 + p - 20$

(d) $a^2 - 10a + 21$

(e) $z^2 + 3z - 10$

(f) $k^2 - 16k + 64$

(g) $y^2 - 17y + 42$

(h) $54 - 15x - x^2$

5. Factorise the following quadratic expressions:

(a) $4a^2 - ab - 14b^2$

(b) $5x^2 - 38xy + 21y^2$

(c) $2x^2 - 19xy + 17y^2$

(d) $12m^2 - 20mn + 3n^2$

(e) $6a^2 - 2ab - 28b^2$

(f) $56k^2 - 19kp - 10p^2$

(g) $22a^2 + 75ab - 7b^2$

(h) $3x^2 - 25xy + 52y^2$

6. Factorise using difference of two squares:

(a) $(x + y)^2 - z^2$

(b) $(b + c)^2 - d^2$

(c) $(m - n)^2 - 4$

(d) $x^4 - (y + z)^2$

(e) $16x^4 - (x + 1)^2$

(f) $(a + b)^2 - (x - y)^2$

(g) $a^2 - 4(x + y)^2$

(h) $4b^2 - (b^2 + c^2)^2$

7. Simplify using the difference of two squares:

(a) $(28)^2 - (22)^2$

(b) $(56\frac{1}{2})^2 - (33\frac{1}{2})^2$

(c) $(101)^2 - 1$

(d) $(337)^2 - (163)^2$

(e) $(73)^2 - (27)^2$

(f) $(84\frac{3}{4})^2 - (15\frac{1}{4})^2$

(g) $(163.52)^2 - (36.48)^2$

(h) $(178.43)^2 - (78.43)^2$

8. Using the remainder theorem or otherwise find the remainder for the following divisions:

(a) $a^2 - 6a - 4 \div (a - 2)$

(b) $6x^2 + 9x - 11 \div (x + 3)$

(c) $p^3 - 11p + 5 \div (p + 2)$

(d) $3m^3 - 4m - 13 \div (m - 3)$

(e) $x^4 + 2x^3 - 3x^2 + 5x - 8 \div (x + 2)$

(f) $2x^4 + 3x^3 - 4x^2 + 6x - 7 \div (x - 3)$

(g) $a^4 + 3a^3 + 7a^2 + 6a + 7 \div (a^2 + 2a + 3)$

(h) $y^4 + 3y^3 - 8y^2 + 7y - 4 \div (y^2 - 2y + 3)$

ANSWERS TO PRACTICE SET 2

1.(a) $4x + 8y - 12 = 4(x + 2y - 3)$

(b) $7a + 14b + 21c = 7(a + 2b + 3c)$

(c) $2am - 6an + 4al = 2a(m - 3n + 2l)$

(d) $a^2 - a^3 + a^4 = a^2(1 - a + a^2)$

(e) $4p^3 + 8p^2 + 20p = 4p(p^2 + 2p + 5)$

(f) $x^3 + x^2y - xy^2 = x(x^2 + xy - y^2)$

(g) $8x^2 + 20x + 4 = 4(2x^2 + 5x + 1)$

(h) $2xy^2 - 6x^2y - 2x^2 = 2x(y^2 - 3xy - x)$

2.(a) $5x^2y^2 - 10xy^2 + 15xy = 5xy(xy - 2y + 3)$

(b) $2am^4 - 6a^2m^2 + 8am^2 = 2am^2(m^2 - 3a + 4)$

(c) $8x^4 - 8x^2y^2 + 16x^2y^2 = 8x^2(x^2 - y^2 + 2y^2)$

(d) $14a^3b^4 + 28a^4b^2 - 7a^3b^2 = 7a^3b^2(2b^2 + 4a - 1)$

(e) $18l^2m^3n + 27lm^2n^2 - 9l^3m^3n^3 = 9lm^2n(2lm + 3n - l^2mn^2)$

(f) $2x^2yz^3 - 8xy^2z^2 - 6yz^3 = 2yz^2(x^2z - 4xy - 3z)$

(g) $3x^3y + 2x^2y^2 - 4x^2yz = x^2y(3x + 2y - 4z)$

(h) $6a^4bc - 3a^2b^3c - 3a^2bc^3 = 3a^2bc(2a^2 - b^2 - c^2)$

3.(a) $a^4 - a^3 - 2a + 2 = a^3(a - 1) - 2(a - 1) = (a^3 - 2)(a - 1)$

(b) $(x + 2)^2 - 5x - 10 = (x + 2)^2 - 5(x + 2) = (x + 2)(x + 2 - 5) = (x + 2)(x - 3)$

(c) $x^2 - (2 - 5y)x - 10y = x^2 - 2x + 5xy - 10y = x(x - 2) + 5y(x - 2) = (x + 5y)(x - 2)$

(d) $3x^2 - y(x + 1) + 3x = 3x(x + 1) - y(x + 1) = (3x - y)(x + 1)$

(e) $2a^2b - 1 - a^2 + 2b = 2a^2b + 2b - 1 - a^2 = 2b(a^2 + 1) - 1(1 + a^2) = (2b - 1)(a^2 + 1)$

(f) $x^2 - 1 + 3x^5 - 3x^3 = x^2 - 1 + 3x^3(x^2 - 1) = (x^2 - 1)(1 + 3x^3)$

(g) $ax + bx - a^2 - ab + cx - ac = ax - a^2 + bx - ab + cx - ac$
$= a(x - a) + b(x - a) + c(x - a) = (x - a)(a + b + c)$

(h) $ax + bx - a^2 - ab - x + a = ax - a^2 + bx - ab - x + a$
$= a(x - a) + b(x - a) - (x - a) = (x - a)(a + b - 1)$

4.(a) $3 - 2a - a^2 = (3 + a)(1 - a)$

(b) $2 - x - x^2 = (2 + x)(1 - x)$

(c) $p^2 + p - 20 = (p + 5)(p - 4)$

(d) $a^2 - 10a + 21 = (a - 3)(a - 7)$

(e) $z^2 + 3z - 10 = (z + 5)(z - 2)$

(f) $k^2 - 16k + 64 = (k - 8)(k - 8)$

(g) $y^2 - 17y + 42 = (y - 3)(y - 14)$

(h) $54 - 15x - x^2 = (3 - x)(18 + x)$

5.(a) $4a^2 - ab - 14b^2 = (a - 2b)(4a + 7b)$

(b) $5x^2 - 38xy + 21y^2 = (x - 7y)(5x - 3y)$

(c) $2x^2 - 19xy + 17y^2 = (2x - 17y)(x - y)$

(d) $12m^2 - 20mn + 3n^2 = (2m - 3n)(6m - n)$

(e) $6a^2 - 2ab - 28b^2 = (a + 2b)(6a - 14b)$

(f) $56k^2 - 19kp - 10p^2 = (7k + 2p)(8k - 5p)$

(g) $22a^2 + 75ab - 7b^2 = (2a + 7b)(11a - b)$

(h) $3x^2 - 25xy + 52y^2 = (x - 4y)(3x - 13y)$

6.(a) $(x + y)^2 - z^2 = (x + y + z)(x + y - z)$

(b) $(b + c)^2 - d^2 = (b + c + d)(b + c - d)$

(c) $(m - n)^2 - 4 = (m - n + 2)(m - n - 2)$

(d) $x^4 - (y + z)^2 = (x^2 + y + z)(x^2 - y - z)$

(e) $6x^4 - (x + 1)^2 = (4x^2 + x + 1)(4x^2 - x - 1)$

(f) $(a + b)^2 - (x - y)^2 = (a + b + x - y)(a + b - x + y)$

(g) $a^2 - 4(x + y)^2 = (a + 2x + 2y)(a - 2x - 2y)$

(h) $4b^2 - (b^2 + c^2)^2 = (2b + b^2 + c^2)(2b - b^2 - c^2)$

7.(a) $(28)^2 - (22)^2 = (28 + 22)(28 - 22) = 50 \times 6 = 300$

(b) $(56\frac{1}{2})^2 - (33\frac{1}{2})^2 = (56\frac{1}{2} + 33\frac{1}{2})(56\frac{1}{2} - 33\frac{1}{2}) = 90 \times 23 = 2{,}070$

(c) $(101)^2 - 1 = (101 + 1)(101 - 1) = 102 \times 100 = 10{,}200$

(d) $(337)^2 - (163)^2 = (337 + 163)(337 - 163) = 500 \times 174 = 87{,}000$

(e) $(73)^2 - (27)^2 = (73 + 27)(73 - 27) = 100 \times 46 = 4{,}600$

(f) $(84\frac{3}{4})^2 - (15\frac{1}{4})^2 = (84\frac{3}{4} + 15\frac{1}{4})(84\frac{3}{4} - 15\frac{1}{4}) = 100 \times 69\frac{1}{2} = 6{,}950$

(g) $(163.52)^2 - (36.48)^2 = (163.52 + 36.48)(163.52 - 36.48) = 200 \times 127.04 = 25{,}408$

(h) $(178.43)^2 - (78.43)^2 = (178.43 + 78.43)(178.43 - 78.43) = 256.86 \times 100 = 25{,}686$

8.(a) $f(a) = a^2 - 6a - 4 \div (a - 2)$,

$R = f(2) = 4 - 12 - 4 = -12$

(b) $f\ x) = 6x^2 + 9x - 11 \div (x + 3)$,

$R = f(-3) = 54 - 27 - 11 = 16$

(c) $f(p) = p^3 - 11p + 5 \div (p + 2)$,

$R = f(-2) = -8 + 22 + 5 = 19$

(d) $f(m) = 3m^3 - 4m - 13 \div (m - 3)$,

$R = f(3) = 81 - 12 - 13 = 56$

(e) $f(x) = x^4 + 2x^3 - 3x^2 + 5x - 8 \div (x + 2)$,

$R = f(-2) = 16 - 16 - 12 - 10 - 8 = -30$

(f) $f(x) = 2x^4 + 3x^3 - 4x^2 + 6x - 7 \div (x - 3)$,

$R = f(3) = 162 + 81 - 36 + 18 - 7 = 218$

(g) $a^4 + 3a^3 + 7a^2 + 6a + 7 \div (a^2 + 2a + 3)$

$$
\begin{array}{r}
a^2 \quad +a \quad +2 \\
\hline
a^2 + 2a + 3 \,\big)\, a^4 + \quad +7a^2 \quad +6a \quad +7 \\
3a^3 \\
a^4 + \\
2a^2 \quad +3a^2 \\
\hline
a^3 \quad +4a^2 \quad +6a \\
a^3 \quad +2a^2 \quad +3a \\
\hline
2a^2 \quad +3a \quad +7
\end{array}
$$

Remainder = $-a + 1$

(h) $y^4 + 3y^3 - 8y^2 + 7y - 4 \div (y^2 - 2y + 3)$

$$
\begin{array}{r}
y^2 \quad +5y \quad -1 \\
\hline
y^2 - 2y + 3 \,\big)\, y^4 \quad +3y^3 \quad -8y^2 \quad +7y \quad -4 \\
y^4 \quad -2y^3 \quad +3y^2 \\
\hline
 \\
5y^3 \quad 11y^2 \quad +7y \\
 \\
5v^3 \quad 10v^2 \quad +15v
\end{array}
$$

Remainder = $-10y - 1$

51

3. PARTIAL FRACTIONS – DECOMPOSING ALGEBRAIC FRACTIONS

It is possible to split or decompose many algebraic fractions into the sum or difference of two or more fractions. The method of splitting depends on the type of algebraic expressions in the numerator and denominator of the fraction.

An algebraic expression where every term in it is a multiple of a power of a variable (e.g. x) is called a **polynomial**. The highest power of the variable in the expression is the **degree** of the polynomial. When the highest power is 1, the algebraic expression is linear.

Examples:

- $ax^4 + bx^3 + cx^2 + dx + e$ = a polynomial of degree 4 (quartic)

- $ax^3 + bx^2 + cx + d$ = a polynomial of degree 3 (cubic)

- $ax^2 + bx + c$ = a polynomial of degree 2 (quadratic)

- $ax + b$ = a linear function

The letters in front of the terms in each of the above expressions are called their respective **coefficients**.

If the numerator of a fraction is a polynomial of lower degree than the denominator then we call it a **proper fraction**. If the numerator is equal to or of a higher degree than the denominator, we call it an **improper fraction**.

Remember that a fraction can be decomposed into partial fractions only if the degree of the numerator is strictly less than the degree of the denominator.

Examples:

- $\dfrac{x^2 + 3x + 1}{2x^3 - 3x^2 + 2x - 3} = \dfrac{(x+2)(x+1)}{(x^2+1)(2x-3)}$ | Proper fraction |

- $\dfrac{2x^4 + 3x - 5}{x^2 + 2}$ | Improper fraction |

Where possible, the numerator and denominator must be factorised.

This method is used when the factors in the denominator of the fraction are linear (in other words, when they do not have any square, cube terms, etc.).

Example 1:

Express $\dfrac{9}{(x + 1)(x - 2)}$ as partial fractions.

Method:

Let $\dfrac{9}{(x + 1)(x - 2)} = \dfrac{A}{x + 1} + \dfrac{B}{x - 2}$

Multiply both sides of the equation by $(x + 1)(x - 2)$:

$9 = A(x - 2) + B(x + 1) = Ax - 2A + Bx + B = (A + B)\,x + B - 2A$

Equating the coefficient of x on both sides:

$A + B = 0$ .... (1)

Equating the constants on both sides:

$B - 2A = 9$ .... (2)

Solving (1) and (2), we get:

$A = -3$ and $B = 3$

Therefore: $\dfrac{9}{(x + 1)(x - 2)} = \dfrac{-3}{x + 1} + \dfrac{3}{x - 2} = \dfrac{3}{x - 2} - \dfrac{3}{x + 1}$

Alternate Method

A short cut to finding A and B when the factors are linear is as follows:

In the fraction $\dfrac{9}{(x + 1)(x - 2)}$, substitute $x = -1$ by covering up $(x + 1)$ to get the value of A.

$[x = -1$ makes $(x + 1) = 0]$.

Then substitute $x = 2$ by covering up $(x - 2)$ to get the value of B.

$[x = 2$ makes $(x - 2) = 0]$.

Therefore:

$A = \dfrac{9}{(x + 1)(x - 2)} = \dfrac{9}{\blacksquare(-1 - 2)} = -3$

$B = \dfrac{9}{(x + 1)(x - 2)} = \dfrac{9}{(2 + 1)\blacksquare - \blacksquare} = 3$

This short cut is referred to as the "**cover up**" rule. It can only be used when the denominator of a given fraction has only linear factors.

Example 2:

Express: $\dfrac{3x-7}{(2x+1)(x-1)}$ as partial fractions.

This is a proper fraction with linear factors in the denominator. Therefore, we express it as the sum of the following partial fractions:

$$\frac{3x-7}{(2x+1)(x-1)} = \frac{A}{2x+1} + \frac{B}{x-1}$$

Multiply both sides of the equation by $(2x+1)(x-1)$ to get:

$$3x-7 = A(x-1) + B(2x+1)$$

Expand the right-hand side and regroup:

$$3x-7 = (A+2B)x + B - A$$

Equate the coefficients of x and the constants:

$$A + 2B = 3$$

$$B - A = -7$$

Solving for A and B:

$$A + 2(A-7) = 3$$

$$A + 2A - 14 = 3$$

$$3A - 14 = 3$$

$$3A = 17$$

$$A = \frac{17}{3}$$

Therefore:

$$B - \frac{17}{3} = -7$$

$$B = \frac{-4}{3}$$

Therefore:

$$\frac{3x-7}{(2x+1)(x-1)} = \frac{A}{2x+1} + \frac{B}{x-1} = \frac{17}{3(2x+1)} - \frac{4}{3(x-1)}$$

QUADRATIC FACTOR IN THE DENOMINATOR

This method is used when one or more of the factors of the denominator is quadratic.

Example:

Express $\dfrac{3x}{(x+1)(x^2+3)}$ as partial fractions.

We write: $\dfrac{3x}{(x+1)(x^2+3)} = \dfrac{A}{x+1} + \dfrac{Bx+C}{x^2+3}$

> Note that since $x^2 + 3$ is a quadratic factor, the numerator must be a linear factor of the form: $Bx + C$

Now multiply both sides of the equation by $(x+1)(x^2+3)$:

We get: $3x = A(x^2+3) + (x+1)(Bx+C)$

$3x = Ax^2 + 3A + Bx^2 + Cx + Bx + C$

$3x = (A+B)x^2 + (B+C)x + 3A + C$

Equate the coefficients of x^2, x and the constants:

$A + B = 0$

$B + C = 3$

$3A + C = 0$

Therefore, $A = \dfrac{-3}{4}$, $B = \dfrac{3}{4}$, $C = \dfrac{9}{4}$,

Hence:

$$\dfrac{3x}{(x+1)(x^2+3)} = \dfrac{A}{x+1} + \dfrac{Bx+C}{x^2+3} = \dfrac{\frac{-3}{4}}{x+1} + \dfrac{\frac{3}{4}x+\frac{9}{4}}{x^2+3}$$

$$= \dfrac{-3}{4(x+1)} + \dfrac{3x+9}{4(x^2+3)} = \dfrac{-3}{4(x+1)} + \dfrac{3(x+3)}{4(x^2+3)}$$

REPEATED LINEAR FACTOR IN THE DENOMINATOR

When there is a repeated linear factor in the denominator such as $(x + 1)^2$ or $(x - 4)^3$, the decomposition (or partial fractions) will take the following forms:

Example:

Express $\dfrac{7x}{(x + 1)(x - 3)^2}$ as partial fractions.

Here, $x + 1$ is a linear factor and $x - 3$ is a repeated linear factor in the denominator.

We write: $\dfrac{7x}{(x + 1)(x - 3)^2} = \dfrac{A}{x + 1} + \dfrac{B}{x - 3} + \dfrac{C}{(x - 3)^2}$

Notice the two partial fractions for the repeated factor $(x - 3)$. Multiplying both sides of the equation by $(x + 1)(x - 3)^2$, we get:

$7x = A(x - 3)^2 + B(x + 1)(x - 3) + C(x + 1)$

$= A(x^2 - 6x + 9) + B(x^2 - 2x - 3) + C(x + 1)$

$= (A + B)x^2 + (-6A - 2B + C)x + 9A - 3B + C$

Equating the coefficients of x^2, x and then the constants,

$A + B = 0$ .... (1)

$-6A - 2B + C = 7$ .... (2)

$9A - 3B + C = 0$ .... (3)

(2) − (3) gives:

$-15A + B = 7$ .... (4)

(1) − (4) gives:

$16A = -7$

$A = \dfrac{-7}{16}$, $B = \dfrac{7}{16}$

From (2), $C = 7 + 6A + 2B$

$= 7 - \dfrac{42}{16} + \dfrac{14}{16} = \dfrac{112}{16} - \dfrac{42}{16} + \dfrac{14}{16} = \dfrac{84}{16}$

Note: The coverup rule won't work

Therefore: $\dfrac{7x}{(x + 1)(x - 3)^2} = \dfrac{A}{x + 1} + \dfrac{B}{x - 3} + \dfrac{C}{(x - 3)^2}$

$= \dfrac{-7}{16(x + 1)} + \dfrac{7}{16(x - 3)} + \dfrac{84}{16(x - 3)^2} = \dfrac{-7}{16(x + 1)} + \dfrac{7}{16(x - 3)} + \dfrac{21}{4(x - 3)^2}$

DECOMPOSING A FRACTION WITH QUADRATIC FACTORS

Example 1:

Express $\dfrac{x^2 + 9}{x(x^2 + 2x + 6)}$ as partial fractions.

We write: $\dfrac{x^2 + 9}{x(x^2 + 2x + 6)} = \dfrac{A}{x} + \dfrac{Bx + C}{x^2 + 2x + 6}$

> Note the Bx + C in the numerator of the second partial fraction. Also, the denominator is not factorable.

Multiplying both sides of the equation by $x(x^2 + 2x + 6)$ we get:

$x^2 + 9 = A(x^2 + 2x + 6) + x(Bx + C)$

$x^2 + 9 = Ax^2 + 2Ax + 6A + Bx^2 + Cx$

$x^2 + 9 = (A + B)x^2 + (2A + C)x + 6A$

Equating the coefficients of x^2, x and then the constants:

$A + B = 1, \quad 2A + C = 0, \quad 6A = 9$

Therefore:

$A = 1.5, \quad B = -0.5, \quad C = -3$

Hence: $\dfrac{x^2 + 9}{x(x^2 + 2x + 6)} = \dfrac{1.5}{x} + \dfrac{-0.5x - 3}{x^2 + 2x + 6} = \dfrac{3}{2x} - \dfrac{x + 6}{2(x^2 + 2x + 6)}$

Example 2:

Express $\dfrac{3x^2 + 2x + 1}{(2x^2 - 3x - 2)(x^2 - x - 6)}$ as partial fractions.

Before we proceed, we examine to see whether any or all of the given quadratics could be reduced to linear factors. The numerator has no linear factors but each of the expressions in the denominator could be factorised to give linear factors as follows:

$$\dfrac{3x^2 + 2x + 1}{(2x^2 - 3x - 2)(x^2 - x - 6)} = \dfrac{3x^2 + 2x + 1}{(x - 2)(2x + 1)(x + 2)(x - 3)}$$

Therefore:

$$\dfrac{3x^2 + 2x + 1}{(x - 2)(2x + 1)(x + 2)(x - 3)} = \dfrac{A}{x - 2} + \dfrac{B}{2x + 1} + \dfrac{C}{x + 2} + \dfrac{D}{x - 3}$$

Since all the denominators of the partial fractions are linear factors, we can use the shortcut (coverup rule) here to get the values of A, B, C and D:

$$A = \dfrac{-17}{20}, \quad B = \dfrac{2}{35}, \quad C = \dfrac{-3}{20}, \quad D = \dfrac{34}{35}$$

Hence: $\dfrac{3x^2 + 2x + 1}{(2x^2 - 3x - 2)(x^2 - x - 6)} = \dfrac{-17}{20(x - 2)} + \dfrac{2}{35(2x + 1)} + \dfrac{-3}{20(x + 2)} + \dfrac{34}{35(x - 3)}$

DECOMPOSING A FRACTION WHERE THE POLYNOMIAL DEGREE IN THE NUMERATOR IS EQUAL TO OR HIGHER THAN THAT IN THE DENOMINATOR

The first thing to do in cases like this is to divide the numerator by the denominator using long division. The resulting mixed fraction is then examined to see whether any expression can be factorised.

Example:

Express $\dfrac{3x^3 + 2x^2 + 4x + 5}{3x^3 + x^2 + 12x + 4}$ as partial fractions.

$$\dfrac{3x^3 + 2x^2 + 4x + 5}{3x^3 + x^2 + 12x + 4} = \dfrac{(3x^3 + x^2 + 12x + 4) + x^2 - 8x + 1}{3x^3 + x^2 + 12x + 4} = 1 + \dfrac{x^2 - 8x + 1}{3x^3 + x^2 + 12x + 4}$$

$$= 1 + \dfrac{x^2 - 8x + 1}{(3x + 1)(x^2 + 4)}$$

Now let $\dfrac{x^2 - 8x + 1}{(3x + 1)(x^2 + 4)} = \dfrac{A}{3x + 1} + \dfrac{Bx + C}{x^2 + 4}$

Multiplying both sides of the equation by $(3x + 1)(x^2 + 4)$ we get:

$x^2 - 8x + 1 = A(x^2 + 4) + (3x + 1)(Bx + C) = Ax^2 + 4A + 3Bx^2 + 3Cx + Bx + C$

$= (A + 3B)x^2 + (3C + B)x + 4A + C$

Equating the coefficients of x^2, x and then the constants:

$A + 3B = 1$ .... (1)

$3C + B = -8$ .... (2)

$4A + C = 1$ .... (3)

(2) × 3: $9C + 3B = -24$ .... (4)

(1) − (4): $A - 9C = 25$ .... (5)

(3) × 9: $36A + 9C = 9$ .... (6)

(5) + (6): $37A = 34$

$A = \dfrac{34}{37}$

From (1): $3B = 1 - \dfrac{34}{37} = \dfrac{3}{37}$

$B = \dfrac{1}{37}$

From (3): $C = 1 - 4A = 1 - \dfrac{136}{37} = -\dfrac{99}{37}$

Therefore: $\dfrac{A}{3x + 1} + \dfrac{Bx + C}{x^2 + 4} = \dfrac{34}{37(3x + 1)} + \dfrac{x - 99}{37(x^2 + 4)}$

$\dfrac{3x^3 + 2x^2 + 4x + 5}{3x^3 + x^2 + 12x + 4} = 1 + \dfrac{34}{37(3x + 1)} + \dfrac{x - 99}{37(x^2 + 4)}$

Decompose each of the following fractions into partial fractions. Wherever possible use the "cover up" rule.

1. $\dfrac{4x - 21}{x^2 + 2x - 15}$

2. $\dfrac{3 + 3x}{2x^2 + 5x - 12}$

3. $\dfrac{7x^2}{(x + 1)(x - 2)^2}$

4. $\dfrac{8x + 27}{x(x^2 + 3)}$

5. $\dfrac{10x^2 - 15}{x(x^2 + 3x + 28)}$

6. $\dfrac{3x^3 + 7x - 4}{x(x + 2)^2}$

7. $\dfrac{4x^3 - 3x^2 + 2x - 5}{x^3 - 8x^2 + 6x + 1}$

8. $\dfrac{x^3 - 7x - 4}{x(2x - 1)}$

1. $\dfrac{4x-21}{x^2+2x-15} = \dfrac{4x-21}{(x+5)(x-3)} = \dfrac{A}{(x+5)} + \dfrac{B}{(x-3)}$

Using the "cover up" rule: $A = \dfrac{41}{8}$, $B = \dfrac{-9}{8}$

Therefore: $\dfrac{4x-21}{x^2+2x-15} = \dfrac{41}{8(x+5)} - \dfrac{9}{8(x-3)}$

---

2. $\dfrac{3+3x}{2x^2+5x-12} = \dfrac{3+3x}{(2x-3)(x+4)} = \dfrac{A}{(2x-3)} + \dfrac{B}{(x+4)}$

Using the "cover up" rule: $A = \dfrac{15}{11}$, $B = \dfrac{9}{11}$

Therefore: $\dfrac{3+3x}{2x^2+5x-12} = \dfrac{15}{11(2x-3)} + \dfrac{9}{11(x+4)}$

---

3. $\dfrac{7x^2}{(x+1)(x-2)^2}$

Let $\dfrac{7x^2}{(x+1)(x-2)^2} = \dfrac{A}{(x+1)} + \dfrac{B}{(x-2)} + \dfrac{C}{(x-2)^2}$

Multiplying both sides of the equal sign by $(x+1)(x-2)^2$:

$7x^2 = A(x-2)^2 + B[(x+1)(x-2)] + C(x+1)$

$7x^2 = A(x^2-4x+4) + B(x^2-x-2) + C(x+1)$

$7x^2 = (A+B)x^2 + (-4A-B+C)x + 4A-2B+C$

Therefore: $A + B = 7$ .... (1)

$-4A - B + C = 0$ .... (2)

$4A - 2B + C = 0$ .... (3)

(2) − (3): $-8A + B = 0$ .... (4)

(1) − (4): $9A = 7$

$A = \dfrac{7}{9}$, $B = \dfrac{56}{9}$, $C = \dfrac{28}{3}$

Hence:

$\dfrac{7x^2}{(x+1)(x-2)^2} = \dfrac{7}{9(x+1)} + \dfrac{56}{9(x-2)} + \dfrac{28}{3(x-2)^2}$

4. $\dfrac{8x + 27}{x(x^2 + 3)}$

Let $\dfrac{8x + 27}{x(x^2 + 3)} = \dfrac{A}{x} + \dfrac{Bx + C}{x^2 + 3}$

Multiplying both sides of the equal sign by $x(x^2 + 3)$:

$8x + 27 = A(x^2 + 3) + x(Bx + C)$

$8x + 27 = (A + B)x^2 + Cx + 3A$

Therefore: $A + B = 0$

$C = 8$

$3A = 27$

$A = 9, \; B = -9, \; C = 8$

Hence:

$\dfrac{8x + 27}{x(x^2 + 3)} = \dfrac{9}{x} - \dfrac{9x - 8}{x^2 + 3}$

---

5. $\dfrac{10x^2 - 15}{x(x^2 + 3x + 28)}$

Let $\dfrac{10x^2 - 15}{x(x^2 + 3x + 28)} = \dfrac{A}{x} + \dfrac{Bx + C}{x^2 + 3x + 28}$

Multiplying both sides of the equal sign by $x(x^2 + 3x + 28)$:

$10x^2 - 15 = A(x^2 + 3x + 28) + x(Bx + C)$

$10x^2 - 15 = (A + B)x^2 + (3A + C)x + 28A$

Therefore: $A + B = 10$

$3A + C = 0$

$28A = -15$

$A = \dfrac{-15}{28}, \; B = \dfrac{295}{28}, \; C = \dfrac{45}{28}$

Hence:

$\dfrac{10x^2 - 15}{x(x^2 + 3x + 28)} = \dfrac{-15}{28x} + \dfrac{295x + 45}{28(x^2 + 3x + 28)}$

6. $\dfrac{3x^3 + 7x - 4}{x(x+2)^2}$

The degree of the expressions in both numerator and denominator are the same. So, we have to do a long division first.

$$\frac{3x^3 + 7x - 4}{x(x+2)^2} = \frac{3x^3 + 7x - 4}{x^3 + 4x^2 + 4x}$$

Now:

$$
\begin{array}{r}
3 - 12x - 1 \\
x^3 + 4x^2 + 4x \overline{)\,3x^3 \qquad\quad + 7x \quad - 4} \\
\underline{3x^3 + 12x^2 + 12x} \\
-12x^2 - 5x \quad - 4 \\
\underline{-12x^2 - 48x - 48} \\
43x + 44
\end{array}
$$

Therefore:

$$\frac{3x^3 + 7x - 4}{x(x+2)^2} = 3 - \frac{12}{x} + \frac{43x + 44}{x(x+2)^2}$$

Now, let $\dfrac{43x + 44}{x(x+2)^2} = \dfrac{A}{x} + \dfrac{B}{x+2} + \dfrac{C}{(x+2)^2}$

Multiplying both sides of the equal sign by $x(x+2)^2$:

$43x + 44 = A(x+2)^2 + Bx(x+2) + Cx$

$43x + 44 = (A + B)x^2 + (4A + 2B + C)x + 4A$

Therefore:

$A + B = 0$

$4A + 2B + C = 43$

$4A = 44$

$A = 11, \ B = -11, \ C = 21$

Hence:

$$\frac{43x + 44}{x(x+2)^2} = \frac{11}{x} - \frac{11}{x+2} + \frac{21}{(x+2)^2}$$

$$\frac{3x^3 + 7x - 4}{x(x+2)^2} = 3 - \frac{1}{x} - \frac{11}{x+2} + \frac{21}{(x+2)^2}$$

7. $\dfrac{4x^3 - 3x^2 + 2x - 5}{x^3 - 8x^2 + 6x + 1}$

Both the numerator and denominator are of degree three. We therefore do a long division:

$$
\begin{array}{r}
4 \\
x^3 - 8x^2 + 6x + 1 \overline{)\, 4x^3 - \ \ 3x^2 + \ \ 2x - 5} \\
\underline{4x^3 - 32x^2 + 24x + 4} \\
29x^2 - 22x - 9
\end{array}
$$

Therefore: $\dfrac{4x^3 - 3x^2 + 2x - 5}{x^3 - 8x^2 + 6x + 1} = 4 + \dfrac{29x^2 - 22x - 9}{x^3 - 8x^2 + 6x + 1}$

Check now to see if the denominator could be factorised.

Let $f(x) = x^3 - 8x^2 + 6x + 1$

$f(1) = 1 - 8 + 6 + 1 = 0$

Therefore $(x - 1)$ is a factor of $f(x)$.

$$
\begin{array}{r}
x^2 - 7x - 1 \\
x - 1 \overline{)\, x^3 - 8x^2 + 6x + 1} \\
\underline{x^3 - \ \ x^2} \\
-7x^2 + 6x \\
\underline{-7x^2 + 7x} \\
-x + 1 \\
\underline{-x + 1} \\
0
\end{array}
$$

Therefore: $\dfrac{29x^2 - 22x - 9}{x^3 - 8x^2 + 6x + 1} = \dfrac{29x^2 - 22x - 9}{(x - 1)(x^2 - 7x - 1)}$

Now, let $\dfrac{29x^2 - 22x - 9}{(x - 1)(x^2 - 7x - 1)} = \dfrac{A}{x - 1} + \dfrac{Bx + C}{x^2 - 7x - 1}$

Multiplying both sides of the equal sign by $(x - 1)(x^2 - 7x - 1)$

$29x^2 - 22x - 9 = A(x^2 - 7x - 1) + (x - 1)(Bx + C)$

$= (A + B)x^2 + (-7A - B + C)x - A - C$

Therefore: $A + B = 29$ .... (1)

$-7A - B + C = -22$ .... (2)

$-A - C = -9$ .... (3)

(2) + (3): $-8A - B = -31$ .... (4)

(1) + (4): $-7A = -2$

$A = \dfrac{2}{7},\ B = \dfrac{201}{7},\ C = \dfrac{61}{7}$

Hence: $\dfrac{4x^3 - 3x^2 + 2x - 5}{x^3 - 8x^2 + 6x + 1} = 4 + \dfrac{2}{7(x - 1)} + \dfrac{201x + 61}{7(x^2 - 7x - 1)}$

8. $\dfrac{x^3 - 7x - 4}{x(2x - 1)}$

The degree of the denominator is greater than that of the denominator, so we divide first.

$$\require{enclose}
\begin{array}{r}
\tfrac{1}{2}x + \tfrac{1}{4} \\
2x^2 - x \enclose{longdiv}{x^3 -7x -4} \\
\underline{x^3 \tfrac{1}{2}x^2 } \\
\tfrac{1}{2}x^2 -7x \\
\underline{\tfrac{1}{2}x^2 \tfrac{1}{4}x } \\
-6\tfrac{3}{4}x -4
\end{array}$$

$$\frac{x^3 - 7x - 4}{x(2x - 1)} = \frac{1}{2}x + \frac{1}{4} - \frac{6\tfrac{3}{4}x + 4}{x(2x - 1)}$$

Now, let $\dfrac{6\tfrac{3}{4}x + 4}{x(2x - 1)} = \dfrac{A}{x} + \dfrac{B}{2x - 1}$

Using the 'cover up' rule:

$A = -4,\ B = \dfrac{59}{4}$

Hence:

$$\frac{6\tfrac{3}{4}x + 4}{x(2x - 1)} = \frac{-4}{x} + \frac{59}{4(2x - 1)}$$

$$\frac{x^3 - 7x - 4}{x(2x - 1)} = \frac{1}{2}x + \frac{1}{4} + \frac{4}{x} - \frac{59}{4(2x - 1)}$$

4. MATRICES

A **matrix** is a rectangular or square grid of numbers arranged into rows and columns. Each number in the matrix is called an element. The numbers are arranged in an array. The plural of "matrix" is "**matrices**".

If there are two rows and two columns in a matrix, it is referred to as a **2×2** (two by two) matrix. If there are two rows and three columns, then it is a **2×3** (two by three) matrix. In general **m×n** matrix will have m rows and n columns. When the number of rows and columns are the same (i.e. m = n) then the matrix is called a **square matrix**.

Examples:

| This is a 2 × 2 square matrix: | $A = \begin{bmatrix} 1 & 2 \\ 2 & 3 \end{bmatrix}$ |

| This is a 2 × 3 matrix: | $B = \begin{pmatrix} 2 & -1 & 3 \\ 1 & 4 & 5 \end{pmatrix}$ |

| This is a 3 × 3 square matrix: | $C = \begin{bmatrix} 3 & 2 & 0 \\ -1 & 1 & -2 \\ 4 & 3 & 0 \end{bmatrix}$ |

- A matrix is usually assigned an alphabet for easy reference.
- A matrix which is not a square matrix is a **rectangular matrix**.
- Notice the different types of enclosures used for the elements of a matrix.

EASY REFERENCING OF AN ELEMENT IN A MATRIX

Consider the matrix $\begin{bmatrix} a & b & c \\ d & e & f \\ g & h & i \end{bmatrix}$

Rows of a matrix are identified by naming them i_1, i_2, i_3 and so on.

- That is, the row containing the elements "a", "b", "c" is i_1
- The row containing the elements "d", "e", "f" is i_2 and so on

Similarly, **the columns of a matrix** are denoted by j_1, j_2, j_3 and so on

- That is, the column containing the elements "a", "d", "g" is j_1
- The column containing the elements "b", "e", "h" is j_2

Thus, the position of the element "a" for example can be referenced as i_1j_1. The position of the element "h" is i_3j_2 etc. The position of the nth element is therefore referenced i_nj_n.

SPECIAL MATRICES

- If a matrix has only one row, it is called a **row** matrix.

e.g. $\begin{bmatrix} 1 & 2 \end{bmatrix}$, $\begin{bmatrix} 3 & -1 & 0 \end{bmatrix}$

- A matrix that has only one column is a **column** matrix.

e.g. $\begin{bmatrix} 2 \\ 3 \end{bmatrix}$, $\begin{bmatrix} 4 \\ 2 \\ 1 \end{bmatrix}$

- A matrix with all its elements 0 is called a **zero or a null** matrix.

e.g. $\begin{pmatrix} 0 & 0 \\ 0 & 0 \end{pmatrix}$

- A square matrix with all its non-diagonal elements zero is a **diagonal** matrix.

e.g. $\begin{vmatrix} a & 0 & 0 \\ 0 & b & 0 \\ 0 & 0 & c \end{vmatrix}$

A **unit matrix** is every square matrix with all elements zero except for the elements of the main diagonal (or a leading diagonal) that are all ones. The unit matrix is also called the **identity matrix**.

- $\begin{bmatrix} 1 & 0 \\ 0 & 1 \end{bmatrix}$

- $\begin{vmatrix} 1 & 0 & 0 \\ 0 & 1 & 0 \\ 0 & 0 & 1 \end{vmatrix}$

The main diagonal is the line joining the **top left** element to the **bottom right** element.

A **triangular matrix** is one with every element above or below the main diagonal is zero.	$\begin{bmatrix} 1 & 0 & 0 \\ 0 & 4 & 0 \\ 0 & 0 & -3 \end{bmatrix}$

If the elements below the main diagonal only are zero, the matrix is an **upper triangular matrix**.	$\begin{bmatrix} 1 & 2 & 3 \\ 0 & 4 & 5 \\ 0 & 0 & 6 \end{bmatrix}$

If the elements above the main diagonal only are zero, the matrix is a **lower triangular matrix**.	$\begin{bmatrix} 1 & 0 & 0 \\ 2 & 5 & 0 \\ 4 & 3 & 7 \end{bmatrix}$

The **negative of a matrix (-A)** is obtained by multiplying each element of matrix A by -1.

ADDITION OF MATRICES

Two matrices of the same type (or order) can only be added by adding the corresponding elements. That is, matrices must be conformable for addition. The addition is **commutative** (i.e. A + B = B + A) and **associative** (i.e. [A + (B + C) = (A + B) + C].

Example 1:

If $A = \begin{bmatrix} 2 & 3 \\ 1 & 4 \end{bmatrix}$ and $B = \begin{bmatrix} 4 & 1 \\ 5 & 3 \end{bmatrix}$ then: $A + B = \begin{bmatrix} 6 & 4 \\ 6 & 7 \end{bmatrix}$

Example 2:

If $X = \begin{bmatrix} 2 & 1 & 3 \\ 0 & 5 & 2 \\ 1 & 0 & 4 \end{bmatrix}$ and $Y = \begin{bmatrix} 3 & 0 & 5 \\ 2 & 1 & 4 \\ 7 & 4 & 3 \end{bmatrix}$ then: $X + Y = \begin{bmatrix} 5 & 1 & 8 \\ 2 & 6 & 6 \\ 8 & 4 & 7 \end{bmatrix}$

SUBTRACTION OF MATRICES

When subtracting a matrix B from matrix A, each element of matrix B is subtracted from the corresponding element of matrix A.

Example 1:

If $A = \begin{bmatrix} 2 & 3 \\ 1 & 4 \end{bmatrix}$ and $B = \begin{bmatrix} 4 & 1 \\ 5 & 3 \end{bmatrix}$ then: $A - B = \begin{bmatrix} -2 & 2 \\ -4 & 1 \end{bmatrix}$

Example 2:

If $X = \begin{bmatrix} 2 & 1 & 3 \\ 0 & 5 & 2 \\ 1 & 0 & 4 \end{bmatrix}$ and $Y = \begin{bmatrix} 3 & 0 & 5 \\ 2 & 1 & 4 \\ 7 & 4 & 3 \end{bmatrix}$ then: $X - Y = \begin{bmatrix} -1 & 1 & -2 \\ -2 & 4 & -2 \\ -6 & -4 & 1 \end{bmatrix}$

SCALAR MULTIPLICATION OF A MATRIX

Multiplying a matrix by a **scalar number** (positive, negative and fractional) means each element of the matrix is multiplied by that number.

Example 1:

$$3 \times \begin{bmatrix} 2 & 1 & 3 \\ 0 & 5 & 2 \\ 1 & 0 & 4 \end{bmatrix} = \begin{bmatrix} 6 & 3 & 9 \\ 0 & 15 & 6 \\ 3 & 0 & 12 \end{bmatrix}$$

Example 2:

$$\frac{1}{2} \times \begin{bmatrix} -2 & 2 \\ -4 & 1 \end{bmatrix} = \begin{bmatrix} 1 & -1 \\ 2 & -\frac{1}{2} \end{bmatrix}$$

MULTIPLICATION OF TWO MATRICES

A certain condition has to be satisfied to be able to multiply two matrices: **the number of columns in the 1st matrix must equal the number of rows in the 2nd matrix.**

Example 1:

Let the first matrix be A = $\begin{bmatrix} 3 & 2 \\ 5 & 1 \end{bmatrix}$ and the second be B = $\begin{bmatrix} 1 & 2 & 3 \\ 0 & 4 & 5 \end{bmatrix}$

Here the first matrix has two columns and the second matrix has two rows. The condition is satisfied for the product AB (i.e. a 2×**2** matrix is multiplied by a **2**×3 matrix. The bolded numbers must be the same. The result of the product AB will be a 2×3 matrix).

In general, (**m**×n matrix) × (n×**p** matrix) = m×**p** matrix

If we want to find the product BA, the first matrix has three columns and the second matrix has only two rows. The condition is not satisfied for the product to be valid (i.e. a 2×**3** matrix is multiplied by a **2**×2 matrix. The bolded numbers are not the same).

AB is valid. The multiplication is performed by taking each row elements of A and multiplying each of the column elements of B and adding them together as shown below:

$$AB = \begin{bmatrix} 3 \times 1 + 2 \times 0 & 3 \times 2 + 2 \times 4 & 3 \times 3 + 2 \times 5 \\ 5 \times 1 + 1 \times 0 & 5 \times 2 + 1 \times 4 & 5 \times 3 + 1 \times 5 \end{bmatrix} = \begin{bmatrix} 3 & 14 & 19 \\ 5 & 14 & 20 \end{bmatrix}$$

The multiplication of matrices is not commutative. That is, AB is not equal to BA. This is the case even if the number of columns of B (first matrix) equals the number of rows of A (second matrix).

Example 2:

Given two matrices A and B: $\begin{bmatrix} -1 & 0 & -4 \\ -2 & 3 & 2 \\ 0 & 1 & -1 \end{bmatrix}\begin{bmatrix} 2 & 1 & -3 \\ 1 & 3 & 4 \\ -4 & -1 & -4 \end{bmatrix}$, find the value of AB.

Solution:

A is a 3×**3** matrix and B is also a **3**×3 matrix. AB is valid as the bolded numbers are the same. The result will be a 3×3 matrix.

$$AB: \begin{bmatrix} -1 \times 2 + 0 \times 1 + (-4 \times -4) & -1 \times 1 + 0 \times 3 + (-4 \times -1) & -1 \times -3 + 0 \times 4 + (-4 \times -4) \\ -2 \times 2 + 3 \times 1 + 2 \times -4 & -2 \times 1 + 3 \times 3 + 2 \times -1 & -2 \times -3 + 3 \times 4 + 2 \times -4 \\ 0 \times 2 + 1 \times 1 + (-1 \times -4) & 0 \times 1 + 1 \times 3 + (-1 \times -1) & 0 \times -3 + 1 \times 4 + (-1 \times -4) \end{bmatrix}$$

$$= \begin{bmatrix} -2 + 0 + 16 & -1 + 0 + 4 & 3 + 0 + 16 \\ -4 + 3 - 8 & -2 + 9 - 2 & 6 + 12 - 8 \\ 0 + 1 + 4 & 0 + 3 + 1 & 0 + 4 + 4 \end{bmatrix} = \begin{bmatrix} 14 & 3 & 19 \\ -9 & 5 & 10 \\ 5 & 4 & 8 \end{bmatrix}$$

Example 3:

If $A = \begin{bmatrix} 1 & 2 & 3 \\ 2 & 3 & 1 \\ 3 & 1 & 2 \end{bmatrix}$ find the value of A^2.

Solution:

$$A^2 = \begin{bmatrix} 1 & 2 & 3 \\ 2 & 3 & 1 \\ 3 & 1 & 2 \end{bmatrix}\begin{bmatrix} 1 & 2 & 3 \\ 2 & 3 & 1 \\ 3 & 1 & 2 \end{bmatrix} = \begin{bmatrix} 1+4+9 & 2+6+3 & 3+2+6 \\ 2+6+3 & 4+9+1 & 6+3+2 \\ 3+2+6 & 6+3+2 & 9+1+4 \end{bmatrix} = \begin{bmatrix} 14 & 11 & 11 \\ 11 & 14 & 11 \\ 11 & 11 & 14 \end{bmatrix}$$

DETERMINANT OF A MATRIX

Determinant is a special number calculated from a square matrix, the use of which will be seen in the later chapters. In this chapter, how to calculate the determinant of a matrix is only shown.

Determinant of a 2×2 matrix: $\det\begin{bmatrix} a & b \\ c & d \end{bmatrix}$ is $ad - bc$

Determinant of a 3×3 matrix: $\det\begin{bmatrix} a & b & c \\ d & e & f \\ g & h & i \end{bmatrix} = a \times \det\begin{bmatrix} e & f \\ h & i \end{bmatrix} - b \times \det\begin{bmatrix} d & f \\ g & i \end{bmatrix} + c \times \det\begin{bmatrix} d & e \\ g & h \end{bmatrix}$

$\begin{bmatrix} e & f \\ h & i \end{bmatrix}, \begin{bmatrix} d & f \\ g & i \end{bmatrix}, \begin{bmatrix} d & e \\ g & h \end{bmatrix}$ are called **co-factors** of a, b and c respectively.

> Note: "a" multiplies the $\det\begin{bmatrix} e & f \\ h & i \end{bmatrix}$ which is obtained by hiding the row and column containing "a". Similarly, "b" multiplies $\det\begin{bmatrix} d & f \\ g & i \end{bmatrix}$ which is obtained by hiding the row and column containing "b" and "c" multiplies $\det\begin{bmatrix} d & e \\ g & h \end{bmatrix}$ which is obtained by hiding the row and column containing "c". **The sign in front of a, b and c alternate starting with +** (i.e. +ve, -ve, +ve). The same is followed when calculating the determinant of a larger sized matrix.

Example 1:

Calculate the determinant of the 2×2 matrix $\begin{bmatrix} 3 & 2 \\ 5 & 1 \end{bmatrix}$

Solution: $\det\begin{bmatrix} 3 & 2 \\ 5 & 1 \end{bmatrix} = 3 \times 1 - 5 \times 2 = -7$

Example 2:

Calculate the determinant of the 3×3 matrix $\begin{bmatrix} 1 & 2 & 3 \\ 2 & 3 & 1 \\ 3 & 1 & 2 \end{bmatrix}$

Solution: $\det\begin{bmatrix} 1 & 2 & 3 \\ 2 & 3 & 1 \\ 3 & 1 & 2 \end{bmatrix} = +1\det\begin{bmatrix} 3 & 1 \\ 1 & 2 \end{bmatrix} - 2\det\begin{bmatrix} 2 & 1 \\ 3 & 2 \end{bmatrix} + 3\det\begin{bmatrix} 2 & 3 \\ 3 & 1 \end{bmatrix}$

$= (6 - 1) - 2(4 - 3) + 3(2 - 9) = 5 - 2 - 21 = -18$

Some properties of a determinant:

- If each element of a row of a determinant is zero, then the value of the determinant is zero.
- The value of the determinant is zero if two rows are identical.
- Value of a determinant does not change if rows and the columns are interchanged.
- If two adjacent rows of a determinant are interchanged, the sign changes but not the value.
- If every element of a row is multiplied by a constant, then the value of the determinant is the original value multiplied by the constant.
- The value of the determinant of a diagonal matrix is the product of the diagonal elements.

TRANSPOSE OF A MATRIX

From a matrix A, its transpose A^T is obtained by interchanging the rows and columns.

Example 1:

If $A = \begin{bmatrix} 3 & 4 \\ 0 & 2 \\ -1 & 2 \end{bmatrix}$, then $A^T = \begin{bmatrix} 3 & 0 & -1 \\ 4 & 2 & 2 \end{bmatrix}$

A square matrix is said to be **symmetric** if it is equal to its **transpose.**

ADJOINT OF A SQUARE MATRIX

From a given square matrix, a cofactor matrix C is obtained by replacing its elements by their corresponding cofactors. **The adjoint A** (adj A) $= C^T$.

Example 1:

If $A = \begin{bmatrix} 1 & 2 & 3 \\ 2 & 3 & 1 \\ 0 & 1 & 2 \end{bmatrix}$, $C = 1 \times \begin{bmatrix} 3 & 1 \\ 1 & 2 \end{bmatrix} - 2 \times \begin{bmatrix} 2 & 1 \\ 0 & 2 \end{bmatrix} + 3 \times \begin{bmatrix} 2 & 3 \\ 0 & 1 \end{bmatrix}$

$- 2 \times \begin{bmatrix} 2 & 3 \\ 1 & 2 \end{bmatrix} + 3 \times \begin{bmatrix} 1 & 3 \\ 0 & 2 \end{bmatrix} - 1 \times \begin{bmatrix} 1 & 2 \\ 0 & 1 \end{bmatrix}$

$+ 0 \times \begin{bmatrix} 3 & 3 \\ 3 & 1 \end{bmatrix} - 1 \times \begin{bmatrix} 1 & 3 \\ 2 & 1 \end{bmatrix} + 2 \times \begin{bmatrix} 1 & 2 \\ 2 & 3 \end{bmatrix}$

> Observe the alternate positive and negative signs

> Take only the determinants of the cofactors

$C = \begin{bmatrix} 5 & -4 & 2 \\ -1 & 2 & -1 \\ -6 & 5 & -1 \end{bmatrix}$, $C^T = \begin{bmatrix} 5 & -1 & -6 \\ -4 & 2 & 5 \\ 2 & -1 & -1 \end{bmatrix}$

DETERMINANT OF A HIGHER ORDER MATRIX

The determinant of a **4×4** matrix, **5×5** matrix etc. involve tedious calculations and could be easily obtained using a matrix or graphics calculator. However, the manual method is simplified when there are one or more zero elements in the matrix.

Example 1:

Calculate the determinant of the 4 × 4 square matrix:

$A = \begin{bmatrix} 2 & 6 & 6 & 2 \\ 2 & 7 & 3 & 6 \\ 1 & 5 & 0 & 1 \\ 3 & 7 & 0 & 7 \end{bmatrix}$

> Look for zero elements. Take the column (or row) with the most zeros. In this example it is the third column that has the most zeros.

We therefore calculate the determinant with reference to this column's elements as follows:

$\text{Det } A = +6 \begin{bmatrix} 2 & 7 & 6 \\ 1 & 5 & 1 \\ 3 & 7 & 7 \end{bmatrix} - 3 \begin{bmatrix} 2 & 6 & 2 \\ 1 & 5 & 1 \\ 3 & 7 & 7 \end{bmatrix} + 0 \begin{bmatrix} 2 & 6 & 2 \\ 2 & 7 & 6 \\ 3 & 7 & 7 \end{bmatrix} - 0 \begin{bmatrix} 2 & 6 & 2 \\ 2 & 7 & 6 \\ 1 & 5 & 1 \end{bmatrix}$

$= 6(2\det\begin{bmatrix} 5 & 1 \\ 7 & 7 \end{bmatrix} - 7\det\begin{bmatrix} 1 & 1 \\ 3 & 7 \end{bmatrix} + 6\det\begin{bmatrix} 1 & 5 \\ 3 & 7 \end{bmatrix}) - 3(2\det\begin{bmatrix} 5 & 1 \\ 7 & 7 \end{bmatrix} - 6\det\begin{bmatrix} 1 & 1 \\ 3 & 7 \end{bmatrix} + 2\det\begin{bmatrix} 1 & 5 \\ 3 & 7 \end{bmatrix})$

$= 6[2(35 - 7) - 7(7 - 3) + 6(7 - 15)] - 3[2(35 - 7) - 6(7 - 3) + 2(7 - 15)]$

$= 6(56 - 28 - 48) - 3(56 - 24 - 16) = -120 - 48 = -168$

INVERSE OF A MATRIX

Only square matrices have inverses but not all square matrices have inverses.

The inverse of a matrix **A** is written **A⁻¹** where **A×A⁻¹ is equal to the identity matrix** $\begin{bmatrix} 1 & 0 \\ 0 & 1 \end{bmatrix}$.

The determinant of the matrix must not be zero. Refer to the properties of matrices to know when the determinant will be zero. A matrix which does not have an inverse is called **a singular matrix.**

If **A** $= \begin{bmatrix} a & b \\ c & d \end{bmatrix}$, its inverse **A⁻¹** is $\dfrac{1}{\text{Det A}} \begin{bmatrix} d & -b \\ -c & a \end{bmatrix}$

Interchange a and d and then change the signs of b and c

If **A** is a higher order matrix (det A is not equal to zero) we use the formula **A⁻¹** $= \dfrac{\text{Adj A}}{\text{Det A}}$

Example 1:

Calculate the inverse of the 2×2 matrix A $= \begin{bmatrix} 3 & 1 \\ -1 & 2 \end{bmatrix}$. Check to see if A×A⁻¹ = 1.

$$A^{-1} = \frac{1}{(3 \times 2) - (-1 \times 1)} \begin{bmatrix} 2 & -1 \\ 1 & 3 \end{bmatrix} = \frac{1}{7} \begin{bmatrix} 2 & -1 \\ 1 & 3 \end{bmatrix} = \begin{bmatrix} \frac{2}{7} & -\frac{1}{7} \\ \frac{1}{7} & \frac{3}{7} \end{bmatrix}$$

$$A \times A^{-1} = \begin{bmatrix} 3 & 1 \\ -1 & 2 \end{bmatrix} \times \begin{bmatrix} \frac{2}{7} & -\frac{1}{7} \\ \frac{1}{7} & \frac{3}{7} \end{bmatrix} = \begin{bmatrix} 1 & 0 \\ 0 & 1 \end{bmatrix} = 1$$

Example 2:

Calculate the inverse of the 3×3 matrix $X = \begin{bmatrix} 1 & 3 & 2 \\ 2 & 2 & 0 \\ 3 & 1 & 2 \end{bmatrix}$.

Check to see if $X \times X^{-1} = 1$

$DetX = 1(4) - 3(4) + 2(-4) = 4 - 12 - 8 = -16$

$C = \begin{bmatrix} 4 & -4 & -4 \\ -4 & -4 & 8 \\ -4 & 4 & -4 \end{bmatrix}$

The elements are the cofactors of X with alternating signs as shown: $\begin{bmatrix} + & - & + \\ - & + & - \\ + & - & + \end{bmatrix}$

$AdjX = C^T = \begin{bmatrix} 4 & -4 & -4 \\ -4 & -4 & 4 \\ -4 & 8 & -4 \end{bmatrix}$

$X^{-1} = \dfrac{AdjX}{DetX} = \dfrac{-1}{16}\begin{bmatrix} 4 & -4 & -4 \\ -4 & -4 & 4 \\ -4 & 8 & -4 \end{bmatrix} = \begin{bmatrix} -\dfrac{4}{16} & \dfrac{4}{16} & \dfrac{4}{16} \\ \dfrac{4}{16} & \dfrac{4}{16} & -\dfrac{4}{16} \\ \dfrac{4}{16} & -\dfrac{8}{16} & \dfrac{4}{16} \end{bmatrix}$

Check: $X \times X^{-1} = \begin{bmatrix} 1 & 3 & 2 \\ 2 & 2 & 0 \\ 3 & 1 & 2 \end{bmatrix}\begin{bmatrix} -\dfrac{4}{16} & \dfrac{4}{16} & \dfrac{4}{16} \\ \dfrac{4}{16} & \dfrac{4}{16} & -\dfrac{4}{16} \\ \dfrac{4}{16} & -\dfrac{8}{16} & \dfrac{4}{16} \end{bmatrix} = \begin{bmatrix} 1 & 0 & 0 \\ 0 & 1 & 0 \\ 0 & 0 & 1 \end{bmatrix} = 1$

1. Four people **A, B, C** and **D** purchased the following from a supermarket:

	Apples (kg)	Oranges(dozen)	Bananas (Kg)
A	4	2	3
B	2	1	4
C	1	0	3
D	2	3	0

(a) Express the above as a 4 × 3 matrix:

$$X = \begin{array}{c} A \\ B \\ C \\ D \end{array} \begin{bmatrix} 4 & 2 & 3 \\ 2 & 1 & 4 \\ 1 & 0 & 3 \\ 2 & 3 & 0 \end{bmatrix}$$

Apples   Oranges   Bananas

(b) The price of items bought are as follows:

	Price per Kg	Price per dozen
Apples	$3	
Oranges		$4
Bananas	$2	

Write down the price column matrix:

Cost per unit

$$Y = \begin{array}{c} \text{Apple} \\ \text{Oranges} \\ \text{Bananas} \end{array} \begin{bmatrix} 3 \\ 4 \\ 2 \end{bmatrix}$$

(c) Write down the matrix showing the four people's total bill.

$$X \times Y = \begin{bmatrix} 4 & 2 & 3 \\ 2 & 1 & 4 \\ 1 & 0 & 3 \\ 2 & 3 & 0 \end{bmatrix} \begin{bmatrix} 3 \\ 4 \\ 2 \end{bmatrix} = \begin{bmatrix} 26 \\ 18 \\ 9 \\ 18 \end{bmatrix}$$

Total bill for the four people = 26 + 18 + 9 + 18 = $71

2. John is building flats on three blocks of land he owns as follows:

	Block A	Block B	Block C
Number of flats	18	15	12

He plans to furnish the flats as follows:

	Per flat
Lounge Chairs (LC)	4
Kitchen Chairs (KC)	6
Beds (B)	3
Table Lamps (TL)	6

(a) Set out the above information as a 3 × 4 matrix.

$$\begin{array}{c} \\ A \\ B \\ C \end{array} \begin{array}{cccc} LC & KC & B & TL \\ \end{array} \\ \begin{bmatrix} 72 & 108 & 54 & 108 \\ 60 & 90 & 45 & 90 \\ 48 & 72 & 36 & 72 \end{bmatrix}$$

(b) If the cost of a lounge chair is $400, a kitchen chair $120, a bed $800 and a table lamp $75, using appropriate matrices calculate the cost of furnishing the flats on the three blocks.

$$\begin{array}{c} \text{Unit cost (\$)} \quad \text{Total cost (\$)} \end{array}$$

$$\begin{bmatrix} 72 & 108 & 54 & 108 \\ 60 & 90 & 45 & 90 \\ 48 & 72 & 36 & 72 \end{bmatrix} \begin{bmatrix} 400 \\ 120 \\ 800 \\ 75 \end{bmatrix} = \begin{bmatrix} 93,060 & A \\ 77,550 & B \\ 62,040 & C \end{bmatrix}$$

The total cost of furnishing the flats in all three blocks:

= $93,060 + $77,550 + $62,040 = $232,650

3. An investment company offers two types of investments, I and II for clients. Investment I pays 10% per year and investment II with a higher risk pays 20% per year. Clients are able to divide their investment between the two to receive a return between 10% and 20%.

The table below lists total investments by three specific clients A, B and C and an arbitrary client D and their desired returns.

	CLIENT			
	A	B	C	D
Total investment ($)	30,000	60,000	25,000	a
Annual desired return ($)	3,500	9,000	3,000	b

How should each client invest to achieve the desired return?

Solution:

Consider the arbitrary client first. Let the arbitrary client make x_1 in Investment in I and x_2 in investment II.

Therefore: $x_1 + x_2 = a$ ....(1)

$0.1x_1 + 0.2x_2 = b$ .... (2)

The matrix equation representing the above is: $\begin{bmatrix} 1 & 1 \\ 0.1 & 0.2 \end{bmatrix}\begin{bmatrix} x_1 \\ x_2 \end{bmatrix} = \begin{bmatrix} a \\ b \end{bmatrix}$

The inverse of $\begin{bmatrix} 1 & 1 \\ 0.1 & 0.2 \end{bmatrix} = \dfrac{1}{0.2 - 0.1}\begin{bmatrix} 0.2 & -1 \\ -0.1 & 1 \end{bmatrix} = 10\begin{bmatrix} 0.2 & -1 \\ -0.1 & 1 \end{bmatrix} = \begin{bmatrix} 2 & -10 \\ -1 & 10 \end{bmatrix}$

Hence $\begin{bmatrix} x_1 \\ x_2 \end{bmatrix} = \begin{bmatrix} 2 & -10 \\ -1 & 10 \end{bmatrix}\begin{bmatrix} a \\ b \end{bmatrix}$

We can now determine each client 's investments as follows:

Client A: $\begin{bmatrix} x_1 \\ x_2 \end{bmatrix} = \begin{bmatrix} 2 & -10 \\ -1 & 10 \end{bmatrix}\begin{bmatrix} 30,000 \\ 3,500 \end{bmatrix} = \begin{bmatrix} 25,000 \\ 5,000 \end{bmatrix}$

Client A should invest $25,000 in I and $5,000 in II.

Client B: $\begin{bmatrix} x_1 \\ x_2 \end{bmatrix} = \begin{bmatrix} 2 & -10 \\ -1 & 10 \end{bmatrix}\begin{bmatrix} 60,000 \\ 9,000 \end{bmatrix} = \begin{bmatrix} 30,000 \\ 30,000 \end{bmatrix}$

Client B should invest $30,000 in I and $30,000 in II.

Client C: $\begin{bmatrix} x_1 \\ x_2 \end{bmatrix} = \begin{bmatrix} 2 & -10 \\ -1 & 10 \end{bmatrix}\begin{bmatrix} 25,000 \\ 3,000 \end{bmatrix} = \begin{bmatrix} 20,000 \\ 5,000 \end{bmatrix}$

Client B should invest $20,000 in I and $5,000 in II.

1. If $A = \begin{bmatrix} 3 & 2 \\ 2 & -1 \end{bmatrix}$, $B = \begin{bmatrix} 1 & 2 \\ 3 & 0 \end{bmatrix}$, $C = \begin{bmatrix} 3 & 1 & -1 \\ 0 & 2 & 2 \end{bmatrix}$

Calculate, if possible, each of the following:

(a) $A + 3B$

(b) $A - 2B$

(c) AC

(d) CA

(e) A^2

---

2. Find the product AB of the following matrices:

(a) $A = \begin{bmatrix} 3 & 2 & 1 \\ -1 & 2 & 3 \\ 3 & 1 & 4 \end{bmatrix}$, $B = \begin{bmatrix} 1 & 3 & 4 \\ 2 & 4 & 1 \\ -1 & 2 & 3 \end{bmatrix}$

(b) $A = \begin{bmatrix} 1 & 3 & 0 \\ 2 & 4 & -1 \end{bmatrix}$, $B = \begin{bmatrix} 3 & 1 & 4 \\ 2 & 0 & 3 \\ 1 & 2 & -1 \end{bmatrix}$

3.(a) In the determinant $\begin{vmatrix} 6 & -1 & 7 \\ 2 & 3 & -4 \\ -1 & -3 & 5 \end{vmatrix}$, find the cofactors of the elements 7, 2 and -3.

(b) Find the cofactors of a_{21} and a_{32} in $\begin{vmatrix} a_{11} & a_{12} & a_{13} \\ a_{21} & a_{22} & a_{23} \\ a_{31} & a_{32} & a_{33} \end{vmatrix}$

---

4. Calculate the inverses of the following matrices:

(a) $P = \begin{bmatrix} 2 & 3 \\ -1 & 5 \end{bmatrix}$ (b) $Q = \begin{bmatrix} 1 & 2 & 5 \\ 1 & -1 & -1 \\ 2 & 3 & -2 \end{bmatrix}$ (c) $R = \begin{bmatrix} 1 & -1 & 2 \\ 0 & 2 & -3 \\ 3 & -2 & 4 \end{bmatrix}$

5.(a) For what value of m does the matrix $\begin{bmatrix} 8 & m \\ 3 & 6 \end{bmatrix}$ have no inverse?

(b) If $A = \begin{bmatrix} 2 & 3 \\ 5 & -2 \end{bmatrix}$, show that $A^{-1} = \dfrac{1}{19} A$

6. Calculate the determinant of the matrix:

$$X = \begin{bmatrix} 1 & 2 & 1 & 0 \\ 0 & 3 & 1 & 1 \\ -1 & 0 & 3 & 1 \\ 3 & 1 & 2 & 0 \end{bmatrix}$$

7. Evaluate the determinant of matrix $P = \begin{bmatrix} 1 & -3 & -2 \\ 3 & 2 & -1 \\ -1 & 5 & 0 \end{bmatrix}$

(a) by the first row

(b) by the second column

8. Consider the matrix $L = \begin{bmatrix} 4 & 0 & -4 \\ 3 & 4 & 2 \\ -1 & -1 & 1 \end{bmatrix}$

Write the 3 × 3 unit matrix along with L as follows and call it M:

$$M = \begin{bmatrix} 4 & 0 & -4 & 1 & 0 & 0 \\ 3 & 4 & 2 & 0 & 1 & 0 \\ -1 & -1 & 1 & 0 & 0 & 1 \end{bmatrix}$$

(a) Carry out the following operations on M in the given order

(i) Divide the first row by a_{11}

(ii) Row 2 − 3 × Row 1 and Row 3 − (-1) × Row 1

(iii) Divide the second row by a_{22}

(iv) Row 3 − (-1) × Row 2

(v) Divide the third row by a_{33}

(vi) Row 1 − (-1) Row 3 and Row 2 − $\dfrac{5}{4}$ × Row 3

What is the 3 × 3 matrix on the right side of the final result?

(b) Check if this matrix is the inverse of the original matrix L.

1. $A = \begin{bmatrix} 3 & 2 \\ 2 & -1 \end{bmatrix}$, $B = \begin{bmatrix} 1 & 2 \\ 3 & 0 \end{bmatrix}$, $C = \begin{bmatrix} 3 & 1 & -1 \\ 0 & 2 & 2 \end{bmatrix}$

(a) $A + 3B = \begin{bmatrix} 3 & 2 \\ 2 & -1 \end{bmatrix} + 3\begin{bmatrix} 1 & 2 \\ 3 & 0 \end{bmatrix} = \begin{bmatrix} 3 & 2 \\ 2 & -1 \end{bmatrix} + \begin{bmatrix} 3 & 6 \\ 9 & 0 \end{bmatrix} = \begin{bmatrix} 6 & 8 \\ 11 & -1 \end{bmatrix}$

(b) $A - 2B = \begin{bmatrix} 3 & 2 \\ 2 & -1 \end{bmatrix} - 2\begin{bmatrix} 1 & 2 \\ 3 & 0 \end{bmatrix} = \begin{bmatrix} 3 & 2 \\ 2 & -1 \end{bmatrix} - \begin{bmatrix} 2 & 4 \\ 6 & 0 \end{bmatrix} = \begin{bmatrix} 1 & -2 \\ -4 & -1 \end{bmatrix}$

(c) $AC = \begin{bmatrix} 3 & 2 \\ 2 & -1 \end{bmatrix}\begin{bmatrix} 3 & 1 & -1 \\ 0 & 2 & 2 \end{bmatrix} = \begin{bmatrix} 9 & 7 & 1 \\ 6 & 0 & -4 \end{bmatrix}$

(d) $CA = (2 \times \mathbf{3}) \times (\mathbf{2} \times 2)$

The multiplication is not possible as the bolded numbers are different.

(e) $A^2 = A \times A = \begin{bmatrix} 3 & 2 \\ 2 & -1 \end{bmatrix} \times \begin{bmatrix} 3 & 2 \\ 2 & -1 \end{bmatrix} = \begin{bmatrix} 13 & 4 \\ 4 & 5 \end{bmatrix}$

2.(a) $A = \begin{bmatrix} 3 & 2 & 1 \\ -1 & 2 & 3 \\ 3 & 1 & 4 \end{bmatrix}$, $B = \begin{bmatrix} 1 & 3 & 4 \\ 2 & 4 & 1 \\ -1 & 2 & 3 \end{bmatrix}$

$AB = \begin{bmatrix} 6 & 19 & 17 \\ 0 & 11 & 7 \\ 1 & 21 & 25 \end{bmatrix}$

(b) $A = \begin{bmatrix} 1 & 3 & 0 \\ 2 & 4 & -1 \end{bmatrix}$, $B = \begin{bmatrix} 3 & 1 & 4 \\ 2 & 0 & 3 \\ 1 & 2 & -1 \end{bmatrix}$

$AB = \begin{bmatrix} 9 & 1 & 13 \\ 13 & 0 & 21 \end{bmatrix}$

3.(a) In the determinant $\begin{vmatrix} 6 & -1 & 7 \\ 2 & 3 & -4 \\ -1 & -3 & 5 \end{vmatrix}$, the cofactors of the elements 7, 2 and -3 are:

Cofactor of 7 $= \begin{bmatrix} 2 & 3 \\ -1 & -3 \end{bmatrix}$

Cofactor of 2 $= \begin{bmatrix} -1 & 7 \\ -3 & 5 \end{bmatrix}$

Cofactor of -3 $= \begin{bmatrix} 6 & 7 \\ 2 & -4 \end{bmatrix}$

(b) The cofactors of a_{21} and a_{32} in $\begin{vmatrix} a_{11} & a_{12} & a_{13} \\ a_{21} & a_{22} & a_{23} \\ a_{31} & a_{32} & a_{33} \end{vmatrix}$

Cofactor of a_{21} $= \begin{bmatrix} a_{12} & a_{13} \\ a_{32} & a_{33} \end{bmatrix}$, Cofactor of a_{32} $= \begin{bmatrix} a_{11} & a_{13} \\ a_{21} & a_{23} \end{bmatrix}$

4.(a) $P = \begin{bmatrix} 2 & 3 \\ -1 & 5 \end{bmatrix}$

$P^{-1} = \dfrac{1}{Det\ P} \begin{bmatrix} 5 & -3 \\ 1 & 2 \end{bmatrix} = \dfrac{1}{13} \begin{bmatrix} 5 & -3 \\ 1 & 2 \end{bmatrix} = \begin{bmatrix} \dfrac{5}{13} & -\dfrac{3}{13} \\ \dfrac{1}{13} & \dfrac{2}{13} \end{bmatrix}$

(b) $Q = \begin{bmatrix} 1 & 2 & 5 \\ 1 & -1 & -1 \\ 2 & 3 & -2 \end{bmatrix}$

$DetQ = 1(5) - 2(0) + 5(5) = 30$

$C = \begin{bmatrix} 5 & 0 & 5 \\ 19 & -12 & 1 \\ 3 & 6 & -3 \end{bmatrix}$ (The elements are the cofactors of Q)

$AdjQ = C^T = \begin{bmatrix} 5 & 19 & 3 \\ 0 & -12 & 6 \\ 5 & 1 & -3 \end{bmatrix}$

Therefore, $Q^{-1} = \dfrac{Adj\ Q}{Det\ Q} = \dfrac{1}{30} \begin{bmatrix} 5 & 19 & 3 \\ 0 & -12 & 6 \\ 5 & 1 & -3 \end{bmatrix} = \begin{bmatrix} \dfrac{5}{30} & \dfrac{19}{30} & \dfrac{3}{30} \\ 0 & \dfrac{-12}{30} & \dfrac{6}{30} \\ \dfrac{5}{30} & \dfrac{1}{30} & \dfrac{-3}{30} \end{bmatrix}$

(c) $R = \begin{bmatrix} 1 & -1 & 2 \\ 0 & 2 & -3 \\ 3 & -2 & 4 \end{bmatrix}$

$DetR = 1(2) - 1(-9) + 2(-6) = -1$

$C = \begin{bmatrix} 2 & -9 & -6 \\ 0 & -2 & -1 \\ -1 & 3 & 2 \end{bmatrix}$

$AdjR = C^T = \begin{bmatrix} 2 & 0 & -1 \\ -9 & -2 & 3 \\ -6 & -1 & 2 \end{bmatrix}$

Therefore: $R^{-1} = \dfrac{Adj\ R}{Det\ R} = -1 \begin{bmatrix} 2 & 0 & -1 \\ -9 & -2 & 3 \\ -6 & -1 & 2 \end{bmatrix} = \begin{bmatrix} -2 & 0 & 1 \\ 9 & 2 & -3 \\ 6 & 1 & -2 \end{bmatrix}$

5.(a) Let $A = \begin{bmatrix} 8 & m \\ 3 & 6 \end{bmatrix}$

Determinant $= 48 - 3m$

Matrix A will have no inverse if $48 - 3m$ is zero.

Therefore, $m = 16$

(b) If $A = \begin{bmatrix} 2 & 3 \\ 5 & -2 \end{bmatrix}$

$A^{-1} = \dfrac{-1}{19}\begin{bmatrix} -2 & -3 \\ -5 & 2 \end{bmatrix} = \dfrac{1}{19}\begin{bmatrix} 2 & 3 \\ 5 & -2 \end{bmatrix} = \dfrac{1}{19}A$

---

6. $X = \begin{bmatrix} 1 & 2 & 1 & 0 \\ 0 & 3 & 1 & 1 \\ -1 & 0 & 3 & 1 \\ 3 & 1 & 2 & 0 \end{bmatrix}$

Determinant by the 4th column as it has two zeros

$= 1\begin{bmatrix} 1 & 2 & 1 \\ -1 & 0 & 3 \\ 3 & 1 & 2 \end{bmatrix} - 1\begin{bmatrix} 1 & 2 & 1 \\ 0 & 3 & 1 \\ 3 & 1 & 2 \end{bmatrix}$

$= 1(-3 + 22 - 1) - 1(5 + 6 - 9) = 18 - 2 = 16$

---

7. Matrix $P = \begin{bmatrix} 1 & -3 & -2 \\ 3 & 2 & -1 \\ -1 & 5 & 0 \end{bmatrix}$

(a) Determinant calculated by the first row

$= 1\begin{bmatrix} 2 & -1 \\ 5 & 0 \end{bmatrix} - (-3)\begin{bmatrix} 3 & -1 \\ -1 & 0 \end{bmatrix} + (-2)\begin{bmatrix} 3 & 2 \\ -1 & 5 \end{bmatrix}$

$= 5 - 3 - 34 = -32$

(b) Determinant calculated by the second column

$= -(-3)\begin{bmatrix} 3 & -1 \\ -1 & 0 \end{bmatrix} + 2\begin{bmatrix} 1 & -2 \\ -1 & 0 \end{bmatrix} - 5\begin{bmatrix} 1 & -2 \\ 3 & -1 \end{bmatrix}$

$= -3 - 4 - 25 = -32$

83

8. $M = \begin{bmatrix} 4 & 0 & -4 & 1 & 0 & 0 \\ 3 & 4 & 2 & 0 & 1 & 0 \\ -1 & -1 & 1 & 0 & 0 & 1 \end{bmatrix}$

(a)(i) $R1 \div 4$

$= \begin{bmatrix} 1 & 0 & -1 & \frac{1}{4} & 0 & 0 \\ 3 & 4 & 2 & 0 & 1 & 0 \\ -1 & -1 & 1 & 0 & 0 & 1 \end{bmatrix}$

(ii) $R2 - 3 \times R1$ and $R3 - (-1) \times R1$

$= \begin{bmatrix} 1 & 0 & -1 & \frac{1}{4} & 0 & 0 \\ 0 & 4 & 5 & \frac{-3}{4} & 1 & 0 \\ 0 & -1 & 0 & \frac{1}{4} & 0 & 1 \end{bmatrix}$

(iii) $R2 \div 4$

$= \begin{bmatrix} 1 & 0 & -1 & \frac{1}{4} & 0 & 0 \\ 0 & 1 & \frac{5}{4} & \frac{-3}{16} & \frac{1}{4} & 0 \\ 0 & -1 & 0 & \frac{1}{4} & 0 & 1 \end{bmatrix}$

(iv) $R3 - (-1) \times R2$

$= \begin{bmatrix} 1 & 0 & -1 & \frac{1}{4} & 0 & 0 \\ 0 & 1 & \frac{5}{4} & \frac{-3}{16} & \frac{1}{4} & 0 \\ 0 & 0 & \frac{5}{4} & \frac{1}{16} & \frac{1}{4} & 1 \end{bmatrix}$

(v) $R3 \div \frac{5}{4}$

$= \begin{bmatrix} 1 & 0 & -1 & \frac{1}{4} & 0 & 0 \\ 0 & 1 & \frac{5}{4} & \frac{-3}{16} & \frac{1}{4} & 0 \\ 0 & 0 & 1 & \frac{1}{20} & \frac{1}{5} & \frac{4}{5} \end{bmatrix}$

(vi) $R1 - (-1)R3$ and $R2 - \frac{5}{4} \times R3$

$= \begin{bmatrix} 1 & 0 & 0 & \frac{6}{20} & \frac{1}{5} & \frac{4}{5} \\ 0 & 1 & 0 & \frac{-4}{16} & 0 & -1 \\ 0 & 0 & 1 & \frac{1}{20} & \frac{1}{5} & \frac{4}{5} \end{bmatrix}$

8.(Continued)

The final matrix on the right side of the unit matrix from (vi) is:

$$\begin{bmatrix} \dfrac{6}{20} & \dfrac{1}{5} & \dfrac{4}{5} \\[2mm] -\dfrac{4}{16} & 0 & -1 \\[2mm] \dfrac{1}{20} & \dfrac{1}{5} & \dfrac{4}{5} \end{bmatrix}$$

(b) The product of the original matrix L and this matrix is:

$$\begin{bmatrix} 4 & 0 & -4 \\ 3 & 4 & 2 \\ -1 & -1 & 1 \end{bmatrix} \begin{bmatrix} \dfrac{6}{20} & \dfrac{1}{5} & \dfrac{4}{5} \\[2mm] -\dfrac{4}{16} & 0 & -1 \\[2mm] \dfrac{1}{20} & \dfrac{1}{5} & \dfrac{4}{5} \end{bmatrix}$$

$$= \begin{bmatrix} [4 \ \ 0 \ \ -4]\begin{bmatrix}\frac{6}{20}\\ -\frac{4}{16}\\ \frac{1}{20}\end{bmatrix} & -[4 \ \ 0 \ \ -4]\begin{bmatrix}\frac{1}{5}\\ 0\\ \frac{1}{5}\end{bmatrix} & [4 \ \ 0 \ \ -4]\begin{bmatrix}\frac{4}{5}\\ -1\\ \frac{4}{5}\end{bmatrix} \\[6mm] -[3 \ \ 4 \ \ 2]\begin{bmatrix}\frac{6}{20}\\ -\frac{4}{16}\\ \frac{1}{20}\end{bmatrix} & [3 \ \ 4 \ \ 2]\begin{bmatrix}\frac{1}{5}\\ 0\\ \frac{1}{5}\end{bmatrix} & -[3 \ \ 4 \ \ 2]\begin{bmatrix}\frac{4}{5}\\ -1\\ \frac{4}{5}\end{bmatrix} \\[6mm] [-1 \ \ -1 \ \ 1]\begin{bmatrix}\frac{6}{20}\\ -\frac{4}{16}\\ \frac{1}{20}\end{bmatrix} & -[-1 \ \ -1 \ \ 1]\begin{bmatrix}\frac{1}{5}\\ 0\\ \frac{1}{5}\end{bmatrix} & [-1 \ \ -1 \ \ 1]\begin{bmatrix}\frac{4}{5}\\ -1\\ \frac{4}{5}\end{bmatrix} \end{bmatrix}$$

$$= \begin{bmatrix} \left[\dfrac{24}{20}+0-\dfrac{4}{20}\right] & \left[-\dfrac{4}{5}+0+\dfrac{4}{5}\right] & \left[\dfrac{16}{5}+0-\dfrac{16}{5}\right] \\[3mm] \left[-\dfrac{18}{20}+1-\dfrac{2}{20}\right] & \left[\dfrac{3}{5}+0+\dfrac{2}{5}\right] & \left[-\dfrac{12}{5}+4-\dfrac{8}{5}\right] \\[3mm] \left[-\dfrac{6}{20}+\dfrac{4}{16}+\dfrac{1}{20}\right] & \left[\dfrac{1}{5}+0-\dfrac{1}{5}\right] & \left[-\dfrac{4}{5}+1+\dfrac{4}{5}\right] \end{bmatrix} = \begin{bmatrix} 1 & 0 & 0 \\ 0 & 1 & 0 \\ 0 & 0 & 1 \end{bmatrix} = 1$$

Therefore: $L^{-1} = \begin{bmatrix} \dfrac{6}{20} & \dfrac{1}{5} & \dfrac{4}{5} \\[2mm] -\dfrac{4}{16} & 0 & -1 \\[2mm] \dfrac{1}{20} & \dfrac{1}{5} & \dfrac{4}{5} \end{bmatrix}$

5. EQUATIONS AND METHODS OF SOLUTIONS

An equation is a statement of an equality containing one or more variables. Solving the equation consists of determining which value(s) of the variable(s) make the equality true. Variables are also called unknowns and the values of the unknowns that satisfy the equality (i.e. make it true) are called solutions of the equation. An equation is written as two expressions, one on the left hand side and the other on the right hand side of the equal sign ('=').

An example of a simple statement of equality (or simple equation) is: $x + 3 = 10$

- The two expressions $x + 3$ and 10 are connected here by the equal sign '='.

- The expression $x + 3$ is on the left side of the equal sign and 10 is on the right side.

- **x is the variable or the unknown.**

What value of x will make this equation true? Since we know that $7 + 3$ makes 10, the value of x is 7. The solution of this equation is $x = 7$.

> Here 'x' has been used to represent the variable. Any English alphabet could be used to represent the variable.

A formal method of solution for the above equation is as follows:

$x + 3 = 10$

Subtracting 3 from both sides of the equation, we get:

$x + 3 - 3 = 10 - 3$ | The aim is to have the variable x only on the LHS

Simplifying: $x = 10 - 3 = 7$

An arithmetical operation performed on the LHS **must** be performed on the RHS also. This way the balance of the equation is maintained.

Another example of a simple equation is: $3y - 2 = y + 4$

We solve for y as follows:

$3y - 2 = y + 4$

$3y - 2 + 2 = y + 4 + 2$

$3y = y + 6$

$3y - y = y + 6 - y$

$2y = 6$

$y = 3$

> A short cut here is to take the y's to LHS and numbers to the RHS. When doing this remember to change the sign to the opposite sign as shown below.
>
> $3y - 2 = y + 4$
>
> $3y - y = 4 + 2$
>
> $2y = 6$
>
> $y = 3$

LINEAR EQUATIONS

The equations seen above are simple equations; they are also called linear equations with one variable. They take the general form $ax + b = 0$. One equation is enough to find the value of the variable as there is only one value for the variable in question.

- Two variables can be connected by one equation e.g. $y = x + 2$

- A linear equation with **two variables** takes the general form: $ax + by + c = 0$

Here the value of y depends on the value given to 'x'. 'x' is called the independent variable as it assumes any value given to it. 'y' is called the dependent variable as its value depends on the value assigned to 'x'. The solutions for the equation $y = x + 2$ are numerous. If x is given a particular value, then y can be calculated and there will be only one solution. For instance, when $x = 3$, $y = 5$.

CHANGING THE SUBJECT OF AN EQUATION (OR A FORMULA)

A single variable (without coefficient) on the left side of an equation is called its subject (e.g. 'y' is the subject of the equation $y = ax + b$). An equation containing one or more variables is sometimes called a **formula**. Any of the variables in an equation (or formula) could be made its subject.

Example 1:

Make 'x' the subject of: $ax + b = c$

Solution:

$ax + b = c$

$ax + b - b = c - b$

$ax = c - b$

Dividing both sides by 'a', we get:

$$x = \frac{c - b}{a}$$

Example 2:

Make 'a' the subject of: $2abc + 3x = 2a$

Solution:

$2abc + 3x = 2a$

$2a = 2abc + 3x$

$2a - 2abc = 2abc + 3x - 2abc$

$2a(1 - bc) = 3x$

Dividing both sides by $2(1 - bc)$, we get:

$$a = \frac{3x}{2(1 - bc)}$$

Example 3:

Make 'u' the subject of: $v^2 = u^2 + 2as$

$v^2 = u^2 + 2as$

Subtracting 2as from both sides, we get

$v^2 - 2as = u^2 + 2as - 2as$

$v^2 - 2as = u^2$

Therefore, $u = \sqrt{v^2 - 2as}$

Example 4:

Make 'v' the subject of: $\dfrac{1}{u} + \dfrac{1}{v} = \dfrac{1}{f}$

$\dfrac{1}{u} + \dfrac{1}{v} = \dfrac{1}{f}$

Multiplying by the LCM of the denominators uvf we get:

$vf + uf = uv$

$vf + uf - vf = uv - vf$

$uf = uv - vf$

$uf = v(u - f)$

$v(u - f) = uf$

Therefore, $v = \dfrac{uf}{u - f}$

INEQUATIONS

An inequation is a statement that two expressions are not the same.

Examples:

The statement 'seven is greater than 5' is written: $7 > 5$

The statement '3 is less than 8' is written: $3 < 8$

The statement $x - 5$ greater than or equal to 4 is written: $x - 5 \geq 4$

The statement $y - 1$ is less than or equal to -8 is written: $y - 1 \leq -8$

The inequality signs are:

- $>$ (read as greater than)
- $<$ (read as less than)
- $\geq$ (read as greater than or equal to)
- $\leq$ (read as less than or equal to)

Inequations with variables are solved in a manner similar to equations. When we multiply an equation on both sides by a negative sign the equal sign remains as it is. However, in the case of inequations, the inequality symbol switches to the opposite symbol. That is, '>' becomes '<' and '<' becomes '>' when multiplied on both sides by a negative sign.

- When $a > b$ is multiplied on both sides by a negative sign, we would write $-a < -b$
- When $a < b$ is multiplied on both sides by a negative sign, we would write $-a > -b$
- $a > b$ but the reciprocal of 'a' is less than the reciprocal of 'b'.
- $a > -b$ and the reciprocal of 'a' is also greater than the reciprocal of '-b'

The following diagrams show the representation of the solutions to inequations on a number line:

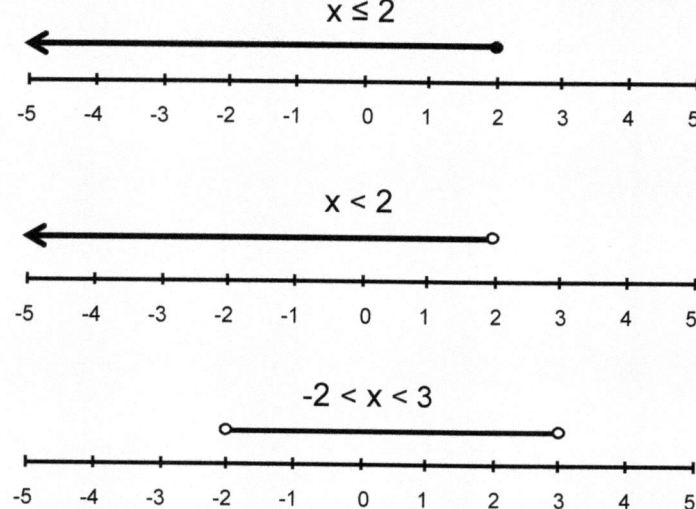

- A **solid circle** above a number indicates that the variable **includes** that number.
- A **hollow circle** above a number **does not include** that number.

Example 1:

$4x + 3 < 9$

$\quad 4x < 6$

$\quad\quad x < 1.5$

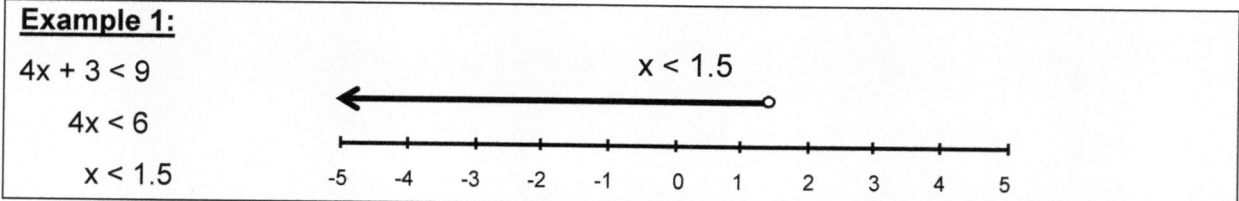

Example 2:

$3a - 5 \geq 4$

$\quad 3a \geq 9$

$\quad\quad a \geq 3$

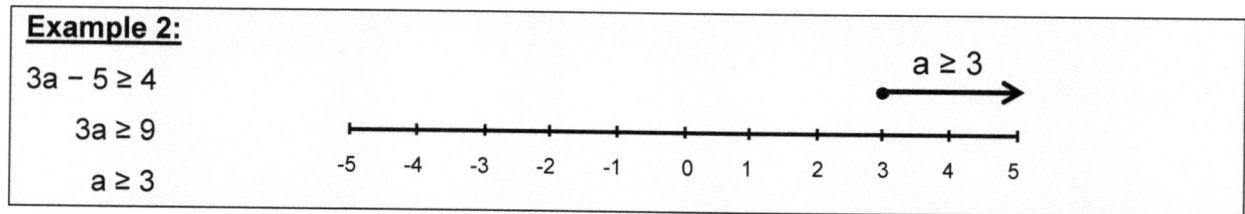

Example 3:

$-2m + 5 < 1 + 6m$

$-8m < -4$

$m > 0.5$

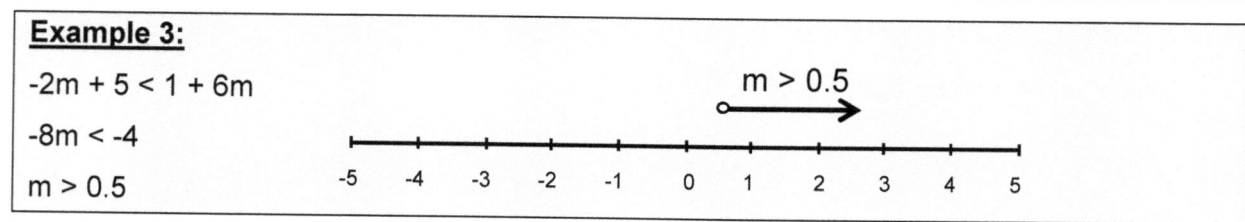

Example 4:

$$\frac{2b - 1}{4} \le \frac{2b + 3}{3}$$

$6b - 3 \le 8b + 12$

$-2b \le 15$

$b \ge -7.5$

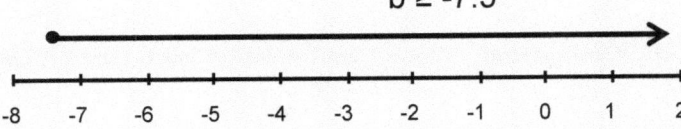

b ≥ -7.5

Example 5:

$|4x + 3| < 7$

This means either $4x + 3 < 7$ or $-4x - 3 < 7$ | Also $7 > -4x - 3$ or $-7 < 4x + 3$

Therefore:

$-7 < 4x + 3 < 7$

$-10 < 4x < 4$

$-2.5 < x < 1$

In other words, x lies between -2.5 and 1

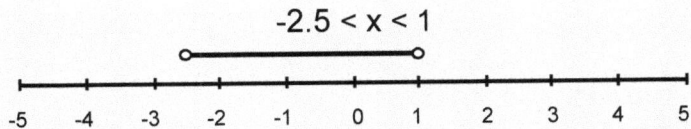

-2.5 < x < 1

We write this as an interval using parenthesis as (-2.5, 1)

Example 6:

$$\frac{2x + 1}{x - 2} > 1$$

When solving a fractional inequality involving an algebraic expression in the denominator **it is necessary to multiply both sides by the square of the denominator.**

Multiplying both sides by $(x - 2)^2$, we get

$(2x + 1)(x - 2) > (x - 2)^2$

$2x^2 - 3x - 2 > x^2 - 4x + 4$

$x^2 + x - 6 > 0$

$(x + 3)(x - 2) > 0$ | Any value of x between -3 and +2 does not satisfy the inequality

$x > 2$ or $x < -3$

(Check whether the original inequality holds for $x > 2$, $x < 2$ and for $x < -3$, $x > -3$)

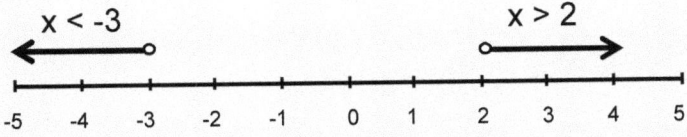

x < -3   x > 2

SIMULTANEOUS LINEAR EQUATIONS (TWO VARIABLES)

In order to solve linear equations with two variables that have a particular solution set, we need to have two linear equations that will be satisfied simultaneously by the values of the two variables.

Consider the case where two numbers have a sum of 15 and a difference of 3. These two conditions must be satisfied simultaneously. We formulate the two linear equations as follows, assuming the two numbers to be x and y.

Thus, we have: $x + y = 15$
$x - y = 3$

By inspection, x is 9 and y is 6. So, $9 + 6 = 15$ and $9 - 6 = 3$. The only solution is $x = 9, y = 6$.

When dealing with more complicated situations, we need to follow formal methods to solve for the values of the two variables as shown below.

Example 1:

Solve the simultaneous equations:

$x + y = 5$
$3x - y = 3$

Substitution Method:

$x + y = 5 \dots\dots\dots (1)$

$3x - y = 3 \dots\dots\dots (2)$

From (1): $y = 5 - x$

$3x - (5 - x) = 3$ Substituting $5 - x$ for y in (2)

$4x = 8$

$x = 2$

$2 + y = 5$ Substituting $x = 2$ in (1)

$y = 3$

The solution is: $x = 2, y = 3$

92

Elimination Method:

$$x + y = 5 \ldots\ldots\ldots (1)$$
$$3x - y = 3 \ldots\ldots\ldots (2)$$

(1) + (2): $4x = 8$ | This can be done only if the algebraic sum of x's or y's is zero |

$x = 2$

$2 + y = 5$ | Substituting $x = 2$ in (1) |

$y = 3$

The solution is: $x = 2$, $y = 3$

Matrix Method:

$$x + y = 5 \ldots\ldots\ldots (1)$$
$$3x - y = 3 \ldots\ldots\ldots (2)$$

The matrix representation of the two equations is:

$$\begin{bmatrix} 1 & 1 \\ 3 & -1 \end{bmatrix} \begin{bmatrix} x \\ y \end{bmatrix} = \begin{bmatrix} 5 \\ 3 \end{bmatrix}$$

Inverse of $\begin{bmatrix} 1 & 1 \\ 3 & -1 \end{bmatrix} = \dfrac{-1}{4} \begin{bmatrix} -1 & -1 \\ -3 & 1 \end{bmatrix} = \begin{bmatrix} \dfrac{1}{4} & \dfrac{1}{4} \\ \dfrac{3}{4} & -\dfrac{1}{4} \end{bmatrix}$

Multiplying both sides of the equation by the inverse:

$$\begin{bmatrix} 1 & 1 \\ 3 & -1 \end{bmatrix} \begin{bmatrix} \dfrac{1}{4} & \dfrac{1}{4} \\ \dfrac{3}{4} & -\dfrac{1}{4} \end{bmatrix} \begin{bmatrix} x \\ y \end{bmatrix} = \begin{bmatrix} \dfrac{1}{4} & \dfrac{1}{4} \\ \dfrac{3}{4} & -\dfrac{1}{4} \end{bmatrix} \begin{bmatrix} 5 \\ 3 \end{bmatrix}$$

$$\begin{bmatrix} 1 & 0 \\ 0 & 1 \end{bmatrix} \begin{bmatrix} x \\ y \end{bmatrix} = \begin{bmatrix} 2 \\ 3 \end{bmatrix}$$

The solution is: $x = 2$, $y = 3$

Example 2:

Solve the simultaneous equations:

$$5x + 4y = \frac{1}{2} \quad \ldots \ldots \ldots (1)$$

$$3x - 2y = -3 \quad \ldots \ldots \ldots (2)$$

Substitution Method

From (1): $y = \dfrac{\frac{1}{2} - 5x}{4} = \dfrac{1 - 10x}{8}$

$$3x - 2\left(\dfrac{1 - 10x}{8}\right) = -3$$

> Substitute $\dfrac{1 - 10x}{8}$ for y in (2)

$$3x - \left(\dfrac{1 - 10x}{4}\right) = -3$$

$$12x - (1 - 10x) = -12$$

$$12x - 1 + 10x = -12$$

$$22x = -11$$

$$x = -\frac{1}{2}$$

$$5\left(-\frac{1}{2}\right) + 4y = \frac{1}{2}$$

> Substituting $x = -\dfrac{1}{2}$ in (1)

$$\dfrac{-5}{2} + 4y = \frac{1}{2}$$

$$4y = 3$$

$$y = \frac{3}{4}$$

The solution is: $x = -\dfrac{1}{2}, \quad y = \dfrac{3}{4}$

Elimination Method:

$$5x + 4y = \frac{1}{2} \ldots \ldots \ldots (1)$$

$$3x - 2y = -3 \ldots \ldots \ldots (2)$$

(2) × 2: $6x - 4y = -6 \ldots \ldots \ldots (3)$

(1) + (3): $11x = -\dfrac{11}{2}$

> Here we cannot perform addition or subtraction to eliminate one variable without some manipulation. Let us eliminate y.

$$x = -\frac{1}{2}$$

Elimination Method (Continued):

$$5\left(-\tfrac{1}{2}\right) + 4y = \tfrac{1}{2}$$

| Substituting $x = -\tfrac{1}{2}$ in (1) |

$$-\tfrac{5}{2} + 4y = \tfrac{1}{2}$$

$$4y = 3$$

$$y = \tfrac{3}{4}$$

The solution is: $x = \tfrac{1}{2}$, $y = \tfrac{3}{4}$

Matrix Method:

$$5x + 4y = \tfrac{1}{2} \quad \cdots\cdots (1)$$

$$3x - 2y = -3 \quad \cdots\cdots (2)$$

The matrix representation of the two equations is:

$$\begin{bmatrix} 5 & 4 \\ 3 & -2 \end{bmatrix}\begin{bmatrix} x \\ y \end{bmatrix} = \begin{bmatrix} \tfrac{1}{2} \\ -3 \end{bmatrix}$$

Inverse of $\begin{bmatrix} 5 & 4 \\ 3 & -2 \end{bmatrix} = -\tfrac{1}{22}\begin{bmatrix} -2 & -4 \\ -3 & 5 \end{bmatrix} = \begin{bmatrix} \tfrac{2}{22} & \tfrac{4}{22} \\ \tfrac{3}{22} & -\tfrac{5}{22} \end{bmatrix}$

Multiplying both sides of the equation by the inverse:

$$\begin{bmatrix} 5 & 4 \\ 3 & -2 \end{bmatrix}\begin{bmatrix} \tfrac{2}{22} & \tfrac{4}{22} \\ \tfrac{3}{22} & -\tfrac{5}{22} \end{bmatrix}\begin{bmatrix} x \\ y \end{bmatrix} = \begin{bmatrix} \tfrac{1}{2} \\ -3 \end{bmatrix}\begin{bmatrix} \tfrac{2}{22} & \tfrac{4}{22} \\ \tfrac{3}{22} & -\tfrac{5}{22} \end{bmatrix}$$

$$\begin{bmatrix} 1 & 0 \\ 0 & 1 \end{bmatrix}\begin{bmatrix} x \\ y \end{bmatrix} = \begin{bmatrix} -\tfrac{1}{2} \\ \tfrac{3}{4} \end{bmatrix}$$

The solution is: $x = -\tfrac{1}{2}$, $y = \tfrac{3}{4}$

SIMULTANEOUS LINEAR EQUATIONS (THREE VARIABLES)

When there is a linear relationship between three variables, **three equations** are required to solve for the **three variables**. The strategy used to solve three variables from three equations is to reduce the three equations to two equations with two variables by a process of elimination of one of the three variables. Once we get two equations with two variables, we could apply any of the three methods for solving simultaneous equations with two variables.

Example 3:

Solve the simultaneous equations:

$$2x + y + z = 9 \quad \text{............} \quad (1)$$
$$x - y + z = 2 \quad \text{............} \quad (2)$$
$$x + 2y - z = 6 \quad \text{............} \quad (3)$$

Eliminate z:

$(1) - (2)$: $x + 2y = 7$ ....(4)

$(2) + (3)$: $2x + y = 8$ ....(5)

Elimination Method:

$(5) \times 2$: $4x + 2y = 16$ ....(6)

$(6) - (4)$: $3x = 9$

Therefore: $x = 3$

$3 + 2y = 7$ | Substitute x = 3 in (4) |

$2y = 4$

$y = 2$

$z = 1$ | Substitute x = 3, y = 2 in (1) |

The solution is: $x = 3$, $y = 2$, $z = 1$

Example 4:

Solve the simultaneous equations:

$$a + 2b - c = 10 \quad \text{...........} (1)$$
$$6a + 3b - 4c = 18 \quad \text{.............} (2)$$
$$-2a + b - 3c = 15 \quad \text{.............} (3)$$

Eliminate a:

$(1) \times 2$: $2a + 4b - 2c = 20$ ....(4)

$(3) + (4)$: $5b - 5c = 35$

$b - c = 7$ ....(5)

$(1) \times 6$: $6a + 12b - 6c = 60$ ....(6)

$(6) - (2)$: $9b - 2c = 42$ ....(7)

96

Substitution Method:

From (5): $b = c + 7$

$9(c + 7) - 2c = 42$ $\boxed{\text{Substituting in (7)}}$

$9c + 63 - 2c = 42$

$7c = -21$

$c = -3$

$b + 3 = 7$ $\boxed{\text{Substitute } c = -3 \text{ in (5)}}$

$b = 4$

$a + 8 + 3 = 10$ $\boxed{\text{Substitute } b = 4 \text{ and } c = -3 \text{ in (1)}}$

$a = -1$

The solution is: $a = -1$, $b = 4$, $c = -3$

Matrix Method:

The above two examples are now solved using the matrix method.

(1) Solve the simultaneous equations:

$2x + y + z = 9$ .... (1)

$x - y + z = 2$ .... (2)

$x + 2y - z = 6$ .... (3)

The matrix representation of the three equations is:

$$\begin{bmatrix} 2 & 1 & 1 \\ 1 & -1 & 1 \\ 1 & 2 & -1 \end{bmatrix} \begin{bmatrix} x \\ y \\ z \end{bmatrix} = \begin{bmatrix} 9 \\ 2 \\ 6 \end{bmatrix}$$

The determinant of matrix A $= \begin{vmatrix} 2 & 1 & 1 \\ 1 & -1 & 1 \\ 1 & 2 & -1 \end{vmatrix} = 2(-1) - 1(-2) + 1(3) = 3$

$$C = \begin{bmatrix} -1 & 2 & 3 \\ 3 & -3 & -3 \\ 2 & -1 & -3 \end{bmatrix}$$

$$C^T = \begin{bmatrix} -1 & 3 & 2 \\ 2 & -3 & -1 \\ 3 & -3 & -3 \end{bmatrix}$$

$$A^{-1} = \frac{1}{3}\begin{bmatrix} -1 & 3 & 2 \\ 2 & -3 & -1 \\ 3 & -3 & -3 \end{bmatrix} = \begin{bmatrix} -\frac{1}{3} & 1 & \frac{2}{3} \\ \frac{2}{3} & -1 & -\frac{1}{3} \\ 1 & -1 & -1 \end{bmatrix}$$

Therefore: $\begin{bmatrix} 2 & 1 & 1 \\ 1 & -1 & 1 \\ 1 & 2 & -1 \end{bmatrix}\begin{bmatrix} -\frac{1}{3} & 1 & \frac{2}{3} \\ \frac{2}{3} & -1 & -\frac{1}{3} \\ 1 & -1 & -1 \end{bmatrix}\begin{bmatrix} x \\ y \\ z \end{bmatrix} = \begin{bmatrix} -\frac{1}{3} & 1 & \frac{2}{3} \\ \frac{2}{3} & -1 & -\frac{1}{3} \\ 1 & -1 & -1 \end{bmatrix}\begin{bmatrix} 9 \\ 2 \\ 6 \end{bmatrix}$

$$\begin{bmatrix} 1 & 0 & 0 \\ 0 & 1 & 0 \\ 0 & 0 & 1 \end{bmatrix}\begin{bmatrix} x \\ y \\ z \end{bmatrix} = \begin{bmatrix} -\frac{1}{3} & 1 & \frac{2}{3} \\ \frac{2}{3} & -1 & -\frac{1}{3} \\ 1 & -1 & -1 \end{bmatrix}\begin{bmatrix} 9 \\ 2 \\ 6 \end{bmatrix} = \begin{bmatrix} 3 \\ 2 \\ 1 \end{bmatrix}$$

The solution is: $x = 3$, $y = 2$, $z = 1$

(2) Solve the simultaneous equations:

$a + 2b - c = 10$ .... (1)

$6a + 3b - 4c = 18$ .... (2)

$-2a + b - 3c = 15$ .... (3)

The matrix representation of the three equations is:

$$\begin{bmatrix} 1 & 2 & -1 \\ 6 & 3 & -4 \\ -2 & 1 & -3 \end{bmatrix}\begin{bmatrix} a \\ b \\ c \end{bmatrix} = \begin{bmatrix} 10 \\ 18 \\ 15 \end{bmatrix}$$

The determinant of matrix $X = \begin{vmatrix} 1 & 2 & -1 \\ 6 & 3 & -4 \\ -2 & 1 & -3 \end{vmatrix} = 1(-5) - 2(-26) + (-1)(12) = 35$

$$C = \begin{bmatrix} -5 & 26 & 12 \\ 5 & -5 & -5 \\ -5 & -2 & -9 \end{bmatrix}$$

$$C^T = \begin{bmatrix} -5 & 5 & -5 \\ 26 & -5 & -2 \\ 12 & -5 & -9 \end{bmatrix}$$

$$X^{-1} = \frac{1}{35}\begin{bmatrix} -5 & 5 & -5 \\ 26 & -5 & -2 \\ 12 & -5 & -9 \end{bmatrix} = \begin{bmatrix} -\frac{5}{35} & \frac{5}{35} & -\frac{5}{35} \\ \frac{26}{35} & -\frac{5}{35} & -\frac{2}{35} \\ \frac{12}{35} & -\frac{5}{35} & -\frac{9}{35} \end{bmatrix}$$

Therefore:
$$\begin{bmatrix} 1 & 2 & -1 \\ 6 & 3 & -4 \\ -2 & 1 & -3 \end{bmatrix}\begin{bmatrix} -\frac{5}{35} & \frac{5}{35} & -\frac{5}{35} \\ \frac{26}{35} & -\frac{5}{35} & -\frac{2}{35} \\ \frac{12}{35} & -\frac{5}{35} & -\frac{9}{35} \end{bmatrix}\begin{bmatrix} a \\ b \\ c \end{bmatrix} = \begin{bmatrix} 10 \\ 18 \\ 15 \end{bmatrix}\begin{bmatrix} -\frac{5}{35} & \frac{5}{35} & -\frac{5}{35} \\ \frac{26}{35} & -\frac{5}{35} & -\frac{2}{35} \\ \frac{12}{35} & -\frac{5}{35} & -\frac{9}{35} \end{bmatrix}$$

$$\begin{bmatrix} 1 & 0 & 0 \\ 0 & 1 & 0 \\ 0 & 0 & 1 \end{bmatrix}\begin{bmatrix} a \\ b \\ c \end{bmatrix} = \begin{bmatrix} -1 \\ 4 \\ -3 \end{bmatrix}$$

The solution is: a = -1, b = 4, c = -3

NON−LINEAR EQUATIONS

- A simple linear equation takes the form ax + b = 0

- A linear equation in two variables is of the form ax + by + c = 0

'a', 'b' and 'c' are positive or negative numbers. 'a' and 'b' are called the coefficients of x^2 and x respectively. 'c' is called a **constant**. When the coefficient is '1', the 1 is left out.
For example, $1x^2$ is written as x^2 and 1x as x.

When the highest power of the single variable in an equation is 2, it is referred to as a **quadratic equation.** A quadratic equation takes the form: $ax^2 + bx + c = 0$ when there is only one variable e.g. $x^2 + 2x + 3 = 0$, $2a^2 - 4a + 1 = 0$.

Similarly, an equation with highest power 3 is a **cubic equation** ($ax^3 + bx^2 + cx + d = 0$), highest power 4, a **quartic equation** ($ax^4 + bx^3 + cx^2 + dx + e = 0$) and so on. It is customary to refer to the non-linear equations as second degree, third degree equations etc. depending on the highest power contained in them.

More than one variable could also be present in non-linear equations:

- $x^2 + y^2 = K$ (a circle)

- $ax^2 + by^2 = 1$ (an ellipse)

- $ax^2 - by^2 = 1$ (a hyperbola)

The distinguishing feature is that while each variable has a highest power of 1 only in a linear equation, a non-linear equation will have a power greater than 1. In the above non-linear equations, the highest power of the variable is 2. Any equation having a variable with a power greater than 1 is a non-linear equation.

A linear equation when represented by graph will take the form of a line. A non- linear equation will not be a line but a curve. This will be made clearer in the next chapter.

QUADRATIC EQUATIONS

The general form of a quadratic equation as seen above is, $ax^2 + bx + c = 0$. There are **two** values of the variable satisfying the quadratic equation. We call them the **roots** of the equation. The two values can be real, distinct and different; real, distinct and equal; or complex (i.e. imaginary). An imaginary root means that its value cannot be easily determined e.g. square root of -3.

> If we call the roots α and β (alpha and beta) each will satisfy the equation:
>
> $$a\alpha^2 + b\alpha + c = 0 \text{ and } a\beta^2 + b\beta + c = 0$$

SOLVING QUADRATIC EQUATIONS

There are different methods for solving a quadratic equation. The method adopted depends on the values for, a, b and c in the general quadratic equation.

FACTOR METHOD

A simple quadratic equation will have no term in x.
The general quadratic equation $ax^2 + bx + c = 0$ reduces to $ax^2 + c = 0$.

Example 1:

If a = 1 and c = -4, find the roots of the equation $ax^2 + c = 0$

If we substitute a = 1, and c = -4, the equation becomes $x^2 - 4 = 0$

This is a **simple quadratic equation**. The LHS is $(x + 2)(x - 2)$.

Therefore $(x + 2)(x - 2) = 0$

The solution is: x = 2 or x = -2

Both 2 and - 2 are roots of the equation $x^2 - 4 = 0$

> Another way to solve $x^2 - 4 = 0$ is to write the equation as $x^2 = 4$ and them find the square root on both sides of the equation. Thus $x = \pm 2$.

Example 2:

Find the roots of the equation $2x^2 - 18 = 0$

Here a = 2. To make 'a' become 1, we divide the equation by 2.

The result is $x^2 - 9 = 0$

i.e. $x^2 = 9$

$x = \pm 3$

Example 3:

Find the roots of the equation $3x^2 - 39 = 0$

$x^2 - 13 = 0$ | Divide by 3 |

$x^2 = 13$

$x = \pm\sqrt{13}$

$x = \pm 3.61$

Example 4:

Find the roots of $x^2 - 3x + 2 = 0$

The LHS can be factored as $(x - 2)(x - 1)$

Therefore: $(x - 2)(x - 1) = 0$

The roots are x = 2 or 1 | The roots are rational, real and different |

Example 5:

Find the roots of $6x^2 + 7x - 3 = 0$

The LHS can be factored as $(3x - 1)(2x + 3)$

Therefore: $(3x - 1)(2x + 3) = 0$

The roots are $x = \dfrac{1}{3}$ or $-\dfrac{3}{2}$ | The roots are rational, real and different |

Example 6:

Find the roots of $16a^2 - 24a + 9 = 0$

The LHS can be factored as $(4a - 3)(4a - 3)$

Therefore: $(4a - 3)(4a - 3) = 0$

The roots are $a = \dfrac{3}{4}$ or $\dfrac{3}{4}$ | The roots are rational, real and equal |

Example 7:

Find the roots of $x^2 + 3x + 1 = 0$

The LHS cannot be factored but the roots are irrational, real and different. The methods described in the next page will help determine the values of the roots (a root is rational if it can be expressed in the form $\dfrac{a}{b}$, e.g, $\dfrac{1}{2}, \dfrac{3}{4}$ etc).

COMPLETING THE SQUARE METHOD

Consider the general quadratic equation $ax^2 + bx + c = 0$.

Divide the equation by 'a', the coefficient of x^2.

Therefore, $x^2 + \dfrac{b}{a}x + \dfrac{c}{a} = 0$

$x^2 + \dfrac{b}{a}x = \dfrac{-c}{a}$

Calculate half the coefficient of x, square it, and add to both sides as shown:

$x^2 + \dfrac{b}{a}x + (\dfrac{b}{2a})^2 = \dfrac{-c}{a} + (\dfrac{b}{2a})^2$

Use the knowledge: $(a + b)^2 = a^2 + 2ab + b^2$ to get LHS as a complete square.

That is: $(x + \dfrac{b}{2a})^2 = \dfrac{-c}{a} + (\dfrac{b}{2a})^2$

Let $(x + \dfrac{b}{2a})^2 = m$

$x + \dfrac{b}{2a} = \pm\sqrt{m}$

$x = -\dfrac{b}{2a} \pm \sqrt{m}$

The roots are: $-\dfrac{b}{2a} + \sqrt{m}$ or $-\dfrac{b}{2a} - \sqrt{m}$

Example 1:

By completing the square, find the roots of $x^2 - 2x - 3 = 0$

$x^2 - 2x - 3 = 0$

$x^2 - 2x = 3$

$x^2 - 2x + (-1)^2 = 3 + (-1)^2$ | Calculate half the coefficient of x, square it, and add it to both sides |

$x^2 - 2x + 1 = 3 + 1$

$(x - 1)^2 = 4$ | Complete the square on LHS |

Square root both sides: $x - 1 = \pm 2$

Therefore: $x = 1 \pm 2$

The roots are: 3 or -1

<u>**Example 2:**</u>

By completing the square, find the roots of $3p^2 - 4p - 5 = 0$

$3p^2 - 4p - 5 = 0$

$p^2 - \dfrac{4}{3}p - \dfrac{5}{3} = 0$ $\boxed{\text{Divide by 3}}$

$p^2 - \dfrac{4}{3}p = \dfrac{5}{3}$

$p^2 - \dfrac{4}{3}p + \left(\dfrac{2}{3}\right)^2 = \dfrac{5}{3} + \left(\dfrac{2}{3}\right)^2$ $\boxed{\begin{array}{l}\text{Calculate half the coefficient of } p,\\ \text{square it, and add it to both sides}\end{array}}$

$\left(p - \dfrac{2}{3}\right)^2 = \dfrac{5}{3} + \dfrac{4}{9} = \dfrac{19}{9} = 2.11$ $\boxed{\text{Complete the square on LHS}}$

Square root both sides: $p - \dfrac{2}{3} = \pm\sqrt{2.11} = \pm 1.4525$

$p - 0.6667 = \pm 1.4525$

$p = 0.6667 \pm 1.4525$

$p = 2.1192 \text{ or } -0.7858$

Therefore the roots are: 2.12 or -0.79 (corrected to 2 decimal places)

THE FORMULA METHOD

From above, we have: $\left(x + \dfrac{b}{2a}\right)^2 = \dfrac{c}{a} + \left(\dfrac{b}{2a}\right)^2$

$\left(x + \dfrac{b}{2a}\right)^2 = \dfrac{c}{a} + \dfrac{b^2}{4a^2} = \dfrac{-4ac + b^2}{4a^2}$ $\boxed{\text{Simplify the fraction on RHS}}$

$x + \dfrac{b}{2a} = \pm\dfrac{\sqrt{b^2 - 4ac}}{2a}$ $\boxed{\text{Find the square root on both sides}}$

Therefore: $x = -\dfrac{b}{2a} \pm \dfrac{\sqrt{b^2 - 4ac}}{2a} = \dfrac{-b \pm \sqrt{b^2 - 4ac}}{2a}$

The roots are: $\dfrac{-b + \sqrt{b^2 - 4ac}}{2a}$ or $\dfrac{-b - \sqrt{b^2 - 4ac}}{2a}$

$x = \dfrac{-b \pm \sqrt{b^2 - 4ac}}{2a}$ is called the **quadratic formula**

Example 1:

By using the quadratic formula find the roots of $x^2 - 2x - 3 = 0$

$x^2 - 2x - 3 = 0$

$$x = \frac{-b \pm \sqrt{b^2 - 4ac}}{2a}$$

Where, a = 1, b = -2 and c = -3

$$x = \frac{-(-2) \pm \sqrt{(-2)^2 - 4 \times 1 \times (-3)}}{2 \times 1} = \frac{2 \pm \sqrt{4 + 12)}}{2} = \frac{2 \pm 4}{2}$$

$x = 1 \pm 2$

The roots are: 3 or -1

Example 2:

By using the quadratic formula, find the roots of $3p^2 - 4p - 5 = 0$

$$p = \frac{-b \pm \sqrt{b^2 - 4ac}}{2a}$$

Where a = 3, b = -4 and c = -5

$$p = \frac{-(-4) \pm \sqrt{(-4)^2 - 4 \times 3 \times (-5)}}{2 \times 3} = \frac{4 \pm \sqrt{16 + 60}}{6} = \frac{4 \pm \sqrt{76}}{6} = \frac{2 \pm \sqrt{19}}{3} = \frac{2 \pm 4.3589}{3}$$

= 2.12 or -0.79

Therefore the roots are: 2.12 or -0.79 (corrected to 2 decimal places)

Some useful facts about quadratic equations:

- The general form of quadratic equations is: $ax^2 + bx + c = 0$

- $b^2 - 4ac$ in the quadratic formula is called "discriminant" as its value decides the nature of the two roots of the equation

- The sum of the two roots is: $\dfrac{-b}{a}$

- The product of the two roots is: $\dfrac{c}{a}$

- The equation whose roots are α and β is: $x^2 - (\alpha + \beta)x + \alpha\beta = 0$

NON-LINEAR SIMULTANOUS EQUATIONS (TWO VARIABLES)

Simultaneous equations with two variables are non-linear when at least one of the two equations is nonlinear.

Example 1:

Solve the simultaneous equations: $x + y = 4$ and $x^2 + y^2 = 10$

$$x + y = 4 \quad \ldots\ldots\ldots(1)$$
$$x^2 + y^2 = 10 \quad \ldots\ldots(2)$$

Only one equation is non-linear

The method used here is substitution.

From (1): $y = 4 - x$

$x^2 + (4 - x)^2 = 10$ Substitute $4 - x$ for y in (2)

$x^2 + 16 - 8x + x^2 = 10$

$2x^2 - 8x + 6 = 0$

$x^2 - 4x + 3 = 0$

Factorise: $(x - 1)(x - 3) = 0$

Therefore: $x = 1$ or 3

Substitute in (1) to get the solution:

When $x = 1$, $y = 3$ and when $x = 3$, $y = 1$

Example 2:

Solve the simultaneous equations $y = x^2$ and $y = 18 - x^2$

$$y = x^2 \quad \ldots\ldots\ldots\ldots(1)$$
$$y = 18 - x^2 \quad \ldots\ldots(2)$$

Both equations are non-linear

The method used here is elimination. We could also use substitution.

$0 = 2x^2 - 18$ (1) − (2) eliminates y

$2x^2 = 18$

$x^2 = 9$

Therefore: $x = \pm 3$

Substitute $x = \pm 3$ in (1) to get the solution:

When $x = 3$, $y = 9$ and when $x = -3$, $y = 9$

Example 3:

Solve the simultaneous equations $y = x^2 + 3x - 2$ and $y = 3x^2 - 4x + 1$

$$y = x^2 + 3x - 2 \ldots\ldots\ldots(1)$$

$$y = 3x^2 - 4x + 1 \ldots\ldots(2)$$

$0 = -2x^2 + 7x - 3$ | (1) − (2) eliminates y |

$2x^2 - 7x + 3 = 0$

$(2x - 1)(x - 3) = 0$ | LHS can be factorised |

$2x - 1 = 0$ or $x - 3 = 0$

$x = \dfrac{1}{2}$ or 3

Substitute for x in either (1) or (2) to get y.

Sub in (1): When $x = \dfrac{1}{2}$, $y = \dfrac{1}{4} + \dfrac{3}{2} - 2 = \dfrac{7}{4} - 2 = -\dfrac{1}{4}$

When $x = 3$, $y = 9 + 9 - 2 = 16$

The solution is: $x = \dfrac{1}{2}$, $y = -\dfrac{1}{4}$ and $x = 3$, $y = 16$

Example 4:

Solve the simultaneous equations: $y = 2x^2 - 9x + 4$ and $y = 3x^2 + 2x - 5 = 0$

$$y = 2x^2 - 9x + 4 \ldots\ldots\ldots(1)$$

$$y = 3x^2 + 2x - 5 \ldots\ldots\ldots(2)$$

$3x^2 + 2x - 5 = 2x^2 - 9x + 4$ | Since LHS are the same |

$x^2 + 11x - 9 = 0$

Solve using the quadratic formula as LHS cannot be factorised.

$x = \dfrac{-b \pm \sqrt{b^2 - 4ac}}{2a}$ | a = 1, b = 11, c = -9 |

$x = \dfrac{-11 \pm \sqrt{121 - 4 \times 1 \times (-9)}}{2 \times 1} = \dfrac{-11 \pm \sqrt{121 + 36}}{2} = \dfrac{-11 \pm \sqrt{157}}{2} = \dfrac{-11 \pm \sqrt{157}}{2}$

Therefore, $x = \dfrac{(-11 + \sqrt{157})}{2}$ or $\dfrac{(-11 - \sqrt{157})}{2}$

| Accuracy is increased if more decimal places are used |

$x = 0.765$ or -11.765 (corrected to 3 decimal places)

The solution is: $x = 0.765$, $y = 1.715$ and $x = -11.765$, $y = 386.715$

1. (a) Solve the following equations:

(i) $4x - 5 = 2x + 3$

(ii) $\dfrac{1}{y - 1} = 2y$

(iii) $4m^2 + 4m = 3$

(b) Change the subject of the following formulae to the letter shown in brackets:

(i) $A = \dfrac{1}{2}(a + b)h$ **(b)**

(ii) $Pt = m(v - u)$ **(u)**

(iii) $\dfrac{F - 32}{9} = \dfrac{C}{5}$ **(F)**

(c) Solve the following inequations:

(i) $\dfrac{-7 - 3c}{4} \le 5$

(ii) $9 - p \le |7 - 2p|$

(iii) $\dfrac{c - 2}{c + 2} > 3$

2. Solve the following simultaneous linear equations in two variables. Use the method of substitution.

(a) $5a + 3b = 7$ and $4a + 5b = 3$ (b) $5x + 7y = 8$ and $7x - 4y = 25$

3. Solve the following simultaneous equations in two linear variables. Use the method of elimination.

(a) $4p + 3q = 5\dfrac{1}{2}$ and $9p - 5q = -17$ (b) $5x + 7y = 8$ and $7x - 4y = 25$

4. Solve the following simultaneous equations in three linear variables.

(a) $a + 2b = 4$

$b + 3c = 5$

$2b - c = 1$

(b) $x + y - 2z = -1$

$2x - 3y + z = 13$

$3x - y + 2z = 17$

5. Solve the following quadratic equations using "completing the square" method. Check using the quadratic formula (Leave the answer in surd form).

(a) $1 + x - 3x^2 = 0$

(b) $2c^2 - 7c + 4 = 0$

6. Solve the following quadratic equations using the quadratic formula.

(a) $x^2 - 6x + 4 = 0$

(b) $4y^2 - 12y - 9 = 0$

7. Solve the following non-linear simultaneous equations.

(a) $y - x = 1$ and $x^2 + y^2 = 5$

(b) $ab + b^2 = 2$ and $2a + b = 3$

8.(a) If α and β are the roots of the equation $x^2 - 4x + 1 = 0$,
Find the values of $\alpha + \beta$ and $\alpha - \beta$.

(b) What is meant by "root" of an equation?

If 1 and 3 are roots of the cubic equation $x^3 + ax + b = 0$, find the third root.

(c) Without solving the equation, determine the nature of the roots of each equation.

(i) $a^2 - 4a - 7 = 0$

(ii) $3x^2 + 4x + 2 = 0$

(iii) $y^2 - 6y + 9 = 0$

1.(a)(i) $4x - 5 = 2x + 3$

$4x - 5 + 5 = 2x + 3 + 5$

$4x = 2x + 8$

$4x - 2x = 2x + 8 - 2x$

$2x = 8$

$x = 4$

(ii) $\dfrac{1}{y - 1} = 2y$

$1 = 2y(y - 1)$ | Multiply both sides by $y - 1$ |

$1 = 2y^2 - 2y$

$2y^2 - 2y - 1 = 0$

$y^2 - y - \dfrac{1}{2} = 0$ | Divide by 2 |

$y^2 - y = \dfrac{1}{2}$

$(y - \dfrac{1}{2})^2 = \dfrac{1}{2} + \dfrac{1}{4} = \dfrac{3}{4}$ | Complete the square on LHS |

$y - \dfrac{1}{2} = \pm\dfrac{\sqrt{3}}{2}$ | Square root both sides |

$y = \dfrac{1}{2} \pm \dfrac{\sqrt{3}}{2}$

$y = \dfrac{1 + \sqrt{3}}{2}$ or $\dfrac{1 - \sqrt{3}}{2}$

(iii) $4m^2 + 4m = 3$

$4m^2 + 4m - 3 = 0$

Factorising: $(2m - 1)(2m + 3) = 0$

Therefore: $2m - 1 = 0$ or $2m + 3 = 0$

$m = \dfrac{1}{2}$ or $\dfrac{-3}{2}$

1.(b)

(i) $A = \frac{1}{2}(a + b)h$ **(b)**

$2A = (a + b)h$

$a + b = \frac{2A}{h}$

$b = \frac{2A}{h} - a$

(ii) $Pt = m(v - u)$ **(u)**

$v - u = \frac{Pt}{m}$

$u = v - \frac{Pt}{m}$

(iii) $\frac{F - 32}{9} = \frac{C}{5}$ **(F)**

$F - 32 = \frac{9C}{5}$

$F = \frac{9C}{5} + 32$

(c)

(i) $\frac{-7 - 3c}{4} \leq 5$

$-7 - 3c \leq 20$

$-3c \leq 27$

$C \geq -9$

(ii) $9 - p \leq |7 - 2p|$

That is, $9 - p \leq 7 - 2p$ or $9 - p \leq -7 + 2p$

$p \leq -2$ or $-3p \leq -6$

$-2 \geq p$ or $p \geq 5.33$

Therefore, the solution is: $-2 \geq p \geq 5.33$

1.(c)(iii) $\dfrac{c-2}{c+2} > 3$

Multiplying both sides by $(c + 2)^2$, we get

$(c - 2)(c + 2) > 3(c + 2)^2$

$c^2 - 4 > 3(c^2 + 4c + 4)$

$c^2 - 4 > 3c^2 + 12c + 12$

That is, $2c^2 + 12c + 16 < 0$

$c^2 + 6c + 8 < 0$

$(c + 4)(c + 2) < 0$

Therefore, c lies between -4 and - 2

The solution is: $-4 < c < -2$

2.(a) $5a + 3b = 7$ and $4a + 5b = 3$

$5a + 3b = 7$ .... (1)

$4a + 5b = 3$ ....(2)

<u>Substitution Method:</u>

From (1): $a = \dfrac{7 - 3b}{5}$

Sub in (2): $4\dfrac{7 - 3b}{5} + 5b = 3$

$4(7 - 3b) + 25b = 15$ | Multiply by 5 |

$28 - 12b + 25b = 15$

$13b = -13$

$b = -1$

$5a - 3 = 7$ | Substitute b = -1 in (1) |

$5a = 10$

$a = 2$

The solution is: a = 2 and b = -1

2.(b) $5x + 7y = 8$ and $7x - 4y = 25$

$5x + 7y = 8$ .... (1)

$7x - 4y = 25$ .... (2)

Substitution Method:

From (1): $x = \dfrac{8 - 7y}{5}$

Sub in (2): $7\dfrac{8 - 7y}{5} - 4y = 25$

$7(8 - 7y) - 20y = 125$ | Multiply by 5 |

$56 - 49y - 20y = 125$

$-69y = 69$

$y = -1$

$7x + 4 = 25$ | Substitute y = -1 in (2) |

$7x = 21$

$x = 3$

The solution is $x = 3$ and $y = -1$

3.(a) $4p + 3q = 5\dfrac{1}{2}$ and $9p - 5q = -17$

$4p + 3q = 5\dfrac{1}{2}$ .... (1)

$9p - 5q = -17$ .... (2)

Elimination Method:

Let us eliminate q:

(1) × 5: $20p + 15q = 27.5$ .... (3)

(2) × 3: $27p - 15q = -51$ .... (4)

(3) + (4): $47p = -23.5$

$p = -\dfrac{1}{2}$

Substitute for $p = -\dfrac{1}{2}$ in (1):

$4 \times -\dfrac{1}{2} + 3q = 5\dfrac{1}{2}$

$-2 + 3q = 5\dfrac{1}{2}$

$3q = 7\dfrac{1}{2}$

$q = 2\dfrac{1}{2}$

The solution is: $p = -\dfrac{1}{2}$ and $q = 2\dfrac{1}{2}$

3.(b) $5x + 7y = 8$ and $7x - 4y = 25$

$5x + 7y = 8$ .... (1)

$7x - 4y = 25$ .... (2)

Let us eliminate y:

(1) × 4: $20x + 28y = 32$ .... (3)

(2) × 7: $49x - 28y = 175$ .... (4)

(3) + (4): $69x = 207$

$x = 3$

$5 \times 3 + 7y = 8$ | Substitute $x = 3$ in (1) |

$15 + 7y = 8$

$7y = -7$

$y = -1$

The solution is: $x = 3$ and $y = -1$

4.(a) $a + 2b = 4$ .... (1)

$b + 3c = 5$ .... (2)

$2b - c = 1$ .... (3)

(2) and (3) only have b and c. We can therefore solve easily for b and c:

(3) × 3: $6b - 3c = 3$ ....(4)

(2) + (4): $7b = 8$

$b = 1\frac{1}{7}$

$2 \times 1\frac{1}{7} - c = 1$ | Substitute $b = 1\frac{1}{7}$ in (3) |

$c = 1\frac{2}{7}$

$a + 2\frac{2}{7} = 4$ | Substitute $b = 1\frac{1}{7}$ in (1) |

$a = 4 - 2\frac{2}{7}$

$a = 1\frac{1}{7}$

The solution is: $a = 1\frac{1}{7}$, $b = 1\frac{1}{7}$ and $c = 1\frac{2}{7}$

4.(b) $x + y - 2z = -1$ .... (1)

$2x - 3y + z = 13$ .... (2)

$3x - y + 2z = 17$ .... (3)

(1) + (3): $4x = 16$

$x = 4$

$8 - 3y + z = 13$ | Substitute $x = 4$ in (2) |

$-3y + z = 5$ .... (4)

$12 - y + 2z = 17$ | Substitute $x = 4$ in (3) |

$-y + 2z = 5$ .... (5)

(4) × 2: $-6y + 2z = 10$ .... (6)

(5) − (6): $5y = -5$

$y = -1$

$3 + z = 5$ | Substitute for $y = -1$ in (4) |

$z = 2$

The solution is: $x = 4$, $y = -1$ and $z = 2$

5.(a) $1 + x - 3x^2 = 0$

$3x^2 - x - 1 = 0$ | Multiply throughout by -1 and rearrange |

$x^2 - \frac{1}{3}x - \frac{1}{3} = 0$ | Divide by 3 (coefficient of x^2) |

$x^2 - \frac{1}{3}x = \frac{1}{3}$

$(x - \frac{1}{6})^2 = \frac{1}{3} + \frac{1}{36}$ | Complete the square on LHS |

$(x - \frac{1}{6})^2 = \frac{13}{36}$

$x - \frac{1}{6} = \pm\frac{\sqrt{13}}{6}$ | Square root both sides |

$x = \frac{1}{6} \pm \frac{\sqrt{13}}{6}$

The solution is: $x = \dfrac{1 + \sqrt{13}}{6}$ or $\dfrac{1 - \sqrt{13}}{6}$

5.(a)(Continued) Check:

$$x = \frac{-b \pm \sqrt{b^2 - 4ac}}{2a}$$

$\boxed{a = 3, \; b = -1, \; c = -1}$

$$x = \frac{1 \pm \sqrt{1 + 12}}{6}$$

$$x = \frac{1 + \sqrt{13}}{6} \;\text{ or }\; \frac{1 - \sqrt{13}}{6}$$

(b) $2c^2 - 7c + 4 = 0$

$c^2 - \dfrac{7}{2}c + 2 = 0$ $\boxed{\text{Divide by 2 (coefficient of } x^2 \text{)}}$

$c^2 - \dfrac{7}{2}c = -2$

$(c - \dfrac{7}{4})^2 = -2 + \dfrac{49}{16}$ $\boxed{\text{Complete the square on LHS}}$

$(c - \dfrac{7}{4})^2 = \dfrac{17}{16}$

$c - \dfrac{7}{4} = \pm\dfrac{\sqrt{17}}{4}$ $\boxed{\text{Square root both sides}}$

$c = \dfrac{7}{4} \pm \dfrac{\sqrt{17}}{4}$

The solution is: $c = \dfrac{7 + \sqrt{17}}{4} \;\text{ or }\; \dfrac{7 - \sqrt{17}}{4}$

Check:

$$x = \frac{-b \pm \sqrt{b^2 - 4ac}}{2a}$$

$\boxed{a = 2, \; b = -7, \; c = 4}$

$$x = \frac{7 \pm \sqrt{49 - 32}}{4}$$

$$x = \frac{7 + \sqrt{17}}{4} \;\text{ or }\; \frac{7 - \sqrt{17}}{4}$$

6.(a) $x^2 - 6x + 4 = 0$

$$x = \frac{-b \pm \sqrt{b^2 - 4ac}}{2a}$$ $\boxed{a = 1, \; b = -6, \; c = 4}$

$$x = \frac{6 \pm \sqrt{36 - 16}}{2} = \frac{6 \pm \sqrt{36 - 16}}{2} = \frac{6 \pm \sqrt{20}}{2} = \frac{6 \pm 2\sqrt{5}}{2} = 3 \pm \sqrt{5}$$

The solution is: $x = 3 + \sqrt{5} \;\text{ or }\; 3 - \sqrt{5}$

6.(b) $4y^2 - 12y - 9 = 0$

$$x = \frac{-b \pm \sqrt{b^2 - 4ac}}{2a}$$

$\boxed{a = 4, \ b = -12, \ c = -9}$

$$y = \frac{12 \pm \sqrt{144 + 144}}{8} = \frac{12 \pm \sqrt{288}}{8} = \frac{12 \pm 12\sqrt{2}}{8} = \frac{3 \pm 3\sqrt{2}}{2}$$

The solution is: $y = \dfrac{3 + 3\sqrt{2}}{2}$ or $\dfrac{3 - 3\sqrt{2}}{2}$

7.(a) $y - x = 1$ and $x^2 + y^2 = 5$

$y - x = 1$ .... (1)

$x^2 + y^2 = 5$ .... (2)

From (1): $y = x + 1$

Substitute in (2): $x^2 + (x + 1)^2 = 5$

$x^2 + x^2 + 2x + 1 = 5$

$2x^2 + 2x - 4 = 0$

$x^2 + x - 2 = 0$

Factorising: $(x + 2)(x - 1) = 0$

$x = -2$ or 1

Substitute in (1): When $x = -2$, $y = -1$ and when $x = 1$, $y = 2$

The solution is: $x = -2, y = -1$ and $x = 1, y = 2$

(b) $ab + b^2 = 2$ and $2a + b = 3$

$ab + b^2 = 2$ ....(1)

$2a + b = 3$ ....(2)

From (2): $b = 3 - 2a$ ....(3)

Substitute in (1): $a(3 - 2a) + (3 - 2a)^2 = 2$

$3a - 2a^2 + 9 - 12a + 4a^2 = 2$

$2a^2 - 9a + 7 = 0$

$(2a - 7)(a - 1) = 0$

Therefore: $a = 3\frac{1}{2}$ or 1

Substitute in (3): When $a = 3\frac{1}{2}$, $b = -4$ and when $a = 1$, $b = 1$

The solution is: $a = 3\frac{1}{2}, b = -4$ or $a = 1, b = 1$

8.(a) $x^2 - 4x + 1 = 0$

If α and β are the roots of this equation then:

$\alpha + \beta = 4$ .... (1)

$\alpha\beta = 1$ .... (2)

Now $(\alpha - \beta)^2 = (\alpha + \beta)^2 - 4\alpha\beta = 4^2 - 4 \times 1 = 12$

Therefore: $\alpha - \beta = \pm\sqrt{12} = \pm2\sqrt{3}$

(b) The "root" of an equation is the value of the variable that will satisfy the equation.

$x^3 + ax + b = 0$

If 1 is a root then $1 + a + b = 0$

$a + b = -1$ .... (1)

If 3 is a root then $27 + 3a + b = 0$

$3a + b = -27$ .... (2)

(3) – (1): $2a = -26$

$a = -13$

Substitute in (1): $-13 + b = -1$

$b = 12$

Substitute the values for a and b in the original equation to get:

$x^3 - 13x + 12 = 0$

Since 1 and 3 are the roots of this equation, $(x - 1)$, $(x - 3)$ are factors. That is, $x^2 - 4x + 3$ is a factor. In order to get the third factor we divide $x^3 - 13x + 12$ by $x^2 - 4x + 3$ as follows.

$$
\begin{array}{r}
x + 4 \\
x^2 - 4x + 3 \overline{\smash{)}x^3 - 13x + 12} \\
\underline{x^3 - 4x^2 + 3x } \\
4x^2 - 16x + 12 \\
\underline{4x^2 - 16x + 12} \\
0
\end{array}
$$

The third factor is $x + 4$. Therefore, the third root is -4.

(c)(i) $a^2 - 4a - 7 = 0$

Discriminant $= 16 + 28 = 44$ — The roots are therefore: irrational, real, and different

(ii) $3x^2 + 4x + 2 = 0$

Discriminant $= 16 - 24 = -8$ — The roots are therefore: imaginary

(iii) $y^2 - 6y + 9 = 0$

Discriminant $= 36 - 36 = 0$ — The roots are, therefore: rational, real and equal

6. THE CARTESIAN CO-ORDINATE SYSTEM

In the diagram below, two number lines intersect. The point of intersection is called the **origin**. The horizontal number line is called the **x-axis** and the vertical number line is called the **y-axis**. Distances measured to the right of the origin on the x-axis are positive and those measured to the left are negative. Similarly, distances measured up from the origin on the y-axis are positive and those measured down from the origin are negative.

To get to the point A in the diagram below we measure 4 units from the origin to the right and then measure 5 units upwards. Point A is then referred to as A(4, 5). The number 4 is called the **x-coordinate** (or abscissa) and the number 5 is called the **y-coordinate** (or ordinate). Similarly, the point B is referred to as (5, 0), C as (0, -4) and D as (-3, 2).

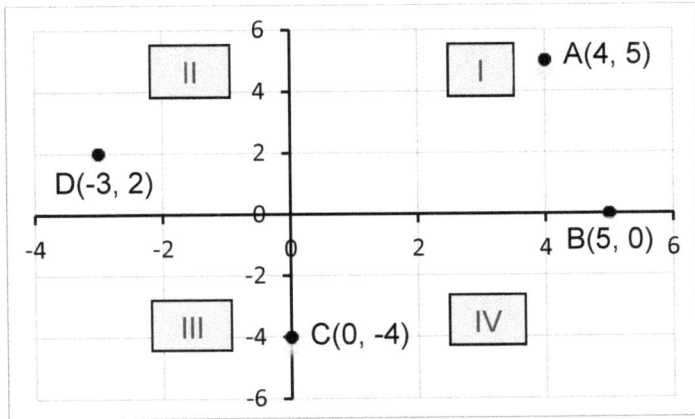

The space between the axes where A is located is called **Quadrant I**. Going in the anticlockwise direction, the other three are **Quadrant II, Quadrant III** and **Quadrant IV**.

Point B lies on the positive x-axis and is therefore written B(5, 0) as its y-distance from the x-axis is zero. Point C lies on the negative y-axis and is therefore written as C(0, -4) as its x distance from the y-axis is zero. Placing a given point on a graph is described as **plotting the point.**

THE DISTANCE BETWEEN TWO POINTS

The two points (4, 3) and (-2, 1) is connected by a straight line in the diagram below. The length of the line can be obtained by using the Pythagoras formula. The distance AB is calculated as $\sqrt{6^2 + 2^2} = \sqrt{40}$ using the Pythagoras Theorem.

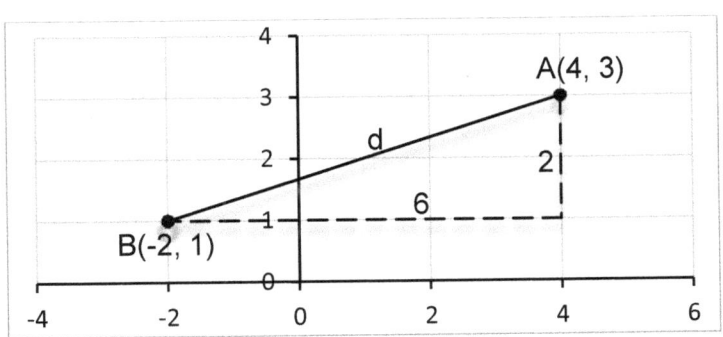

THE DISTANCE FORMULA

The distance 'd' between two points $A(x_1, y_1)$ and $B(x_2, y_2)$ can be calculated by the formula:

$$d = \sqrt{(x_1 - x_2)^2 + (y_1 - y_2)^2}$$

Example:

Using the distance formula, calculate the distance between A(4, 3) and B(-2, 1)

Distance AB $= \sqrt{[4 - (-2)]^2 + (3 - 1)^2} = \sqrt{36 + 4} = \sqrt{40}$

THE CO-ORDINATES OF THE MID-POINT

The coordinates of the **mid-point** on the line joining two points $A(x_1, y_1)$ and $B(x_2, y_2)$ are calculated as:

$$\left(\frac{x_1 + x_2}{2}, \frac{y_1 + y_2}{2}\right)$$

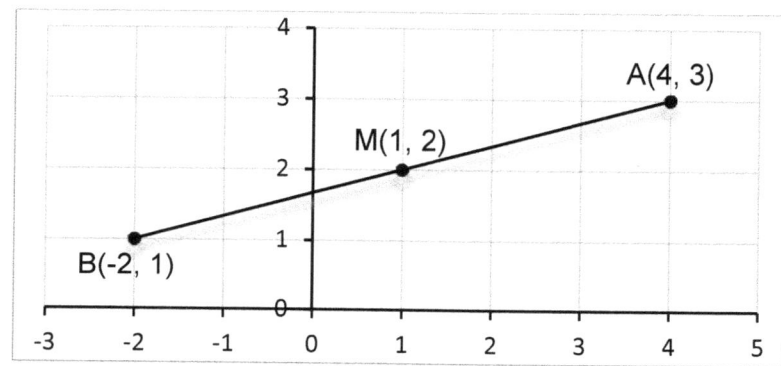

Example:

Calculate the co-ordinates of M, the midpoint joining A(4, 3) and B(-2, 1).

$$M = \left(\frac{x_1 + x_2}{2}, \frac{y_1 + y_2}{2}\right) = \left(\frac{4 - 2}{2}, \frac{3 - 1}{2}\right) = (1, 2)$$

Therefore, the co-ordinates of the midpoint joining A and B are (1, 2).

COORDINATES OF ANY POINT THAT DIVIDES A LINE INTERNALLY IN THE RATIO M: N

$$R = (\frac{mx_2 + nx_1}{m+n}, \frac{my_2 + ny_1}{m+n})$$

Example:

Find the coordinates of the point R that divides the line joining P(3, 1) and Q(2, 4) internally in the ratio 2:1

$$R = (\frac{2 \times 2 + 1 \times 3}{2+1}, \frac{2 \times 4 + 1 \times 1}{2+1})$$

$$R = (\frac{7}{3}, \frac{9}{3})$$

$$R = (2.33, 3)$$

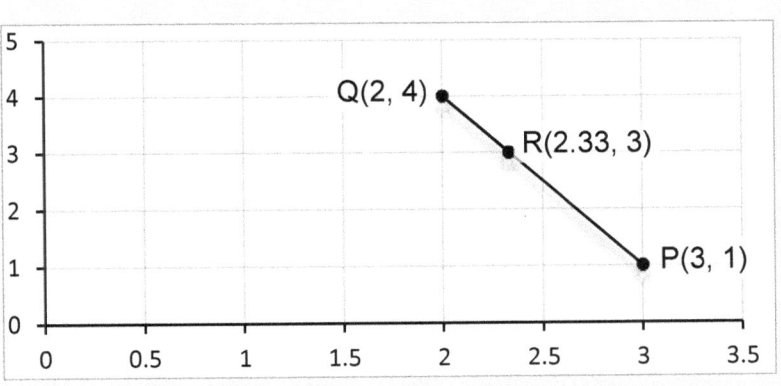

GRADIENT OF A STRAIGHT LINE

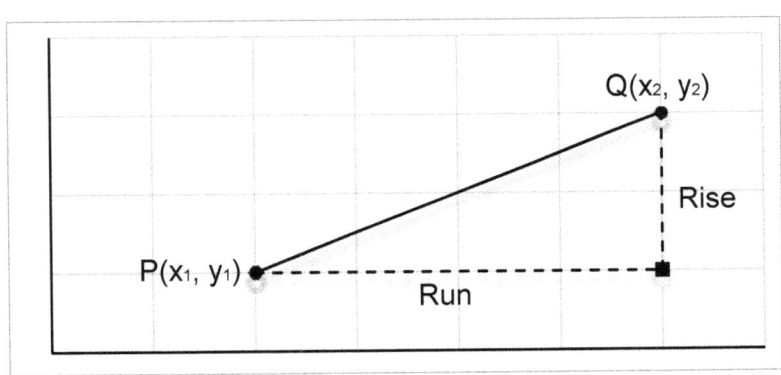

In the diagram above, the points P and Q are joined by a straight line. The distance marked "**Run**" is the difference between the x-coordinates of P and Q (i.e. $x_2 - x_1$). Similarly, the distance marked "**Rise**" is the difference between the y-coordinates of P and Q ($y_2 - y_1$).

The ratio "$\frac{Rise}{Run}$" is the **slope** (or **gradient**) of the line PQ and is denoted by the letter '**m**'.

$$\text{Gradient of PQ} = m = \frac{Rise}{Run} = \frac{y_2 - y_1}{x_2 - x_1}$$

The sign of the gradient depends on where the two points are located. The gradient can be positive, negative, zero or infinity(undefined).

- The gradient is **positive** if the line slopes to the **right**, it is **negative** if the line slopes to the **left**.

- The gradient is **zero** if the line is **parallel to the x-axis**.

- The gradient is **infinity** if the line is **parallel to the y-axis**.

- The gradient of the x-axis itself is zero and that of the y-axis is infinity

Example 1:

Calculate the gradient of A(-1, 3) and B(4, 5).

Solution: Gradient of AB $= m = \dfrac{y_2 - y_1}{x_2 - x_1}$

$= \dfrac{5 - 3}{4 - (-1)} = \dfrac{2}{5} = 0.4$

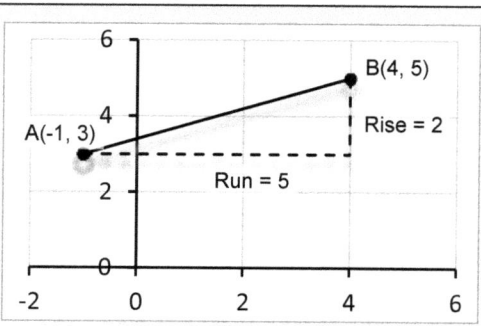

Example 2:

Calculate the gradient of X(-2, 4) and Y(3, -2).

Solution: Gradient of XY $= m = \dfrac{y_2 - y_1}{x_2 - x_1}$

$= \dfrac{-2 - 4}{3 - (-2)} = \dfrac{-6}{5} = -1.2$

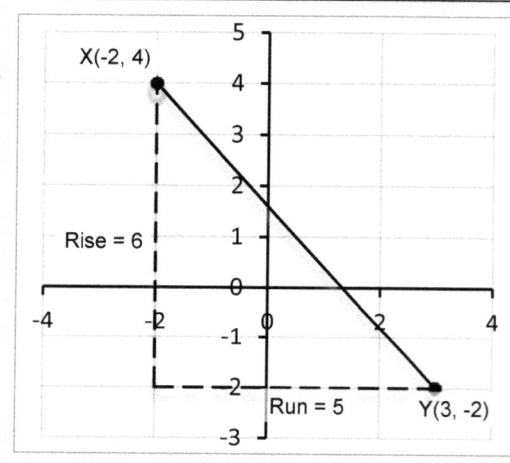

Example 3:

Calculate the gradient of the line joining P (-4, 4) and Q (6, 4).

Solution: Gradient of PQ $= m = \dfrac{y_2 - y_1}{x_2 - x_1}$ or $m = \dfrac{y_1 - y_2}{x_1 - x_2}$

$= \dfrac{4 - 4}{6 - (-4)} = \dfrac{0}{10} = 0$

If a line has a zero gradient, it is either the x-axis or a line parallel to the x-axis

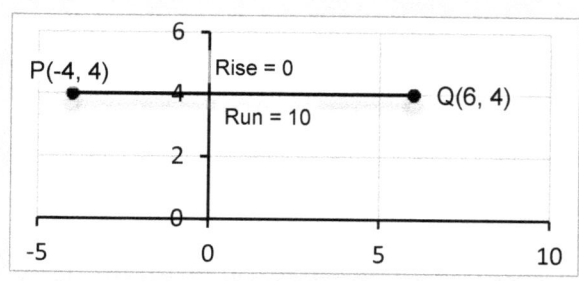

Example 4:

Calculate the gradient of the line joining M(2, 4) and N(2, -5).

Solution: Gradient of MN = m = $\dfrac{y_2 - y_1}{x_2 - x_1}$

$$= \dfrac{-5 - 4}{2 - 2} = \dfrac{-9}{0} = \text{undefined (or infinity)}$$

If a line has an undefined gradient, it is either the y-axis or a line parallel to the y-axis)

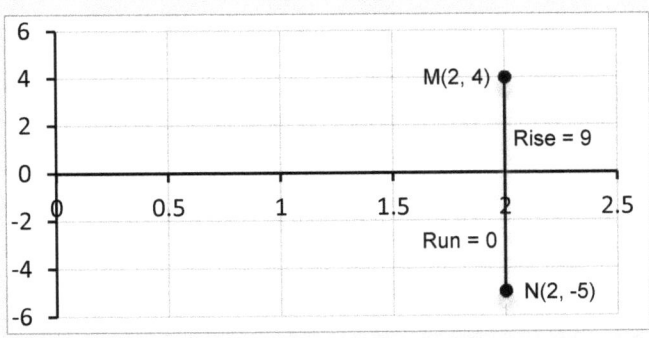

The Gradients Of Two Parallel Lines

- If two lines are parallel, their gradients are equal
- If m_1 and m_2 are the **gradients of two parallel lines**, then $m_1 = m_2$
- If m_1 and m_2 are the **gradients of two perpendicular lines**, then $m_1 \times m_2 = -1$

THE X- INTERCEPT AND Y- INTERCEPT

If a line drawn cuts the x-axis and y axis, the distance from the origin to the point of intersection of the line and x-axis is called the **x-intercept**. Similarly, the distance from the origin to the point of intersection of the line and y-axis is called the **y-intercept**.
This is shown in the diagram below (The x-intercept = 3 and the y-intercept = 4).

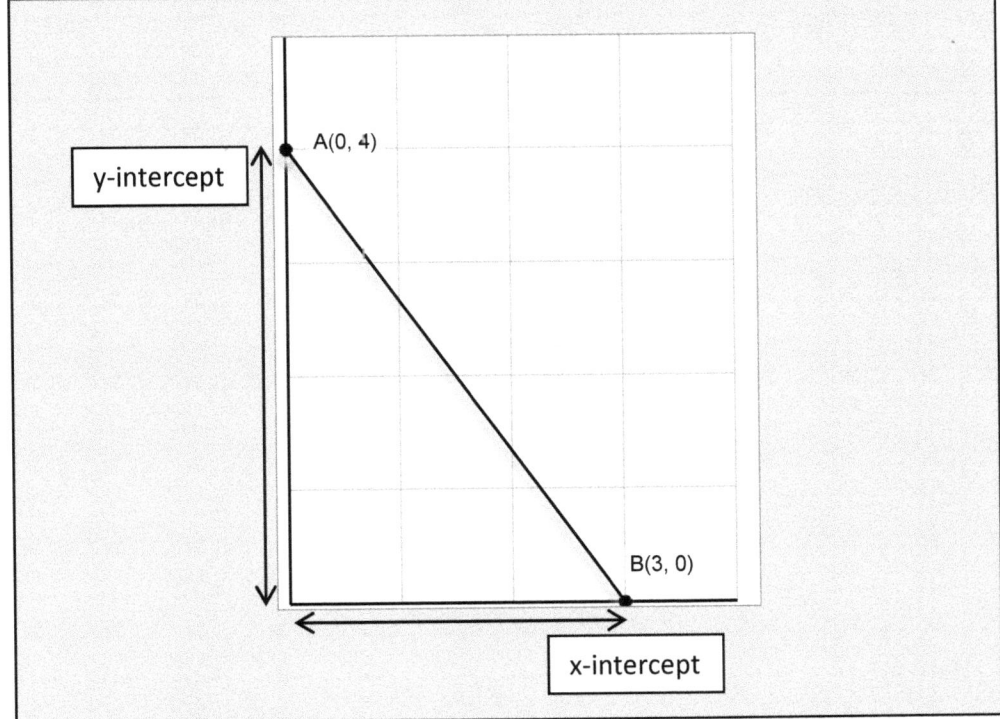

EQUATION OF A LINE

We can draw numerous lines through a given point. These lines can be differentiated if we know the gradient of each line and its y-intercept. Each such line is then defined by an equation.

- Generally, If a line has a gradient "m" and y-intercept "c", then the equation is:
  y = mx + c
- Two points are enough to define a line

Example 1:
Write down the equation of the line having a gradient 2 and a y-intercept of 3 units.

Solution: y = 2x + 3

Example 2:
Write down the equation of the line having a gradient -3 and a y-intercept of 1.5 units.

Solution: y = -3x + 1.5

Example 3:
Write down the equation of the line having a gradient 1 and a y-intercept of -2 units.

Solution: y = x − 2

Example 4:
Write down the equation of the line having a gradient 3 and a y-intercept of 0 units.

Solution: y = 3x

Example 5:
Write down the equation of the line parallel to x-axis and a y-intercept of 1.5 units.

Solution: y = 1.5

Example 6:
Write down the equation of the line perpendicular to the x-axis and having an x-intercept of 4 units.

Solution: x = 4

FINDING THE X AND Y INTERCEPTS OF A LINE

Consider the equation of a line $2y = 6x - 9$

The x intercept is obtained by substituting $y = 0$ in the equation.

That is: $0 = 6x - 9$

Therefore: $6x = 9$

$x = 1.5$

The y intercept is obtained by substituting $x = 0$ in the equation.

That is, $2y = 0 - 9$

Therefore $2y = -9$

$y = -4.5$

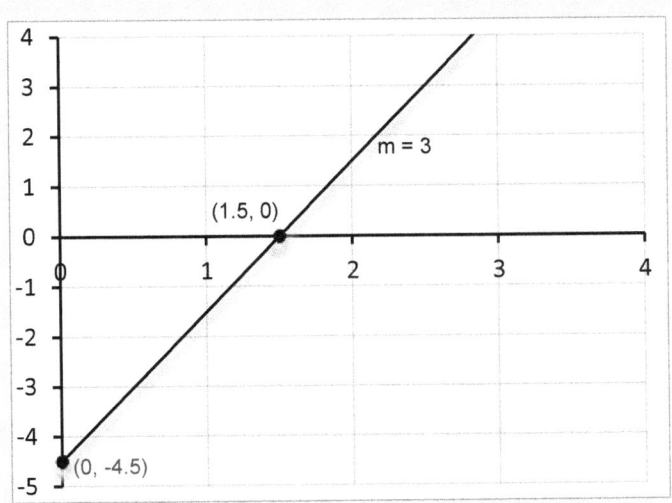

EQUATION OF A LINE IF X AND Y INTERCEPTS ARE GIVEN

Let the x intercept is 'a' and y intercept 'b'. The equation of the line is: $\dfrac{x}{a} + \dfrac{y}{b} = 1$

Proof: Using the proportionality theorem for similar triangles.

$\dfrac{a - x}{a} = \dfrac{y}{b}$

There are two triangles in the diagram

That is: $1 - \dfrac{-x}{a} = \dfrac{y}{b}$ or $\dfrac{x}{a} + \dfrac{y}{b} = 1$

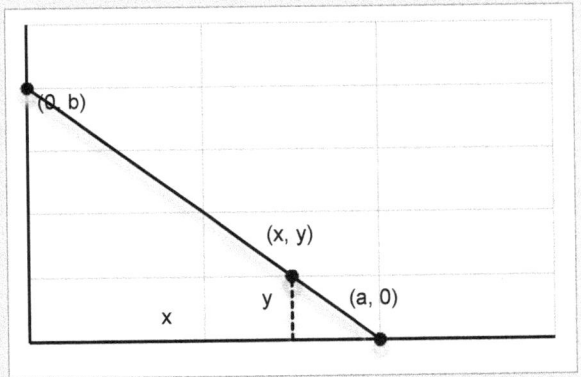

Example:

Find the equation of a line with x intercept $= 2$ and y intercept $= 3$.

Solution: $\dfrac{x}{2} + \dfrac{y}{3} = 1$

$3x + 2y = 6$ Multiply by 6 throughout

The equation in $y = mx + c$ form is: $y = -1.5x + 3$

EQUATION OF A LINE GIVEN ITS SLOPE AND ONE POINT ON IT

If m is the gradient and the point on it is (x_1, y_1), then the equation is: $y - y_1 = m(x - x_1)$

Example:

Find the equation of the line with a gradient of 2 and passing through the point (3, - 1).

Solution: The required equation is:

$y - (-1) = 2(x - 3)$

$y + 1 = 2x - 6$

$y = 2x - 7$

EQUATION OF A LINE GIVEN TWO POINTS ON IT

If the line passes through two points (x_1, y_1) and (x_2, y_2), then its equation is:

$$y - y_1 = \frac{y_1 - y_2}{x_1 - x_2}(x - x_1) \quad \text{or} \quad y - y_2 = \frac{y_1 - y_2}{x_1 - x_2}(x - x_2)$$

Example 1:

Find the equation of the line passing through the two points (3, 1) and (4, 4).

Solution: The required equation is:

$y - 1 = \frac{1 - 4}{3 - 4}(x - 3) = \frac{-3}{-1}(x - 3) = 3(x - 3) = 3x - 9$

$y - 1 = 3x - 9$

$y = 3x - 8$

Example 2:

Find the equation of the line passing through the two points (2, -2) and (0, 1).

Solution: The required equation is:

$y - 1 = \frac{1 + 2}{0 - 2}(x - 0) = -1.5x$

$y + 1 = -1.5x$ Multiply throughout by -2

$y = -1.5x + 1$

• **A line is parallel to another line, if the gradients are the same**

The lines $y = mx + c_1$ and $y = mx + c_2$ are parallel because the gradients are the same

Example 3:

Determine which of the following pairs of lines are parallel:

(i) $y = 3x + 7$ and $y = -3x + 5$ (ii) $y = 2x + 1.5$ and $2y = 4x + 9$

Solution:

In (i) the gradients are 3 and -3. The two lines are not parallel.

In (ii) the gradients are 2 and 2. The two lines are parallel.

To determine the gradient of a line, its equation must be written in the form $y = mx + c$

- A line is perpendicular to another line if the product of the gradients $= -1$

- If the two lines $y = m_1 x + c_1$ and $y = m_2 x + c_2$ have the product of their gradients equal to -1, (i.e. $m_1 \times m_2 = -1$) then the two lines are perpendicular.

- $m_1 = \dfrac{-1}{m_2}$ or $m_2 = \dfrac{-1}{m_1}$

Example 4:

Determine which of the following pairs of lines are perpendicular:

(i) $y = 4x + 7$ and $y = -4x - 1$ (ii) $y = 2x + 1.5$ and $4y = -2x + 3$

Solution:

In (i) the gradients are 4 and -4. The product of the gradients is -16.

The two lines are not perpendicular.

In (ii) the gradients are 2 and $-\dfrac{1}{2}$. The product of the gradients is -1.

The two lines are perpendicular.

EQUATION OF A LINE PARALLEL TO A GIVEN LINE AND PASSING THROUGH A GIVEN POINT

Let the given line be: $y = 2x + 3$

Therefore, the equation of the line parallel to this is: $y = 2x + c$ | Same gradient but different y-intercept |

If the parallel line passes through, say (1, -1) it will satisfy $y = 2x + c$.

Therefore, $-1 = 2 + c$ or $c = -3$.

The equation of the required parallel line is: $y = 2x - 3$

EQUATION OF A LINE PERPENDICULAR TO A GIVEN LINE AND PASSING THROUGH A GIVEN POINT

Let the given line be: $y = 2x + 3$

Therefore, the equation of the line perpendicular to this is: $y = -\dfrac{1}{2}x + c$ | Different gradient and different y-intercept |

If the perpendicular line passes through, say (1, -1) it will satisfy $y = -\dfrac{1}{2}x + c$

Therefore: $-1 = -\dfrac{1}{2} + c$ or $c = -\dfrac{1}{2}$

The equation of the required perpendicular line is: $y = -\dfrac{1}{2}x - \dfrac{1}{2}$ or $2y = -x - 1$

DRAWING LINEAR GRAPHS

A linear graph is simply a representation of an equation of a straight line on the graph paper

Example 1:

Graph the equation y = 3x − 6

In order to graph this equation, choose a minimum of two pints that would lie on the line. This is done as follows: Assign any two values, say 1 and 2 for x and determine the corresponding values of y by substituting in the given equation. Show the results as depicted in the grid below:

y = 3x − 6	x	1	2
	y	-3	0

Thus, the two points have co-ordinates (1, -3) and (2, 0). Plot these points on the graph paper and join them (extending on both sides) to get the required graph.
The line has a gradient of 3 and a y-intercept of -6.

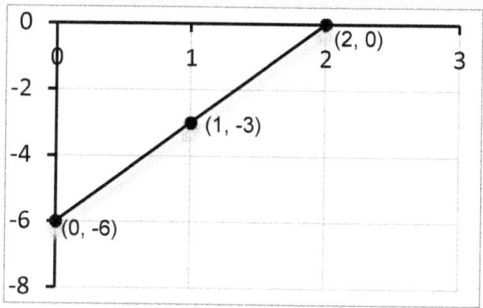

Example 2:

Graph the equation 3x + 2y = -4

Solution: Rewrite the equation in the form y = mx + c as follows:

$$y = \frac{-4 - 3x}{2} = -2 - 1.5x = -1.5x - 2$$

Give any two values, say -2 and 3 for x and determine the corresponding values of y by substituting in the given equation. The results are as shown in the grid below:

y = -1.5x − 2	x	-2	3
	y	1	-6.5

The two points have coordinates (-2, 1) and (3, -6.5)

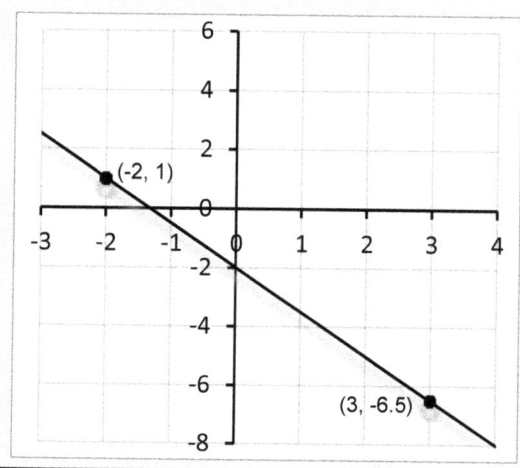

SOLVING LINEAR SIMULTANEOUS EQUATIONS GRAPHICALLY

A graphical method could be used to solve two linear simultaneous equations. The two equations are graphed on the same graph paper. The point of intersection of the two graphs is the solution. This point lies on both the lines and hence satisfies them simultaneously. We proceed as before but we need to have two grids.

Example 1:

Solve graphically the following simultaneous equations:

$$y = -2x \text{ and } y = 4x + 6$$

Solution:

The two grids with the same values of x (say x = 0 and 2) used for both are:

$y = -2x$	x	0	2
	y	0	-4

$y = 4x + 6$	x	0	2
	y	6	14

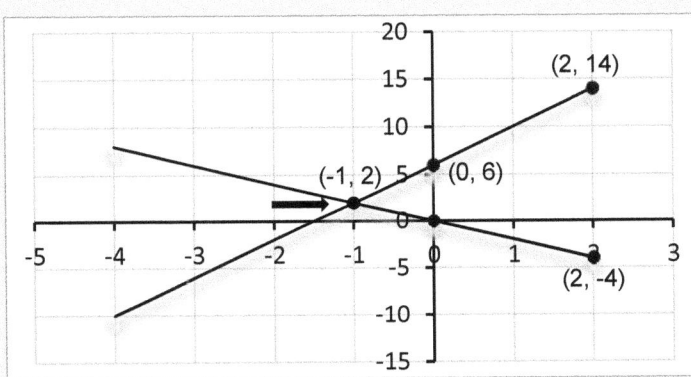

From the graph, the point of intersection of the two lines has coordinates (-1, 2).
Therefore, the solution to the simultaneous equations is: x = -1, y = 2.

Example 2:

Solve graphically the following simultaneous equations:

$$5x - y = -5 \quad \text{and} \quad x + y = -19$$

Solution:

Rewrite the equations in the form $y = mx + c$

$5x - y = -5$ becomes $y = 5x + 5$

$x + y = -19$ becomes $y = -x - 19$

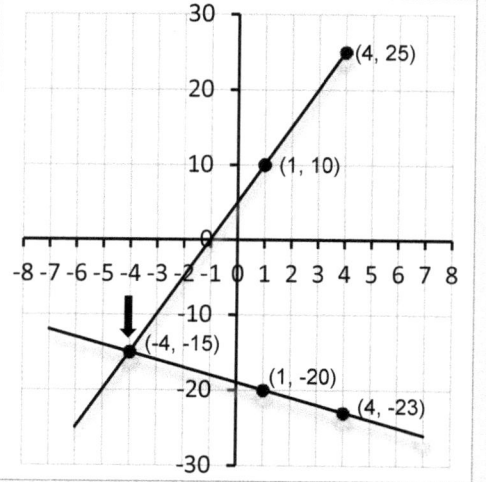

y = 5x + 5	x	1	4
	y	10	25

The same values for x are used in both grids

y = -x - 19	x	1	4
	y	-20	-23

From the graph, the point of intersection of the two lines has coordinates (-4, -15).
Therefore, the solution to the simultaneous equations is: x = -4, y = -15

Example 3:

Solve graphically the following simultaneous equations:

$$3x - y + 8 = 0 \quad \text{and} \quad 4x + 2y - 21 = 0$$

Solution:

Rewrite the equations in the form $y = mx + c$ as shown below:

$3x - y + 8 = 0$ becomes $y = 3x + 8$

$4x + 2y - 21 = 0$ becomes $y = -2x + 10.5$

The two grids with the same values of x (say x = 1 and 3) used for both are:

y = 3x + 8	x	1	3
	y	11	17

y = -2x + 10.5	x	1	3
	y	8.5	4.5

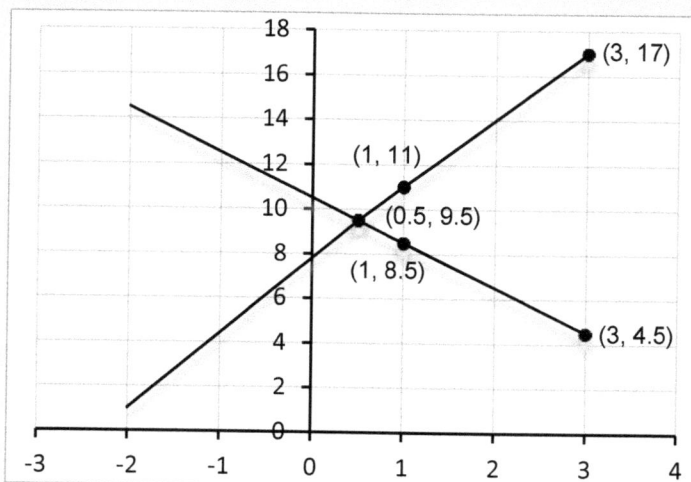

From the graph, the point of intersection of the two lines has coordinates (0.5, 9.5).

Therefore, the solution to the simultaneous equation is: x = 0.5, y = 9.5

NON-LINEAR GRAPHS

A non-linear graph is any graph that is not a straight line. Its equation cannot be written in the form $y = mx + c$. In order to draw an accurate non-linear graph, we need to plot a number of points.(or use a graphics calculator). Generally, if a variable in an equation has a power greater than 1, then it is a non-linear equation.

TRANSFORMATION OF PARABOLAS

The equation $y = ax^2 + bx + c$ when graphed gives a bell-shaped graph, often described as a **parabola**. The basic form is $y = x^2$ (where $a = 1, b = 0, c = 0$).

The basic graph undergoes transformation, namely:

- **Dilation**
- **Translation**
- **Reflection**
- **Rotation**

Dilation of a parabola refers to stretching or compressing it. Stretching occurs if "a" is less than 1 and compressing occurs if "a" is greater than 1.

Example:

Show the graphs of $y = ax^2$ when $a = 1$, $a > 1$ and $a < 1$

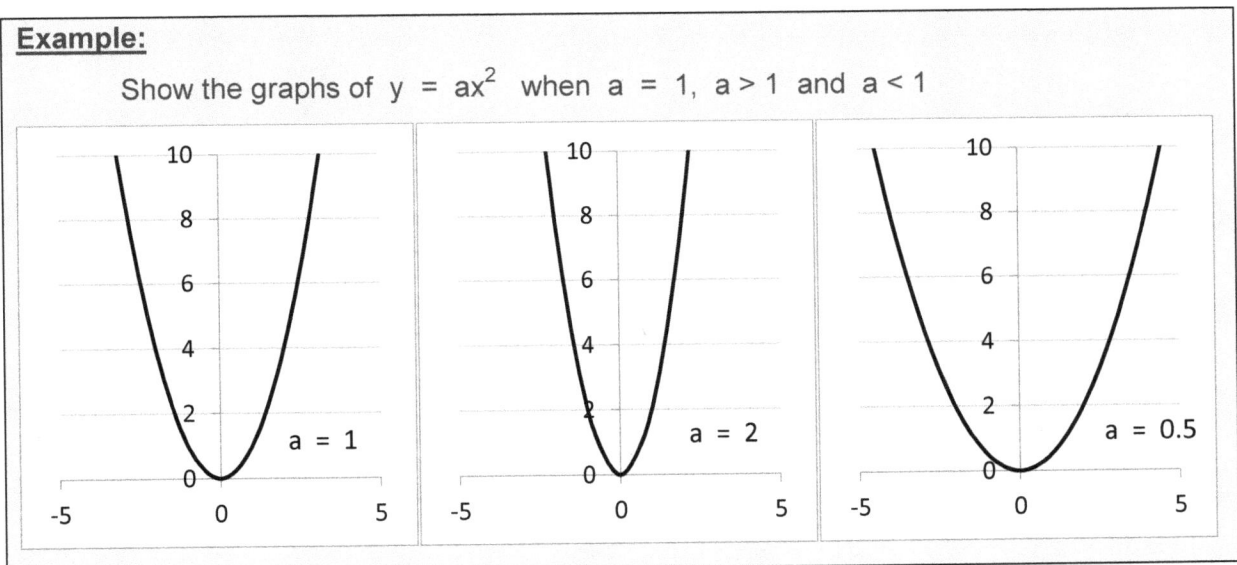

In the equation $y = ax^2 + bx + c$, If the coefficient "a" is negative, the curve is inverted. That is, it is **reflected** in the x-axis.

Example:

Show in the same diagram how the basic graph $y = x^2$ will look like when dilated by a factor of 2 and by a factor of 0.5 in the direction of y-axis. Also, show its reflection in the x-axis.

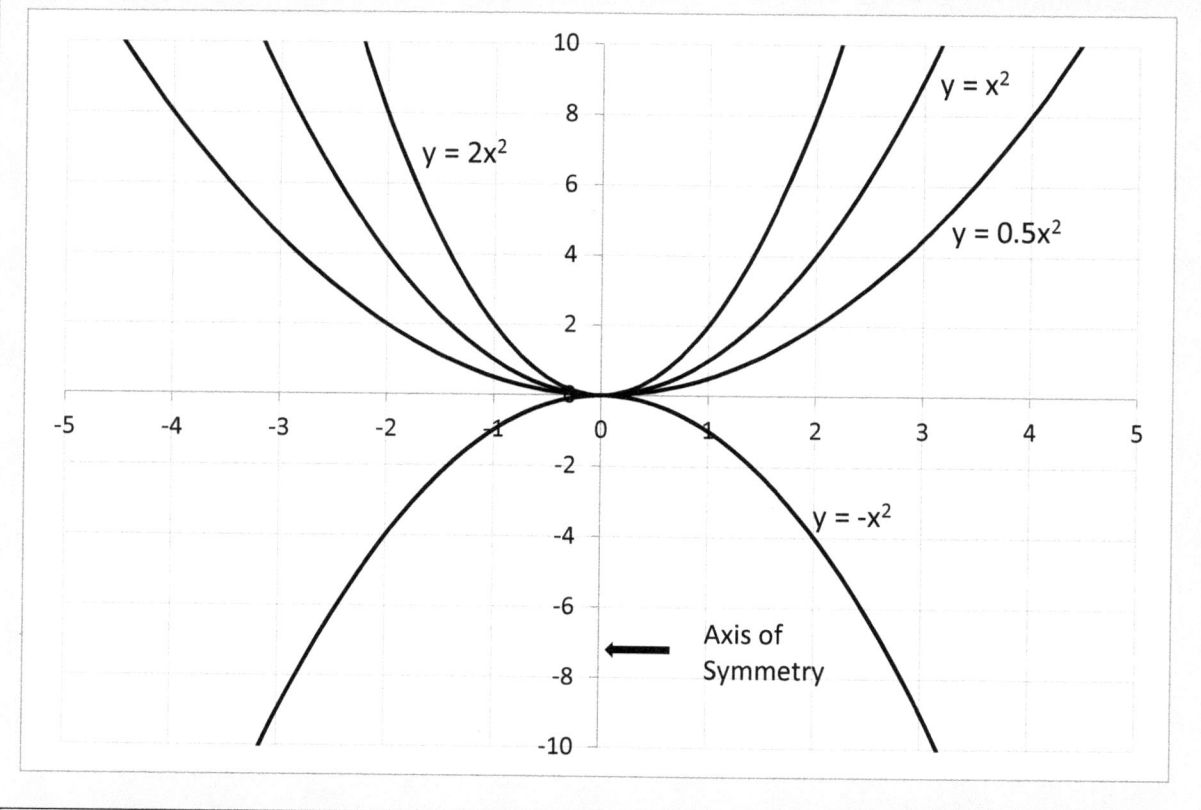

When a graph is moved **horizontally or vertically**, it is called **translation**. A basic graph can undergo horizontal or vertical translation. This is illustrated by the diagrams on the next page.

The basic graphs with constants added are shown with their different translations:

- The basic graph with 3 added to x^2 moves vertically up 3 units and moves vertically down 2 units when -2 is added.

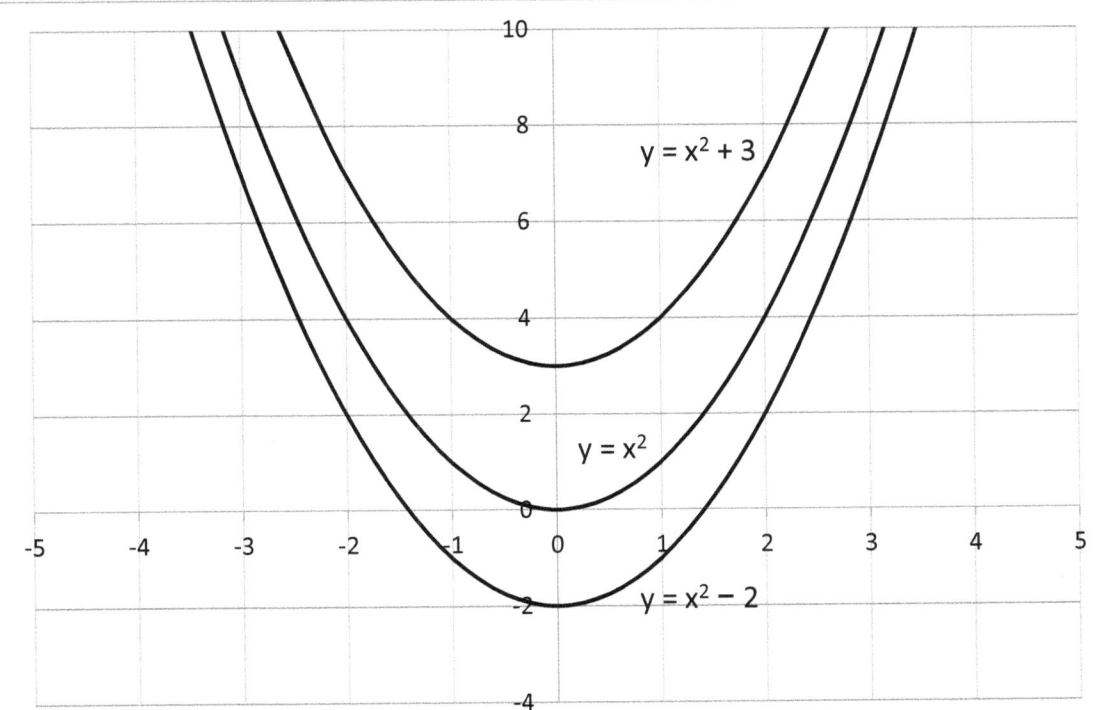

- The basic graph with 2 added to x moves it horizontally 2 units to the left and moves it horizontally to the right 1 unit when -1 is added to x.

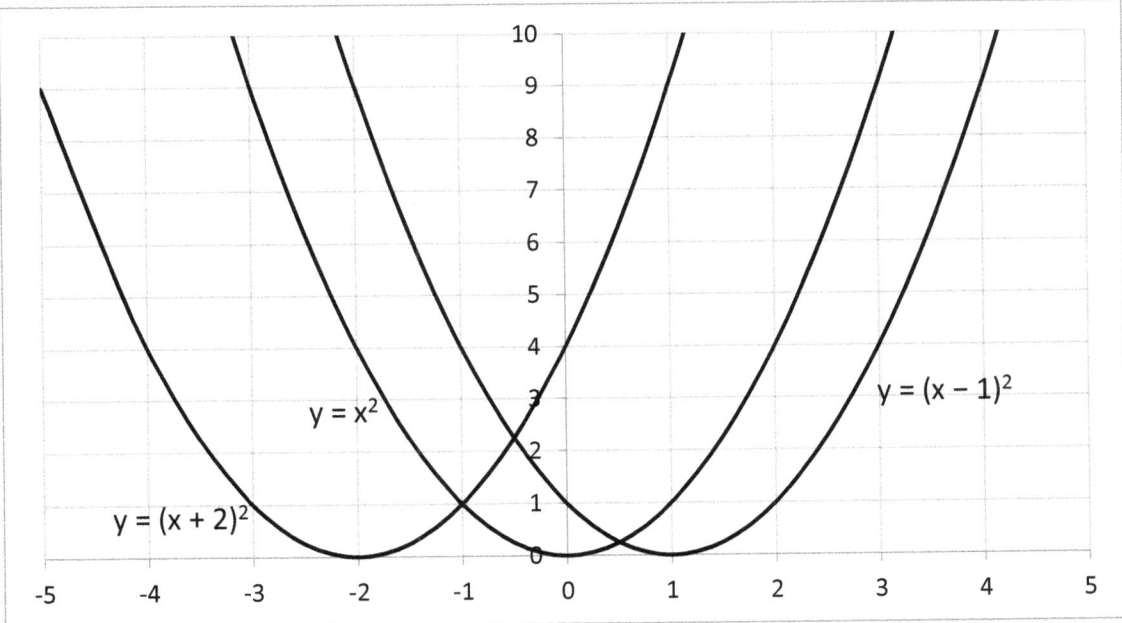

Rotation occurs when a parabola is rotated about the origin.

Example:

Rotate the parabola $y = (x - 2)^2 + 3$ through 180^0 about the origin and state the equation of the new parabola.

The given parabola is the basic parabola shifted 2 units to the right and 3 units upwards. If we replace x by -x and y by -y, we get:

$-y = (-x - 2)^2 + 3$

Multiply both sides of the equation by -1 to get:

$y = -(-x - 2)^2 - 3$

$y = -(x + 2)^2 - 3$

This is the equation of the new parabola obtained by rotating the given parabola through 180 degrees about the origin.

LINEAR VS NON-LINEAR RELATIONSHIP

While a linear equation has one basic form $(y = mx + c)$, nonlinear equations can take many different graphical forms. Unlike a straight line, which has a constant slope or gradient, a nonlinear line has multiple slopes or gradients which depend on the point at which it is determined.

In order to determine if a table of values represents a non-linear equation, check the **rate of change** of the variables. If the rate of change is not constant, then it represents a non-linear equation. The rate of change is given by $\dfrac{y_1 - y_2}{x_1 - x_2}$.

Example:

Determine whether the tables of values below represent a linear or non-linear equation.

(a)

x	1	2	3	4	5	6
y	3	5	7	9	11	13

(b)

x	1	2	3	4	5	6
y	3	9	19	33	51	73

Solution:

In (a), the rate of change is constant and equal to 2 $(\dfrac{5 - 3}{2 - 1}, \dfrac{7 - 5}{3 - 2},$ etc.).

Therefore, the values given represent a linear equation.

In (b) the rate of change is not constant $(\dfrac{9 - 3}{2 - 1}, \dfrac{19 - 9}{3 - 2},$ etc.).

Therefore, the values represent a non-linear equation.

- The set of all possible x-values (i.e. values for the independent variable) is called the **domain** of x. In other words, the **horizontal** extent of graph.
- The spread of possible dependent y-values (minimum y-value to maximum y-value) Is called the **range.** In other words, the **vertical** extent of the graph.

Example 1:

Graph showing the domain and range:

The domain is (-3, 1) and the range is (0, -4).

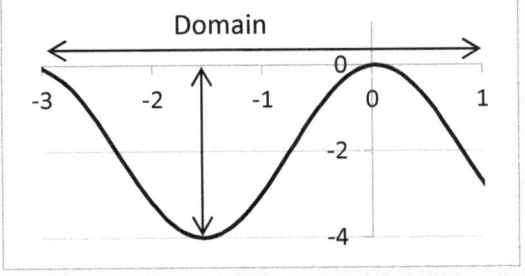

Example 2:

State the domain and range of the following: (1, 2), (3, 8), (5, 14), (7, 20)

Domain = (1, 7) and Range = (2, 20)

THE TURNING POINT OF A QUADRATIC GRAPH

The turning point of a quadratic graph is the point at which the curve changes direction. It is also called the **stationary point**. On a quadratic graph where the concavity faces upwards, the turning point is the **minimum point (coefficient of x^2 will be positive)**. In the case of a quadratic curve where the concavity faces downwards, the turning point is **the maximum point (coefficient of x^2 will negative)**.

The completing the square method is used to determine the coordinates of the turning point. The following examples illustrate this method. A vertical line through the turning point is called the **Line of Symmetry.**

MAXIMUM, MINIMUM POINTS OF A QUADRATIC GRAPH

Minimum point

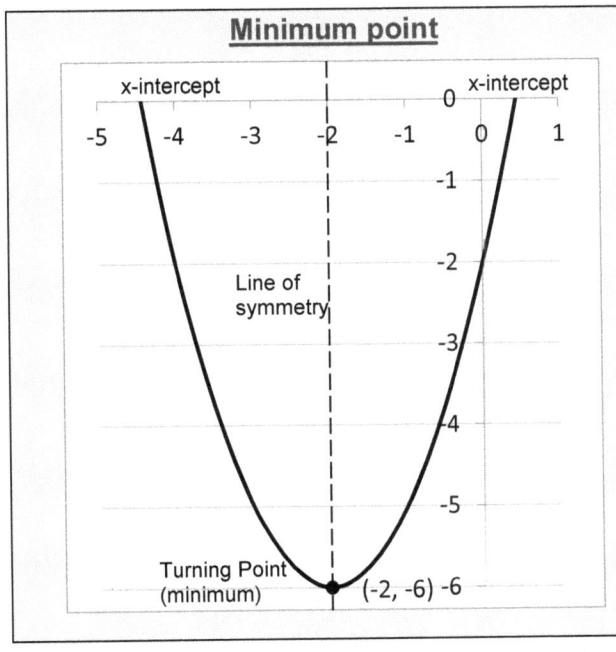

Maximum point

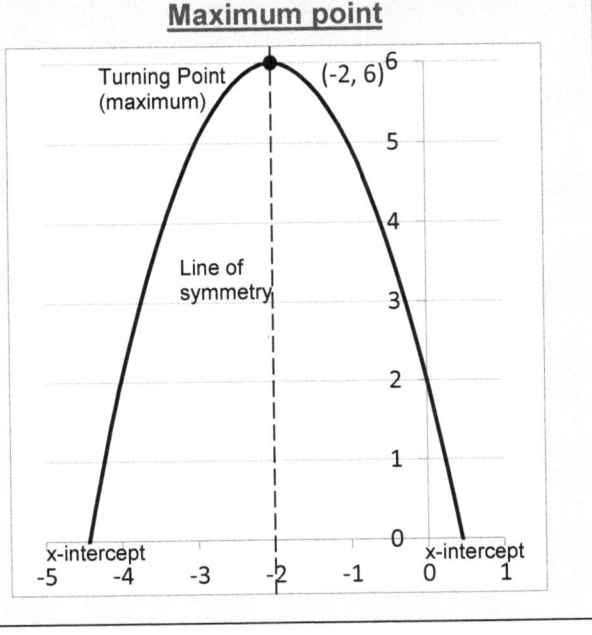

THE TURNING POINT FORM OF A QUADRATIC EQUATION

If the quadratic equation can be written in the form $y = a(x - h)^2 + k$, then the turning point would be (h, k).

Example 1:

Find the turning point of the graph: $y = x^2 - 4x + 2$

$y = x^2 - 4x + 2 = (x - 2)^2 - 2$

Since the coefficient of x^2 is positive, this equation has a minimum point.
The coordinates of the turning point are $(2, -2)$.

Example 2:

Find the turning point of the graph: $y = -2x^2 + 3x - 1$

$y = -2x^2 + 3x - 1 = -2[x^2 - \dfrac{3}{2}x + \dfrac{1}{2}]$

$y = -2[(x - \dfrac{3}{4})^2 - \dfrac{9}{16} + \dfrac{1}{2}] = -2[(x - \dfrac{3}{4})^2 - \dfrac{1}{16}] = -2(x - \dfrac{3}{4})^2 + \dfrac{1}{8}$

Since the coefficient of x^2 is negative, this equation has a maximum point.

Therefore, the coordinates of the turning point are $(\dfrac{3}{4}, \dfrac{1}{8})$

FORMULA METHOD OF FINDING THE TURNING POINT

If $y = ax^2 + bx + c$:

- The x co-ordinate of the turning point $= \dfrac{b}{2a}$
- The y coordinate is obtained by substituting the value of x in the equation.

Example 1:

$y = x^2 - 4x + 2$

x-coordinate of TP $= \dfrac{-4}{2 \times 1} = 2$

y-coordinate of TP $= 2^2 - 4 \times 2 + 2 = -2$

Therefore, the coordinates of the turning point are $(2, -2)$

Example 2:

$y = -2x^2 + 3x - 1$

x-coordinate of TP $= \dfrac{3}{2 \times (-2)} = \dfrac{3}{4}$

y-coordinate of TP $= -2(\dfrac{3}{4})^2 + 3 \times \dfrac{3}{4} - 1 = \dfrac{9}{8} + \dfrac{9}{4} - 1 = \dfrac{9}{8} - 1 = \dfrac{1}{8}$

Therefore, the coordinates of the turning point are $(\dfrac{3}{4}, \dfrac{1}{8})$

THE GRAPH OF A QUADRATIC EQUATION

The general equation of a quadratic equation is $y = ax^2 + bx + c$

A quadratic equation gives a graph (or curve) that is bell shaped. The concavity of the curve can be turned upwards or downwards. If the coefficient of x^2 is positive it will be turned upwards, if negative, it will be turned downwards. The curve will cut the x-axis in two places if $b^2 - 4ac$ (i.e. the discriminant) is greater than zero. If the discriminant is zero, it will touch the x axis. The curve will not cut the x-axis if $b^2 - 4ac$ is negative.

Example 1:

Complete the grid below, plot the points and draw the graph.

$$y = x^2 - 4$$

x	0	1	2	3	4	5	6
y							

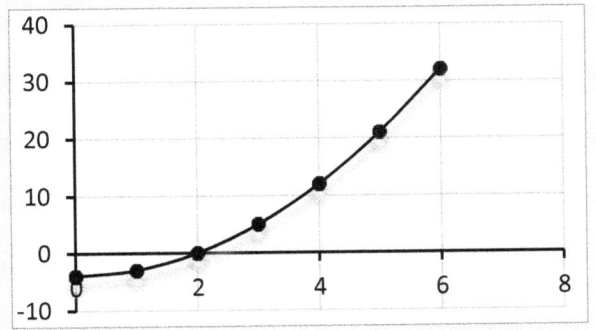

Solution:

$$y = x^2 - 4$$

x	0	1	2	3	4	5	6
y	-4	-3	0	5	12	21	32

Example 2:

By first finding the x and y intercepts and turning point, sketch the graph of:

$$y = x^2 + 4x + 3$$

Solution:

When $x = 0$, $y = 3$.

Thus the y-intercept $= 3$.

When $y = 0$, $(x + 1)(x + 3) = 0$.

That is, $x = -1$ or -3

Therefore, the x-intercepts are -1 and -3.

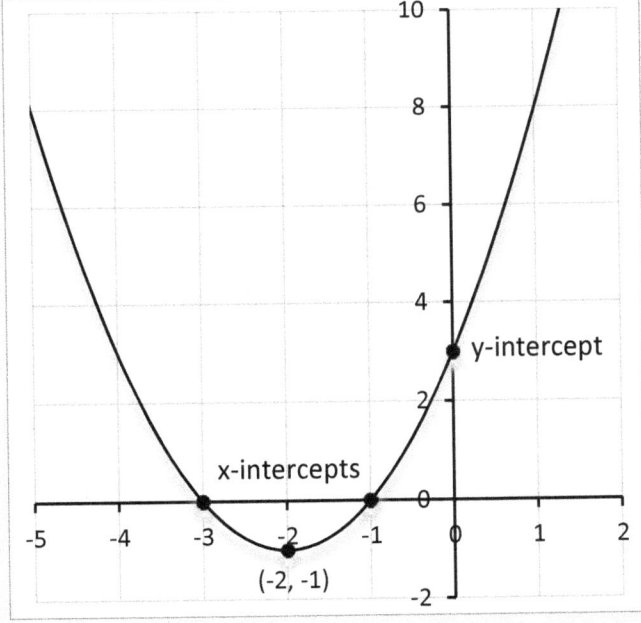

The x-coordinate of the turning point $= -\dfrac{b}{2a} = -2$

The y-coordinate of the turning point $= (-2)^2 + 4(-2) + 3 = -1$

I.e. The coordinates of the turning point are (-2, -1)

Example 3:

Complete the grid below, plot the points and sketch the graph

$$y = 3x^2 - 2x - 3$$

x	-3	-2	-1	0	1	2	3
y							

Solution:　　$y = 3x^2 - 2x - 3$

x	-3	-2	-1	0	1	2	3
y	30	13	2	-3	-2	5	18

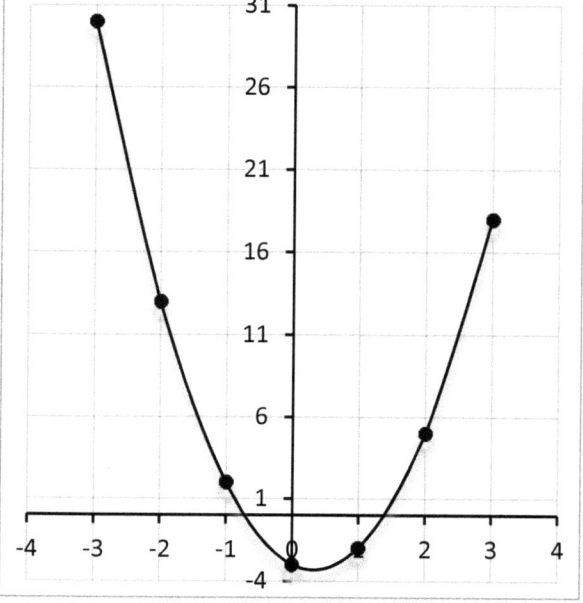

Example 4:

By first finding the x and y intercepts and the turning point, sketch the graph

$$y = -2x^2 - 5x - 6$$

Solution:

When $x = 0$, $y = -6$

Thus, the y-intercept $= -6$

When $y = 0$, $-2(x + 2)(x + 3) = 0$

The discriminant $= -23$

Therefore, there are no x-intercepts

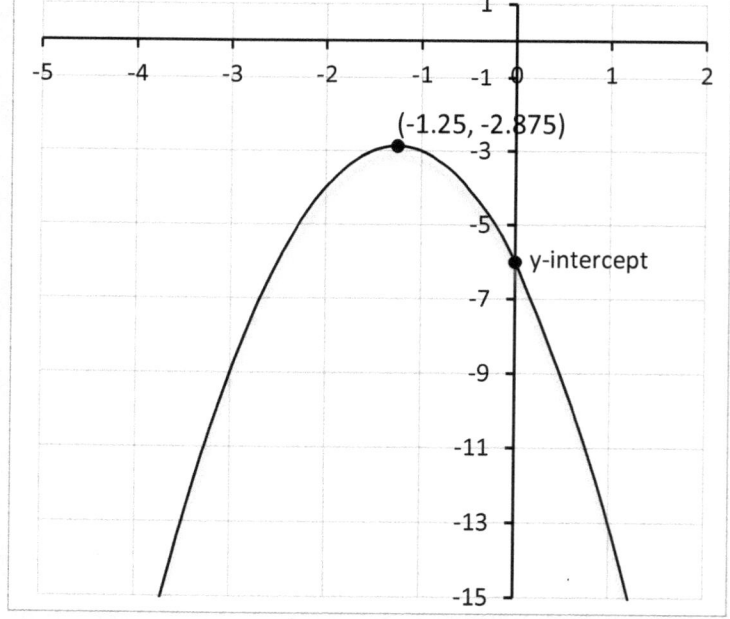

The x-coordinate of the turning point $= -\dfrac{b}{2a} = -\dfrac{5}{4} = -1.25$

The y-coordinate of the turning point $= -2(-1.25)^2 - 5(-1.25) - 6$

$= -3.125 + 6.25 - 6 = -2.875$

I.e. The coordinates of the turning point are (-1.25, -2.875)

SOLVING A NON-LINEAR SIMULTANEOUS EQUATION BY GRAPH

Example:

Solve the equations $y = 2x + 1$ and $3y = x^2 - 9$ using a graph.

Solution:

$y = 2x + 1$ is a straight line graph with gradient 2 and y-intercept of 1.

The graph of $3y = x^2 - 9$ will cut the y-axis at (0, -3) and the x axis at (-3, 0) and (3, 0).

The diagram below illustrates this. The point where the two graphs intersect gives the solution to the problem.

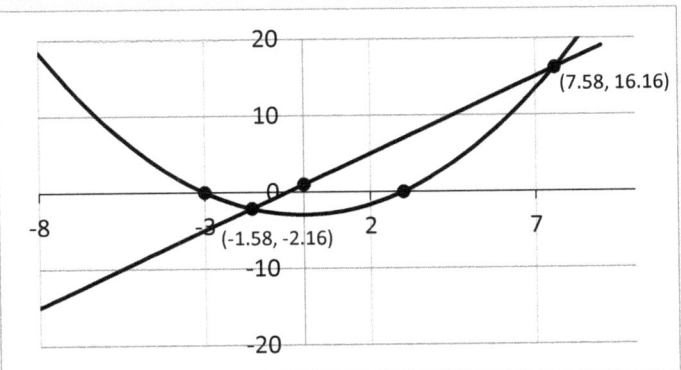

Therefore, the solution is: $x = 7.58$ and $y = 16.16$ or $x = -1.58$ and $y = -2.16$

CUBIC GRAPHS

A **cubic graph** represents a polynomial of **degree three.**
- The general equation is $y = ax^3 + bx^2 + cx + d$

Graph of the basic cubic
$y = x^3$

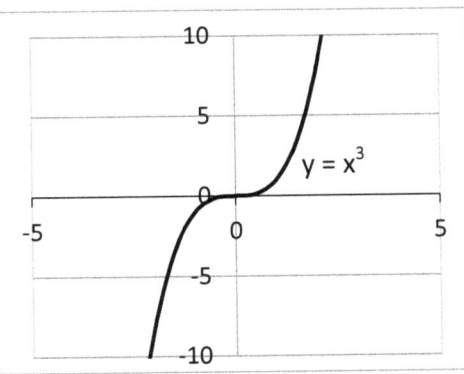

This graph has a special stationary point called the **point of inflection.** An **inflection point** is where a curve changes from concave upward to concave downward (or vice versa).

A graph of the general cubic equation will generally have three x-intercepts. They are obtained by making $y = 0$. Sometimes we can have two coincident x-values. This will mean that the curve touches the x-axis instead of cutting it. In order to draw an accurate graph, the turning points of the graph need to be known.

This is easily determined using calculus (by equating the derivative to zero) as we will see in chapter 15. For the purpose of this topic, we will use some **critical points** that would make it easy to see that the graph is continuous from left to right.

Example 1:

Draw the graph of $y = x^3 + 2x^2 - 5x - 6$

We first determine one root by trial and error. The possible roots are ±1, ±2, ±3 and ±6

Let us try $x = 2$. Therefore, $y = 8 + 8 - 10 - 6 = 0$

Therefore, $x - 2$ is a factor of y. Now, using long division we get the other (quadratic) factor as follows:

$$
\begin{array}{r}
x^2 + 4x \quad + 3 \\
x - 2 \overline{\smash{\big)}\, x^3 + 2x^2 - 5x - 6} \\
\underline{x^3 - 2x^2} \\
4x^2 - 5x \\
\underline{4x^2 - 8x} \\
3x - 6 \\
\underline{3x - 6} \\
0
\end{array}
$$

Therefore, $y = (x - 2)(x^2 + 4x + 3)$

That is, $y = (x - 2)(x + 1)(x + 3)$ | Using the method of inspection |

Steps to draw the graph:

1. Find the values of x when $y = 0$ (x values are: 2, -1 and -3).
   Plot them on the x–axis.

2. Find the value of y when $x = 0$ (y value = -2 × 1 × 3 = -6).
   Plot it on the y-axis.

3. Select four (suitable) values — one less than -3 (say -4), another between -3 and -1 (say -2), another between -1 and 2 (say 1) and the last one greater than 2 (say 3). Find the corresponding y-values and plot them [(-4, -18), (-2, 4), (1, -8), (3, 24)].

4. Draw the graph as shown below.

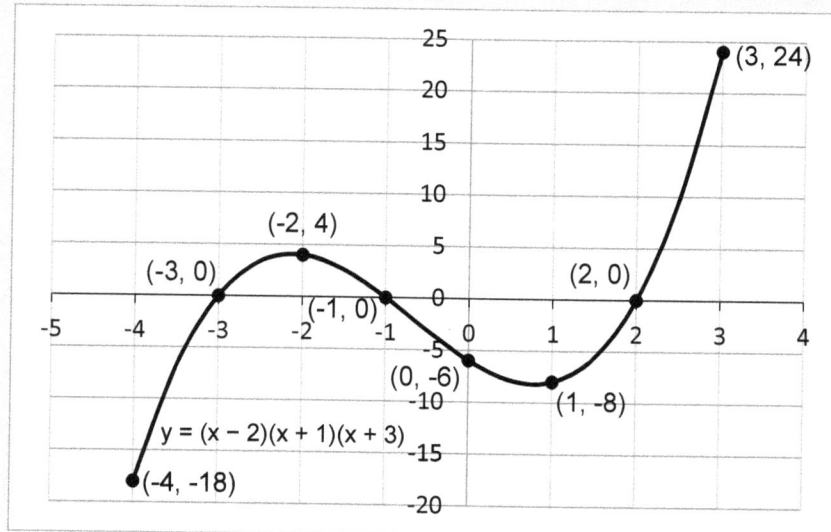

140

Example 2:

        Draw the graph of $y = 2x^3 + 5x^2 + 4x + 1$

Multiply 2 (coefficient of x^3) by 1. The result is 2.

The trial root that would satisfy the given equation is one of: ± 1 and ± 2

Let us try $x = 1$. This gives y a value of 12 and not zero. Therefore, it is not a root.

Now, try $x = -1$. This makes y equal to 0. Therefore, it is a root.

Therefore, one factor of y is $(x + 1)$.

Carry out long division to get the other factor which will be a quadratic.

$$\begin{array}{r}
2x^2 + 3x + 1 \\
\hline
x + 1 \overline{)\ 2x^3 + 5x^2 + 4x + 1} \\
\underline{2x^3 + 2x^2} \\
3x^2 + 4x \\
\underline{3x^2 + 3x} \\
x + 1 \\
\underline{x + 1} \\
0
\end{array}$$

Therefore: $y = (x + 1)(2x^2 + 3x + 1)$

That is: $y = (x + 1)(2x + 1)(x + 1)$ | Using the method of inspection |

Steps to draw the graph:

1. Find the values of x when $y = 0$ (x values are: -1(twice), -0.5)
   Plot them on the x-axis

2. Find the value of y when $x = 0$ (y value $= 1 \times 1 \times 1 = 1$)
   Plot it on the y-axis.

3. Select 3 values — one less than -1 (say -2), another between -1 and -0.5 (say -0.75), and the last one greater than -0.5 (say 0). Find the corresponding y-values and plot them
   [(-2, -3), (-0.75, -0.03125), (0, 1)].

4. Draw the graph as shown:

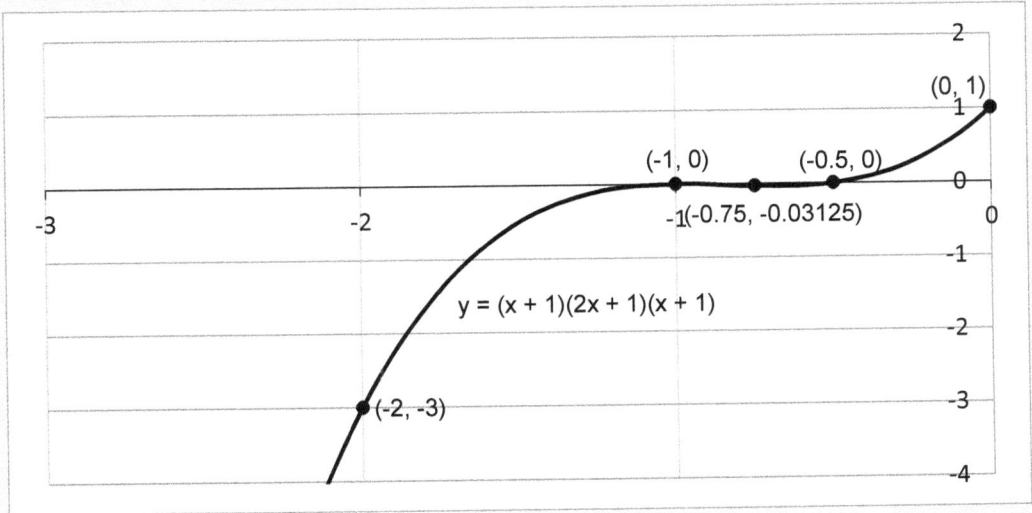

1. (a) Find the gradient and y-intercept of the following straight lines:

   (i) $y = 2x + 5$ (ii) $y = -3x - 2$ (iii) $2x - 3y - 4 = 0$ (iv) $x - 3y = 6$

   (b) Find the equation of a line passing through (-3, 1) that:

   (i) has a gradient of -2

   (ii) makes an intercept of 3 on the y-axis

   (iii) is parallel to the x-axis

   (iv) is parallel to the y-axis

2. (a) Find the point of intersection of each of the following pairs of straight lines by using graphs.

   (i) $x + 2y - 3 = 0$ and $3y - 2x - 8 = 0$

   (ii) $2y = -3x + 2$ and $4x + 5y + 2 = 0$

   (b) Find algebraically the equation of the line that is concurrent with the lines:

   $2y + 3x = 16$ and $3y - 4x = 7$ and is parallel to the line $2y + x = 4$

3. (a) Find the distance between the following pairs of points.

   (i) (2, 4) and (6, 2)   (ii) (2, -1) and (-2, 3)

   (iii) (-4, -6) and (-8, -5)   (iv) (-3, 1) and (4, 4)

   (b) Find the equation of the line that passes through the point of intersection of the lines

   $3x - 2y + 14 = 0$ and $5x + y + 6 = 0$ and:

   (i) passes through the point (3, -2)

   (ii) is parallel to the line $x + y + 3 = 0$

   (iii) is perpendicular to the line $2x - 3y + 5 = 0$

4. Write down the equation of the line passing through the points:

   (a)(i) (0, 0) and (3, 1)   (ii) (1, 5) and (3, 0)   (iii) (-1, 4) and (-3, -4)

   (b) Find the equation of the perpendicular bisector of the line joining

   (i) (0, 1) and (3, 4)   (ii) (2, -1) and (-4, 2)   (iii) (6, -1) and (0, 4)

5. (a) By first finding the x and y intercepts and the turning point, sketch the graphs of the following.

   (i) $y = x^2 + x - 12$ (ii) $y = 5 + 6x^2 - 13x$ (iii) $y = -x^2 - 2x - 1$

   (b) A quadratic graph has a turning point (2, 1) and y-intercept of (0, 9).
   What is its equation?

   (c) Using the equation $y = x^2 + 4x - 9$, complete a table of coordinates.
   Use these coordinates to plot the graph between $x = -5$ and $x = 2$.

6 (a) State the changes required to transform $y = x^2$ into the graph of each of the following:

(i) $y = -4x^2$ (ii) $y = 2(2 - x)^2$ (iii) $y = (x + 3)^2 - 2$ (iv) $y = 1 - 3(2 + x)^2$

(b) Sketch each of the following cubic curves:

(i) $y = (x + 6)(x - 6)(2x + 3)$

(ii) $y = (4x - 1)^2(x + 5)$

(iii) $y = 3x^2(x + 4)$

---

7. (a) Using transformations of the graph $y = x^2$, describe how you would arrive at the graph of $y = 3(x + 1)^2 + 4$

(b) Given the following table of values, graphically determine the equation of the quadratic graph described by the table.

x	0	1	2	3	4	5	6
y	16	11	8	7	8	11	16

8.(a) Write the equations that result from the following transformations:

(i) $y = x^2$ is reflected in the x-axis and translated 1 unit to the right

(ii) $y = x^2$ is reflected in the x-axis and translated 2 unit to the left

(iii) $y = x^2$ is dilated by a factor of 2 in the y-direction and translated 5 units up

(iv) $y = x^2$ is dilated by a factor of 0.5 in the y-direction and translated 1 unit down

(v) $y = x^2$ is reflected in the x-axis and translated 2 unit to the left and 1 unit up

(vi) $y = x^2$ is translated 5 units upwards and 3 units to the right

(b) By finding the discriminant, determine the number of roots and their nature, of each of the following:

(i) $x^2 - 3x + 2 = 0$

(ii) $2x^2 + 3x - 5 = 0$

(iii) $5x^2 - 3x + 2 = 0$

(iv) $3x^2 + 6x - 7 = 0$

(v) $4x^2 - 12x + 9 = 0$

1.(a)(i) y = 2x + 5 (Gradient = 2, y-intercept = 5)

(ii) y = -3x − 2 (Gradient = -3, y-intercept = -2)

(iii) 2x − 3y − 4 = 0

Rewriting this in the form of y = mx + c = $\frac{2}{3}$x − $\frac{4}{3}$ (Gradient = $\frac{2}{3}$, y-intercept = -$\frac{4}{3}$)

(iv) x − 3y = 6

Rewriting this in the form of y = mx + c = $\frac{1}{3}$x − 2 (Gradient = $\frac{1}{3}$, y-intercept = -2)

(b)(i) The equation of a line passing through (-3, 1) is:
y − 1 = -2(x + 3) = -2x − 6

y = -2x − 5

(ii) When making an intercept of 3 on the y-axis, the line passes through (0, 3).

The gradient of the line is: $\frac{3-1}{0+3}$ = $\frac{2}{3}$

The required equation of the line is:

y − 3 = $\frac{2}{3}$(x − 0) = $\frac{2}{3}$x

y = $\frac{2}{3}$x + 3

(iii) A line parallel to x-axis has gradient 0. Therefore, the required equation is: y = 1

(iv) A line parallel to y-axis has an undefined gradient.
Therefore, the required equation is: x = -3

---

2. (a)

(i) x + 2y − 3 = 0

y = -$\frac{1}{2}$x + $\frac{3}{2}$

x	-1	2	4
y	2	0.5	-0.5

3y − 2x − 8 = 0

y = $\frac{2}{3}$x + $\frac{8}{3}$

x	-1	2	4
y	2	4	5.33

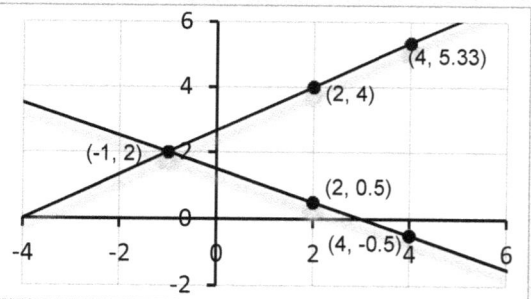

(ii) 2y = -3x + 2

y = -$\frac{3}{2}$x + 1

x	0	2
y	1	-2

4x + 5y + 2 = 0

y = -$\frac{4}{5}$x − $\frac{2}{5}$

x	0	2
y	-0.4	-2

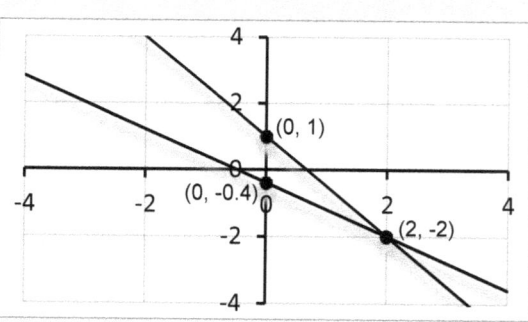

2. (b) $2y + 3x = 16$ ---------- (1)

　　　 $3y - 4x = 7$ ---------- (2)

(1) × 3: $6y + 9x = 48$ ---------- (3)

(2) × 2: $6y - 8x = 14$ ---------- (4)

(3) − (4): $17x = 34$

$x = 2$

$2y + 6 = 16$ | Sub x = 2 in (1) |

$y = 5$

The point of intersection of (1) and (2) = (2, 5)

If the line parallel to the line $2y + x = 4$ is concurrent with (1) and (2), (2, 5) must lie on it.

Now, the line parallel to $2y + x = 4$ is $2y + x = c$

Therefore: $10 + 2 = c$

$c = 12$

The equation of the required line is $2y + x = 12$

---

3. (a) The distance between the points.

(i) (2, 4) and (6, 2): $d = \sqrt{(2-6)^2 + (4-2)^2} = \sqrt{16 + 4} = \sqrt{20} = 2\sqrt{5}$

(ii) (2, -1) and (-2, 3): $d = \sqrt{(2+2)^2 + (-1-3)^2} = \sqrt{16 + 16} = \sqrt{32} = 4\sqrt{2}$

(iii) (-4, -6) and (-8, -5): $d = \sqrt{(-4+8)^2 + (-6+5)^2} = \sqrt{16 + 1} = \sqrt{17}$

(iv) (-3, 1) and (4, 4): $d = \sqrt{(-3-4)^2 + (1-4)^2} = \sqrt{49 + 9} = \sqrt{58}$

3.(b) $3x - 2y + 14 = 0$ ---------- (1)

　　　 $5x + y + 6 = 0$ -------------- (2)

(2) × 2: $10x + 2y + 12 = 0$ --------- (3)

(1) + (3): $13x + 26 = 0$

$13x = -26$

$x = -2$

$-6 - 2y + 14 = 0$ | Sub x = -2 in (1) |

$2y = 8$

$y = 4$

The coordinates of the point of intersection of (1) and (2) are (-2, 4)

(i) The equation of the line passing through (-2, 4) and (3, -2) is:

$$y - 4 = \frac{-2 - 4}{3 - (-2)}(x + 2) = -\frac{6}{5}(x + 2)$$

$5y - 20 = -6x - 12$

$5y + 6x = 8$

3.(b)(ii) The equation of the line parallel to the line $x + y + 3 = 0$ is:

$x + y + c = 0$

Since this line passes through (-2, 4):

$-2 + 4 + c = 0$

$c = -2$

The equation of the required line is: $x + y - 2 = 0$

(iii) The gradient of the line perpendicular to the line $2x - 3y + 5 = 0$ is $-\dfrac{3}{2}$

The equation of the required line is: $y - 4 = -\dfrac{3}{2}(x + 2)$

$2y - 8 = -3x - 6$ or $2y + 3x - 2 = 0$

---

4. (a)(i) The equation of the line passing through the points (0, 0) and (3, 1) is:

$y - 0 = \dfrac{1 - 0}{3 - 0}(x - 0)$

$y = \dfrac{1}{3}x$

(ii) The equation of the line passing through the points (1, 5) and (3, 0) is:

$y - 0 = \dfrac{5 - 0}{1 - 3}(x - 3)$

$y = \dfrac{5}{-2}(x - 3)$

$-2y = 5x - 15$

$5x + 2y - 15 = 0$

(iii) The equation of the line passing through the points (-1, 4) and (-3, -4) is:

$y - 4 = \dfrac{-4 - 4}{-3 - (-1)}(x + 1) = 4(x + 1)$

$y = 4x + 8$ or $4x - y + 8 = 0$

(b)(i) The equation of the perpendicular bisector of the line joining (0, 1) and (3, 4):

```
A————————————————————B        | Let C be the midpoint of AB |
(0, 1)        C        (3, 4)
```

Therefore, the coordinates of C are $(\dfrac{0 + 3}{2}, \dfrac{1 + 4}{2})$ i.e. $(\dfrac{3}{2}, \dfrac{5}{2})$

Gradient of AB $= \dfrac{4 - 1}{3 - 0} = 1$

Gradient of a line perpendicular to AB $= -1$

The equation of the line perpendicular to AB and passing through C is:

$y - \dfrac{5}{2} = -1(x - \dfrac{3}{2})$

$2y - 5 = -2x + 3$

$2x + 2y - 8 = 0$

$x + y - 4 = 0$

4.(b)(ii) The equation of the perpendicular bisector of the line joining (2, -1) and (-4, 2):

A————————————————B   Let C be the midpoint of AB
(2, -1)   C   (-4, 2)

Therefore, the coordinates of C are: $(\dfrac{2-4}{2}, \dfrac{-1+2}{2})$ i.e. (-1, 0.5)

Gradient of AB $= \dfrac{-1-2}{2-(-4)} = \dfrac{-1}{2}$

Gradient of a line perpendicular to AB $= 2$

The equation of the line perpendicular to AB and passing through C is:

$y - \dfrac{1}{2} = 2(x + 1)$

$2y - 1 = 4x + 4$

$4x - 2y + 5 = 0$

(iii) The equation of the perpendicular bisector of the line joining (6, -1) and (0, 4):

A————————————————B   Let C be the midpoint of AB
(6, -1)   C   (0, 4)

Therefore, the coordinates of C are: $(\dfrac{6+0}{2}, \dfrac{-1+4}{2})$ i.e. $(3, 1\dfrac{1}{2})$

Gradient of AB $= \dfrac{-1-4}{6-0} = -\dfrac{5}{6}$

Gradient of a line perpendicular to AB $= \dfrac{6}{5}$

The equation of the line perpendicular to AB and passing through C is:

$y - 1\dfrac{1}{2} = \dfrac{6}{5}(x - 3)$

$10y - 15 = 12x - 36$ | Multiply both sides by 10

$12x - 10y - 21 = 0$

5. (a)(i) $y = x^2 + x - 12$

When x = 0, y = -12

When y = 0, $x^2 + x - 12 = 0$

$(x - 4)(x + 3) = 0$

Therefore: x = 4 or x = -3

The x-intercepts are 4 and -3, y-intercept = -12

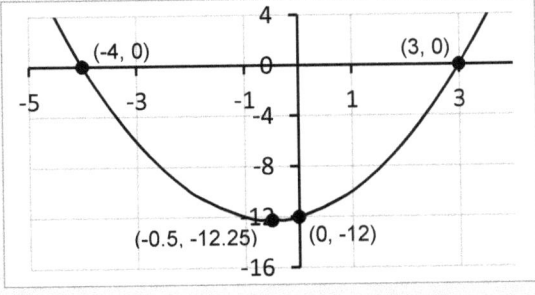

Write the given equation in turning point form as follows:

$y = (x + \dfrac{1}{2})^2 - \dfrac{1}{4} - 12$

$y = (x + \dfrac{1}{2})^2 - 12\dfrac{1}{4}$

Therefore, the coordinates of the turning point are: (-0.5, -12.25)

147

5.(a)(ii) $y = 5 + 6x^2 - 13x$

$y = 6x^2 - 13x + 5$

When $x = 0$, $y = 5$

When $y = 0$, $6x^2 - 13x + 5 = 0$

That is $(2x - 1)(3x - 5) = 0$

Therefore: $x = \dfrac{1}{2}$ or $x = \dfrac{5}{3}$

The x-intercepts are $\dfrac{1}{2}$ and $\dfrac{5}{3}$, y-intercept $= 5$

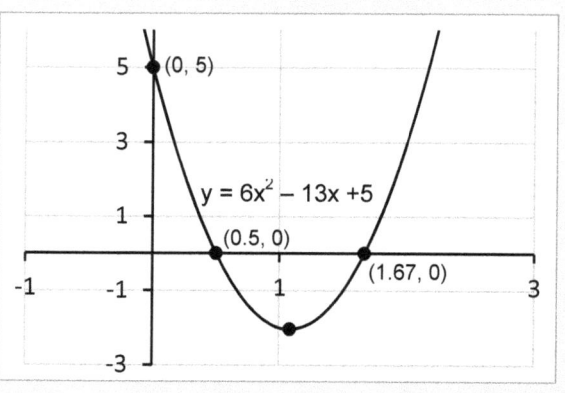

Write the given equation in turning point form as follows:

$y = 6(x^2 - \dfrac{13}{6}x + \dfrac{5}{6}) = 6[(x - \dfrac{13}{12})^2 - \dfrac{169}{144} + \dfrac{5}{6} = 6[(x - \dfrac{13}{12})^2 - \dfrac{169}{144} + \dfrac{120}{144}]$

$y = 6[(x - \dfrac{13}{12})^2 - \dfrac{49}{144}] = 6(x - \dfrac{13}{12})^2 - (6 \times \dfrac{49}{144})$

$y = 6(x - \dfrac{13}{12})^2 - \dfrac{49}{24}$

Therefore the coordinates of the turning point are: $(\dfrac{13}{12}, -\dfrac{49}{24})$ or $(1\dfrac{1}{12}, -2\dfrac{1}{24})$ $\boxed{(1, -2) \text{ approx}}$

(iii) $y = -x^2 - 2x - 1$

When $x = 0$, $y = -1$

When $y = 0$, $x^2 + 2x + 1 = 0$

That is: $(x + 1)(x + 1) = 0$

Therefore $x = -1$(twice)

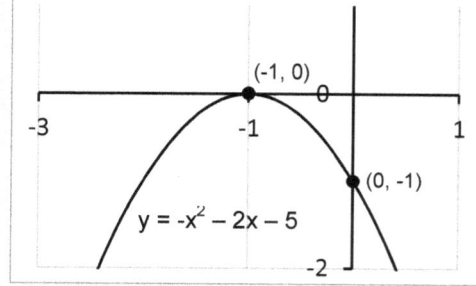

The x – coordinate of the turning point is $\dfrac{-b}{2a} = \dfrac{2}{-2} = -1$

The y co-ordinate of the turning point $= -(-1)^2 - 2(-1) - 1 = 0$

That is, the turning point is $(-1, 0)$

5.(b) Let the equation be: $y = a(x - h)^2 + k$

Since $h = 2$, $k = 1$, $y = a(x - 2)^2 + 1$

Since $(0, 9)$ lies on the graph: $9 = a(0 - 2)^2 + 1$

$9 = 4a + 1$

$8 = 4a$

$a = 2$

Therefore, the equation of the graph is: $y = 2(x - 2)^2 + 1$

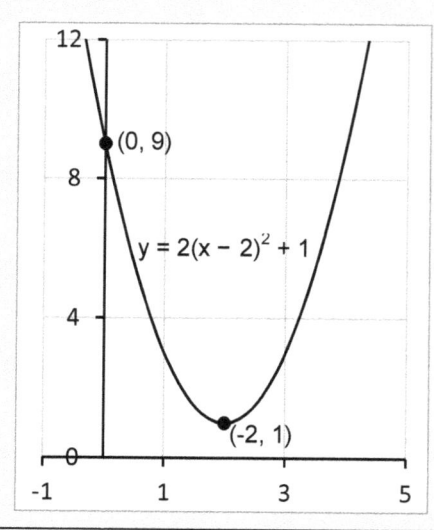

5. (c) $y = x^2 + 4x - 9$

x	-5	-4	-3	-2	-1	0	1	2
y	-4	-9	-12	-13	-12	-9	-4	3

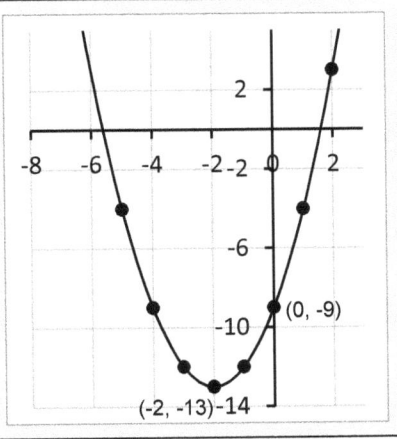

6.(a)(i) In order to transform $y = x^2$ to get the graph of $y = -4x^2$
Dilate by a factor of 4 in the y-direction and reflect in the x-axis

(ii) In order to transform $y = x^2$ to get the graph of $y = 2(2 - x)^2$
Dilate by a factor of 2 in the y-direction and translate 2 units to the right

(iii) In order to transform $y = x^2$ to get the graph of $y = (x + 3)^2 - 2$
Translate 3 units to the left and then translate 2 units down.

(iv) In order to transform $y = x^2$ to get the graph of $y = 1 - 3(2 + x)^2$
Dilate by the factor of 3 in the y-direction, translate 2 units to the left and 1 unit up.

6.(b) Sketching cubic curves

(i) $y = (x + 6)(x - 6)(2x + 3)$

Steps to sketch the graph:

1. The values of x when $y = 0$ (x values are: -6, 6 and -1.5)
    Plot them on the x-axis

2. The value of y when $x = 0$ (y value = 6 × -6 × 3 = -108)
    Plot it on the y-axis.

3. Select four (suitable) values – one less than -6 (say, -7), another between -6 and -1.5
    (say, -3), another between -1.5 and 6 (say, 3) and the last one greater than 6 (say, 7).
    Find the corresponding y-values and plot these also [(-7, -143), (-3, 81), (7, 221)].

4. Sketch the graph as shown below.

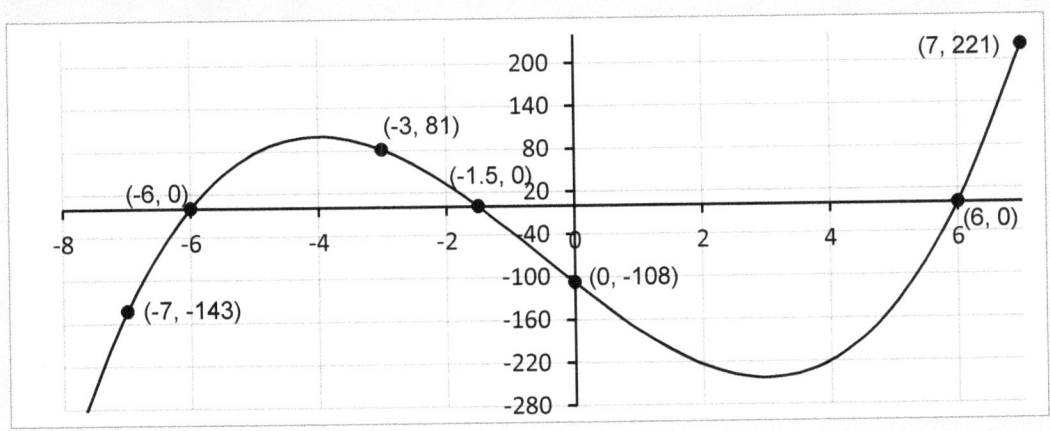

6.(b)(ii) $y = (4x - 1)^2(x + 5)$

Steps to sketch the graph:

1. The values of x when y = 0 (x values are: 0.25(twice) and -5)
    Plot them on the x-axis

2. The value of y when x = 0 (y value = 5)
    Plot it on the y-axis.

3. Select three (suitable) values — one, less than -5 (say, -6), another between -5 and 0.25 (say, -1), and the last one greater than 0.25 (say, 1). Find the corresponding y-values and plot these also [(-6, -625), (-1, 100), (1, 54)].

4. Sketch the graph as shown below.

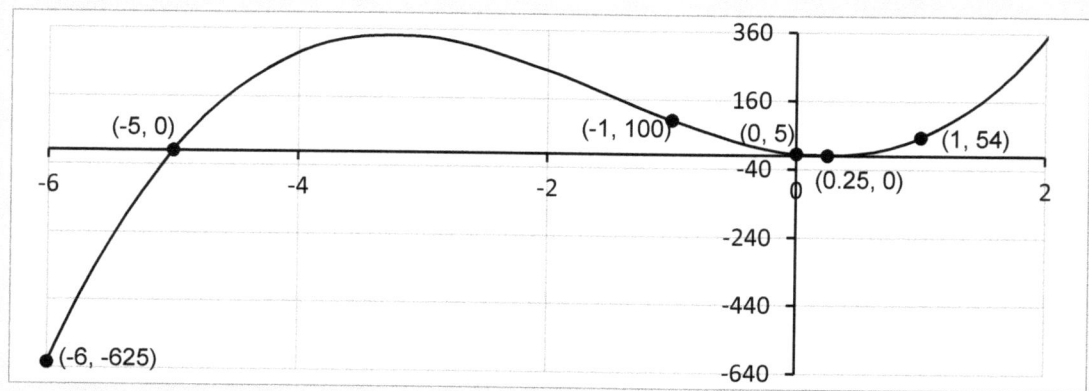

(iii) $y = 3x^2(x + 4)$

Steps to sketch the graph:

1. The values of x when y = 0 (x values are: 0 (twice) and -4)
    Plot them on the x-axis.

2. The value of y when x = 0 (y value = 0)
    Plot it on the y-axis.

3. Select three (suitable) values — one, less than -4 (say, -5), another between -4 and 0 (say, -2), and the last one greater than 0 (say, 1). Find the corresponding y-values and plot these also [(-5, -75), (-2, 24), and (1, 15)].

4. Sketch the graph as shown below.

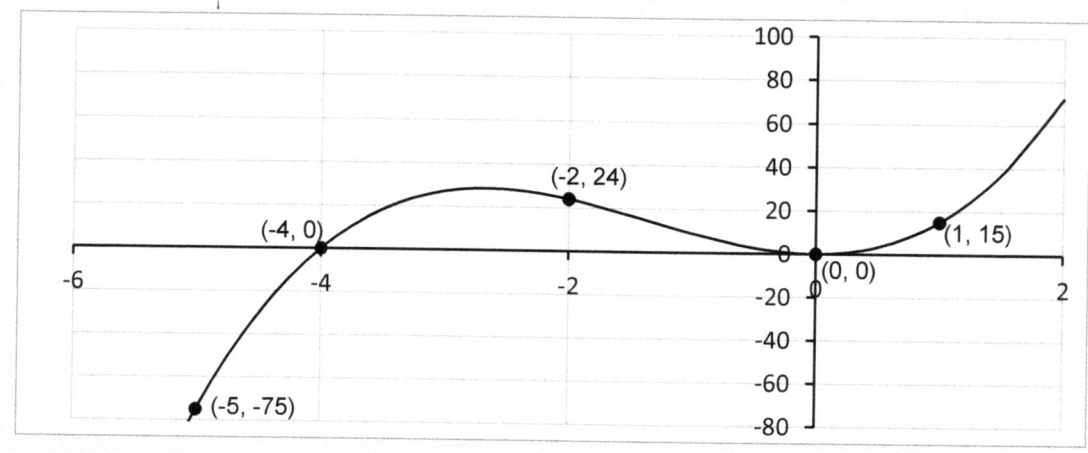

7. (a) The graph of $y = x^2$ is first dilated by a factor of 3 in the y-direction, then translated 1 unit to the left, and finally translated 4 units upwards.

The equation of the new graph is: $y = 3(x + 1)^2 + 4$

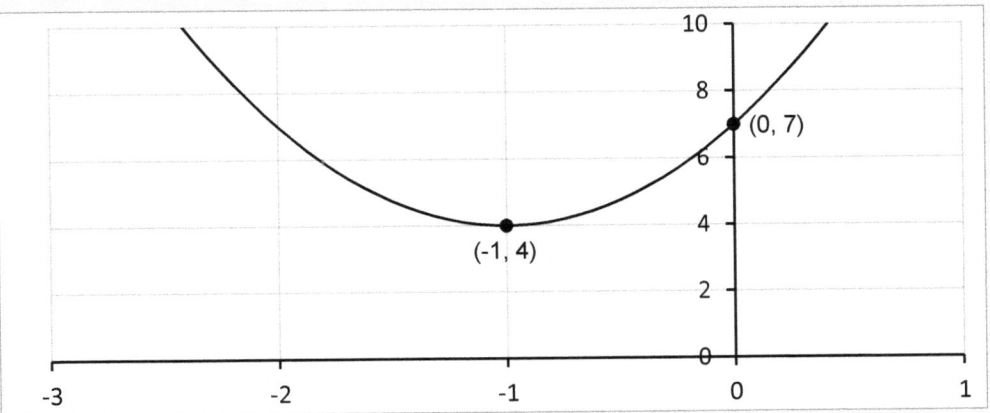

(b)

x	0	1	2	3	4	5	6
y	16	11	8	7	8	11	16

Draw the graph and find where it cuts the x-axis.

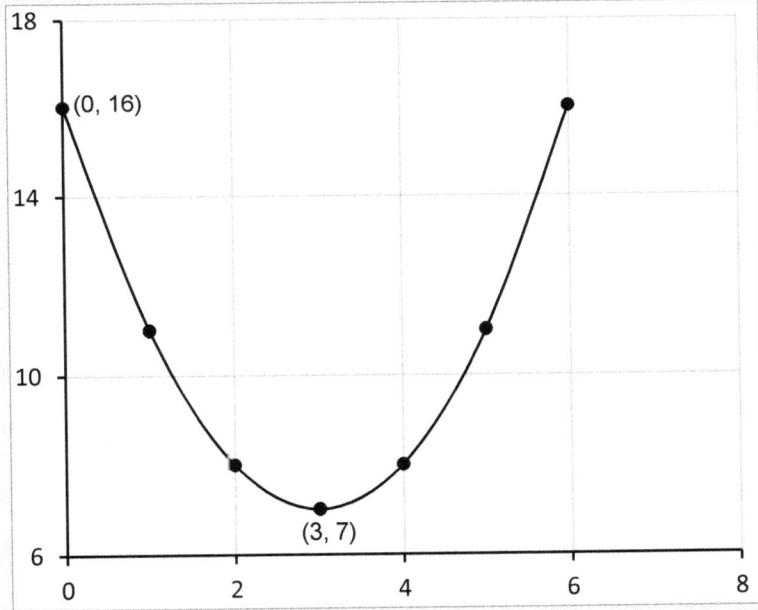

The curve is a parabola and does not cut the x axis. Its turning point is (3, 7).

Therefore, the required equation is $y = (x - 3)^2 + 7$

In the general formula $y = a(x - h)^2 + k$, $a = 1$, $h = 3$ and $k = 7$

"a" is obtained by substituting any of the points given in the formula

8.(a) The equations that result from the given transformations:

(i) $y = x^2$ is reflected in the x-axis and translated 1 unit to the right.

Equation of the transformed graph is: $y = -(x - 1)^2$

(ii) $y = x^2$ is reflected in the x-axis and translated 2 unit to the left.

Equation of the transformed graph is: $y = -(x + 2)^2$

(iii) $y = x$ is dilated by a factor of 2 in the y-direction and translated 5 units upwards.

Equation of the transformed graph is: $y = 2x + 5$

(iv) $y = x$ is dilated by a factor of 0.5 in the y-direction and translated 1 unit downwards.

Equation of the transformed graph is: $y = 0.5x - 1$

(v) $y = x$ is reflected in the x-axis and translated 2 unit to the left and 1 unit upwards.

Equation of the transformed graph is: $y = -(x + 2) + 1$

(vi) $y = x$ is translated 5 units upwards and 3 units to the right.

Equation of the transformed graph is: $y = (x - 3) + 5$

(b)(i) $x^2 - 3x + 2 = 0$

Discriminant $= b^2 - 4ac = 9 - 8 = 1$

There are two roots which are both real, rational and different.

(ii) $2x^2 + 3x - 5 = 0$

Discriminant $= b^2 - 4ac = 9 + 40 = 49$

There are two roots which are both real, rational and different.

(iii) $5x^2 - 3x + 2 = 0$

Discriminant $= b^2 - 4ac = 9 - 40 = -31$

There are two roots which are both imaginary (or complex)

> Graphs of equations with imaginary roots won't make x-intercepts

(iv) $3x^2 + 6x - 7 = 0$

Discriminant $= b^2 - 4ac = 36 + 84 = 120$

There are two roots which are both real, irrational and different

(v) $4x^2 - 12x + 9 = 0$

Discriminant $= b^2 - 4ac = 144 - 144 = 0$

There are two roots which are both real, rational and equal.

7. ALGEBRAIC FUNCTIONS

In order to understand algebraic functions, knowledge of the terms "Set" and "Relation" used in mathematics is essential.

SETS, RELATIONS AND FUNCTIONS

In mathematics, a **set** is a collection of well-defined distinct objects. It is just things grouped together with a certain property in common. The different objects that form a set are called the **elements** or members of a set. A set can have **sub sets**.

SETS

Consider the set of first five even numbers: 2, 4, 6, 8, 10

This is written as X = {2, 4, 6, 8, 10}

- The member "4" of this set, for example is written as: $4 \in X$ (i.e. 4 belongs to X).

- The number, say 5 does not belong to this set and is written as: $5 \notin X$
  (That is, 5 does not belong to X)

- The set Y = (2, 4, 6} is a **proper subset** of X.

- The set Y contains some but not all elements of X.

- If Y had elements 2, 4, 6, 8, 10 then Y would be a subset of X

  (but not a proper subset of X)

- The set Z = {2, 5, 8} is not a subset of X, since 5 is not an element of set X.

- The notation $Y \subseteq X$ means Y is a subset of X.

- An empty set is a set with no elements and is written {∅}.

- $\emptyset \subseteq X$ means, a null set is a subset of X.

UNION AND INTERSECTION OF SETS

- The **union** of 2 sets X and Y is denoted by **X∪Y**. This is the set of all distinct elements that are in **X or Y**.
- The **intersection** of 2 sets X and Y is denoted by **X∩Y**. This is the set of all distinct elements that are in both **X and Y**.

If the set of all numbers under consideration are 1, 2, 3 and 4, they are called the **Universal set U.** Out of this, X = {1, 2} and Y = {2, 3}.

Therefore, X∪Y = {1, 2, 3} and X∩Y = {2} and U = {1, 2, 3, 4}

The above information is presented in a **Venn diagram** below:

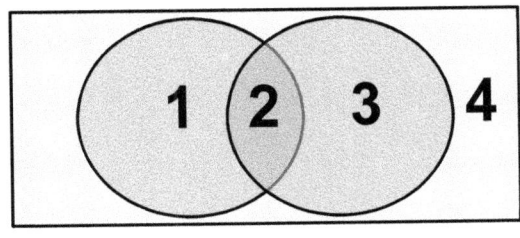

A Venn diagram showing the various intersections involving three sets are shown below:

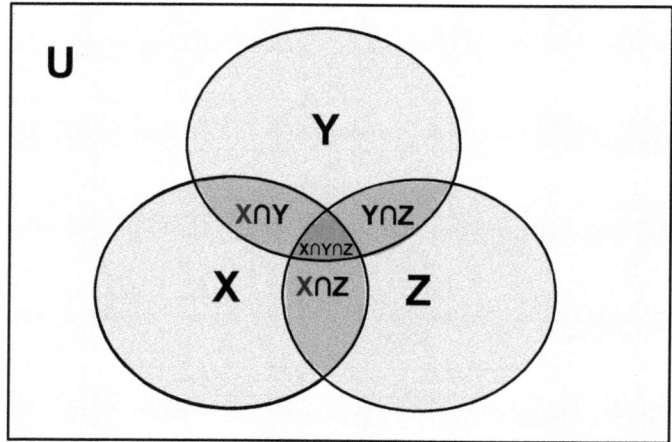

If U is a universal set and A is a subset of U, then the set of all elements in U that are not in A is called the **complement** of A and is denoted by **A^c**.

In the diagrams below, the shaded areas represent different things.

- In Diagram A, the shaded area contains members common to all three sets, **x, y and z**.
- In Diagram B, the shaded area contains members of **x only**
- In Diagram C, the shaded contains members common to **x and z**.

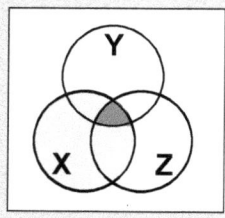
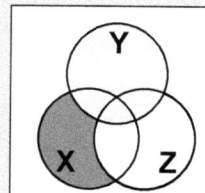
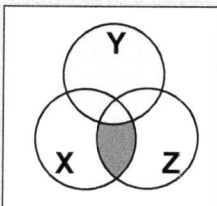

Diagram A   **Diagram B**   **Diagram C**

Example 1:

Let U = {1, 2, 3, 4, 5, 6, 7}, X = {1, 2, 3}, Y = {3, 4, 5, 6}, Z = {2, 3, 4}

Find the following sets:

(i) X^c (ii) $X \cup Y$ (iii) $Y \cap Z$ (iv) $(X \cup Y) \cap Z$ (v) $(X \cap Y) \cup Z$ (vi) $X \cap Y \cap Z$ (vii) $X^c \cap (Y \cup Z)^c$

Solution:

(i) {4, 5, 6, 7} (ii) {1, 2, 3, 4, 5, 6} (iii) {3, 4} (iv) {2, 3, 4} (v) {2, 3, 4} (vi) {3} (vii) {7}

In dealing with sets, a useful formula is:

$$n(A \cup B) = n(A) + n(B) - n(A \cap B)$$

'n' is the number of elements in the set concerned.

Example 2:

In a survey of 100 coffee drinkers it was found that 70 take sugar, 60 take milk, and 50 take both sugar and milk. How many coffee drinkers take sugar or milk with their coffee?

Solution: Let A represent sugar takers and B represent Milk takers.

Therefore n(A) = 70 and n(B) = 60 and n(A∩B) = 50

Now, n(A∪B) = n(A) + n(B) − n(A∩B)

= 70 + 60 − 50

= 80

Therefore, out of 100 coffee drinkers 80 take either sugar or milk.

(A∪B) = A or B
(A∩B) = A and B

Example 3:

A survey of students eating at the college Cafeteria revealed the following:
- 130 ate breakfast, 180 ate lunch and 275 ate dinner
- 68 ate breakfast and lunch
- 112 ate breakfast and dinner
- 94 ate lunch and dinner
- 58 ate all three meals

Determine the following:
(a) Number of students who ate at least one meal
(b) Number who ate exactly one meal
(c) Number who ate dinner only
(d) Number who ate exactly two meals.

n(Breakfast) = 130

n(Lunch) = 180

n(Dinner) = 275

n(Breakfast + Lunch) = 68

n(Breakfast + Dinner) = 112

n(Lunch + Dinner) = 94

n(Breakfast + Lunch + Dinner) = 58

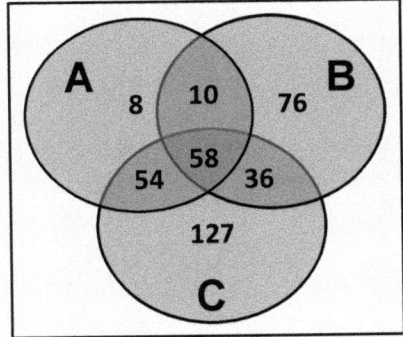

A = Breakfast
B = Lunch
C = Dinner

Solution:

(a) Number of students who ate at least one meal

= n(Breakfast∪Lunch∪Dinner) = 8 + 10 + 76 + 54 + 58 + 36 + 127 = 369

(b) Number who ate exactly one meal = 8 + 76 + 127 = 211

(c) Number who ate dinner only = 127

(d) Number who ate exactly two meals = 54 + 36 + 10 = 100

RELATIONS

A "relation" is just a relationship between **sets** of information. A relation between **two sets** is a collection of ordered pairs containing one object from each set. An **ordered pair** is two numbers written in a certain order usually within parenthesis. For example, the coordinate of a point is written with its distance from the y-axis first and the distance from the x-axis next. The point (5, 3) on a graph means it is 5 units from the y-axis and 3 units from the x-axis.

A relation may be described by a listed set of ordered pairs, a graph or a rule and is generally represented by a mapping diagram and graph. The mapping diagram of a relation is shown below.

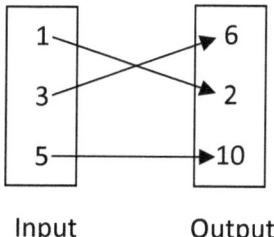

The rule here is: Output = 2 × Input

It can be represented by a graph of y = 2x

Input   Output

There are **four types of relations.** Using x and y coordinates, the different relation can be understood.

- **One-to-one relation** exists when there is only one y value corresponding to one x-value e.g. $y = 2x - 1$.

- **One-to-many relation** exists when there is more than one value of y for a given x value but for any y value there is only one x-value e.g. $y^2 = 4x$.

- **Many-to-one relation** exists when there is more than one x-value for a given y-value but for any x-value there is only one y-value e.g. $y = x^2$.

- **Many-to-many relations** exist when there is more than one y value for any x-value and there is more than one x-value for any y-value e.g. $x^2 + y^2 = 9$.

FUNCTIONS

A function is something that takes in some specific information, works on it and then gives back some other information. In mathematics, the word function means the value of some quantity is determined by the value of some other quantity. **In other words, a function relates an input to an output.** We have already seen examples of functions. The linear and non-linear equations are all examples of functions.

When the variable y depends on the values of the variable x, we say that y is a function of x. The symbol "f(x)" is sometimes used instead of "y". That is, instead of writing say: $y = 3x + 5$, we write $f(x) = 3x + 5$.

Like a "relation", a "function" is also a set of **ordered pairs**, however, every x-value must be associated to **only one** y-value. A function $y = f(x)$ may thus be regarded as a rule that assigns to each value of x, one and only one value of y.

There are two ways to decide whether a relation is a function or not.

1. Examine each element in the domain (independent variable) and ensure that it only appears once.

2. Draw a Vertical Line through the given graph to see if it intersects the graph only once. If it does, then the graph represents a function. Otherwise the graph is not a function.

Example:

Which of the following sets of ordered pairs represents a function?

(A) {2, 4, 4, 8, 8, 16, 16, 32}

(B) {(0, 0), (1, 1), (1, -1), (2, 2), (2, -2)}

(C) {(5, -10), (5, -3), (5, 0), (5, 2), (5, 17)}

(D) {(-2, 2), (-1, 1), (0, 0), (1, 1), (2, 2)}

Solution:

(A) {2, 4, 4, 8, 8, 16, 16, 32}
Not a function. These numbers are not grouped into ordered pairs.

(B) {(0, 0), (1, 1), (1, -1), (2, 2), (2, -2)}
Not a function. Some x-coordinates are repeated and have different y-coordinates.

(C) {(5, -10), (5, -3), (5, 0), (5, 2), (5, 17)}
Not a function since a function requires each input to have only one output.

(D) {(-2, 2), (-1, 1), (0, 0), (1, 1), (2, 2)}
A function. No x-coordinate is repeated and each has exactly one y-coordinate.

POLYNOMIAL FUNCTIONS

A polynomial function is defined by: $y = a_0 + a_1x + a_2x^2 + \ldots + a_nx^n$
where n is a non-negative integer and $a_0, a_1, a_2, \ldots, a_n \in \mathbf{R}$

($\in \mathbf{R}$ stands for elements of the set of all real numbers)

The **highest power** in the expression is **the degree** of the polynomial function. Polynomial functions are further classified based on their highest degrees:

- Constant Function: If the highest degree is zero
- Linear Function: If the highest degree is 1
- Quadratic Function: If the highest degree is 2
- Cubic Function: If the highest degree is 3
- Quartic Function: If the highest degree is 4
- Quintic function: If the highest degree is 5

POWER FUNCTIONS

A function of the form **y = ax^n** is called a **power function.**

Example:

Is $f(x) = 3x^2 \times 2x^3$ a power function?

Solution:

$f(x) = 3x^2 \times 2x^3 = 6x^5$

This is of the form $y = ax^n$ where $a = 6$ and $n = 5$
Therefore $f(x)$ is a power function.

RATIONAL FUNCTIONS

A function is a rational function if it can be represented by a rational fraction say, $\dfrac{f(x)}{g(x)}$ in which the numerator, $f(x)$ and denominator, $g(x)$ are polynomial functions of x, where $g(x)$ cannot be zero. A rational function must have a variable in the denominator. In a rational function, an excluded value is any x-value that makes the function value y undefined.

Example:

$y = \dfrac{x + 4}{2x - 3}$

This is a rational function except when $x = 1.5$, y is undefined as the denominator becomes zero. Thus, $x = 1.5$ is an excluded value.

MODULUS FUNCTIONS (ABSOLUTE VALUE FUNCTIONS)

The **absolute value** of any number, c is represented in the form of **|c|**. A function defined by $f(x) = |x|$ is known as a **modulus function**. It means for each positive value of x, $f(x) = x$ and for each negative value of x, $f(x) = -x$. We can write the same thing as follows:

$$|x| = \begin{cases} x & \text{if } x \geq 0 \\ -x & \text{if } x < 0 \end{cases}$$

Example 1:

If $|x + 3| = 9$, then
(a) $x + 3 = 9$ i.e. $x = 6$ or   (b) $x + 3 = -9$ i.e. $x = -12$

Example 2:

If $\left|\dfrac{x}{3} + 5\right| = 8$, then

(a) $\dfrac{x}{3} + 5 = 8$ or   (b) $\dfrac{x}{3} + 5 = -8$

$x + 15 = 24$ $x + 15 = -24$

$x = 9$ $x = -39$

158

Example 3:

　　　Graph y = |x + 1|

Solution: The basic parent function y = |x| is moved 1 unit to the left.

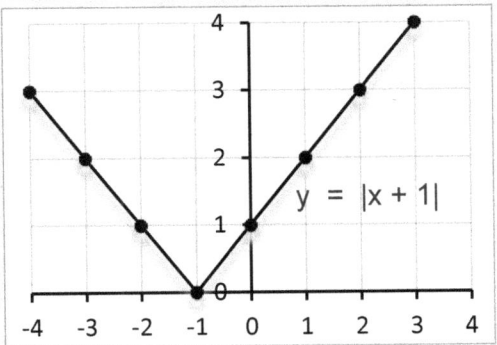

A general equation for the absolute value function is: $f(x) = a|x - h| + k$ where "a", "h" and "k" have the usual meaning i.e. "a" means degree of dilation or inversion, "h" the left or right shift and "k" the vertical shift.

Example 4:

　　　Graph the function $f(x) = |x - 1| + 5$

Solution: The basic parent function is moved 1 unit to the right and 5 units upwards.

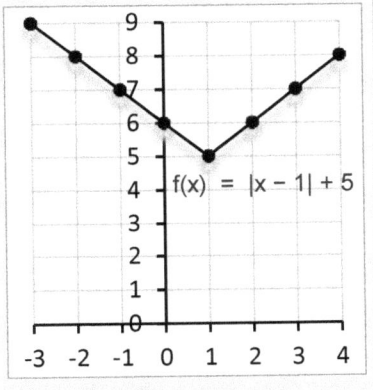

COMPOSITE FUNCTION (FUNCTION OF A FUNCTION)

The output of a function "f" can be the input for a function "g" and vice versa. They then become composite functions. A composite function of f(x) and g(x) is written as:

$$(f \circ g)(x) \quad \text{and} \quad (g \circ f)(x)$$

The above is interpreted as follows:

$$(f \circ g)(x) = f(g(x))$$
$$(g \circ f)(x) = g(f(x))$$

Example 1:

　　　If $f(x) = 3x + 1$ and $g(x) = x^2 + 4$
　　　Find the value of: (a) $(f \circ g)(x)$　　　(b) $(g \circ f)(x)$

Solution:

(a) $(f \circ g)(x) = f(g(x)) = 3(x^2 + 4) + 1$ 　 $\boxed{\text{Replace x in f(x) with } (x^2 + 4)}$

$= 3x^2 + 13$

(b) $(g \circ f)(x) = g(f(x)) = (3x + 1)^2 + 4$ 　 $\boxed{\text{Replace x in g(x) with } 3x + 1}$

$= 9x^2 + 6x + 5$

Example 2:

If $f(x) = 2x - 1$ and $g(x) = x^3$, find the value of: (a) $(g \circ f)(3)$ (b) $(f \circ g)(2)$

Solution:

(a) $(g \circ f)(x) = g(f(x)) = (2x - 1)^3$

$(g \circ f)(3) = (6 - 1)^3 = 5^3 = 125$

(b) $(f \circ g)(x) = f(g(x)) = 2x^3 - 1$

$(f \circ g)(2) = 2 \times 8 - 1 = 15$

INVERSE FUNCTIONS

If a function f takes x to y, so that $f(x) = y$, an **inverse function**, which we call f^{-1}, is another function that takes y back to x. So $\mathbf{f^{-1}(y) = x}$.

Example 1:

Find the inverse $f^{-1}(x)$ of the function $f(x) = 2x - 1$

Write, $y = 2x - 1$

Swap x and y to get $x = 2y - 1$

That is, $2y = x + 1$

$y = \dfrac{x + 1}{2}$ or $f^{-1}(x) = \dfrac{x + 1}{2}$

If we take say, a point (2, 3) on $f(x) = 2x - 1$, then the point (3, 2) will be a point on $f^{-1}(x) = \dfrac{x + 1}{2}$

The graphs of $f(x)$ and $f^{-1}(x)$ are mirror images of each other with respect to the line $y = x$. The graph below helps understand the above explanation.

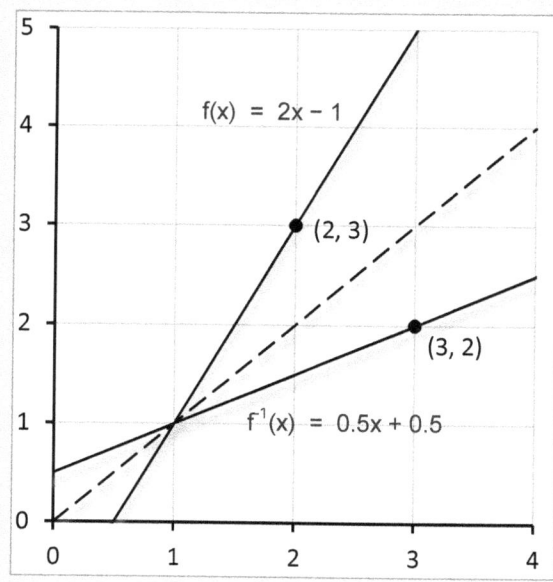

The functions $f(x)$ and $g(x)$ are inverse functions if, $f(g(x)) = x$ and $g(f(x)) = x$, for all x in the domains of g and f respectively.

Example 2:

If $f(x) = 2x - 1$ and $g(x) = \dfrac{x + 1}{2}$ Show that, $f(x)$ and $g(x)$ are inverse functions.

$f(g(x)) = 2(\dfrac{x + 1}{2}) - 1 = x + 1 - 1 = x$

$g(f(x)) = (\dfrac{2x - 1 + 1}{2}) = \dfrac{2x}{2} = x$

Therefore, $f(x)$ and $g(x)$ are inverse functions.

Example 3:

Find the inverse of $f(x) = \dfrac{1}{x}$ for $x > 0$ and sketch its curve

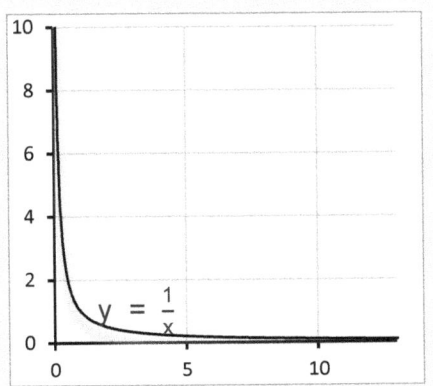

Let $y = \dfrac{1}{x}$

Swap x and y to get: $x = \dfrac{1}{y}$

That is, $y = \dfrac{1}{x}$

Therefore, the required inverse is the same as the original function.

HYBRID FUNCTIONS (PIECEWISE FUNCTIONS)

Functions can be created to behave differently depending on the input value.

Example 1:

A function with two pieces: When x is less than 0, the y-value is 5
When x is 0 or more, the y-value is x^2

x	-2	-1	0	1	2	3	4
y	5	5	0	1	4	9	16

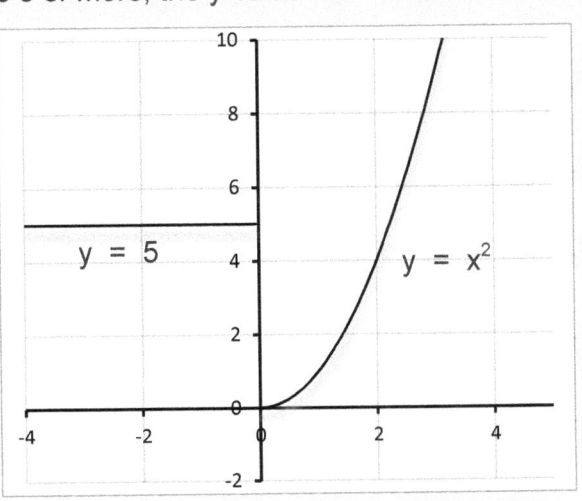

The above information is written as: $f(x) =$

$\begin{cases} 5 & \text{if } x < 0 \quad \text{(i.e. } x \text{ is less than 0)} \\ x^2 & \text{if } x \geq 0 \quad \text{(i.e. } x \text{ is greater than or equal to 0)} \end{cases}$

Example 2:

A function with three pieces: When x ≤ -1, the y-value is x + 3

When -1 > x < 2, the y-value is 2

When x ≥ 2, the y-value is $0.5x^2$

$$f(x) = \begin{cases} x + 3: & x \le -1 \\ 2: & -1 < x < 2 \\ 0.5x^2: & x \ge 2 \end{cases}$$

This is illustrated in the graph:

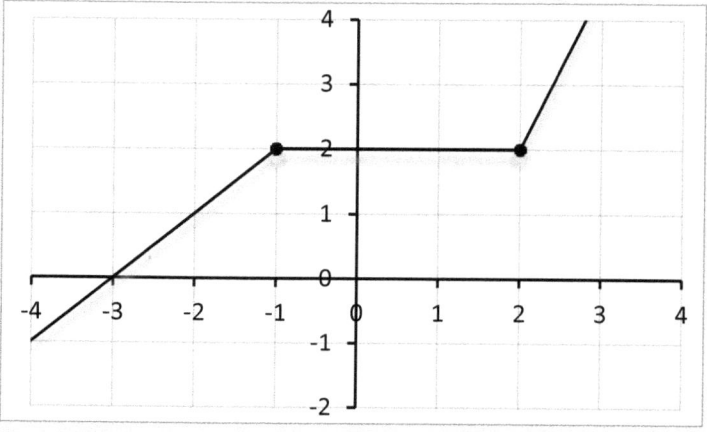

EXPONENTIAL FUNCTIONS

A function of the form $y = a^x$ is called an **exponential function**. The graph of these functions will make a y-intercept of 1. The graph will touch the x-axis at infinity (i.e. x-axis is an asymptote.)

Example:

Graph the exponential function $y = 2^x$

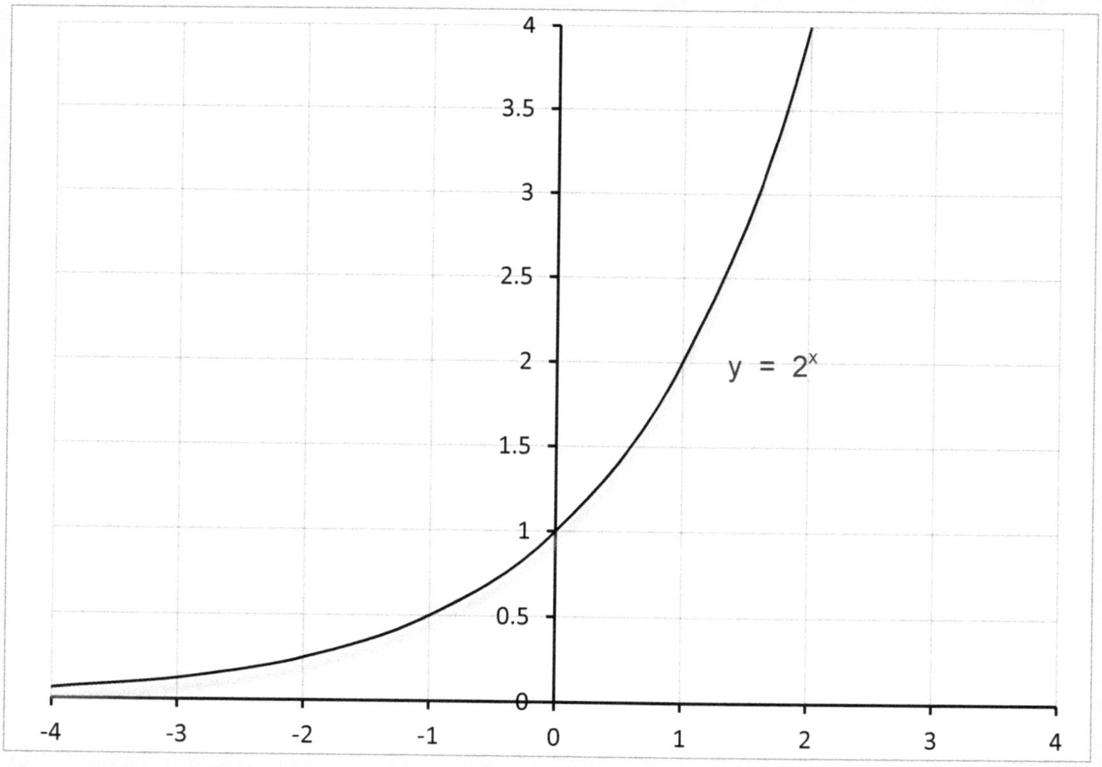

$y = 2^x$

EVEN FUNCTIONS

If $f(x) = f(-x)$, then the function is an even function. The graph of an even function that is reflected in the y-axis results in the same graph. The following are even functions:

- $y = x^2$
- $y = |x|$
- $y = x^4$

Example:

Show that $5x^2 - 2x^4$ is an even function

Solution:

$f(x) = 5x^2 - 2x^4$

$f(-x) = 5(-x)^2 - 2(-x)^4 = 5x^2 - 2x^4$

Since $f(x) = f(-x)$, the function is even.

ODD FUNCTIONS

If $f(-x) = -f(x)$, then the function is an odd function. The graph of an odd function that is reflected in the y-axis results in an upside-down version of the same graph. The following are odd functions:

- $y = x$
- $y = x^3$
- $y = \dfrac{1}{x}$

Example:

Show that $3x - 4x^3$ is an odd function.

Solution:

$f(x) = 3x - 4x^3$

$f(-x) = 3(-x) - 4(-x)^3 = -3x + 4x^3$

$-f(x) = -(3x - 4x^3) = -3x + 4x^3$

Since $f(-x) = -f(x)$, the function is odd.

1.(i) Set A = {1, 2, 3, 4, 5}, Set B = {1, 2, 7} and Set U = {1, 2, 3, 4, 5, 6 ,7}

(a) List Set A∪B and Set A∩B

(b) Find n(A), n(B) and n(A∪B)

(ii) The Venn diagram shows the number of people playing Tennis (T) and Hockey (H).

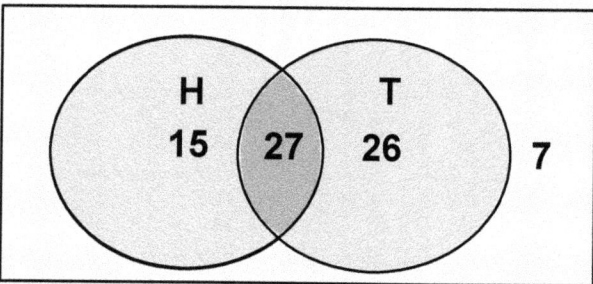

Determine the number of people:

(a) in the club

(b) who play hockey

(c) who play both sports

(d) who play at least one sport

(e) who play neither sport

---

2. In a survey of 120 customers conducted in a shopping mall, 80 customers indicated that they buy brand A of a certain product, 68 buy brand B and 42 buy both brands.

Determine the number of consumers participating in the survey who buy:

(a) at least one of these brands

(b) exactly one of these brands

(c) only brand A

(d) none of these brands

Show the results clearly in a Venn diagram.

---

3. By calculating (f ° g)(x) and (g ° f)(x):

• Prove that $f(x) = x^{0.5}$ is the inverse of $g(x) = x^2$

• Sketch the graphs of the two functions

• Draw the line $y = x$ and mark any two points on one curve and the corresponding reflections of these in the line lying on the other curve.

4.(a) Which of the following is not a relation?

$$y = x^2, \qquad \{1, 2, 4, 6, 8\}, \qquad \{(1, 1), (2, 1), (3, 2), (4, 3)\}$$

(b) Which of the following is not a function?

$$y = \frac{x}{2}, \qquad y = 3x^2 - 5, \qquad x = 9$$

(c) Which of the following is not a one to one relation?

$$f(x) = 3 - x^2, \qquad \{(4, 4), (5, 6), (6, 7)\}, \qquad \{(6, 8), (7, 9), (8, 8), (9, 10)\}$$

(d) What is the range of the function $y = 2(x - 6)^{0.5}$

(e) State the domain and range of each of the following:

   (i) $\{(2, 7), (3, 9), (4, 11), (5, 13), (6, 15)\}$

   (ii) $\{(1.1, 2), (1.3, 1.8), (1.5, 1.6), (1.7, 1.4)\}$

---

5. (i) Sketch the graph of $f(x) = (x - 4)^2 + 1$ for all real x greater than 4.

(ii) Find $f^{-1}(x)$

(iii) On the same diagram sketch the graph of $y = f^{-1}(x)$

(iv) Write down the equation of the line in which the graph of $y = f(x)$ must be reflected in order to obtain the graph of $y = f^{-1}(x)$

(v) Find the exact solution of the equation $f(x) = f^{-1}(x)$

---

6. Graph the piecewise functions showing clearly the "boundary lines" and the open and closed endpoints:

(a) $f(x) = \begin{cases} 1.2x - 2 & \text{if } x < 5 \\ 0.4x + 2 & \text{if } x \geq 5 \end{cases}$

(b) $f(x) = \begin{cases} -2x - 4 & \text{if } x < -2 \\ x^2 - 2 & \text{if } -2 \leq x < 1 \\ 2 & \text{if } x \geq 1 \end{cases}$

---

7. Show that the equation $y = \dfrac{2x + 7}{x + 2}$ can be written as $y = A + \dfrac{B}{x + 2}$ where A and B are constants. Hence state the sequence of transformations which transform the graph of $y = \dfrac{1}{x}$ to the graph of $y = \dfrac{2x + 7}{x + 2}$.

Sketch the graph of $y = \dfrac{2x + 7}{x + 2}$, giving the equations of any asymptotes and the coordinates of any points of intersection with the x and y-axes.

---

8. (i) Sketch the graph of $f(x) = x^3 + x^2 - 2x - 4$

(ii) Find the integer solution of $f(x) = 4$ and prove that there are no other real solutions.

(iii) State the integer solution of the equation: $(x + 3)^3 + (x + 3)^2 - 2(x + 3) - 4 = 4$

(iv) Write down two different cubic equations which between them give the roots of the equation $|f(x)| = 4$. Hence find all the roots of this equation.

1.(i) A∪B = {1, 2, 3, 4, 5, 7}

A∩B = {1, 2}

n(A) = 5

n(B) = 3

n(A∪B) = 6

(ii)(a) The number of people in the club = 15 + 27 + 26 + 7 = 75
(b) The number of people who play hockey = 15 + 27 = 42
(c) The number of people who play both sports = 27
(d) The number of people who play at least one sport = 15 + 27 + 26 = 68
(e) The number of people who play neither sport = 7

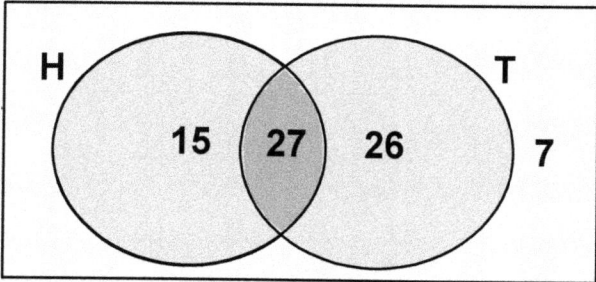

2. (a) Number of customers that buy at least one brand = 38 + 26 + 42 = 106
   (b) Number that buy exactly one brand = 38 + 26 = 64
   (c) Number that buy only brand A = 38
   (d) Number that buy none of the brands = 120 − 106 = 14

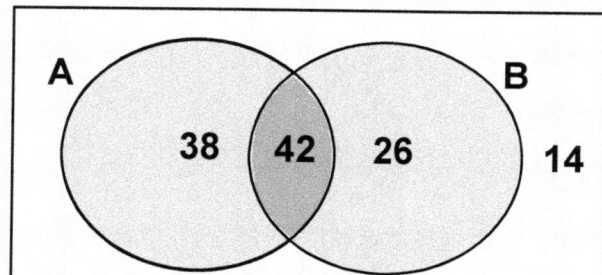

3. $f(x) = x^{0.5}$ and $g(x) = x^2$

$(f \circ g)(x) = (x^2)^{0.5} = x$

$(g \circ f)(x) = (x^{0.5})^2 = x$

Therefore, $f(x)$ is the inverse of $g(x)$.

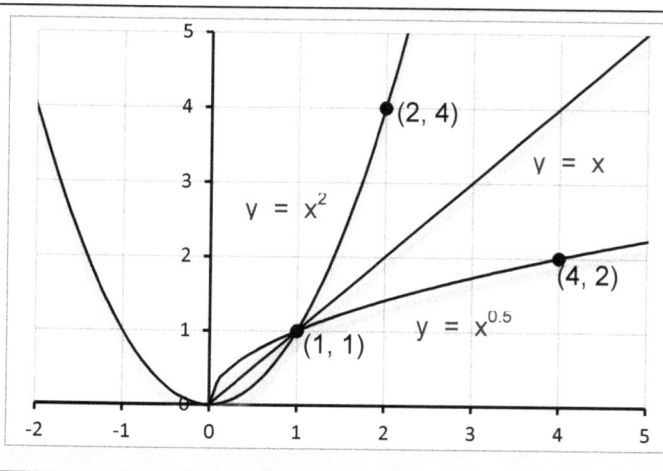

4.(a) {1, 2, 4, 6, 8} is not a relation because the numbers are not ordered pairs.

(b) $x = 9$ is not a function because there is no input output relationship.

(c) {(6, 8), (7, 9), (8, 8), (9, 10)} has the many-to-one relationship,
    i.e. (6, 8) and (8, 8) violate the one-to-one rule.

(d) The range of the function $y = 2(x - 6)^{0.5}$ is {0, ∞}.

(e) The domain and range of:

(i) {(2, 7), (3, 9), (4, 11), (5, 13), (6, 15)}

Domain = {2, 3, 4, 5, 6}

Range = {7, 9, 11, 13, 15}

(ii) {(1.1, 2), (1.3, 1.8), (1.5, 1.6), (1.7, 1.4)}

Domain = {1.1, 1.3, 1.5, 1.7}

Range = {1.4, 1.6, 1.8, 2}

5.(i) The graph of $f(x) = (x - 4)^2 + 1$ for all real x greater than 4 is the basic graph of
    $f(x) = x^2$ translated to the right by 4 units and upwards by 1 unit.

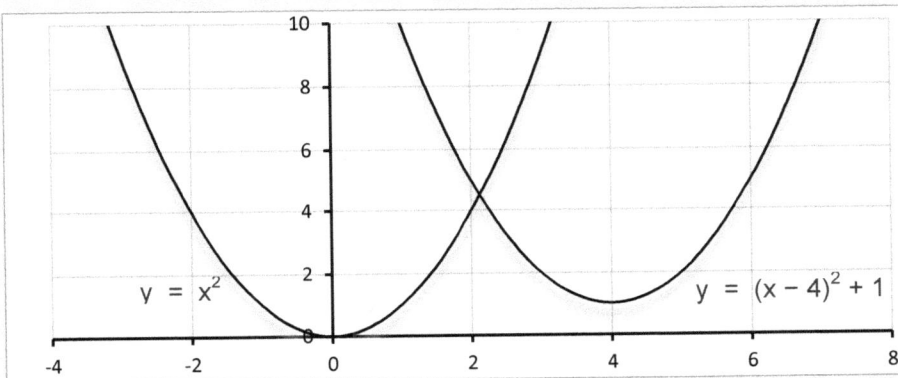

(ii) Find $f^{-1}(x)$

$y = (x - 4)^2 + 1$

Swap x and y

Therefore: $x = (y - 4)^2 + 1$

$(y - 4)^2 = x - 1$

$y - 4 = (x - 1)^{0.5}$

$y = (x - 1)^{0.5} + 4$

Therefore, $f^{-1}(x) = (x - 1)^{0.5} + 4$

(iii) Sketch of the graph of $y = f^{-1}(x)$

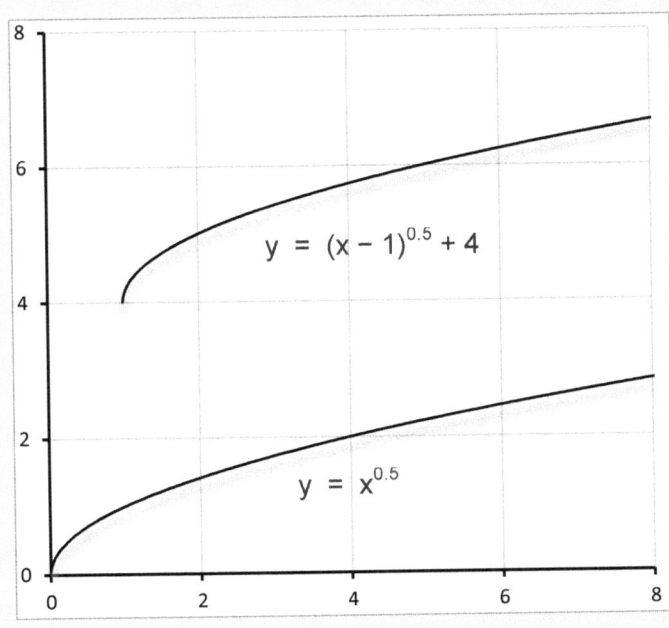

5. (iv) The equation of the line in which the graph of $y = f(x)$ must be reflected in order to obtain the graph of $y = f^{-1}(x)$ is $y = x$.

(v) Find the exact solution of the equation $f(x) = f^{-1}(x)$

$(x - 4)^2 + 1 = (x - 1)^{0.5} + 4$

$(x - 1)^{0.5} = (x - 4)^2 - 3$

By inspection: $x = 5$ is a solution to this equation.

Substituting 5 for x in: $y = (x - 4)^2 + 1$

$y = 2$

Therefore, the exact solution is: $x = 5$, $y = 2$

6.

(a)

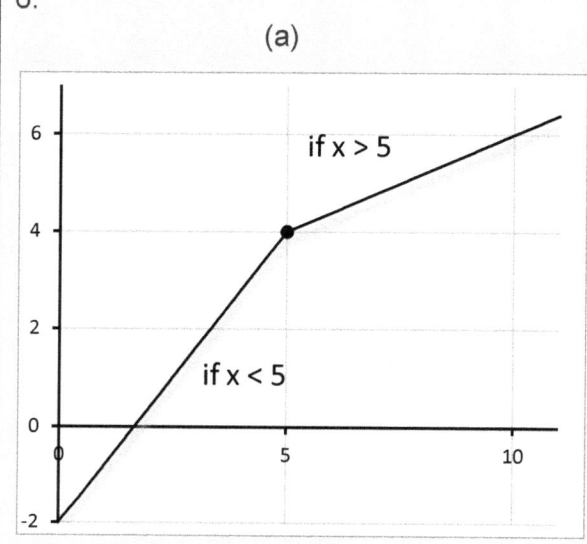

if x > 5

if x < 5

(b)

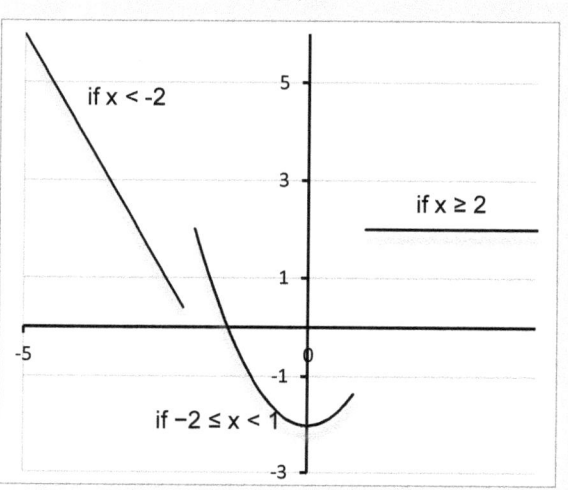

if x < -2

if x ≥ 2

if −2 ≤ x < 1

---

7. $y = \dfrac{2x + 7}{x + 2}$

That is, $y = 2 + \dfrac{3}{x + 2}$

The sequence of transformations which transform the graph of $y = \dfrac{1}{x}$ to the graph of

$y = \dfrac{2x + 7}{x + 2}$ are:

(i) dilated by a factor of 3

(ii) moved to the left by 2 units

(iii) moved upwards 2 units

x-intercept = -3.5

y–intercept = 3.5

Asymptotes:

when x tends to infinity, y tends to 2 i.e. $y = 2$

y tends to infinity, when x tends to -2 i.e. $x = -2$

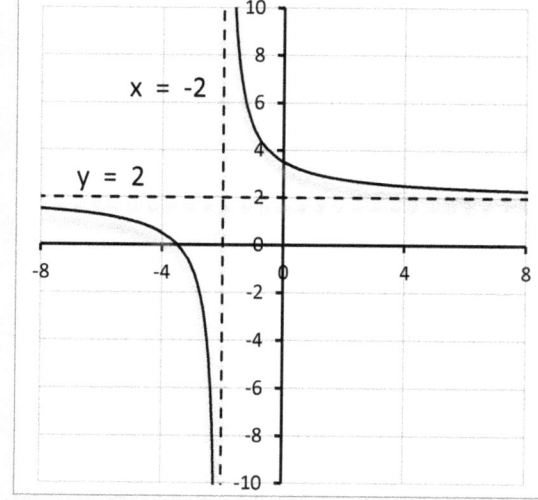

x = -2

y = 2

8.(i) The graph of $f(x) = x^3 + x^2 - 2x - 4$

When $x = 0$, $y = -4$ | y-intercept = -4 |

When $y = 0$, $x^3 + x^2 - 2x - 4 = 0$

x	-4	-3	-2	-1	0	1	2	3	4
y	-44	-16	-4	-2	-4	-4	4	26	68

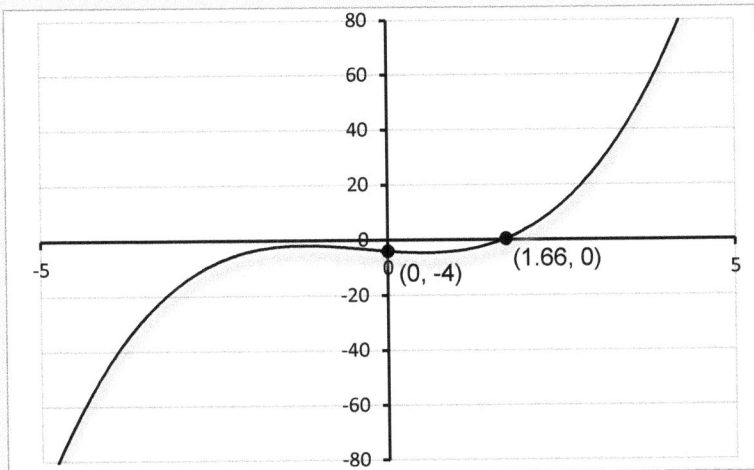

(ii) Finding the integer solution of $f(x) = 4$ and proving that there are no other real solutions.

$x^3 + x^2 - 2x - 4 = 4$

$x^3 + x^2 - 2x - 8 = 0$

By inspection, $x = 2$ is a root (i.e. an integer solution)

Therefore: $x - 2$ is a factor of $x^3 + x^2 - 2x - 8$

The other (quadratic) factor is obtained by long division as follows:

$$
\begin{array}{r}
x^2 + 3x + 4 \\
x - 2 \overline{)x^3 + x^2 - 2x - 8} \\
\underline{x^3 - 2x^2} \quad\quad\quad\quad\quad \\
3x^2 - 2x \quad\quad \\
\underline{3x^2 - 6x} \quad\quad \\
4x - 8 \\
\underline{4x - 8} \\
0
\end{array}
$$

The other quadratic factor is: $x^2 + 3x + 4$

The discriminant of this is: $9 - 16 = $ negative

Therefore, there are no other real solutions.

8.(iii) The integer solution of the equation:

$(x + 3)^3 + (x + 3)^2 - 2(x + 3) - 4 = 4$ is obtained as follows:

Let $X = x + 3$

Therefore, $X^3 + X^2 - 2X - 8 = 0$

An integer solution is $X = 2$

i.e. $x + 3 = 2$

$x = 1$

The required integer solution is $x = 1$

(iv) Write down two different cubic equations which between them give the roots of the equation $|f(x)| = 4$. Hence find all the roots of this equation.

$x^3 + x^2 - 2x - 4 = 4$ .... (1)

$x^3 + x^2 - 2x - 4 = -4$ .... (2)

Solution to (1) is: $x = 2$

$x^3 + x^2 - 2x = 0$ $\boxed{\text{From (2)}}$

That is: $x(x^2 + x - 2) = 0$

$x(x + 2)(x - 1) = 0$

Solutions to (2) are: $x = 0, -2,$ or 1

Therefore, all the roots of $|f(x)| = 4$ are: $0, -2, -1,$ and 2

8. PERMUTATION, COMBINATION AND PROBABILITY

In this chapter we look at the three topics:

- **Permutation** deals with the <u>arrangement</u> of a set of items or people in a specified way
- **Combination** deals with the <u>selection</u> of items or people in a desired manner from a group of these
- **Probability** tells us the <u>likelihood</u> of some event happening. In order to ascertain this sometimes we need to know the possible number of arrangements or selection

FACTORIAL

The factorial of a **positive integer 'n'**, denoted by **n!**, is the product of all positive integers less than or equal to 'n'. That is: **n!** = n × (n − 1) × (n − 2) × (n − 3) ....3 × 2 × 1

Example:

6! = 6 × 5 × 4 × 3 × 2 × 1

12! = 12 × 11 × 10 × 9 ×.........1

1! = 1

0! = 1 | This generally accepted value is proved when we learn about combinations

n! can be written as n × (n − 1)! or n × (n − 1) × (n − 2)! and so on.

For example, 5! = 5 × 4! or 5 × 4 × 3! and so on.

PERMUTATION

Permutation is the number of ways of arranging the desired number of members from a given set (where each member is unique). Putting this another way, permutation is the number of arrangements of a set of 'n' dis-similar, non-repeated items taken 'r' at a time.
It is written as ^nP_r.

$$^nP_r \text{ is evaluated as } \frac{n!}{(n-r)!}$$

Example 1:

Evaluate $^7P_3$

$$^7P_3 = \frac{7!}{(7-3)!} = \frac{7!}{4!}$$

$$= \frac{7 \times 6 \times 5 \times 4 \times 3 \times 2 \times 1}{4 \times 3 \times 2 \times 1} = 7 \times 6 \times 5 = 210$$

Example 2:

If A = {a, b, c,} calculate the number of permutations of A. List them.

Number of permutations = $^3P_3 = \frac{3!}{(3-3)!} = \frac{3!}{0!} = 3 \times 2 \times 1 = 6$

The 6 possible permutations are: <u>a, b, c</u>, <u>a, c, b</u>, <u>b, a, c</u>, <u>b, c, a</u>, <u>c, a, b</u>, <u>c, b, a</u>

Example 3:

If A = {a, b, c, d}, calculate the number of permutations of A.

Number of permutations $= {}^4P_4 = \dfrac{4!}{(4-4)!} = \dfrac{4!}{0!} = \dfrac{4 \times 3 \times 2 \times 1}{1} = 24$

(i.e. the number of permutations of n items taken all at a time = n!)

Example 4:

If A = {a, b, c, d, e}, calculate the number of permutations of A taken 3 at a time.

Number of permutations $= {}^5P_3 = \dfrac{5!}{(5-3)!} = \dfrac{5!}{2!} = 5 \times 4 \times 3 = 60$

PERMUTATIONS WITH REPETITIONS

Take for example the word **DAD**. In how many ways can we arrange the three letters? If we said that the answer is 3! or six ways it would be wrong. This is because there are two D's; D is repeated. The only acceptable arrangements are: **DAD, ADD** and **DDA**. That is, the number of permutations is 3. This answer could be obtained by dividing 3! by 2! (where 3 is the total number of letters in DAD and 2, the number of repeated letter D).

Take another word, **ACCURACY**. Here, **A** occurs twice and **C** occurs thrice.

The number of permutations in this case is $\dfrac{8!}{2! \times 3!} = 3{,}360$ (A and C are repeated)

The number of permutations of n objects with n_1 identical objects of type 1, n_2 identical objects of type 2....... and n_k identical objects of type k is:

$$\dfrac{n!}{n_1! \times n_2! \times n_3! \times \ldots\ldots n_k!}$$

PERMUTATIONS WHEN ARRANGEMENT IS IN A CIRCLE

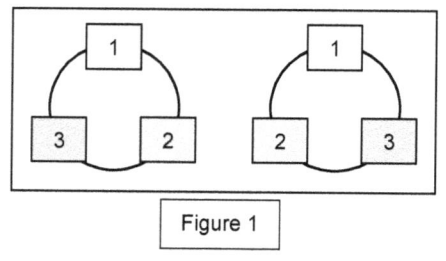

Figure 1

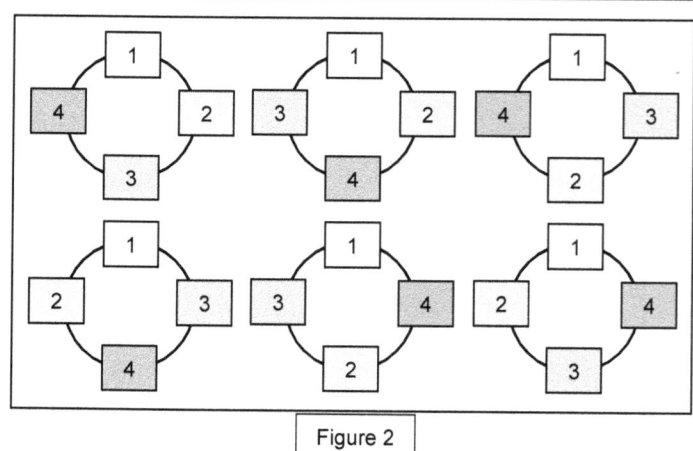

Figure 2

In Figure 1, three people are seated in a circle in **2 ways only** (not 6 as in a straight-line seating arrangement). The formula is: Number of circular permutations = **(n − 1)!**
Figure 2, shows the number of ways 4 people are seated in a circle.
The number of ways = **(4 − 1)! = 3! = 3 × 2 × 1 = 6**

To find the number of ways in which n objects can be arranged in a circle, we need to fix the position of one of the objects and then calculate the number of ways in which the remaining positions may be filled.

COMBINATION

Combination refers to the selection of a desired number of items or people from a given set. Common examples:

- Selection of 11 cricketers for the national team from 20 qualified players
- Selection of 5 people to be in an executive committee from 12 eligible men and women

Combination is number of ways of selecting the desired number of members from a given set. Putting this another way, combination is the number of ways of selecting r items from a set of n items. It is written as ^nC_r.

^nC_r is evaluated as $\dfrac{n!}{r! \times (n-r)!}$

Evaluating ^nC_r gives the same result as evaluating $^nC_{n-r}$ (e.g. $^6C_4 = {}^6C_2$)

Example 1:

Evaluate $^7C_3$

$$^7C_3 = \frac{7!}{(3!) \times (7-3)!} = \frac{7!}{3! \times 4!} = \frac{7 \times 6 \times 5 \times 4 \times 3 \times 2 \times 1}{(3 \times 2 \times 1) \times (4 \times 3 \times 2 \times 1)} = 7 \times 5 = 35$$

Example 2:

If A = {a, b, c,}, calculate the number of combinations of A. List them.

$$\text{Number of combinations} = {}^3C_3 = \frac{3!}{3! \times (3-3)!} = \frac{3!}{3! \times 0!} = 1$$

There is only one possible combination **a, b, c**. That is, there is only **one selection** containing the three members from the given set of 3 (taken all three at a time).

In general: $^nC_n = 1$ (i.e. selecting n people at a time from n people)

i.e. $\dfrac{n!}{n! \times 0!} = 1$. It follows $\dfrac{1}{0!} = 1$. That is, **0! = 1.**

Example 3:

If A = {a, b, c, d}, calculate the number of combinations of A taken 3 at a time. List them.

$$\text{Number of combinations} = {}^4C_3 = \frac{4!}{3! \times 1!} = 4$$

The four combinations are: <u>a, b, c</u>,   <u>a, b, d</u>,   <u>a, c, d</u>,   <u>b, c, d</u>

Example 4:

If A = {a, b, c, d, e}, calculate the number of combinations of A taken 3 at a time.

Number of combinations = $^5C_3$ = $^5C_2$

= $\dfrac{5 \times 4}{2 \times 1}$ = 10 | Note the short cut |

When confused as to whether a problem involves permutation or combination, use the following as a guide:

- When the **order doesn't matter**, it is a **Combination** problem.
- When the **order does matter** it is a **Permutation** problem.

SITUATIONS WHERE THERE ARE NO RESTRICTIONS

r letters when chosen from **n** letters to form a code with repetitions allowed, would result in n^r codes.

Example:

A vehicle license plate is to consist of three digits followed by three English alphabets. How many license plates are possible if there are no restrictions?

The first digit can be any of the 10 and so can the second and third one.

Number of combinations of digits is therefore 10 × 10 × 10 = 10^3

Now, for each of these combinations, the number of combination of three letters to be used can be similarly calculated as 26^3.

Therefore, the total number of license plates = $10^3 \times 26^3$ = 17,576,000

SITUATIONS WHERE THERE ARE RESTRICTIONS

Example:

A vehicle license plate is to consist of three digits followed by three English alphabets. ow many license plates are possible?

(i) If there was a restriction that no letter or digit is to appear more than once.

(ii) If there was a restriction that no letter is to appear more than once but no such restriction for the digits.

(iii) If there was no restriction for the letters but no digit is to appear more than once.

Solution:

(i) Total number of license plates = (10 × 9 × 8) × (26 × 25 × 24) = 11,232,000

(ii) Total number of license plates = (10^3) × 26 × 25 × 24 = 15,600,000

(iii) Total number of license plates = (10 × 9 × 8) × 26^3 = 12,654,720

Multiplication Rule: If there are **m** ways to do A and **n** ways to do B, then there are (**m × n**) ways to do A and B.

MISCELLANEOUS PROBLEMS

1. In how many ways can the first and second places be filled by 8 competitors?

The first place can be filled in 8 ways. Corresponding to each way the first place gets filled, the second place can be filled in 7 ways. Therefore, both first and second places can be filled in 8 × 7 = 56 ways. The same result can be obtained by using the formula:

$$^nP_r = \frac{n!}{(n-r)!}$$

Number of ways = $^8P_2 = \frac{8!}{(8-2)!} = \frac{8!}{6!} = 8 \times 7 = 56$

2. The 10 nominees for the Board of Directors of an organisation include 6 men and 4 women. In how many ways can:

(i) any two nominees be elected
(ii) two males be elected
(iii) one male and one female be elected

Solution:

(i) Number of ways possible for any two nominees = $^{10}C_2 = \frac{10 \times 9}{2 \times 1} = 45$

(ii) Number of ways possible for any two male nominees = $^6C_2 = \frac{6 \times 5}{2 \times 1} = 15$

(iii) Number of ways possible for one male and one female = $^6C_1 \times {}^4C_1 = 6 \times 4 = 24$

3. A shipment of 12 items of a product contains one that is defective. In how many ways can an inspector choose three of the items for inspection so that:

(i) the defective item is not included
(ii) the defective item is included

Solution:

(i) The number of ways of choosing if defective is not included = $^{11}C_3$

$= \frac{11 \times 10 \times 9}{3 \times 2 \times 1} = 165$ (i.e. leave out the defective and select **three** from the rest)

(ii) The number of ways of choosing if defective is included = $^{11}C_2 = \frac{11 \times 10}{2 \times 1} = 55$

   (i.e. count in the defective and select **two** from the rest)

4. A vehicle license plate is to consist of three digits, the first of which cannot be 0, followed by two letters of the English alphabet, the only restriction is that the first letter cannot be I, O or Q. How many license plates are possible?

Solution:
As to the digits, the first one can be chosen in 9 ways (i.e. leave zero out), the second and third one can be chosen in 10 ways each.

Total number of ways for digits = 9 × 10 × 10 = 900

4.(Continued)

As to the letters, the first letter can be chosen in 23 ways and corresponding to each of these ways, the second letter can be chosen in 26 ways.

Total number of ways for letters = 23 × 26 = 598

Therefore, the possible number of license plates = 900 × 598 = 538,200

---

5. It is required to seat 5 men and 4 women in a row so that the women occupy the even places. How many arrangements are possible?

Solution:

The men can be seated in the odd places in $^5P_5$ ways. The women can be seated in the even places in $^4P_4$ ways. Therefore, the possible number of arrangements:

$$= {}^5P_5 \times {}^4P_4 = \frac{5!}{(5-5)!} \times \frac{4!}{(4-4)!} = 120 \times 24 = 2,880.$$

---

6. (a) In how many ways can the letters of the word **MATHEMATICS** be arranged?
   (b) In how many ways can they be arranged if the first letter is H, the last letter is S and letters E, C and I are together?

Solution:
(a) There are altogether 11 letters, two A's, two M's and two T's.

Number of ways of arranging the 11 letters $= \dfrac{11!}{2! \times 2! \times 2!} = 4,989,600$

(b) H M̲ M̲ A̲ A̲ T̲ T̲ E̲ C̲ I̲ S

Number of ways $= \dfrac{7!}{2! \times 2! \times 2!} \times 3! = 3,780$

---

7. 6 men and 6 women are to be seated at a round table. There are 3 married couples among these and they all must sit together. Find the number of ways of seating the 12 if:

(a) the seats are not numbered
(b) the seats are numbered.

Solution:
$$X\,X\,X \quad **\ **\ ** \quad X\,X\,X$$
(a) Number of ways of seating $= (9-1)! \times (2!)\,(2!)\,(2!) = 322,560$

(b) Number of ways of seating $= (9-1)! \times (2!)\,(2!)\,(2!) \times 12 = 3,870,720$
   (If the seats are numbered, the actual seating position matters)

---

8. Find the number of ways in which the letters of the word **MATHEMATICS** be arranged if the vowels are separated.

Solution:
$* M * T * H * M * T * C * S *$ (* represents a vowel's place)

Number of ways $= \dfrac{7!}{2! \times 2!} \times {}^8C_4 \times \dfrac{4!}{2!} = 1,058,400.$

PROBABILITY

Probability in mathematics is the study of the chance or likelihood of an event happening. It is expressed as a number between 0 and 1, a number closer to 0 (zero) means that the event is less likely to happen and a number closer to 1 (one) means that there is a greater certainty of the event happening.

A number of techniques are available for computing the probability of a certain event happening. Before looking at these techniques it is important to get an understanding of the terms used in connection with the study of probability. Two words commonly used are **Experiment** and **Outcome**.

An experiment is an observable activity such as tossing a coin, casting a die (or dice) and drawing a card from a pack of playing cards. When tossing a coin, we can get either a "Head" or a "Tail", when casting a die we can get any one of the numbers 1, 2, 3, 4, 5, and 6 uppermost etc. These results from the experiment performed are called **"Outcomes"**.

An outcome of an experiment is called the **sample point**, and all possible outcomes of that experiment (set of all possible sample points), **the sample space**. For example, in the experiment of tossing a coin, the sample point is either **head** or **tail and** sample space is **Head and Tail** (two sample points). In the casting of a die, the sample point is any one of the numbers 1, 2, 3, 4, 5, 6 and the sample space is all of these numbers (six sample spaces).

The probability of an event happening is calculated as: **sample point divided by the sample space.** Thus, the probability of obtaining a head when tossing a coin is $\frac{1}{2}$ and the probability of say '4' turning uppermost when casting a die is $\frac{1}{6}$.

If we conduct an experiment n times (called trials) and an event **E** occurs with a frequency **F(E)**, then the approximate probability of occurrence of that event **P(E)** is written as:

$$P(E) = \frac{\text{Frequency of occurence of E}}{\text{Total number of trials}}$$

Example:

Two coins are tossed 50 times with the following frequencies of outcomes:

Outcome	2 heads	1 head	0 heads
Frequency	10	28	12

Calculate the probability for each outcome.

Solution:

P (2 heads) $= \frac{10}{50} = 0.2$

P (1 head) $= \frac{28}{50} = 0.56$

P (0 heads) $= \frac{12}{50} = 0.24$

If the probability of an event **E** happening (success) is denoted by P(E) and the probability of that event not happening (failure) is denoted by Q(E), then Q(E) = 1 − P(E) or simply:

$$p = 1 - q \quad \text{or} \quad p + q = 1$$

Sometimes the probability of an event E not happening is denoted by P(E'). Here E' is said to be the complement of E. A table of the outcomes with their respective frequencies is called a frequency distribution table. If, instead of frequencies, the respective probabilities are used, then the table will be called a **probability distribution** table.

The term **Relative frequency** when used refers to the ratio of the frequency of an event to the total of the frequencies of all the events. It is the same thing as the probability of occurrence of that event.

PROBABILITIES AND ODDS

The odds that an event will occur are given by the ratio of the probability that it will occur to the probability that it will not occur.

Example 1:

What are the odds for the occurrence of an event if its probability of success is $\frac{5}{9}$?

Solution:

The probability of success is $\frac{5}{9}$. Therefore, the probability of failure $= \frac{4}{9}$.
The odds for the occurrence (or the odds in favour) of the event is 5 to 4 (or 5:4).
We can also state the same thing as the odds against success. The answer will then be 4:5.

Example 2:

If the probability that a certain shipment will arrive on time is $\frac{7}{15}$, what are the odds that it will not arrive on time?

Solution:

The probability of success is $\frac{7}{15}$. The probability of failure is $\frac{8}{15}$.

Therefore, the odds that the shipment will not arrive on time is 8:7

Example 3:

A die is rolled once. What are the odds:
(i) in favour of getting a 5
(ii) against getting a 5

Solution:

(i) Odds in favour of getting a "5" $= \dfrac{\text{Probability of success}}{\text{Probability of failure}} = \dfrac{1/6}{5/6} = \dfrac{1}{5}$ (or 1:5)

(ii) Odds against getting a "5" $= \dfrac{5/6}{1/6} = 5:1$

RULES OF PROBABILITY

1. Probability of events A or B happening = P(A) + P(B)
   The probability of A or B is defined to be P(A∪B)

   The rules are also referred to as addition and multiplication laws

2. Probability of events A and B happening = P(A) × P(B)
   The probability of A and B is defined to be P(A∩B)

Example 1:

A six-sided die is rolled once. What is the probability of getting 1 or 5?

Solution:

Probability of getting a "1" = $\frac{1}{6}$

Probability of getting a "5" = $\frac{1}{6}$

The final answer for probability is to be expressed in its lowest terms

Therefore, the probability of getting 1 or 5 = $\frac{1}{6} + \frac{1}{6} = \frac{2}{6} = \frac{1}{3}$

Example 2:

A six-sided die is rolled twice. What is the probability of getting "1" followed by "5"?

Solution:

Probability of getting a "1" = $\frac{1}{6}$

Probability of getting a "5" = $\frac{1}{6}$

Therefore, the probability of getting 1 followed by 5 = $\frac{1}{6} \times \frac{1}{6} = \frac{1}{36}$

INDEPENDENT AND DEPENDENT EVENTS

Two events are **independent** if the probability that one event occurs does not affect the other event occurring e.g. rolling a die and tossing a coin at the same time. Here the outcome of the rolling of the die does not affect that of the tossing of the coin.

Two events are **dependent** if the outcome of the first event affects the outcome of the second event e.g. the probability of drawing a black card second time from a pack of 52 playing cards without replacing the first black card that was drawn.

If the first black card drawn is replaced, the probability of drawing the second black card is the same (i.e. $\frac{26}{52} = \frac{1}{2}$). On the other hand, if the first card drawn was not replaced, the probability of drawing the second card is $\frac{25}{51}$. Here the drawing of the first black card affects the probability outcome of the second card and the two events are dependent (see conditional probability below).

Two events are **mutually exclusive**, if one event happens and the other event cannot happen at the same time.

CONDITIONAL PROBABILITY

The probability of the occurrence of an event B, given the occurrence of another event A is, called a conditional probability. This is written as 'P(B|A)' and read probability of B given A.

$$P(B|A) = \frac{P(A \cap B)}{P(A)} \quad \text{or} \quad P(A \cap B) = P(A) \times P(B|A)$$

Example:

What is the probability of drawing 2 Queens from a pack of playing cards without replacement?

Solution:

Let the probability of drawing the first Queen = P(A)

And probability of drawing the second Queen = P(B|A)

Where $P(A) = \frac{4}{52}$ and $P(B|A) = \frac{3}{51}$

Therefore: $P(A \cap B) = P(A) \times P(B|A) = \frac{4}{52} \times \frac{3}{51} = \frac{1}{221}$

BAYES' FORMULA

Bayes' Formula is used to find the probability when certain other probabilities are also known. The formula is:

$$P(A|B) = \frac{P(A) \times P(B|A)}{P(B)}$$

Example:

There were two types of food items A and B in a restaurant. Customers ate either A or B but not both.

The probability of customers who ate A = 0.4 {i.e. P(A)}

The probability of customers who ate B = 0.6 {i.e. P(B)}

The probability of those who fell sick after eating A = 0.3 {i.e. P(S|A)}

The probability of those who fell sick after eating B = 0.25 {i.e. P(S|B)}

Calculate: (i) P(A|S)   (ii) P(B|S)

Solution:

Let us first find p(S) using the formula:

$p(S) = p(S|A)\} \times p(A) + p(S|B) \times p(B) = 0.3 \times 0.4 + 0.25 \times 0.6 = 0.12 + 0.15 = 0.27$

(i) $P(A|S) = \frac{P(A) \times P(S|A)}{P(S)} = \frac{0.4 \times 0.3}{0.27} = 0.44$ (i.e. $\frac{4}{9}$)

(ii) $P(B|S) = \frac{P(B) \times P(S|B)}{P(S)} = \frac{0.6 \times 0.25}{0.27} = 0.55$ (i.e. $\frac{5}{9}$)

PROBABILITY DIAGRAMS

Some probability questions are best illustrated and solved easily using Venn diagrams and Tree diagrams. A Venn diagram is a diagram with two or more overlapping circles or rectangles used to indicate where items or sets have something in common.

Example 1:

In a class of 30 students, 12 like Mathematics only, 10 like English only and 8 like both subjects. Illustrate this information using a Venn diagram and hence state:
(i) the probability that a student chosen at random likes mathematics or English
(ii) the probability that the student likes both maths and English
(iii) the probability that the student likes English given that the student likes Maths

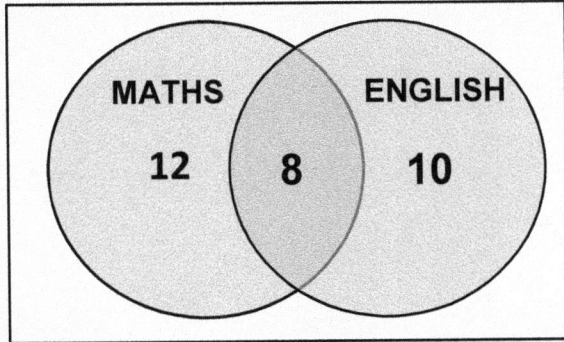

Solution:

(i) The probability that the student chosen likes mathematics or English:

$$= \frac{12}{30} + \frac{10}{30} = \frac{22}{30} = \frac{11}{15}$$

(ii) The probability that the student chosen likes both mathematics and English:

$$= \frac{8}{30} = \frac{4}{15}$$

(iii) Probability that the student likes English given that the student likes Maths:

$$= P(E|M) = \frac{P(M \cap E)}{P(M)} = \frac{8/30}{12/30} = \frac{8}{12} = \frac{2}{3}$$

TREE DIAGRAM (DECISION TREE)

A Tree diagram displays all the possible outcomes of an event. A dot represents the start of an event and each branch in the diagram represents a possible outcome.

Example 1:

A coin is tossed twice. Show the outcomes using a tree diagram.
What are the probabilities of getting:
(i) two heads   (ii) two tails   (iii) one head and one tail?

Solution:

(i) $P(2H) = \dfrac{1}{2} \times \dfrac{1}{2} = \dfrac{1}{4}$

(ii) $P(2T) = \dfrac{1}{2} \times \dfrac{1}{2} = \dfrac{1}{4}$

(iii) $P(1H, 1T) = \dfrac{1}{2} \times \dfrac{1}{2} + \dfrac{1}{2} \times \dfrac{1}{2} = \dfrac{1}{2}$

$\boxed{\text{P(Head and Tail) + P(Tail and Head)}}$

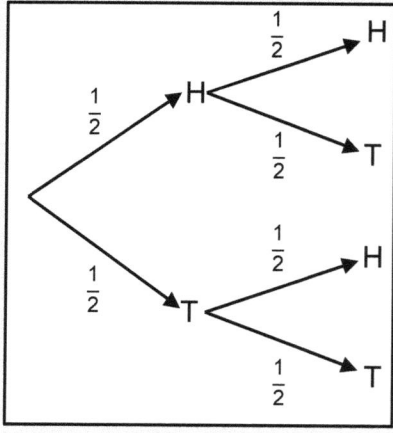

Example 2:

A bag contains 4 Black marbles and 3 white marbles. What are the probabilities of picking randomly one at time: (i) two black marbles   (ii) two white marbles ?
if the first marble picked is: (a) replaced   (b) not replaced

Solution:

(i)(a) $= \dfrac{4}{7} \times \dfrac{4}{7} = \dfrac{16}{49}$

(b) $= \dfrac{4}{7} \times \dfrac{3}{6} = \dfrac{12}{42} = \dfrac{2}{7}$

(ii)(a) $= \dfrac{3}{7} \times \dfrac{3}{7} = \dfrac{9}{49}$

(b) $= \dfrac{3}{7} \times \dfrac{2}{6} = \dfrac{1}{7}$

EXPECTED VALUE

The expected value of X is denoted by E(X). If the outcome is x_i and its probability is $P(x_i)$:

$$E(X) = \text{Sum of } [x_i \times P(x_i)]$$

Example 1:

In a gambling game, the payout depends on the outcome of rolling a die. Assume that payout is $2 if an odd number shows up and $3 for an even number. What is the expected (average) value for a roll?

Solution:

There are 3 possibilities for an odd number (i.e. 1, 3, 5) and three possibilities for an even number (i.e. 2, 4, 6). The expected value per roll is:

$$\text{Sum of: } [(2 \times \frac{1}{6}) + (3 \times \frac{1}{6}) + (2 \times \frac{1}{6}) + (3 \times \frac{1}{6}) + (2 \times \frac{1}{6}) + (3 \times \frac{1}{6})]$$

$$= 15 \times \frac{1}{6}$$

$$= \$2.50$$

Example 2:

A raffle ticket sells for $20. Altogether 1500 tickets were sold. The prize awarded for the winner is $10,000. What is the expected value?

Solution:

Loss = $20

Win = $9,980

$$\text{Probability of success} = \frac{1}{1500}$$

$$\text{Probability of failure} = 1 - \frac{1}{1500} = \frac{1499}{1500}$$

$$\text{Expected value} = \text{Sum of } [x_i \times P(x_i)] = \text{Sum of } [(9980 \times \frac{1}{1500}) - (20 \times \frac{1499}{1500})]$$

$$= 6.65 - 19.99 = -\$13.34 \quad \text{(i.e. a loss)}$$

PAYOFF TABLE

A payoff table is a useful way to represent and analyse a scenario where there is a range of possible outcomes and a variety of possible responses.

Example:

There are three Actions A1, A2 and A3 with probabilities 0.3, 0.5 and 0.2 respectively, and three different decisions D1, D2 and D3. The costs associated with the actions for each decision are shown in the following Pay Off Table. Calculate the expected value (i.e. of costs) of each decision and state which decision is preferred.

PAY OFF TABLE (Costs)				
	Actions			
Decisions	A1	A2	A3	Expected
D1	11	8	14	10.1
D2	14	10	7	10.6
D3	6	13	10	10.3
Probability	0.3	0.5	0.2	

Solution:

Expected value for D1 $= (11 \times 0.3) + (8 \times 0.5) + (14 \times 0.2) = 10.1$

Expected value for D2 $= (14 \times 0.3) + (10 \times 0.5) + (7 \times 0.2) = 10.6$

Expected value for D3 $= (6 \times 0.3) + (13 \times 0.5) + (10 \times 0.2) = 10.3$

Therefore, D1 is the preferred decision as it has the lowest expected cost.

MISCELLANEOUS PROBLEMS

1. If the probability that a certain shipment will arrive on time is $\frac{5}{12}$, what are the odds that it will not arrive on time?

    Solution:

    The odds against are $\frac{7}{12}$ to $\frac{5}{12}$ or 7:5.

---

2. Given the mutually exclusive events A and B for which P(A) = 0.44 and P(B) = 0.39, find P(A and B) and P(A or B).

    Solution:

    P (A and B) = 0

    P (A or B) = 0.44 + 0.39 = 0.83

---

3. The probabilities that a student will fail Maths, English or both are P(M) = 0.2, P(E) = 0.15 and P(M and E) = 0.03. What is the probability he will fail Maths given that he will fail English?

    Solution:

    $P(M | E) = \dfrac{P(M \cap E)}{P(E)} = \dfrac{0.03}{0.15} = 0.20$

    Note that P(M|E) = P(M). This means that the probability of the student failing Maths is the same irrespective of whether the student has failed or will fail English.

---

4. What is the probability of rolling a 10 with a pair of balanced dice?

    Solution:

    The sample space in this case is 36. That is, there are 36 possibilities (i.e. for each of the six numbers coming uppermost in one die, there are six corresponding numbers coming uppermost in the other die).

    The possible number pairs adding up to 10 are: 4 and 6, 6 and 4, 5 and 5.

    Therefore, the probability of rolling a 10 is: $\dfrac{3}{36} = \dfrac{1}{12}$

---

5. In an election Mr.A, Ms.B, and Ms.C are running for President, while Mr.D, Ms.E and Mr. F are running for Vice-President. Use a diagram to show the number of ways in which the two officials elected will not be of the same sex.

    Solution:

    5 ways

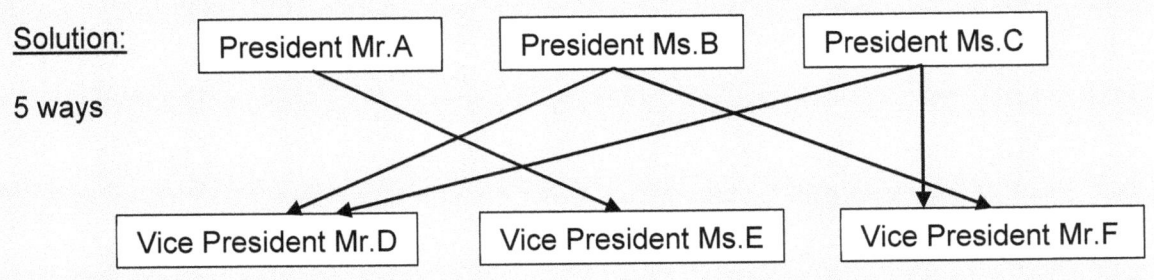

---

6. If P(A) = 0.55, P(B) = 0.40 and P(A and B) = 0.28, are the events A and B independent?

Solution:

If A and B are independent, then P(A and B) must equal P(A) × P(B).

But P(A) × P(B) = 0.55 × 0.4 = 0.22 and not 0.28

Therefore, the two events are not independent.

---

7. Given that P(A) = 0.30, P(B) = 0.50 and P(A and B) = 0.15
   Verify that: (a) P(A|B) = P(A)   (b) P(B|A) = P(B)
               (c) P(A|B') = P(A)   (d) P(B|A') = P(B)

Where A' is the complimentary of A and B' is the complimentary of B.
Show these in a Venn diagram.

Solution:

(a) $P(A|B) = \dfrac{0.15}{0.50} = 0.3 = P(A)$

(b) $P(B|A) = \dfrac{0.15}{0.30} = 0.5 = P(B)$

Note that in this diagram the whole circle represents Probability of A and similarly, Probability of B

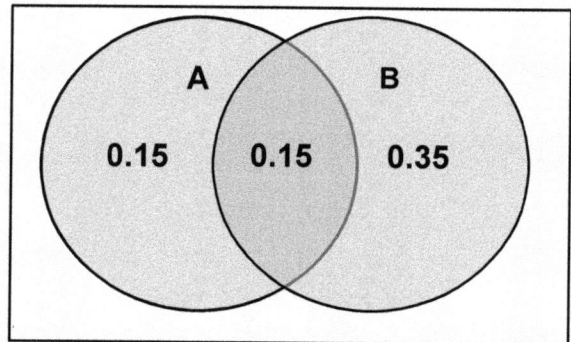

(c) $P(A|B') = \dfrac{0.15}{0.50} = 0.3 = P(A)$

(d) $P(B|A') = \dfrac{0.35}{0.70} = 0.5 = P(B)$

B' = complement of B = 1 − 0.50 = 0.50
A' = complement of A = 1 − 03 = 0.70

---

8. The probability that a bus from A to B will leave on time is 0.8. The probability that it will leave on time and also arrive on time is 0.64. What is the probability that if such a bus does leave on time, it will also arrive on time?

Solution:

$P(A|L) = \dfrac{P(A \cap L)}{P(L)}$

A = arrives on time, L = Leaves on time

$= \dfrac{0.64}{0.80} = 0.8$

1. A Ball is drawn at random from a box containing 6 red balls, 4 white balls and 5 blue balls. Determine the probability that it is:

   (a) Red
   (b) White
   (c) Blue
   (d) not Red
   (e) Red or White

2. An experiment consists of dealing 5 cards from a standard 52 card deck. What is the probability of being dealt:

   (a) only Ace, King, Queen or Jack
   (b) 4 Aces
   (c) Ace, King, Queen and Jack of any suite
   (d) 2 Aces and 3 Queens?

3. Three balls are selected from a box containing 6 yellow balls and 4 red balls. If the ball chosen after each selection is replaced before the next selection:

   (a) find the probability distribution for the number of balls drawn
      (i) 0 yellow balls   (ii) 1 yellow ball   (iii) 2 yellow balls   (iv) 3 yellow balls

   (b) find the probability that 3 yellow balls are chosen, given that more than 1 ball was yellow

   (c) show that the function $p(x) = \dfrac{1}{42}(5x + 3)$ where x = 0, 1, 2, 3 is a probability function.

4. (a) In drawing 5 cards from a deck of 52 cards without replacement, what is the probability of getting 5 hearts?

   (b) A committee of 6 people is to be drawn from 12 men and 16 women. What is the probability it will contain 3 men and 3 women?

5. There were two brands A and B of a product in a supermarket. Customers bought either A or B but not both.

   The probability of customers who bought A = 0.6 {i.e. P(A)}

   The probability of customers who bought B = 0.8 {i.e. P(B)}

   The probability of those who returned the product A = 0.4 {i.e. P(R|A)}

   The probability of those who returned the product B = 0.2 {i.e. P(R|B)}

   Calculate: (i) P(A|R)   (ii) P(B|R)

6. (i) The diagram below illustrates the transport choices in a small town. If a person were selected at random, what is the probability that:

(a) the person is a cyclist

(b) the person does not drive a car

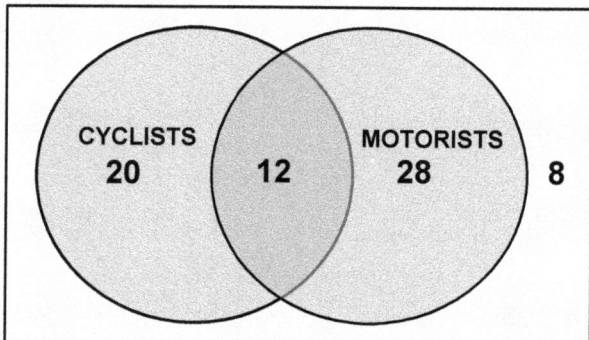

(ii) How many different three letter arrangements may be formed from the letters in the word 'LARGE'. How many of these arrangements are in alphabetical order?

---

7. (a) A pair of dice is cast. What is the probability that the sum of the numbers falling uppermost is 7 if it is known that one of the numbers is 5?

(b) 4 balls are selected randomly without replacement from an urn containing 10 Green balls and 8 Black balls. What is the probability that all the chosen balls are Green?

---

8. (a) The probability distribution of the random Variable X is shown in the following table.

x	-10	-5	0	5	10	15	20
P(X = x)	0.20	0.15	0.05	0.10	0.25	0.10	0.15

Find: (i) $P(X = -10)$ (ii) $P(X \geq 5)$ (iii) $P(-5 \leq X \leq 5)$ (iv) $P(X \leq 20)$

(b) P and Q play a card game with a standard deck of 52 cards. P selects a card from the well-shuffled deck and receives $x from Q if the card selected is a heart; otherwise P pays Q a dollar. Determine the value of x if the game is to be fair.

1.(a) $P(R) = \dfrac{6}{15} = \dfrac{2}{5}$

(b) $P(W) = \dfrac{4}{15}$

(c) $P(B) = \dfrac{5}{15} = \dfrac{1}{3}$

(d) $P(\text{not } R) = 1 - P(R) = \dfrac{3}{5}$

(e) $P(R \text{ or } W) = P(R) + P(W) = \dfrac{6}{15} + \dfrac{4}{15} = \dfrac{10}{15} = \dfrac{2}{3}$

---

2. (a) $P(5 \text{ picture cards}) = \dfrac{16_{C_5}}{52_{C_5}} = \dfrac{\frac{16 \times 15 \times 14 \times 13 \times 12}{5!}}{\frac{52 \times 51 \times 50 \times 49 \times 48}{5!}} = \dfrac{16 \times 15 \times 14 \times 13 \times 12}{52 \times 51 \times 50 \times 49 \times 48}$

$= \dfrac{1}{595} = 0.00168$

(b) $P(4 \text{ Aces}) = \dfrac{48}{52_{C_5}} = \dfrac{48}{\frac{52 \times 51 \times 50 \times 49 \times 48}{5!}} = \dfrac{1}{13 \times 17 \times 5 \times 49} = \dfrac{1}{54145} = 0.0000184$

(c) $P(\text{Ace, King, Queen or Jack}) = \dfrac{4 \times 48}{52_{C_5}} = \dfrac{4 \times 48}{\frac{52 \times 51 \times 50 \times 49 \times 48}{5!}} = \dfrac{4}{54145} = 0.0000739$

(d) $P(2 \text{ Aces and } 3 \text{ Queens}) = {}^4C_2 \times \dfrac{4_{C_3}}{52_{C_5}} = 6 \times \dfrac{4}{\frac{52 \times 51 \times 50 \times 49 \times 48}{5!}}$

$= \dfrac{1}{108\ 290} = 0.0000092$

3. (a)

x	0	1	2	3
P(x)	= P(RRR) = 0.064	= P(YRR) +P(RYR) +P(RRY) = 0.288	= P(YYR) +P(YRY) +P(RYY) = 0.432	= P(YYY) = 0.216

Check: Sum of probabilities = 1

(b) $P(Y = 3 \mid Y > 1) = \dfrac{P(Y = 3 \text{ and } Y > 1)}{P(Y > 1)} = \dfrac{0.216}{0.432 + 0.216} = \dfrac{0.216}{0.648} = \dfrac{1}{3}$

(c) $P(x) = \dfrac{1}{42}(5x + 3)$

$P(0) = \dfrac{1}{14}, \quad P(1) = \dfrac{4}{21}, \quad P(2) = \dfrac{13}{42}, \quad P(3) = \dfrac{3}{7}$

Check: (i) All probabilities are between 0 and 1

(ii) Sum of all probabilities $= \dfrac{1}{14} + \dfrac{4}{21} + \dfrac{13}{42} + \dfrac{3}{7} = \dfrac{3 + 8 + 13 + 18}{42} = 1$

Therefore, the given function is a probability function.

---

4. (a) Probability of getting 5 hearts $= \dfrac{13_{C_5}}{52_{C_5}}$

$= \dfrac{\frac{13 \times 12 \times 11 \times 10 \times 9}{5!}}{\frac{52 \times 51 \times 50 \times 49 \times 48}{5!}} = \dfrac{13 \times 12 \times 11 \times 10 \times 9}{52 \times 51 \times 50 \times 49 \times 48} = \dfrac{99}{199920} = 0.0005$

(b) The required probability $= \dfrac{12_{C_3} \times 16_{C_3}}{28_{C_6}} = \dfrac{\frac{12 \times 11 \times 10}{3 \times 2 \times 1} \times \frac{16 \times 15 \times 14}{3 \times 2 \times 1}}{\frac{28 \times 27 \times 26 \times 25 \times 24 \times 23}{6 \times 5 \times 4 \times 3 \times 2 \times 1}} = \dfrac{880}{2691} = 0.327$

---

5. Let us first find P(R) using the formula:

$P(R) = P(R|A) \times P(A) + P(R|B) \times P(B) = 0.4 \times 0.6 + 0.2 \times 0.8 = 0.24 + 0.16 = 0.40$

(i) $P(A|R) = \dfrac{P(A) \times P(R|A)}{P(R)} = \dfrac{0.6 \times 0.4}{0.4} = 0.6 \quad (\text{i.e. } \dfrac{3}{5})$

(ii) $P(B|R) = \dfrac{P(B) \times P(R|B)}{P(R)} = \dfrac{0.8 \times 0.2}{0.4} = 0.4 \quad (\text{i.e. } \dfrac{2}{5})$

6.(i)(a) The probability that the person is a cyclist $= \dfrac{32}{68} = \dfrac{8}{17}$

(b) The probability that the person does not drive a car $= \dfrac{28}{68} = \dfrac{7}{17}$

(ii)(a) Number of combinations $= {}^{5}C_3 = 10$

Number of arrangements for each combination $= 3! = 6$

Total number of arrangements $= 10 \times 6 = 60$

(b) Number of arrangements in alphabetical order $= 10$ (i.e. one for each combination)

---

7. (a) Let A denote the event that the sum of numbers is 7 and B the event that one of the numbers is 5.

$A = \{(6,1), (5, 2), (4, 3), (3, 4), (2, 5), (1, 6)\}$

$B = \{(5, 1), (5, 2), (5, 3), (5, 4), (5, 5), (5, 6), (1, 5), (2, 5), (3, 5), (4, 5), (6, 5)\}$

$A \cap B = \{(5, 2), (2, 5)\}$

$P(A \cap B) = P(A \text{ and } B) = \dfrac{2}{36} = \dfrac{1}{18}$

$P(B) = \dfrac{11}{36}$

Therefore: $P(A|B) = \dfrac{P(A \cap B)}{P(B)} = \dfrac{2/36}{11/36} = \dfrac{2}{11}$

(b) The probability that all chosen balls are Green $= \dfrac{{}^{10}C_4}{{}^{18}C_4}$

$= \dfrac{10 \times 9 \times 8 \times 7}{18 \times 17 \times 16 \times 15} = \dfrac{7}{102} = 0.069$

8.(a)(i) $P(X = -10) = 0.20$

(ii) $P(X \geq 5) = 0.10 + 0.25 + 0.10 + 0.15 = 0.60$

(iii) $P(-5 \leq X \leq 5) = 0.15 + 0.05 + 0.10 = 0.30$

(iv) $P(X \leq 20) = 0.20 + 0.15 + 0.05 + 0.10 + 0.25 + 0.10 + 0.15 = 1$

(b) $P(X = x) = \dfrac{13}{52} = \dfrac{1}{4}$

$P(X = -1) = \dfrac{3}{4}$

If the game is to be fair, the expected value E(X) of P's winnings is zero.

That is: $\dfrac{1}{4}(x) + \dfrac{3}{4}(-1) = 0$

$x - 3 = 0$

$x = 3$

The game will be fair if Q makes a $3 payoff for a winning bet of $1 placed by P.

9. SURDS, INDICES AND LOGARITHMS

SURDS

Any number whose exact value can only be expressed by using the nth root sign $\sqrt[n]{}$ is called a **surd.**

Example 1:

Express in the simplest form the cube root of 81.

$\sqrt[3]{81} = 3\sqrt[3]{3}$ ($81 = 3 \times 3 \times 3 \times 3$)

If the nth root results in a whole number, it is not a surd.

Example 2:

Express in the simplest form the fourth root of 256.

$\sqrt[4]{256} = 4$ ($256 = 4 \times 4 \times 4 \times 4$)

ADDITION AND SUBTRACTION OF SURDS

Surds can be added together, if they are similar.

Examples:

$\sqrt[2]{5} + \sqrt[2]{5} = 2\sqrt[2]{5}$

$\sqrt[5]{2} + 4\sqrt[5]{2} - 2\sqrt[5]{2} = 3\sqrt[5]{2}$

$\sqrt[n]{a} + \sqrt[n]{a} = 2\sqrt[n]{a}$

$2\sqrt[3]{3} + \sqrt[3]{3} + 4\sqrt[3]{3} = 7\sqrt[3]{3}$

MULTIPLICATION AND ADDITION OF SURDS

The nth root of a number multiplied by the nth root of another number is the nth root of the **product of the two numbers**. Multiplication of surds can sometimes result in a rational number.

Examples:

$\sqrt[n]{a} \times \sqrt[n]{b} = \sqrt[n]{ab}$

$\sqrt[4]{8} \times \sqrt[4]{20} = \sqrt[4]{160} = 2\sqrt[4]{10}$ | Surd |

$\sqrt[5]{2} \times \sqrt[5]{16} = \sqrt[5]{32} = 2$ | Rational number |

$\sqrt[n]{a} \times \sqrt[n]{a} = \sqrt[n]{a^2}$ | Surd |

$\sqrt[3]{8} \times \sqrt[3]{8} = \sqrt[3]{64} = 4$ | Rational number |

$\sqrt[6]{16} \times \sqrt[6]{25} = \sqrt[6]{400}$ | Surd |

The square root of a number multiplied by itself gives the number itself.

In general: $\sqrt{a} \times \sqrt{a} = a$

Examples:

- $\sqrt{2} \times \sqrt{2} = 2$ • $\sqrt{3} \times \sqrt{3} = 3$ • $\sqrt[2]{5} \times \sqrt[2]{5} = 5$

The product of the nth root of a number and the mth root of the same number cannot be expressed in the above manner.

THE DISTRIBUTIVE LAW OF SURDS

$$\sqrt{x}(\sqrt{y} + \sqrt{z}) = \sqrt{x} \times \sqrt{y} + \sqrt{x} \times \sqrt{z} = \sqrt{xy} + \sqrt{xz}$$

Examples:

$\sqrt{5}(\sqrt{3} + \sqrt{8}) = \sqrt{15} + \sqrt{40}$

$\sqrt{2}(\sqrt{8} - \sqrt{6}) = \sqrt{16} - \sqrt{12} = 4 - 2\sqrt{3}$

CONJUGATE SURDS

$\sqrt{a} - \sqrt{b}$ is the conjugate of $\sqrt{a} + \sqrt{b}$

$\sqrt{a} + \sqrt{b}$ is the conjugate of $\sqrt{a} - \sqrt{b}$

When $(\sqrt{a} + \sqrt{b})$ is multiplied by $(\sqrt{a} - \sqrt{b})$, the result is $(a - b)$.

Examples:

$(\sqrt{3} + \sqrt{2})(\sqrt{3} - \sqrt{2}) = 3 - 2 = 1$

$(\sqrt{12} + \sqrt{7})(\sqrt{12} - \sqrt{7}) = 12 - 7 = 5$

FRACTIONAL SURDS AND RATIONALISATION

A fraction with a surd in the denominator (or in both the numerator and the denominator) is called a **fractional surd**. The surd in the denominator can be rationalised (i.e. made a whole number) by multiplying the numerator and denominator by that surd.

A **surd in the denominator** can be a simple surd of the form $\sqrt{x}$ or of any of the following forms: $a + \sqrt{b}$, $\sqrt{a} + b$, $\sqrt{a} + \sqrt{b}$

Example 1:

Rationalise $\dfrac{2}{\sqrt{3}}$

$= \dfrac{2}{\sqrt{3}} \times \dfrac{\sqrt{3}}{\sqrt{3}} = \dfrac{2\sqrt{3}}{3}$ (multiply the numerator and denominator by $\sqrt{3}$)

Example 2:

Rationalise $\dfrac{3\sqrt{2}}{\sqrt{5}}$

$= \dfrac{3\sqrt{2}}{\sqrt{5}} \times \dfrac{\sqrt{5}}{\sqrt{5}} = \dfrac{3\sqrt{10}}{5}$ (multiply the numerator and denominator by $\sqrt{5}$)

In order to rationalise a complex denominator, we multiply the numerator and denominator by the **conjugate of the denominator**.

Example 3:

Rationalise $\dfrac{2}{\sqrt{3}+1}$

$= \dfrac{2}{\sqrt{3}+1} \times \dfrac{\sqrt{3}-1}{\sqrt{3}-1} = \dfrac{2(\sqrt{3}-1)}{3-1} = \sqrt{3}-1$

Example 4:

Rationalise $\dfrac{\sqrt{7}}{\sqrt{2}+3}$

$= \dfrac{\sqrt{7}}{\sqrt{2}+3} \times \dfrac{\sqrt{2}-3}{\sqrt{2}-3} = \dfrac{\sqrt{7}(\sqrt{2}-3)}{2-9} = \dfrac{\sqrt{7}(\sqrt{2}-3)}{-7} = \dfrac{\sqrt{7}(\sqrt{3}-\sqrt{2})}{7}$

Example 5:

Rationalise $\dfrac{5\sqrt{2}}{\sqrt{8}-\sqrt{3}}$

$= \dfrac{5\sqrt{2}}{\sqrt{8}-\sqrt{3}} \times \dfrac{\sqrt{8}+\sqrt{3}}{\sqrt{8}+\sqrt{3}} = \dfrac{5\sqrt{2}(\sqrt{8}+\sqrt{3})}{8-3} = \sqrt{2}(\sqrt{8}+\sqrt{3}) = \sqrt{16}+\sqrt{6} = 4+\sqrt{6}$

SURD EQUATIONS

We usually encounter equations with one to three surds.

- When there is only one surd, isolate it to one side.
- If there are two surds, keep one on either side of the equal sign.
- When there are three surds keep one on one side and the other two on the other side of the equal sign.

In all cases we have to square both sides of the equation and square as many times as needed to get rid of the surd. When we get a solution for the variable, check it with the original equation to see whether it satisfies the equation.

Example 1:

Solve: $\sqrt{3x-2} + 3 = 7$

By isolating the surd to one side we get:

$\sqrt{3x-2} = 4$ (Subtracting 3 from both sides)

Squaring both sides of the equation we get:

$3x - 2 = 16$

$3x = 18$

$x = 6$

Example 2:

Solve: $\sqrt{x+8} - \sqrt{x} = 2$

$\sqrt{x+8} = \sqrt{x} + 2$ | Rewriting the equation by keeping one surd on either side |

$x + 8 = x + 4\sqrt{x} + 4$ | Squaring both sides |

$4\sqrt{x} = 4$

$\sqrt{x} = 1$

$x = 1$

Example 3:

Solve $\sqrt{4x+13} - \sqrt{x} = \sqrt{x+7}$

$\sqrt{4x+13} = \sqrt{x} + \sqrt{x+7}$ | Keeping one surd on one side, two on the other side |

$4x + 13 = x + x + 7 + 2\sqrt{x} \times \sqrt{x+7}$

$2x + 6 = 2\sqrt{x} \times \sqrt{x+7}$

$x + 3 = \sqrt{x} \times \sqrt{x+7}$

$x^2 + 6x + 9 = x(x+7)$ | Squaring both sides |

$x^2 + 6x + 9 = x^2 + 7x$

$x = 9$

Example 4:

Solve: $\sqrt{8m + 9} = m + 2$

$8m + 9 = m^2 + 4m + 4$ $\boxed{\text{Squaring both sides}}$

$m^2 - 4m - 5 = 0$

$(m - 5)(m + 1) = 0$

The values of m satisfying this equation are either 5 or -1. Therefore, m = 5 or -1
Now we check these values to see whether they satisfy the original equation.

For m = 5:

$\sqrt{40 + 9} = 5 + 2$

$7 = 7$ $\boxed{\text{5 is a solution}}$

For m = -1:

$\sqrt{-8 + 9} = -1 + 2$

$1 = 1$ $\boxed{\text{-1 is a solution}}$

MISCELLANEOUS PROBLEMS

1. Write the following as simpler surds:

(a) $\sqrt{12}$ (b) $\sqrt{45}$ (c) $\sqrt{63}$ (d) $\sqrt{72}$

(e) $\sqrt{98}$ (f) $\sqrt{300}$ (g) $\sqrt{512}$ (h) $\sqrt{648}$

2. Simplify the following:

(a) $\sqrt{a^2b}$

(b) $\sqrt{x^3y^5}$

(c) $2\sqrt{x} + 5\sqrt{x}$

(d) $a\sqrt{75} - 3a\sqrt{3}$

(e) $x\sqrt[3]{24} + x\sqrt[3]{192}$

(f) $15y\sqrt[5]{32} - 2y\sqrt[4]{256}$

(g) $\sqrt{x}(2\sqrt{x} - \sqrt{y})$

(h) $2\sqrt{x}(3\sqrt{xy} + 5\sqrt{x})$

3. Rationalise the following:

(a) $\dfrac{1}{\sqrt{2}}$ (b) $\dfrac{3}{\sqrt{5}}$ (c) $\dfrac{\sqrt{a}}{\sqrt{b}}$ (d) $\dfrac{3\sqrt{x}}{\sqrt{3y}}$

(e) $\dfrac{\sqrt{m}}{\sqrt{m} + \sqrt{n}}$ (f) $\dfrac{\sqrt{a} - b}{\sqrt{a} + b}$ (g) $\dfrac{x}{\sqrt{xy} - \sqrt{x}}$ (h) $\dfrac{\sqrt{c}}{2\sqrt{cd} + \sqrt{c}}$

4. Find the solutions of the following equations

(a) $\sqrt{2x + 4} = 3$

(b) $\sqrt{5x - 1} + 2 = 5$

(c) $\sqrt{3x - 7} = \sqrt{x}$

(d) $\sqrt{3a + 1} - 3 = \sqrt{a - 4}$

(e) $\sqrt{3m + 4} - 2 = \sqrt{2m - 4}$

(f) $\sqrt{3x + 7} - 1 = \sqrt{2x + 3}$

(g) $\sqrt{4l + 2} - \sqrt{4l - 2} = 2$

(h) $\sqrt{8y + 25} = y + 2$

1.

(a) $\sqrt{12} = 2\sqrt{3}$ (b) $\sqrt{45} = 3\sqrt{5}$ (c) $\sqrt{63} = 3\sqrt{7}$ (d) $\sqrt{72} = 6\sqrt{2}$

(e) $\sqrt{98} = 7\sqrt{2}$ (f) $\sqrt{300} = 10\sqrt{3}$ (g) $\sqrt{512} = 16\sqrt{2}$ (h) $\sqrt{648} = 18\sqrt{2}$

2.

(a) $\sqrt{a^2 b} = a\sqrt{b}$ (b) $\sqrt{x^3 y^5} = xy^2 \sqrt{xy}$

(c) $2\sqrt{x} + 5\sqrt{x} = 7\sqrt{x}$ (d) $a\sqrt{75} - 3a\sqrt{3} = 5a\sqrt{3} - 3\sqrt{3} = 2a\sqrt{3}$

(e) $x\sqrt[3]{24} + x\sqrt[3]{192} = 2x\sqrt[3]{3} + 4x\sqrt[3]{3} = 6x\sqrt[3]{3}$ (f) $15y\sqrt[5]{32} - 2y\sqrt[4]{256} = 30y - 8y = 22y$

(g) $\sqrt{x}(2\sqrt{x} - \sqrt{y}) = 2x - \sqrt{xy}$ (h) $2\sqrt{x}(3\sqrt{xy} + 5\sqrt{x}) = 6x\sqrt{y} + 10x$

3.

(a) $\dfrac{1}{\sqrt{2}} = \dfrac{\sqrt{2}}{2}$ (b) $\dfrac{3}{\sqrt{5}} = \dfrac{3\sqrt{5}}{5}$ (c) $\dfrac{\sqrt{a}}{\sqrt{b}} = \dfrac{\sqrt{ab}}{b}$ (d) $\dfrac{3\sqrt{x}}{\sqrt{3y}} = \dfrac{\sqrt{3xy}}{y}$

(e) $\dfrac{\sqrt{m}}{\sqrt{m} + \sqrt{n}} = \dfrac{\sqrt{m}}{\sqrt{m} + \sqrt{n}} \times \dfrac{\sqrt{m} - \sqrt{n}}{\sqrt{m} - \sqrt{n}} = \dfrac{m - \sqrt{mn}}{m - n}$

(f) $\dfrac{\sqrt{a} - b}{\sqrt{a} + b} = \dfrac{\sqrt{a} - b}{\sqrt{a} + b} \times \dfrac{\sqrt{a} - b}{\sqrt{a} - b} = \dfrac{a - 2b\sqrt{a} + b^2}{a - b^2}$

(g) $\dfrac{x}{\sqrt{xy} - \sqrt{x}} = \dfrac{x}{\sqrt{xy} - \sqrt{x}} \times \dfrac{\sqrt{xy} + \sqrt{x}}{\sqrt{xy} + \sqrt{x}} = \dfrac{x\sqrt{xy} + x\sqrt{x}}{xy - x} = \dfrac{\sqrt{xy} + \sqrt{x}}{y - 1}$

(h) $\dfrac{\sqrt{c}}{2\sqrt{cd} + \sqrt{c}} = \dfrac{\sqrt{c}}{2\sqrt{cd} + \sqrt{c}} \times \dfrac{2\sqrt{cd} - \sqrt{c}}{2\sqrt{cd} - \sqrt{c}} = \dfrac{2c\sqrt{d} - c}{4cd - c} = \dfrac{2\sqrt{d} - 1}{4d - 1}$

4.

(a) $\sqrt{2x + 4} = 3$

$2x + 4 = 9$ | Squaring both sides |

$2x = 5$

$x = 2.5$

(b) $\sqrt{5x - 1} + 2 = 5$

$\sqrt{5x - 1} = 3$

$5x - 1 = 9$ | Squaring both sides |

$5x = 10$

$x = 2$

(c) $\sqrt{3x - 7} = \sqrt{x}$

$3x - 7 = x$ | Squaring both sides |

$2x = 7$

$x = 3.5$

(d) $\sqrt{3a + 1} - 3 = \sqrt{a - 4}$

$3a + 1 - 6\sqrt{3a + 1} + 9 = a - 4$ | Squaring both sides |

$-6\sqrt{3a + 1} = -2a - 14$

$36(3a + 1) = 4a^2 + 56a + 196$ | Squaring both sides again |

$108a + 36 = 4a^2 + 56a + 196$

$4a^2 - 52a + 160 = 0$

$a^2 - 13a + 40 = 0$

$(a - 5)(a - 8) = 0$

$a = 5$ or 8

(e) $\sqrt{3m + 4} - 2 = \sqrt{2m - 4}$

$3m + 4 - 4\sqrt{3m + 4} + 4 = 2m - 4$ | Squaring both sides |

$-4\sqrt{3m + 4} = -m - 12$

$16(3m + 4) = m^2 + 24m + 144$ | Squaring both sides again |

$48m + 64 = m^2 + 24m + 144$

$m^2 - 24m + 80 = 0$

$(m - 4)(m - 20) = 0$

$m = 4$ or 20

4.(f) $\sqrt{3x+7} - 1 = \sqrt{2x+3}$

$3x + 7 - 2\sqrt{3x+7} + 1 = 2x + 3$ | Squaring both sides |

$-2\sqrt{3x+7} = -x - 5$

$4(3x+7) = x^2 + 10x + 25$ | Squaring both sides again |

$12x + 28 = x^2 + 10x + 25$

$x^2 - 2x - 3 = 0$

$(x-3)(x+1) = 0$

$x = 3$ or -1

(g) $\sqrt{4I+2} - \sqrt{4I-2} = 2$

$\sqrt{4I+2} = \sqrt{4I-2} + 2$

$4I + 2 = 4I - 2 + 4\sqrt{4I-2} + 4$ | Squaring both sides |

$4\sqrt{4I-2} = 0$

$16(4I-2) = 0$ | Squaring both sides again |

$4I - 2 = 0$

$I = 0.5$

(h) $\sqrt{8y+25} = y + 2$

$8y + 25 = y^2 + 4y + 4$ | Squaring both sides |

$y^2 - 4y - 21 = 0$

$(y-7)(y+3) = 0$

$y = 7$ or -3 | $y = -3$ is admissible if we consider the negative value of a square root |

The nth root of a number x, $\sqrt[n]{x}$ can also be expressed as $x^{\frac{1}{n}}$.

e.g.
- $\sqrt{x} = x^{\frac{1}{2}}$
- $\sqrt[3]{a} = a^{\frac{1}{3}}$
- $\sqrt[5]{m} = m^{\frac{1}{5}}$

We know that a variable multiplied by itself a number of times is expressed as the power of that number, for example: $b \times b \times b = b^3$. The numbers that are raised as powers of the variables in the above examples are **positive fractional numbers**. Powers can also be positive or negative whole numbers and positive or **negative fractional numbers**. The negative indices can be derived from following a rule to express fractions such as the ones shown below.

- $\dfrac{1}{x}$ is written as x^{-1}

- $\dfrac{1}{x^n}$ is written as x^{-n}

- $\dfrac{1}{\sqrt{x}}$ which is the same as $\dfrac{1}{x^{1/2}}$ is written as $x^{-1/2}$

- $\dfrac{1}{\sqrt[n]{x}}$ which is the same as $\dfrac{1}{x^{1/n}}$ is written as $x^{-1/n}$

The power of a variable is generally referred to as its **index** or **exponent.** The plural of index is indices.

RULES OF INDICES

A set of rules for dealing with indices are shown below with examples:

1. The product of a variable raised to different indices (**m** and **n**) is the same as the variable raised to the sum of those indices.

$$a^m \times a^n = a^{(m+n)}$$

e.g.
- $a^5 \times a^{-2} = a^3$
- $m^{\frac{1}{2}} \times m^{\frac{5}{2}} = m^3$
- $p^{\frac{-1}{3}} \times p^2 = p^{\frac{5}{3}}$

2. When a variable raised to the power **m** is divided by the same variable raised to the power **n**, the result is the variable raised to the difference between the powers.

$$a^m \div a^n = a^{(m-n)}$$

3. When a variable raised to the power m is further raised to the power **n**, the result is the variable raised to the product of the two powers m and n.

$$(a^m)^n = a^{mn}$$

4. A variable raised to a power is the same as the inverse of that variable raised to the same power but with an opposite sign.

$$a^m = \frac{1}{a^{-m}} \quad \text{and} \quad a^{-m} = \frac{1}{a^m}$$

5. Any variable or a number raised to the power zero is equal to 1.

- $a^0 = 1$
- $x^0 = 1$
- $1000^0 = 1$

INDEX (OR EXPONENTIAL) EQUATIONS

Equate both sides of the equation as the power of the same base. If the base is the same on either side, we could equate the exponents on either side. Solve the following exponential equations:

Example 1:

Solve: $2x = 8$

$2x = 2^3$ | Express 8 as a power of 2

$x = 3$

Example 2:

Solve: $3^{2x} = 27$

$3^{2x} = 3^3$

$2x = 3$

$x = 1.5$

Example 3:

Solve: $(9^x)^2 = 81$

$9^{2x} = 9^2$

$2x = 2$

$x = 1$

Example 4:

Solve: $3^x = \dfrac{1}{27}$

$3^x = 3^{-3}$

$x = -3$

Example 5:

Solve: $8^{5x} = 256$

$(2^3)^{5x} = 2^8$

$2^{15x} = 2^8$

$15x = 8$

$x = \dfrac{8}{15}$

Example 6:

Solve: $\left(\dfrac{4}{3}\right)^m = \dfrac{16}{9}$

$\left(\dfrac{4}{3}\right)^m = \left(\dfrac{4}{3}\right)^2$

$m = 2$

Example 7:

Solve: $5^{-x} = \dfrac{1}{125}$

$5^{-x} = 5^{-3}$

$-x = -3$

$x = 3$

Example 8:

Solve: $\left(\dfrac{1}{3}\right)^p = 81$

$3^{-p} = 3^{-4}$

$-p = 4$

$p = -4$

Example 9:

Solve: $2^x \times 2^{4x} = 32$

$2^x \times 2^{4x} = 2^5$

$2^{5x} = 2^5$

$5x = 5$

$x = 1$

Example 10:

Solve: $\dfrac{3^x}{9^2} - 25 = 2$

$\dfrac{3^x}{3^4} = 27$

$3^{(x-4)} = 27$

$3^{(x-4)} = 3^3$

$x - 4 = 3$

$x = 7$

> See Logarithm section for questions with solutions involving irrational numbers

MISCELLANEOUS PROBLEMS

1. Simplify the following:

(a) $9^{1/2}$ (b) $8^{1/3}$ (c) $81^{1/4}$ (d) $25^{3/2}$

(e) $27^{2/3}$ (f) $64^{-1/6}$ (g) $3^{-2} \times 2^3$ (h) $5(4^2 \times 3^3)^0$

2. Simplify the following:

(a) $a^2 \times a^4$ (b) $4y^3 \times 5y^5$ (c) $3p^6q^3 \times 2p^2q^4$ (d) $5m^3n^2 \times 7m^{-2}n^0$

(e) $b^7 \div b^3$ (f) $12a^5 \div 3a^2$ (g) $20e^8 \div 5e^{-1}$ (h) $18c^3d^4 \div -6c^{-2}d^3$

3. Simplify the following:

(a) $(a^3)^4$ (b) $(3a^2)^3$ (c) $3(2x)^4$ (d) $(3p^2q^3)^2$

(e) $b^2 \times (a^3b^4)^2$ (f) $(2c^2d^4)^2 \div 2cd^3$ (g) $8b^2 \div (2b)^2$ (h) $(x^2y^3)^4 \div (x^3y^2)^3$

4. Simplify and express the answer using positive indices:

(a) $a^2 \times (a^{-2}b^3)^2$ (b) $(x^2y^{-3})^2 \div x^{-6}$ (c) $(3a^2b^{-3})^2 \div ab^2$ (d) $(3a^{-1/2})^4 \times b^{-2}$

(e) $2(x^{-2}y^6)^{1/3}$ (f) $4m^{-1/3} \times 5m^{1/4}$ (g) $\dfrac{a^0}{a^2b^{-3}}$ (h) $9c^2 \div (6c^{-2}d)^2$

5. Simplify the following:

(a) $(2a^2b)^3 \div 4a^2b^2$ (b) $(3x^2y)^2 \times (4x^2y^4)^{1/2}$

(c) $(-5cd^2)^3 \div 25c^3d^{-2}$ (d) $\dfrac{12m^2n^3}{4mn} \times (mn)^{-1}$

(e) $81^{1/2} + (3 \times 12)^{-1/2}$ (f) $a^{12}b^9 \div 3^2a^{-4}b^3$

(g) $(16x)^{1/2} \div 8x - 3x^{-1/2}$ (h) $2x^{(n-1)} \div 4x^{-n} \times x^{(n+2)}$

6. Solve the following exponential equations:

(a) $6^{3x} = 6^{(4-5x)}$ (b) $4^{(1-x)} = 16$

(c) $5^{x^2} = 5^{(3x+10)}$ (d) $3^{(3-x)} = 9^{4x}$

(e) $2^{(6x-9)} = \left(\dfrac{1}{16}\right)^{(x-2)}$ (f) $3^{(4x+6)} = \left(\dfrac{1}{27}\right)^{(3x+1)}$

(g) $9 \times 2^{(2x-3)} = 72$ (h) $3^{(4x+4)} = 3^2 \times 9^{(x+1)}$

1.

(a) $9^{1/2} = (3^2)^{1/2} = 3$

(b) $8^{1/3} = (2^3)^{1/3} = 2$

(c) $81^{1/4} = (3^4)^{1/4} = 3$

(d) $25^{3/2} = (5^2)^{3/2} = 125$

(e) $27^{2/3} = (3^3)^{2/3} = 9$

(f) $64^{-1/6} = (2^6)^{-1/2} = 2^{-3} = \dfrac{1}{8}$

(g) $3^{-2} \times 2^3 = \dfrac{1}{9} \times 8 = \dfrac{8}{9}$

(h) $5(4^2 \times 3^3)^0 = 5 \times 1 = 5$

2.

(a) $a^2 \times a^4 = a^6$

(b) $4y^3 \times 5y^5 = 20y^8$

(c) $3p^6q^3 \times 2p^2q^4 = 6p^8q^7$

(d) $5m^3n^2 \times 7m^{-2}n^0 = 35mn^2$

(e) $b^7 \div b^3 = b^4$

(f) $12a^5 \div 3a^2 = 4a^3$

(g) $20e^8 \div 5e^{-1} = 4e^9$

(h) $18c^3d^4 \div -6c^{-2}d^3 = -3c^5d$

3.

(a) $(a^3)^4 = a^{12}$

(b) $(3a^2)^3 = 27a^6$

(c) $3(2x)^4 = 48x^4$

(d) $(3p^2q^3)^2 = 9p^4q^6$

(e) $b^2 \times (a^3b^4)^2 = a^6b^{10}$

(f) $(2c^2d^4)^2 \div 2cd^3 = 4c^6d^6$

(g) $8b^2 \div (2b)^2 = 2$

(h) $(x^2y^3)^4 \div (x^3y^2)^3 = \dfrac{y^6}{x}$

4.

(a) $a^2 \times (a^{-2}b^3)^2 = \dfrac{b^6}{a^2}$

(b) $(x^2y^{-3})^2 \div x^{-6} = \dfrac{x^{10}}{y^6}$

(c) $(3a^2b^{-3})^2 \div ab^2 = \dfrac{9a^3}{b^8}$

(d) $(3a^{-1/2})^4 \times b^{-2} = \dfrac{81}{a^2b^2}$

(e) $2(x^{-2}y^6)^{1/3} = \dfrac{2y^2}{x^{2/3}}$

(f) $4m^{-1/3} \times 5m^{1/4} = \dfrac{20}{m^{1/12}}$

(g) $\dfrac{a^0}{a^2b^{-3}} = \dfrac{b^3}{a^2}$

(h) $9c^2 \div (6c^{-2}d)^2 = \dfrac{c^6}{4d^2}$

5.

(a) $(2a^2b)^3 \div 4a^2b^2 = 8a^6b^3 \div 4a^2b^2 = 2a^4b$

(b) $(3x^2y)^2 \times (4x^2y^4)^{1/2} = 9x^4y^2 \times 2xy^2 = 18x^5y^4$

(c) $(-5cd^2)^3 \div 25c^3d^{-2} = \dfrac{-125c^3d^6}{25c^3d^{-2}} = -5d^8$

(d) $\dfrac{12m^2n^3}{4mn} \times (mn)^{-1} = 3n$

(e) $81^{1/2} + (3 \times 12)^{-1/2} = 9 + \dfrac{1}{6} = 9\dfrac{1}{6}$

(f) $a^{12}b^9 \div 3^2a^{-4}b^3 = \dfrac{a^{16}b^6}{9}$

5.(g) $(16x)^{1/2} \div 8x - 3x^{-1/2} = 4x^{1/2} \div 8x - 3x^{-1/2} = -2\frac{1}{2}x^{-1/2}$

(h) $2x^{(n-1)} \div 4x^{-n} \times x^{(n+2)} = \frac{1}{2}x^{(2n-1)} \times x^{(n+2)} = \frac{1}{2}x^{(3n+1)}$

6.(a)

$6^{3x} = 6^{(4-5x)}$

$3x = 4 - 5x$

$8x = 4$

$x = 0.5$

(b) $4^{(1-x)} = 16$

$4^{(1-x)} = 4^2$

$1 - x = 2$

$x = -1$

(c) $5^{x^2} = 5^{(3x+10)}$

$x^2 = 3x + 10$

$x^2 - 3x - 10 = 0$

$(x - 5)(x - 2) = 0$

$x = 5$ or 2

(d) $3^{(3-x)} = 9^{4x}$

$3^{(3-x)} = (3^2)^{4x}$

$3 - x = 8x$

$9x = 3$

$x = \frac{1}{3}$

(e) $2^{(6x-9)} = (\frac{1}{16})^{(x-2)}$

$2^{(6x-9)} = (\frac{1}{2^4})^{(x-2)}$

$2^{(6x-9)} = 2^{(-4x+8)}$

$6x - 9 = -4x + 8$

$10x = 17$

$x = \frac{10}{17}$

(f) $3^{(4x+6)} = (\frac{1}{27})^{(3x+1)}$

$3^{(4x+6)} = (\frac{1}{3^3})^{(3x+1)}$

$3^{(4x+6)} = 3^{(-9x-3)}$

$4x + 6 = -9x - 3$

$13x = -9$

$x = \frac{-9}{13}$

(g) $9 \times 2^{(2x-3)} = 72$

$2^{(2x-3)} = 8$

$2^{(2x-3)} = 2^3$

$2x - 3 = 3$

$2x = 6$

$x = 3$

(h) $3^{(4x+4)} = 3^2 \times 9^{(x+1)}$

$3^{(4x+4)} = 3^2 \times 3^{2(x+1)}$

$3^{(4x+4)} = 3^{(2x+4)}$

$4x + 4 = 2x + 4$

$2x = 0$

$x = 0$

LOGARITHMS

A number can be raised to a power or **exponent**. The number raised is called the **base**.

Example:

$$2^3 = 8$$

The base here is 2 and the power to which it is raised is 3. The **logarithm** (or log) of a number with respect to a given base is **the power to which we have to raise the base** to obtain the number. So, we say, Logarithm of 8 to the base 2 is equal to 3. This is written as:

$$\log_2 8 = 3$$

When the base used is 10, we refer to the logarithm as a **common logarithm**. The base can be any number and the power does not need to be a whole number.

Examples:

- $\log_2 16 = 4$
- $\log_4 16 = 2$
- $\log_{10} 2 = 0.3010$
- $\log_{10} 3 = 0.4771$
- $\log_{10} 5 = 0.6990$
- $\log_{10} 20 = 1.3010$
- $\log_{10} 300 = 2.4771$
- $\log_{10} 5000 = 3.6990$

The common logarithms of 2, 3 and 5 above are 0.3010, 0.4771 and 0.6990 respectively. These are obtained using the calculator. The common logarithms of 20, 300 and 5000 will be 1.3010, 2.4771 and 3.6990 respectively. We observe that the decimal part of the number in each case is the same as those for 2, 3 and 5 but there is a digit in front when a number whose logarithm we are finding is not a single digit number.

The number in front of each logarithm is called the **characteristic** and is obtained by subtracting 1 from the number of digits in the number whose logarithm is being determined. The decimal part of the number is called the **mantissa**.

For common logarithms of decimal numbers (e.g. 0.2, 0.5), the characteristic is negative and increases by 1 for every additional zero after the decimal point, as shown in the examples below.

Examples:

- $\log_{10} 0.2 = -1 + 0.3010$
- $\log_{10} 0.3 = -1 + 0.4771$
- $\log_{10} 0.5 = -1 + 0.6990$
- $\log_{10} 0.02 = -2 + 0.3010$
- $\log_{10} 0.003 = -3 + 0.4771$
- $\log_{10} 0.0005 = -4 + 0.6990$

Converting the logarithm of a number back to the number is referred to as 'finding the **antilogarithm**'.

Example:

The logarithm of 50 is 1.6990.

The antilogarithm of 1.6990 is 50.

This can be done easily using a calculator

When the base used is a special letter 'e', the logarithm is called a **Natural Logarithm** (or a Napierian Logarithm). **The value of e is 2.71828**. The use of such a base will be seen in later chapters (exponential functions and integration). When a logarithm is written without a base, it is assumed to be common logarithm. For example, $\log 100 = 2$ is assumed to be common logarithm.

> Logarithm to the base 'e' is written **ln**. $\log_e x$ is written as **lnx**.

CONVERTING LOGARITHMS FROM ONE BASE TO ANOTHER

The logarithm of a number to any given base can be converted to common logarithm. The conversion is done as follows:

$$\log_b a = \frac{\log_{10} a}{\log_{10} b}$$

If we let 'a' take the place of 10, then we have:

$$\log_b a = \frac{\log_a a}{\log_a b}$$

Cross multiplying:

$$\log_b a \times \log_a b = 1 \quad \boxed{\text{By definition } \log_a a = 1}$$

Example:

Convert $\log_2 12$ to $\log_{12} 2$

$$\log_{12} 2 = \frac{1}{\log_2 12}$$

THE THREE LAWS OF LOGARITHMS

1. $\log(MN) = \log M + \log N$ (e.g. $\log 12 = \log (3 \times 4) = \log 3 + \log 4$)

2. $\log(\frac{M}{N}) = \log M - \log N$ (e.g. $\log(\frac{3}{4}) = \log 3 - \log 4$)

3. $\log M^k = k \log M$ (e.g. $\log 8^3 = 3 \log 8$)

> The laws are the same for logarithms with any base

Example 1:

Evaluate $\log_5 25$

What power must 5 be raised to get 25? The answer is 2. Therefore: $\log_5 25 = 2$.

Example 2:

Evaluate $\log_6 1$

6 must be raised to zero to get 1. Therefore: $\log_6 1 = 0$.

Example 3:

Evaluate $\log_4 64$

What power must 4 be raised to get 64? The answer is 3. Therefore: $\log_4 64 = 3$.

Example 4:

Find the value of $\log_2 30$

We need to change the base to 10 and then use the calculator to simplify.

$\log_2 30 = \dfrac{\log_{10} 30}{\log_{10} 2}$

$\log_2 30 = \dfrac{0.4771}{0.3010}$

$\log_2 30 = 1.585$

Calculators use only base "10" and base "e"

Example 5:

Simplify: $\log_{10} 4 + \log_{10} 25$

$\log_{10} 4 + \log_{10} 25 = \log_{10}(4 \times 25) = \log_{10} 100 = 2$ Law 1

Example 6:

Simplify: $\log_{10} 80 - \log_{10} 8$

$\log_{10} 80 - \log_{10} 8 = \log_{10}\left(\dfrac{80}{8}\right) = \log_{10} 10 = 1$ Law 2

Example 7:

Simplify: $\log_{10} 5^3$

$\log_{10} 5^3 = 3\log_{10} 5 = 3 \times 0.6990 = 2.097$ Law 3

Example 8:

Simplify: $\log_4 9 - \log_4 18 + \log_4 32$

$\log_4 9 - \log_4 18 + \log_4 32 = \log_4 \dfrac{9 \times 32}{18} = \log_4 16 = 2$

Example 9:

Simplify: $\dfrac{\log_a x^6}{\log_a x^2}$

$\dfrac{\log_a x^6}{\log_a x^2} = \dfrac{6\log_a x}{2\log_a x} = 3$

Example 10:

Simplify: $2\log_4 27 - 3\log_4 3 - \log_4 108$

$2\log_4 27 - 3\log_4 3 - \log_4 108 = \log_4\left(\dfrac{27^2}{3^3 \times 108}\right) = \log_4\left(\dfrac{1}{4}\right) = \log_4 4^{-1} = -1$

LOGARITHMIC EQUATIONS

Example 1:

Solve for x: $2^x = 50$

$\log 2^x = \log 50$ | Taking logarithm on both sides

$x\log 2 = \log 50$ | Law 3

$x = \dfrac{\log 50}{\log 2} = \dfrac{1.6990}{0.3010} = 5.645$ | Assume common logarithm

Example 2:

Solve for x: $\log_9 3 = x$

That is: $9^x = 3$

Therefore: $x = \dfrac{1}{2}$

Example 3:

Solve for x: $\log_3 9 = x$

That is: $3^x = 9 = 3^2$

Therefore: $x = 2$

Example 4:

Solve for: $\log_{10}(8 - 2x) = 1$

That is: $8 - 2x = 10^1$

$2x = -2$

$x = -1$

Example 5:

Solve for x: $\log_{\frac{1}{2}} 4 = x$

That is: $(\frac{1}{2})^x = 4$

$2^{-x} = 4 = 2^2$

$-x = 2$

$x = -2$

Example 6:

Find the value of $\log_a x^2$ if $\log_a x = 0.8$

$\log_a x^2 = 2\log_a x = 2 \times 0.8 = 1.6$

Example 7:

Solve for x: $\log_2 x - \log_2 8 = 13$

That is: $\log_2 x - 3 = 13$

$\log_2 x = 16$

$x = 4$

Example 8:

Solve for x: $\log_5 x + \log_5 x^2 = \log_5 125$

$\log_5 x + 2\log_5 x = \log_5 125$

$3\log_5 x = \log_5 125$

$\log_5 x^3 = \log_5 5^3$

$x = 5$

Example 9:

Solve for x: $\log_6 3 - \log_6 x = \log_6 12$

$\log_6(\frac{3}{x}) = \log_6 12$

$\frac{3}{x} = 12$

$x = \frac{3}{12} = \frac{1}{4}$

Example 10:

Solve for x: $\log_5(x-1) - \log_5(x+2) = \log_5(x-3)$

That is: $\log_5(\frac{x-1}{x+2}) = \log_5(x-3)$

Therefore: $\frac{x-1}{x+2} = x - 3$

$x - 1 = (x+2)(x-3)$ Cross multiplying

$x - 1 = x^2 - x - 6$

$x^2 - 2x - 5 = 0$

$x^2 - 2x = 5$

$(x-1)^2 - 1 = 5$

$(x-1)^2 = 6$

$x - 1 = \pm 2.45$

$x = 1 \pm 2.45$

$x = 3.45$ or -1.45

MISCELLANEOUS PROBLEMS

1. Find the values of the following:

(a) $\log_4 64$ (b) $\log_3 27$ (c) $\log_7 343$ (d) $\log_8 512$

(e) $\log_{10} 1000$ (f) $\log_4 256$ (g) $\log_5 125$ (h) $\log_2 1024$

2. Express the following as a relation in logarithms:

(a) $32 = 2^5$ (b) $625 = 5^4$ (c) $243 = 3^5$ (d) $216 = 6^3$

(e) $a = b^n$ (f) $x = y^{\frac{1}{2}}$ (g) $p^2 = q^m$ (h) $xy = a^{\frac{1}{z}}$

3. Express the following as a relation in indices:

(a) $\log_2 16 = 4$ (b) $\log_3 27 = 3$ (c) $\log_{10} 1 = 0$ (d) $\log_9 27 = 1.5$

(e) $\log_2 x = 3$ (f) $\log_{25} y = 0.5$ (g) $\log_{\frac{1}{3}} 9 = m$ (h) $\log_a 4 = \frac{2}{3}$

4. Simplify the following:

(a) $\dfrac{\log_3 27}{\log_5 25}$ (b) $\dfrac{2}{3}\log_2 8 + \dfrac{1}{2}\log_{\frac{1}{3}} 9$

(c) $\log_{10} 10^5$ (d) $\log_2(16 \times 64)$

(e) $\log_3 3^{-2}$ (f) $\log_2 8 \times \log_8 2$

(g) $\dfrac{\log_{10} 1000}{\log_6 36}$ (h) $\log_{100} 1000$

5. Evaluate using logarithm laws but not simplify.

(a) $\log(12 \times 19)$ (b) $\log\dfrac{98}{23}$

(c) $\log(36 \times 28^2)$ (d) $\log\dfrac{212 \times 18}{56 \times 37}$

(e) $\log(104 \times 73 \times 26)$ (f) $\log(78^2 \times 21^3)$

(g) $\log(37.5 \times 61.3 \times 46.8)$ (h) $\log\dfrac{49 \times 522}{76^2}$

6. Solve the following logarithmic equations

(a) $\log_x 5^3 = 3$ (b) $\log_{\frac{1}{3}} 27 = x$ (c) $2 + \log x = \log 2$ (d) $2^x = 20$

(e) $6^{(3-x)} = \dfrac{3}{4}$ (f) $\log x - \log 4 = \log 2$ (g) $\log_5 x + \log_5 6 = \log_5 21$ (h) $\log_{10} x = 3\log_2 4$

1.

(a) $\log_4 64 = 3$ (b) $\log_3 27 = 3$ (c) $\log_7 343 = 3$ (d) $\log_8 512 = 3$

(e) $\log_{10} 1000 = 3$ (f) $\log_4 256 = 4$ (g) $\log_5 125 = 3$ (h) $\log_2 1024 = 10$

2.

(a) $\log_2 32 = 5$ (b) $\log_5 625 = 4$ (c) $\log_3 243 = 5$ (d) $\log_6 216 = 3$

(e) $\log_b a = n$ (f) $\log_y x = \dfrac{1}{2}$ (g) $\log_q p^2 = m$ (h) $\log_a xy = \dfrac{1}{z}$

3.

(a) $16 = 2^4$ (b) $27 = 3^3$ (c) $1 = 10^0$ (d) $27 = 9^{1.5}$

(e) $x = 2^3$ (f) $y = 25^{0.5}$ (g) $9 = \left(\dfrac{1}{3}\right)^m$ (h) $4 = a^{\frac{2}{3}}$

4.

(a) $\dfrac{3}{2}$ (b) 1

(c) 5 (d) 10

(e) -2 (f) 1

(g) $\dfrac{3}{2}$ (h) $\dfrac{3}{2}$

5.

(a) $\log 12 + \log 19$ (b) $\log 98 - \log 23$

(c) $\log 36 + 2\log 28$ (d) $\log 212 + \log 18 - \log 56 - \log 37$

(e) $\log 104 + \log 73 + \log 26$ (f) $2\log 78 + 3\log 21$

(g) $\log 37.5 + \log 61.3 + \log 46.8$ (h) $\log 49 + \log 522 - 2\log 76$

6. (a) $\log_x 5^3 = 3$

$5^3 = x^3$

$x = 5$

(b) $\log_{\frac{1}{3}} 27 = x$

$\left(\dfrac{1}{3}\right)^x = 27$

$3^{-x} = 3^3$

$-x = 3$

$x = -3$

6.(c) $2 + \log x = \log 2$

$2 = \log 2 - \log x$

$2 = \log(\frac{2}{x})$

$\frac{2}{x} = 10^2 = 100$

$x = \frac{2}{100} = 0.02$

(d) $2^x = 20$

$x\log 2 = \log 20$

$0.3010x = 1.3010$

$x = 4.32$

(e) $6^{(3-x)} = \frac{3}{4}$

$\log 6(3 - x) = \log 3 - \log 4$

$(0.7781)(3 - x) = 0.4771 - 0.6020 = -0.1249$

$3 - x = \frac{-0.1249}{0.7781} = -0.1605$

$x = 3 + 0.1605 = 3.1605$

(f) $\log x - \log 4 = \log 2$

$\log x = \log 2 + \log 4 = \log 8$

$x = 8$

(g) $\log_5 x + \log_5 6 = \log_5 21$

$\log_5 6x = \log_5 21$

$6x = 21$

$x = 3.5$

(h) $\log_{10} x = 3\log_2 4$

$\log_{10} x = 3\log_2 4 = 3\frac{\log_{10} 4}{\log_{10} 2} = 3\frac{0.6020}{0.3010} = 3 \times 2$

$\log_{10} x = 6$

$x = 10^6 = 1,000,000$

1. Simplify the following rationalising the denominator where required:

(a) $2\sqrt{3x} - 4\sqrt{12x} + 3\sqrt{48x}$

(b) $\dfrac{\sqrt{242}}{6} \div \dfrac{\sqrt{32}}{3}$

(c) $(4\sqrt{3} + 2\sqrt{5})(4\sqrt{3} - 2\sqrt{5})$

(d) $\dfrac{7}{\sqrt{5} - 2}$

(e) $\dfrac{4 + \sqrt{5}}{\sqrt{5} + 3}$

(f) $\dfrac{\sqrt{7} + \sqrt{3}}{\sqrt{7} - \sqrt{3}}$

2. Find the solutions of the following surd equations

(a) $3\sqrt{x + 1} = x + 3$

(b) $\sqrt{x + 2} - \sqrt{x - 1} = \sqrt{\dfrac{x}{2}}$

3. Simplify:

(a) $\dfrac{12^{-4} \times 108 \times 4^3}{18^{-2} \times 20^{-1} \times 3^4}$

(b) $\dfrac{9.25 \times 10^6 + 8.75 \times 10^6}{9.25 \times 10^{-6} - 8.75 \times 10^{-6}}$

(c) $\dfrac{2^n \times 8^{(n + 1)} \times 9^{(n - 1)}}{3^{2n} \times 4^{(2n - 1)}}$

4. Simplify:

(a) $\left(\dfrac{81a^{12}}{16b^8}\right)^{\frac{3}{4}}$

(b) $\left(\dfrac{m^{12}}{64m^{18}}\right)^{\frac{1}{6}}$

(c) $\dfrac{9(x^6)^4}{27x^9x^7}$

5. Solve for x:

(a) $5^{(2x + 1)} = \dfrac{1}{625}$

(b) $4^{2x} \times 16^{(x - 2)} = 2^8$

(c) $3^{2x} - 12.3^x = -27$

6. Simplify:

(a) $3\log_3 m^{\frac{1}{3}}$

(b) $\dfrac{1}{2}\log_6 16 + 2\log_6 8 - 3\log_6 12$

(c) $2\log_a x^2 \div \log_a x^6$

7. Determine the value of x:

(a) $\log_3\left(\dfrac{1}{9}\right) = x$

(b) $\log_2 x + \log_2 9 - \log_2 10 = \log_2 18$

(c) $\log_8(x + 6) - \log_8(x - 1) = 1$

8.

(i) If $y = a\log_{10} x$, find the value of x when $a = 3$ and $y = 6$

(ii) Solve for n if $4^n - 2^{(n + 3)} + 16 = 0$

(iii) Given that $\log_{10} 2 = 0.3010$ and $\log_{10} 50 = 1.6990$, find the value of $\log_2 50$ correct to three places of decimals.

1.

(a) $2\sqrt{3x} - 4\sqrt{12x} + 3\sqrt{48x} = 2\sqrt{3x} - 8\sqrt{3x} + 12\sqrt{3x} = 6\sqrt{3x}$

(b) $\dfrac{\sqrt{242}}{6} \div \dfrac{\sqrt{32}}{3} = \dfrac{11\sqrt{2}}{6} \div \dfrac{4\sqrt{2}}{3} = \dfrac{11\sqrt{2}}{6} \times \dfrac{3}{4\sqrt{2}} = \dfrac{11}{8} = 1\dfrac{3}{8}$

(c) $(4\sqrt{3} + 2\sqrt{5})(4\sqrt{3} - 2\sqrt{5}) = (4\sqrt{3})^2 - (2\sqrt{5})^2 = 48 - 20 = 28$

(d) $\dfrac{7}{\sqrt{5} - 2} = \dfrac{7}{\sqrt{5} - 2} \times \dfrac{\sqrt{5} + 2}{\sqrt{5} + 2} = 7(\sqrt{5} + 2)$

(e) $\dfrac{4 + \sqrt{5}}{\sqrt{5} + 3} = \dfrac{4 + \sqrt{5}}{\sqrt{5} + 3} \times \dfrac{\sqrt{5} - 3}{\sqrt{5} - 3} = \dfrac{-(4 + \sqrt{5})(\sqrt{5} - 3)}{4} = \dfrac{-(4\sqrt{5} - 12 + 5 - 3\sqrt{5})}{4} = \dfrac{(7 - \sqrt{5})}{4}$

(f) $\dfrac{\sqrt{7} + \sqrt{3}}{\sqrt{7} - \sqrt{3}} = \dfrac{\sqrt{7} + \sqrt{3}}{\sqrt{7} - \sqrt{3}} \times \dfrac{\sqrt{7} + \sqrt{3}}{\sqrt{7} + \sqrt{3}} = \dfrac{7 + \sqrt{21} + 3}{4} = \dfrac{10 + \sqrt{21}}{4}$

2.

(a) $3\sqrt{x + 1} = x + 3$

$9(x + 1) = x^2 + 6x + 9$ $\boxed{\text{Squaring both sides}}$

$9x + 9 = x^2 + 6x + 9$

$x^2 - 3x = 0$

$x(x - 3) = 0$

$x = 0 \text{ or } 3$

(b) $\sqrt{x + 2} - \sqrt{x - 1} = \sqrt{\dfrac{x}{2}}$

$x + 2 - 2\sqrt{x + 2} \times \sqrt{x - 1} + x - 1 = \dfrac{x}{2}$ $\boxed{\text{Squaring both sides}}$

$-2\sqrt{x + 2} \times \sqrt{x - 1} = \dfrac{3x}{2} - 1$

$4(x + 2)(x - 1) = \dfrac{9x^2}{4} + 3x + 1$ $\boxed{\text{Squaring again}}$

$16(x^2 + x - 2) = 9x^2 + 12x + 4$

$16x^2 + 16x - 32 = 9x^2 + 12x + 4$

$7x^2 + 4x - 36 = 0$

$x = \dfrac{-b \pm \sqrt{b^2 - 4ac}}{2a} = \dfrac{-4 \pm \sqrt{16 + 1008}}{14} = \dfrac{-4 \pm \sqrt{1024}}{14} = \dfrac{-4 \pm 32}{14} = \dfrac{28}{14} \text{ or } \dfrac{-36}{14} = 2 \text{ or } -2\dfrac{4}{7}$

$x = 2$ $\boxed{-2\dfrac{4}{7} \text{ is inadmissible}}$

3. (a) $\dfrac{12^{-4} \times 108 \times 4^3}{18^{-2} \times 20^{-1} \times 3^4} = \dfrac{18^2 \times 108 \times 4^3 \times 20}{12^4 \times 3^4} = \dfrac{18 \times 18 \times 108 \times 64 \times 20}{12 \times 12 \times 12 \times 12 \times 81} = \dfrac{80}{3} = 26\dfrac{2}{3}$

(b) $\dfrac{9.25 \times 10^6 + 8.75 \times 10^6}{9.25 \times 10^{-6} - 8.75 \times 10^{-6}} = \dfrac{10^6(9.25 + 8.75)}{10^{-6}(9.25 - 8.75)} = 10^{12} \times \dfrac{18}{0.5} = 36 \times 10^{12}$

(c) $\dfrac{2^n \times 8^{(n+1)} \times 9^{(n-1)}}{3^{2n} \times 4^{(2n-1)}} = \dfrac{2^n \times 2^{(3n+3)} \times 3^{(2n-2)}}{3^{2n} \times 2^{(4n-2)}} = \dfrac{2^{(n+3n+3-4n+2)}}{3^{(2n-2n+2)}} = \dfrac{2^5}{3^2} = \dfrac{32}{9} = 3\dfrac{5}{9}$

4. (a) $\left(\dfrac{81a^{12}}{16b^8}\right)^{\frac{3}{4}} = \left(\dfrac{3^4 a^{12}}{2^4 b^8}\right)^{\frac{3}{4}} = \dfrac{3^3 a^9}{2^3 b^6} = \dfrac{27a^9}{8b^6}$

(b) $\left(\dfrac{m^{12}}{64m^{18}}\right)^{\frac{1}{6}} = \left(\dfrac{m^{12}}{2^6 m^{18}}\right)^{\frac{1}{6}} = \left(\dfrac{m^2}{2m^3}\right) = \dfrac{1}{2m}$

(c) $\dfrac{9(x^6)^4}{27x^9 x^7} = \dfrac{9x^{24}}{27x^{16}} = \dfrac{x^8}{3}$

5. (a) $5^{(2x+1)} = \dfrac{1}{625}$

$5^{(2x+1)} = 5^{-4}$

$2x + 1 = -4$

$2x = -5$

$x = -2.5$

(b) $4^{2x} \times 16^{(x-2)} = 2^8$

$2^{4x} \times 2^{(4x-8)} = 2^8$

$2^{(8x-8)} = 2^8$

$8x - 8 = 8$

$8x = 16$

$x = 2$

(c) $3^{2x} - 12.3^x = -27$

Let $3^x = y$

Therefore: $y^2 - 12y + 27 = 0$

$(y - 9)(y - 3) = 0$

$y = 9 \text{ or } 3$

That is: $3^x = 3^2 \text{ or } 3^1$

$x = 2 \text{ or } 1$

6.(a) $3\log_3 m^{\frac{1}{3}} = \log_3 (m^{\frac{1}{3}})^3 = \log_3 m$

(b) $\dfrac{1}{2}\log_6 16 + 2\log_6 8 - 3\log_6 12 = \log_6\left(16^{\frac{1}{2}} \times \dfrac{8^2}{12^3}\right) = \log_6\left(4 \times \dfrac{64}{1728}\right) = \log_6\left(\dfrac{3}{27}\right)$

(c) $2\log_a x^2 \div \log_a x^6 = \dfrac{4\log_a x}{6\log_a x} = \dfrac{4}{6} = \dfrac{2}{3}$

7.(a) $\log_3\left(\dfrac{1}{9}\right) = x$

$3^x = 3^{-2}$

$x = -2$

(b) $\log_2 x + \log_2 9 - \log_2 10 = \log_2 18$

$\log_2(0.9x) = \log_2 18$

$0.9x = 18$

$x = 20$

(c) $\log_8(x + 6) - \log_8(x - 1) = 1$

$\log_8 \dfrac{x+6}{x-1} = \log_8 8$

$\dfrac{x+6}{x-1} = 8$

$x + 6 = 8x - 8$

$7x = 14$

$x = 2$

8. (i) $y = a\log_{10}x$

$6 = 3\log_{10}x$ | $a = 3$ and $y = 6$

That is: $2 = \log_{10}x$

Therefore: $x = 10^2 = 100$

(ii) $2^{2n} + 2^n - 12 = 0$

Let $x = 2^n$

Therefore, $x^2 + x - 12 = 0$

That is: $(x + 4)(x - 3) = 0$ | $x = -4$ is inadmissible because $2^n \neq -4$

$x = 3$ or -4

Therefore: $x = 3$ is the solution

That is: $2^n = 3$

$n\log2 = \log3$ | Taking logarithm on both sides

$n = \dfrac{\log3}{\log2} = \dfrac{0.4771}{0.3010} = 1.585$

(iii) $\log_2 50 = \dfrac{\log_{10}50}{\log_{10}2} = \dfrac{\log_{10}50}{\log_{10}2} = \dfrac{1.6990}{0.3010} = 5.645$

10. PATTERNS, SEQUENCES AND SERIES

A **pattern** is the repeated or regular way in which something happens or is done. Pattern is the general term for any recognisable regularity in a given observation. Examples where patterns occur include weather, designs and number sequences. All patterns follow some order or set of rules. There are linear patterns and non-linear patterns and can be represented in a number of ways.

Examples:

- R G Y R G Y R G Y R G Y ....
- White, Black, Red, White, Black, Red ....
- 1, 2, 3, 4, 1, 2, 3, 4, 1, 2, 3, 4 ....

When one or more terms or elements in a pattern build in a systematic way to form a larger pattern, the result is a growth pattern:

- RGY, RRGGYY, RRRGGGYYY ....
- 01, 0011,000111, 00001111 ....

A number pattern follows a formula. If given an initial set of numbers, the next number is predictable. For example: 2, 5, 8, 11, 14 .... is a number pattern where each element is 3 more than the preceding element. In order to find a missing number in a sequence we do the following:

- Determine if the order of numbers is ascending (getting larger in value) or descending (becoming smaller in value).

- Find the difference between numbers that are next to each other.

- Use the difference between numbers to find the missing number.

Example:

Find the missing number: 15, 13, x, 9

The difference between the first two numbers is 2. Therefore, x is 11.

POSITION NUMBERS

Consider the following pattern and the position numbers of each of the three elements A, B and C:

Element:	A	B	C	A	B	C	A	B	C	A	B	C	A	B	C
Position Number:	1	2	3	4	5	6	7	8	9	10	11	12	13	14	15

- A has positions 1, 4, 7, 10 ....
- B has positions 2, 5, 8, 11 ....
- C has positions 3, 6, 9, 12 ....

Each element's position number increases by 3 with reference to its previous position.

DESCRIBING PATTERNS BY A SIMPLE RULE

In the following sets of number patterns, the words in brackets describe each pattern. This is called the **rule**.

Examples:

- 1, 6, 11, 16, ___, ___   (add 5)
- 2, 8, 2, 8, ___, ___   (alternating numbers)
- 28, 24, 20, 16, ___, ___   (subtract 4)
- 5, 10, 15, 20, ___, ___   (skip count by 5)
- 0, 1, 1, 2, 3, 5, 8, 13, ___, ___   (add the two previous numbers)

The last pattern is known as the **Fibonacci sequence**. More examples:

- 1, 3, 7, 15 ……..   (multiply by 2 and add 1)
- 1, 4, 10 ……….   (multiply by 2 and add 2)
- 3, 4, 6 …………   (subtract 1 and then multiply by 2)
- 4, 5, 7 ………..   (multiply by 2 and subtract 3)
- 8, 10, 14 ……..   (subtract 3 and multiply by 2)

SEQUENCES

Sequences are a string of numbers that follow a set of rules which determine the number (or term) next to each other. Any particular term in the sequence is referred to as the nth term. It is usually represented by the notation a_n or T_n. For example, the 3rd term is represented by a_3 or T_3. A sequence is, therefore, a list of numbers, the order in which the numbers are listed is important.

- **Arithmetic Sequence:** This is a sequence where a term is obtained by adding a fixed number to the immediately preceding term

The pattern 3, 5, 7, 9, 11, 13 …. is an arithmetic sequence where the fixed number is 2. The fixed number added is called the **common difference**.

- **Geometric sequence:** This is a sequence where a term is obtained by multiplying the immediately preceding term by a fixed number.

The pattern 2, 6, 18, 54, 162 … is a geometric sequence where the fixed number is 3. The fixed number that multiplies is called the **common ratio**.

- **Fibonacci sequence:** This is a sequence where two immediately preceding terms are added to get the next term.

The pattern 0, 1, 1, 2, 3, 5, 8, 13 …… is called a Fibonacci sequence. When the sequence is from a defined set of numbers, we refer to it as a finite sequence. If the set is open (e.g. all positive integers) then a sequence from that set is an infinite sequence.

FINDING THE SEQUENCE WHEN ITS nth TERM IS KNOWN

Example:

Suppose we have the formula for the nth term as $T_n = 2n - 1$.
Let us substitute 1, 2 and 3, in turn for n:

$T_1 = 2(1) - 1 = 1$

$T_2 = 2(2) - 1 = 3$

$T_3 = 2(3) - 1 = 5$

The sequence for which the nth term is 2n − 1 is: 1, 3, 5 ....

FINDING THE Nth TERM OF A SEQUENCE

Example 1:

Find the nth term of the sequence 4, 7, 10, 13 ....

Now to get 4, which is term 1, we multiply the term number by 3 and add 1. We check to see whether this formula works for the next term as well:

$3 \times 2 + 1 = 7$

The formula works, so we can see that 3n + 1 is the nth term. This is expressed as:

$T_n = 3n + 1$

Example 2:

What term would 58 be in the sequence 4, 7, 10, 13 ....

We can use the formula for the nth term to answer this question.

$T_n = 3n + 1$

$58 = 3n + 1$

$3n = 57$

$n = 19$

Therefore, the 19th term in the given sequence is 58.

Example 3:

Find the nth term of the sequence 7, 11, 15, 19 ....

The difference between consecutive terms is 4. Consider the 4 times table 4, 8, 12, 16, 20... which can be stated as 4n where n = 1, 2, 3 etc. Add 3 to the first number of this to get the first term of the given sequence. Do the same for the other numbers.

Therefore, the nth term of the given sequence is: $T_n = 4n + 3$

THE METHOD OF FINITE DIFFERENCES

The nth term of a sequence can be determined by calculating the differences between successive terms and then the differences between successive differences themselves. We stop when constant differences are obtained.

- The relationship will be **linear** (i.e. of the form $T_n = an + b$) if the **first differences are constant**.

- The relationship will be **quadratic** (i.e. of the form $T_n = an^2 + bn + c$) if the **second differences are constant**.

- The relationship will be **cubic** (i.e. of the form $an^3 + bn^2 + cn + d$) if the **third differences are constant**.

Example 1:

Consider the number sequence: -1, 1, 3, 5, 7, 9 ....

The differences between successive terms are: 2, 2, 2, 2, 2. We have obtained constant difference of 2 between successive terms. Therefore, the relationship is $T_n = an + b$. We need to determine the values of a, b. This is done by substituting any two numbers from the given sequence. If we choose the first two numbers, we have the following equations:

$-1 = a + b$ -------------------- (1)

$1 = 2a + b$ ------------------ (2)

(2) − (1) gives $a = 2$ --------------- (3)

Substituting $a = 2$ into (1), we get: $b = -3$

Therefore: $T_n = 2n - 3$

Example 2:

Consider the number sequence: 5, 12, 21, 32, 45, 60 ....

The first differences between successive terms are 7, 9, 11, 13, 15.

The second differences between successive differences are 2, 2, 2, 2.

We have obtained a constant difference of 2 between successive differences. Therefore, the relationship is: $T_n = an^2 + bn + c$. We need to determine the values of a, b and c. This is done by substituting any three numbers from the given sequence. If we choose the first three numbers, we have three equations:

$5 = a + b + c$ ---------------------- (1)

$12 = 4a + 2b + c$ ------------------ (2)

$21 = 9a + 3b + c$ ------------------ (3)

(2) − (1) gives $7 = 3a + b$ ----------------------- (4)

(3) − (2) gives $9 = 5a + b$ ----------------------- (5)

(5) − (4) gives $2 = 2a$ --------------------------- (6)

Therefore: $a = 1$ From (6)

Substituting $a = 1$ in (4) we get: $b = 4$

Substituting for a and b in (1) we get: $c = 0$

Therefore: $T_n = n^2 + 4n$

Example 3:

Consider the number sequence: 4, 11, 30, 67, 128, 219 ....

The first differences between successive terms are 7, 19, 37, 61, 91.

The second differences between successive differences are 12, 18, 24, 30.

The third differences between successive differences are 6, 6, 6.

We have obtained constant difference of 6 between successive terms. Therefore, the relationship is $T_n = an^3 + bn^2 + cn + d$. We need to determine the values of a, b, c and d. This is done by substituting any four numbers. If we choose the first four numbers, we have the following equations:

$4 = a + b + c + d$ ------------------- (1)

$11 = 8a + 4b + 2c + d$ ------------ (2)

$30 = 27a + 9b + 3c + d$ ----------- (3)

$67 = 64a + 16b + 4c + d$ --------- (4)

Therefore: a = 1 | From (10)

Substituting a = 1 in (8), we get b = 0

Substituting a = 1 and b = 0 in (5), we get: c = 0

Substituting the above values for 'a' 'b' and 'c in (4), we get d = 3

Therefore, $T_n = n^3 + 3$

(2) − (1) gives $7 = 7a + 3b + c$ ---------------- (5)

(3) − (2) gives $19 = 19a + 5b + c$ ------------- (6)

(4) − (3) gives $37 = 37a + 7b + c$ ------------- (7)

(6) − (5) gives $12 = 12a + 2b$ ------------------ (8)

(7) − (6) gives $18 = 18a + 2b$ ------------------ (9)

(9) − (8) gives $6 = 6a$ -------------------------- (10)

ARITHMETIC AND GEOMETRIC SERIES (PROGRESSIONS)

A series is the sum of a finite or infinite set of numbers in a sequence.

The Greek alphabet capital sigma ($\sum$) is used to represent the sum of a sequence.

- $\sum_{i=1}^{4} 3r$ means the sum of 3, 6, 9 and 12 (i.e. substitute 1 to 4 for r in 3r)

- $\sum_{i=1}^{100} i$ represents the sum of a finite sequence of numbers from 1 to 100.

- $\sum_{1}^{\infty} i$ represents the sum of an infinite sequence of numbers.

Example:

Write in detail the sum expressed by $\sum_{1}^{6} r^2$

$$\sum_{1}^{6} r^2 = 1^1 + 2^2 + 3^2 + 4^2 + 5^2 + 6^2$$

ARITHMETIC PROGRESSION (AP)

An Arithmetic Series or Arithmetic Progression (AP) has a common difference. Let us call the first term of an arithmetic progression 'a' and the common difference 'd'.

The sum (S_n) of such a progression with n terms and the last term 'l' can be written as:

$S_n = a + (a + d) + (a + 2d) \ldots\ldots\ldots\ldots (l - 2d) + (l - d) + l$ -------- (1)

We can write the above starting with 'l' as follows:

$S_n = l + (l - d) + (l - 2d) \ldots\ldots\ldots\ldots (a + 2d) + (a + d) + a$ --------- (2)

Adding (1) and (2):

$2S_n = (a + l) + (a + l) + (a + l) \ldots\ldots\ldots\ldots (a + l) + (a + l) + (a + l)$

There are n such (a + l) and therefore:

$2S_n = n(a + l)$

Hence, $S_n = \dfrac{n(a + l)}{2}$

In other words, the sum of an AP is equal to half the number of terms multiplied by the sum of the first term and the last term. We know that 'l' is the nth term T_n and 'l' can be formulated as: $T_n = a + (n - 1)d$ as when n is replaced by 1, 2, 3 etc., we obtain the various terms of the sequence. Thus we can state the formula for the sum of AP, S_n as:

$$S_n = \frac{n(a + a + (n - 1)d)}{2} \quad \text{or} \quad S_n = \frac{n(2a + (n - 1)d)}{2}$$

The formula for the common difference d can be stated as $d = T_n - T_{(n-1)}$

Example 1:

Find the 8th term of the Arithmetic Series: $3 + 5 + 7 + \ldots\ldots$

Here, a = 3 and d = 2 $\boxed{d = 5 - 3 \text{ or } 7 - 5}$

$T_n = a + (n - 1)d$

$T_8 = 3 + (8 - 1) \times 2 = 3 + 14 = 17$

Example 2:

Find the first term and the common difference of an Arithmetic Progression if the 6th term is -10 and the 10th term is -22.

$T_n = a + (n - 1) \times d$

$-10 = a + (6 - 1) \times d$

$-10 = a + 5d$ .... (1)

Similarly: $-22 = a + 9d$ .... (2)

(1) – (2) gives: $12 = -4d$

$d = -3$

$-10 = a + 5 \times -3$ | Substituting 'd' into (1) |

$a = 5$

Therefore, the first term of the AP is 5 and the common difference is -3

Example 3:

Find the sum of $1 + 2 + 3 + 4 + 5 + \ldots + 80$

$S_n = \dfrac{n(a + l)}{2}$

$S_n = \dfrac{80(1 + 80)}{2}$

$S_n = 40 \times 81$

$S_n = 3240$

Example 4:

Find the sum of $4 + 7 + 10 + \ldots$ (50th term)

Here, $n = 50$, $a = 4$ and $d = 3$

$S_n = \dfrac{n(2a + (n - 1)d)}{2}$

$S_n = \dfrac{50(2 \times 4 + (50 - 1) \times 3)}{2}$

$S_n = 25(8 + 49 \times 3)$

$S_n = 25 \times 155$

$S_n = 3875$

ARITHMETIC MEAN

The arithmetic mean of any two numbers is a number inserted between the two numbers to form an **Arithmetic Progression**.

Example 5:

Find the arithmetic mean of 8 and 24

Let the arithmetic mean be x. Then 8, x and 24 will form an AP. That is, the common difference between the first two numbers and the last two numbers are equal. We can express this as the following:

$x - 8 = 24 - x$

$2x = 24 + 8 = 32$

$x = 16$

The arithmetic mean = 16. We have thus inserted 16 between 8 and 24 so that all three numbers form an AP.

The **Arithmetic Mean** of two numbers A and B $= \dfrac{(A + B)}{2}$

We can also insert more than one arithmetic mean between any two numbers so that all the numbers together form an AP.

Example:

Insert three arithmetic means between 5 and 21

Let the three arithmetic means be x_1, x_2 and x_3.

Therefore 5, $x_1, x_2, x_3, 21$ form an AP. That is, a = 5 and $T_5 = 21$.

$T_5 = a + 4d$

$21 = 5 + 4 \times d$

$4d = 16$

$d = 4$

Therefore, $x_1 = 9, x_2 = 13, x_3 = 17$

The three arithmetic means are 9, 13 and 17.

GEOMETRIC PROGRESSION (GP)

Unlike an arithmetic progression, a geometric progression has a common ratio. Let us call the first term of a geometric progression 'a' and the common ratio 'r'. The sum (S_n) of a geometric progression with n terms and the last term 'l' can be written as:

$$S_n = a + ar + ar^2 + ar^3 + \ldots\ldots\ldots + ar^{(n-2)} + ar^{(n-1)} \text{ ----------- (1)}$$

The nth term (or T_n) is $ar^{(n-1)}$ because all terms have 'a' but the power of 'r' of any term is one less than the number of the term (i.e. the third term has r^2, fourth term has r^3 and so on).

$$\text{Therefore: } T_n = ar^{(n-1)}$$

Multiplying each term in equation (1) by r and writing the result under the next term:

$$rS_n = ar + ar^2 + ar^3 + \ldots\ldots\ldots + ar^{(n-1)} + ar^n \text{ --------------- (2)}$$

(1) – (2) gives $S_n - rS_n = a - ar^n$

That is, $(1 - r)S_n = a(1 - r^n)$. Therefore:

$$S_n = \frac{a(1 - r^n)}{1 - r} \qquad \text{(Valid only if r < 1)}$$

When r is less than 1, the sum of a geometric progression converges to a definite value when n is very large (i.e. when n tends to infinity). If r is less than 1 and n tends to infinity, r^n will tend to zero. So, the above formula when n tends to infinity becomes:

$$S_{infinity} = \frac{a}{1 - r}$$

The formula for the sum of n terms of a geometric progression when r is greater than 1 is written as:

$$S_n = \frac{a(r^n - 1)}{1 - r} \qquad \text{(Valid only if r > 1).}$$

A geometric progression is said to be divergent when r is greater than 1 and convergent when r is less than 1.

GEOMETRIC MEAN

Geometric mean of any two numbers is a number inserted between the two numbers which along with the given number will form a geometric progression.

Example:

Find the geometric mean of 2 and 32.

Let the geometric mean be x. Then, 2, x and 32 will form a GP. That is, the common ratio between the first two and the last two numbers are equal.

Therefore: $\dfrac{x}{2} = \dfrac{32}{x}$

$x^2 = 64$

$x = \sqrt{64} = 8$

Therefore, the geometric mean is 8.

The geometric mean of two numbers A and B $= \sqrt{AB}$. We can also insert more than one geometric mean between any two numbers so that all the numbers together form a GP.

Example:

Insert three geometric means between 2 and 162.

Let the three geometric means be x_1, x_2 and x_3. Therefore 2, x_1, x_2, x_3 and 162 form a GP. That is, a = 2 and T_5 = 162.

$T_5 = ar^4$

$162 = 2 \times r^4$

$r^4 = 81$

$r = 3$

Therefore, $x_1 = 6$, $x_2 = 18$ and $x_3 = 54$

The three Geometric Means are 6, 18 and 54.

BINOMIAL SERIES

An expression involving the sum or difference of two numbers is a **binomial**.

Examples:

- $a + b$
- $2a + 4$
- $3x - y$

A binomial can be raised to a power. These when expanded give a binomial series. There are several related series that are known as the **binomial series**.

The most general is:

$$(a + b)^n = {}^nc_0a^n + {}^nc_1a^{(n-1)}b + {}^nc_2a^{(n-2)}b^2 \dots {}^nc_{(n-1)}ab^{(n-1)} + {}^nc_nb^n$$

$T_{(r+1)}$ is called the **General Term** in the binomial expansion. The general term in the binomial expansion of $(a + b)^n$ means any term that may be required to be found.

$$T_{(r+1)} = {}^nC_r a^{(n-r)} b^r \qquad \text{where } r = 0, 1, 2, 3 \dots\dots\dots\dots$$

Example:

Find the third term in the expansion of $(a + b)^5$

$T_3 = {}^5C_2a^3b^2$ | The third term is obtained when $r = 2$

The series is true for any positive integral value of n. Note that the coefficients of the terms are ${}^nc_0, {}^nc_1, {}^nc_2$ etc. This method of finding the coefficients of terms is called the ${}^nc_r$ **method.**

The binomial series is true for negative values and fractional values of n as well if $\left|\dfrac{b}{a}\right| < 1$

PASCAL'S TRIANGLE

The coefficients of the various terms could be easily obtained using Pascal's Triangle.

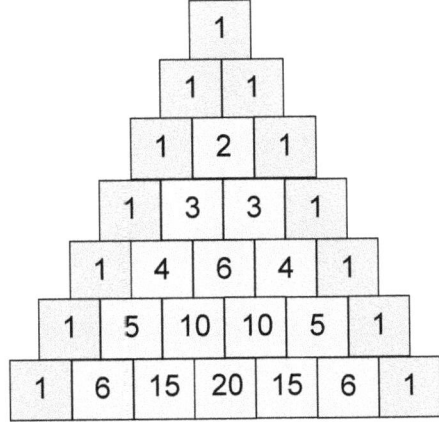

How are the numbers in the Pascal's Triangle built up?

1. Write the number "1" at the top

2. On the next row write two 1's, forming a triangle.

3. On each subsequent row start and end with 1's and compute each interior term by adding together the two numbers above it.

The numbers in the Pascal's triangle, starting with row 3 are the coefficients of the various terms in a given binomial expansion.

> **Example 1:**
>
> $$(a + b)^2 = a^2 + 2ab + b^2$$
>
> Here the coefficients of a^2, ab and b^2 are 1, 2, and 1 respectively. These numbers are seen in row 3 of the Pascal's Triangle.

Notice that in the expansion of $(a + b)^2$, the first term is a^2, in the second term the power of a is reduced by 1 and b is included, and in the third term a's power further reduced by 1 and b's power is increased by 1. In all binomial expansions, this will be the case.

> **Example 2:**
>
> $$(a + b)^3 = a^3 + 3a^2b + 3ab^2 + b^3$$
>
> Here, the coefficients of a^3, a^2b, ab^2 and b^3 are 1, 3, 3, 1 and these numbers are seen in row 4 of the Pascal's triangle.

> **Example 3:**
>
> $$(a - b)^5 = a^5 - 5a^4b + 10\,a^3b^2 - 10a^2b^3 + 5ab^4 - b^5$$
>
> Here, the coefficients of a^5, a^4b, a^3b^2, and a^2b^3, ab^4 and b are: 1, -5, 10, -10, 5, -1. The numbers are taken from row 6 of Pascal's triangle, but the sign alternates starting from positive.

Examples of the **alternative method** of finding values of the coefficients of the terms using ^nC_r are given below. In this case, the positive and negative signs for the coefficients are taken care of automatically.

> **Example 1:**
>
> Expand $(1 + x)^5$
>
> $$(1 + x)^5 = {}^5c_0(1)^5 + {}^5c_1(1)^{(5-1)}x^1 + {}^5c_2(1)^{(5-2)}x^2 + {}^5c_3(1)^{(5-3)}x^3 + {}^5c_4(1)^{(5-4)}x^4 + {}^5c_5x^5$$
>
> $$(1 + x)^5 = 1 + 5x + \frac{5 \times 4}{2}x^2 + \frac{5 \times 4 \times 3}{3 \times 2}x^3 + 5x^4 + x^5$$
>
> $$(1 + x)^5 = 1 + 5x + 10x^2 + 10x^3 + 5x^4 + x^5$$

> **Example 2:**
>
> Expand $(2 - a)^6$
>
> $$(2 - a)^6 = {}^6c_0(2)^6 + {}^6c_1(2)^5(-a)^1 + {}^6c_2(2)^4(-a)^2 + {}^6c_3(2)^3(-a)^3 + {}^6c_4(2)^2(-a)^4 + {}^6c_5(2)^1(-a)^5$$
> $$+ {}^6c_6(2)^0(-a)^6$$
>
> $$(2 - a)^6 = 64 - 192a + 240a^2 - 180a^3 + 60a^4 - 12a^5 + a^6$$

Example 3:

Write down the 4th term of $(p + q)^7$

The 4th term $= 7c_3p^4q^3 = \dfrac{7 \times 6 \times 5}{3 \times 2}p^4q^3 = 35p^4q^3$

Example 4:

Find the value of $\sqrt{1.06}$

$\sqrt{1.06} = (1 + 0.06)^{1/2} = {}^{1/2}c_0(1)^{1/2} + {}^{1/2}c_1(1)^{-1/2}(0.06) + {}^{1/2}c_2(1)^{-3/2}(0.06)^2$

$\qquad + {}^{1/2}c_3(1)^{-5/2}(0.06)^3 + \ldots\ldots$

$= 1 + 0.5 \times (0.06) + \dfrac{0.5 \times -0.5}{2}(0.0036) + \dfrac{0.5 \times -0.5 \times -1.5}{3 \times 2}(0.000216) + \ldots\ldots$

$= 1 + 0.03 - 0.00045 + 0.000013 + \ldots\ldots = 1.02956$

USE OF BINOMIAL EXPANSION TO FIND PROBABILITIES

If p is the probability of success and q the probability of failure then: $q = 1 - p$. The terms in the expansion of $(q + p)^n$ gives the successive probabilities of no success, one success, two successes and so on. The following examples illustrate the use of binomial expansion to find these probabilities.

Example 1:

Find the probability of at least two successes getting a total of 7 in four tosses of a pair of dice.

Probability of a total of seven in a single toss of a pair of dice $= \dfrac{12}{36} = \dfrac{1}{3}$

That is, $p = \dfrac{1}{3}$ and $q = \dfrac{2}{3}$

We now expand $(\dfrac{2}{3} + \dfrac{1}{3})^4$: $(\dfrac{2}{3} + \dfrac{1}{3})^4 = (\dfrac{2}{3})^4 + 4(\dfrac{2}{3})^3(\dfrac{1}{3}) + 6(\dfrac{2}{3})^2(\dfrac{1}{3})^2 + 4(\dfrac{2}{3})(\dfrac{1}{3})^3 + (\dfrac{1}{3})^4$

Now, getting a total of 7 is a success.

Probability of no success $= (\dfrac{2}{3})^4$

Probability of one success $= 4(\dfrac{2}{3})^3(\dfrac{1}{3})$

Probability of two successes $= 6(\dfrac{2}{3})^2(\dfrac{1}{3})^2$

Probability of three successes $= 4(\dfrac{2}{3})(\dfrac{1}{3})^3$

Probability of four successes $= (\dfrac{1}{3})^4$

Probability of at least two successes $= 6(\dfrac{2}{3})^2(\dfrac{1}{3})^2 + 4(\dfrac{2}{3})(\dfrac{1}{3})^3 + (\dfrac{1}{3})^4$

$= 6 \times \dfrac{4}{9} \times \dfrac{1}{9} + 4 \times \dfrac{2}{3} \times \dfrac{1}{27} + \dfrac{1}{81} = \dfrac{24}{81} + \dfrac{8}{81} + \dfrac{1}{81} = \dfrac{33}{81} = \dfrac{11}{27}$

Example 2:

If 10% of an item manufactured are defective, what is the probability that out of five items chosen at random:
(a) none will be defective
(b) one will be defective
(c) at least two will be defective

Let us call getting a defective a success. Then, p = 0.1 and q = 0.9.

We expand $(q + p)^5$

$(0.9 + 0.1)^5 = 1(0.9)^5 + 5(0.9)^4(0.1) + 10(0.9)^3(0.1)^2 + 10(0.9)^2(0.1)^3 + 5(0.9)(0.1)^4 + (0.1)^5$

(a) Probability that none will be defective = $(0.9)^5$ = 0.59049

(b) Probability one will be defective = $5(0.9)^4(0.1)$ = 0.32805

(c) Probability that at least two will be defective = 1 − (0.59049 + 0.32805) = 0.08146

MATHEMATICAL INDUCTION

Mathematical Induction is a special method of proving certain formulae. It is widely used in research. It is especially useful to prove properties of sequences, like the natural numbers as can be seen from the examples given below. The method involves the following steps:

Step 1: We prove that a given formula is true for the base value, usually 1

Step 2: We assume that the formula is true for n = k

Step 3: We show that if it is true for n = k, then it is true for n = k + 1

Step 4: We conclude that the formula is true for all values of n

Example 1:

Use mathematical induction to prove that:

$$1 + 2 + 3 + ... + n = \frac{n(n + 1)}{2}$$ for all positive integers n.

Let P(n) be: $1 + 2 + 3 + ... + n = \frac{n(n + 1)}{2}$

STEP 1: We first show that P(1) is true.

When n = 1, Left Hand Side = 1

Right Hand Side: $\frac{1(1 + 1)}{2}$ = 1

Therefore, P(1) is true.

Example 1(Continued):

STEP 2: We assume that $P(k)$ is true. That is:

$$P(k) = 1 + 2 + 3 + \ldots + k = \frac{k}{2}(k + 1)$$

Add $k + 1$ to both sides:

$$1 + 2 + 3 + \ldots + k + (k + 1) = \frac{k}{2}(k + 1) + (k + 1) = (k + 1)(\frac{k}{2} + 1) = \frac{(k + 1)(k + 2)}{2} = P(k + 1)$$

That is, on assuming that $P(n)$ is true for $n = k$, it is also true for $n = k + 1$.
Therefore, $P(n)$ is true for all positive integer values of n.

Example 2:

Use mathematical induction to prove that:

$$1^2 + 2^2 + 3^2 + \ldots + n^2 = \frac{n}{6}(n + 1)(2n + 1) \text{ for all positive integers n.}$$

Let $P(n)$ be: $1^2 + 2^2 + 3^2 + \ldots + n^2 = \frac{n}{6}(n + 1)(2n + 1)$

STEP 1: We first show that $p(1)$ is true.
When $n = 1$, Left Hand Side $= 1$
Right Hand Side: $\frac{1}{6}(2)(3) = 1$
Therefore, $P(1)$ is true.

STEP 2: We assume that $P(k)$ is true. That is:

$$P(k) = 1^2 + 2^2 + 3^2 + \ldots + k^2 = \frac{k}{6}(k + 1)(2k + 1)$$

Add $(k + 1)^2$ to both sides: $1^2 + 2^2 + 3^2 + \ldots + k^2 + (k + 1)^2 = \frac{k}{6}(k + 1)(2k + 1) + (k + 1)^2$

$$= \frac{1}{6}(k + 1)[k(2k + 1) + 6(k + 1)] = \frac{1}{6}(k + 1)(2k^2 + 7k + 6) = \frac{1}{6}(k + 1)(k + 2)(2k + 3) = P(k + 1)$$

That is, on assuming that $P(n)$ is true for $n = k$, it is also true for $n = k + 1$
Therefore, $P(n)$ is true for all values of n.

Example 3:

Prove that $3^n > n^2$ for $n = 1$, $n = 2$
Use the mathematical induction to prove that $3^n > n^2$ for n, a positive integer greater than 2.

Let $P(n)$ be: $3^n > n^2$

STEP 1: When $n = 1$, LHS $= 3$ and RHS $= 1$

3 is greater than 1 and hence $P(1)$ is true.

Let us also show that $P(2)$ is true.

LHS $= 3^2 = 9$

RHS $= 2^2 = 4$

Hence $P(2)$ is also true.

Example 3(Continued):

STEP 2: We assume that P(k) is true

$3^k > k^2$

$3 \times 3^k > 3 \times k^2$ | Multiply both sides of the inequality by |

For k >, 2, we can write

$k^2 > 2k$ and $k^2 > 1$

That is, $2k^2 > 2k + 1$ | Adding the above together |

Adding k^2 to both sides:

$3k^2 > k^2 + 2k + 1$

$3k^2 > (k + 1)^2$

But, $3 \times 3^k > 3 \times k^2$

i.e. $3^{(k + 1)} > 3k^2$

Therefore: $3^{(k + 1)} > (k + 1)^2$

Hence, P(k + 1) is true.

Therefore P(n) is true for all values of n greater than 2.

ALTERNATIVE METHOD

Example:

      Prove that $7^n - 3^n$ is divisible by 4 for all positive integer values of n.

Let $P(n) = 7^n - 3^n$

When n = 1: $7^n - 3^n = 7 - 3 = 4$

Therefore, the statement is true when n = 1

We assume that it is true for n = k

That is, $P(k) = 7^k - 3^k = 4D$ | 4 times some value |

$7^k = 4D + 3^k$

Now, $P(k + 1) = 7^{(k + 1)} - 3^{(k + 1)} = 7 \times 7^k - 3 \times 3^k = 7(4D + 3^k) - 3 \times 3^k$

$= 28D + 7 \times 3^k - 3 \times 3^k = 28D + 4 \times 3^k = 4(7D + 3^k)$

The statement is true also for n = k + 1

Therefore, the statement is true for all positive integer n.

MISCELLANEOUS PROBLEMS

A1. (a) Three different types of symbols are put on a straight line as shown below. Which two symbols continue this pattern?

$$ĐÑĐÇĐÑĐÇĐÑĐÇ??$$

(b) Study the following pattern and answer the question below:

$X_2 = 2 + 1$

$X_3 = 3 + 2 + 1$

$X_4 = 4 + 3 + 2 + 1$

What is the value of $X_6 - X_2$?

A2. Find the nth term of the sequence: 0, 1, 3, 6, 10

A3.(a) You are to lay the following figures on the floor by repeating the patterns shown covering a length of 52cm. How many squares would be needed?

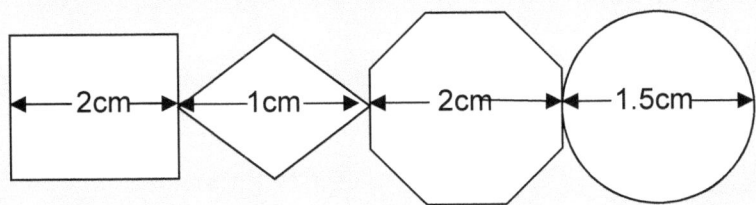

(b) Find the general term of the sequence: 5, 9, 13, 17, ...

A4. (a) Find the next number in the sequence: 21, 25, 33, 49, 81, (?)

(b) Find the general term of the sequence: 0, 3, 8, 15, 24, ...

A5. (a) What is the next term in the number pattern 91, 45, 22, ...?

(b) Fill in the missing figures in the following table:

4	5	9	?	?	?	?	?	?
2	2	4	7	5	7	7	1	3
2	3	5	6	5	8	9	2	4
4	6	?	?	?	?	?	?	?

A6. Find the nth term of the sequence: 2, 0, 0, 2, 6 ....

A7. Find a formula for the general term of the sequence. The sequence starts with $n = 1$.

$$\frac{2}{6}, \frac{4}{9}, \frac{6}{12}, \frac{8}{15}, \ldots$$

Write down the 7th term.

A8. Calculate the first, second and third difference for the sequence:

1, 4, 17, 45, 93, 166, ...

Hence determine the nth term of the sequence.

B1. Find the tenth term and the sum of the first ten terms for each of the following Arithmetic Progressions:

(a) 4, 7, 10, 13, ...

(b) 3, 7, 11, 15, ...

(c) 25, 20, 15, 10, ...

(d) -6, -9, -12, -15, ...

(e) 3, 8, 13, 18, ...

(f) $\frac{1}{2}$, 1, $1\frac{1}{2}$, 2, ...

(g) 1, $\frac{5}{3}$, $\frac{7}{3}$, 3, ...

(h) 4, $3\frac{3}{4}$, $3\frac{1}{2}$, $3\frac{1}{4}$, ...

B2. Insert the indicated number of Arithmetic Means between each of the following pairs of numbers.

(a) 8 and 20 (1 mean)

(b) -3 and 15 (1 mean)

(c) 3 and 39 (5 means)

(d) 12 and 44 (7 means)

(e) 4 and 54 (9 means)

(f) 6.333 and 11 (6 means)

(g) 7.8 and 21 (5 means)

(h) -5.65 and -17.8 (8 means)

B3. Find the eighth term and the sum of the first eight terms for each of the following Geometric Progressions:

(a) 1, 2, 4, 8, ...

(b) 3, 6, 12, 24, ...

(c) 2, 6, 18, 54, ...

(d) 9, 3, 1, $\frac{1}{3}$, ...

(e) 2, 1, $\frac{1}{2}$, $\frac{1}{4}$, ...

(f) 5, -10, 20, -40, ...

(g) $\frac{1}{6}$, $\frac{1}{8}$, $\frac{3}{32}$, $\frac{9}{128}$, ...

(h) 0.2, 0.8, 3.2, 12.8, ...

B4. Insert the indicated number of Geometric Means between each of the following pairs of numbers:

(a) 4 and 16 (1)

(b) 2 and 162 (3)

(c) 3 and -96 (4)

(d) 5 and $\frac{5}{64}$ (5)

(e) 6 and 6144 (4)

(f) $\frac{1}{2}$ and $\frac{1}{162}$ (3)

(g) 7 and 112 (3)

(h) -4 and $\frac{1}{32}$ (6)

B5. Use the formula $S_n = \dfrac{n(2a + (n-1)\,d)}{2}$ to find the sum of each of the following AP's:

(a) $2 + 7 + 12 +$ .... to 10 terms

(b) $6 + 8 + 10 +$ .... to 12 terms

(c) $3 + 5 + 7 +$ .... to 20 terms

(d) $8 + 9\frac{1}{2} + 11 +$ .... to 14 terms

(e) $-8 - 11 - 14 -$ .... to 9 terms

(f) $1\frac{1}{6} + 2 + 2\frac{5}{6} +$ ... to 8 terms

(g) $4 + 6.5 + 9 +$ .... 18 terms

(h) $-4.4 - 2.3 - 0.2 +$ ... to 16 terms

B6.(a) In an arithmetic progression with a common difference of 3, the 12th term is 38. Find the first term.

(b) In an arithmetic progression, the fourth term is 21 and the 9th term is 56. Find the 15th term.

(c) In an arithmetic progression the first term is -7 and the 14th term is 58. Find the sum of the first 12 terms

(d) The sum of n terms of an arithmetic progression is $\dfrac{n(3n-15)}{2}$. What are the first four terms?

(e) The ninth term of an Arithmetic progression is 1 and the sum of the first five terms equals the sum of the first eleven terms. Find the 17th term.

(f) How many terms of the series $3 + 8 + 13 + 18 +$ ... will add up to 255?

(g) Find the sum of all the integers between 1 and 100 that are divisible by 7.

(h) The sum of n terms of an AP is $\dfrac{n(3n+7)}{2}$. What is the 8th term?

B7. Using the formula $T_n = ar^{(n-1)}$, find the number of terms in each of the following Geometric Series. Find also the sum in each case.

(a) $1 + 3 + 9 +$ .... $+ 729$

(b) $2 + 4 + 8 +$ .... $+ 2048$

(c) $8 + 4 + 2 +$ .... $+ 0.125$

(d) $\dfrac{1}{2}, \dfrac{1}{4}, \dfrac{1}{8} +$ .... $+ \dfrac{1}{256}$

(e) $1\frac{1}{2} + 4\frac{1}{2} + 13\frac{1}{2} +$ .... $+ 3280\frac{1}{2}$

(f) $2 + 0.6 + 0.18 +$ .... $+ 0.00486$

(g) $2 + 10 + 50$ .... $+ 31250$

(h) $\dfrac{1}{8} - \dfrac{1}{4} + \dfrac{1}{2} +$ .... -64

B8. (a) The 5th term of a GP is $\dfrac{64}{81}$ and the 7th term is $\dfrac{256}{729}$. Find the first term and the common ratio.

(b) The first term of a geometric sequence is 8 and the sum to infinity is 12. Find the common ratio.

C1. Write out the expansion of each of the following:

(a) $(1 + x)^3$

(b) $(2 + x)^4$

(c) $(m - n)^5$

(d) $(a + 2)^6$

(e) $(2a - 3b)^7$

(f) $(1 + 0.2)^4$

(g) $(2 + 0.05)^3$

(h) $(3p + 1)^6$

C2. What is the 4th term in the expansion of $(2x + 3y)^7$?

C3. Using the binomial expansion find the value of $(1.02)^{1/2}$?

C4. What is the 5th term in the expansion of $(1 + 0.04)^{-3}$?

C5. Write down the 4th term in the expansion of $(1 + x^2)^{1/2}$?

C6. What is the probability that in five throws of a die, 3 appears twice?

C7. Use mathematical induction to prove that: $1^3 + 2^3 + 3^3 + \dots n^3 = \dfrac{n^2(n + 1)^2}{4}$ for all positive integers n.

C8. Use mathematical induction to prove that $17^n - 12^n$ is divisible by 5.

PRACTICAL APPLICATIONS

1. A land purchased for $120,000 appreciates in value at the rate of 6% per annum. What would be its value after 8 years?

$T_8 = ar^7 = 120{,}000 \times (1.06)^7 = 180435.61$

Value after 8 years $= \$180{,}435.61$

2. A motor car bought for $45,000 depreciates in value at the rate of 20% per year of the original value. What would be its value at the end of 4 years?

$a = 45{,}000,\ d = -9000,\ n = 3$

$T_4 = a + 3d = 45000 - 3 \times 9000 = 45000 - 27000 = \$18{,}000$

The value of the motor car at the end of 4 years $= \$18000$

3. Peter deposited $100 in his bank savings account on the first day of January and thereafter made deposits every month increasing the previous month's deposit by $40 of $140, $180, $220 and so on. How many such monthly deposits are required to be made to have a total deposit of $5700 in the account?

$a = 100,\ d = 40,\ S_n = 5700$

$$S_n = \frac{n(2a + (n - 1)d)}{2}$$

$$5700 = \frac{n(200 + (n - 1) \times 40)}{2}$$

$$5700 = \frac{n(160 + 40n)}{2}$$

$11400 = 160n + 40n^2$

$40n^2 + 160n - 11400 = 0$

$n^2 + 4n - 285 = 0$

$(n + 19)(n - 15) = 0$

$n = 15$

Number of monthly deposits required $= 15$

A1. (a) Đ and Ñ

(b) $X_6 = 6 + 5 + 4 + 3 + 2 + 1 = 21$

$X_2 = 2 + 1 = 3$

$X_6 - X_2 = 21 - 3 = 18$

A2. 0, 1, 3, 6, 10

The first differences are: 1, 2, 3, 4

The second differences are: 1, 1, 1

Therefore, the relationship is: $T_n = an^2 + bn + c$

The equations to find a, b and c are:

$0 = a + b + c$ -------------------- (1)   (2) − (1): $1 = 3a + b$ -------------- (4)

$1 = 4a + 2b + c$ --------------- (2)   (3) − (2): $2 = 5a + b$ -------------- (5)

$3 = 9a + 3b + c$ --------------- (3)   (5) − (4): $1 = 2a$ ------------------- (6)

$a = \dfrac{1}{2}$ From (6)

$b = \dfrac{1}{2}$ Substituting $a = \dfrac{1}{2}$ in (4)

Therefore: $c = 0$

Hence, $T_n = \dfrac{1}{2}n^2 - \dfrac{1}{2}n + 0 = \dfrac{1}{2}n(n - 1)$

A3. (a) Number of squares required $= 52 \div 6.5 = 8$

(b) $a_1 = 5 = 4 \times 1 + 1$

$a_2 = 9 = 4 \times 2 + 1$

$a_3 = 13 = 4 \times 3 + 1$

$a_4 = 17 = 4 \times 4 + 1$

The general term $a_n = 4n + 1$

A4. (a) 21, 25, 33, 49, 81, (?)

Difference between consecutive numbers: 4, 8, 16, 32, 64

The required number $= 81 + 64 = 145$

(b) $a_1 = 0 = 1^2 - 1$

$a_2 = 3 = 2^2 - 1$

$a_3 = 8 = 3^2 - 1$

$a_4 = 15 = 4^2 - 1$

$a_5 = 24 = 5^2 - 1$

Therefore, the general term $a_n = n^2 - 1$

A5.(a) 91, 45, 22, ...?

The second number is $(91 - 1) \div 2 = 45$

The third number is $(45 - 1) \div 2 = 22$

The fourth number is $(22 - 1) \div 2 = 10.5$

(b) Fill in the missing figures in the following table:

4	5	9	?	?	?	?	?	?
2	2	4	7	5	7	7	1	3
2	3	5	6	5	8	9	2	4
4	6	?	?	?	?	?	?	?

The top row numbers are obtained by adding the second and the third row numbers.

The bottom row numbers are obtained by multiplying the second and the third row numbers

The missing top row numbers are: 13, 10, 15, 16, 3, 7

The missing bottom row numbers are: 20, 42, 25, 56, 63, 2, 12

A6. 2, 0, 0, 2, 6 ....

The first differences are: -2, 0, 2, 4

The second difference are: 2, 2, 2

Therefore, the relationship is: $T_n = an^2 + bn + c$

The equations to find a, b and c are:

$2 = a + b + c$ ------------------- (1)

$0 = 4a + 2b + c$ --------------- (2)

$0 = 9a + 3b + c$ --------------- (3)

$b = -5$ | Substituting $a = 1$ in (4)

(2) − (1): $-2 = 3a + b$ -------------- (4)

(3) − (2): $0 = 5a + b$ ---------------- (5)

(5) − (4): $2 = 2a$

$a = 1$

Therefore: $c = 6$

Hence: $T_n = n^2 - 5n + 6$

A7. The numerators are even numbers, given by 2n. The denominators are multiples of 3, starting at 6 instead of 3. The following list shows how the denominator is obtained.

$a_1 = 6 = 3 \times 1 + 3$

$a_2 = 9 = 3 \times 2 + 3$

$a_3 = 12 = 3 \times 3 + 3$

$a_4 = 15 = 3 \times 4 + 3$

The denominator is given by $3(n + 1)$. Therefore, the general term is $= \dfrac{2n}{3(n + 1)}$

7th Term $= \dfrac{14}{24} = \dfrac{7}{12}$

A8. 1, 4, 17, 45, 93, 166 ....

The first differences between successive terms are 3, 13, 28, 48, 73

The second differences between successive differences are 10, 15, 20, 25

The third differences between successive differences are 5, 5, 5

Therefore, the relationship is $T_n = an^3 + bn^2 + cn + d$. That is:

$1 = a + b + c + d$ ----------------------- (1)

$4 = 8a + 4b + 2c + d$ ------------------ (2)

$17 = 27a + 9b + 3c + d$ ---------------- (3)

$45 = 64a + 16b + 4c + d$ -------------- (4)

(2) − (1): $3 = 7a + 3b + c$ ---------------- (5)

(3) − (2): $13 = 19a + 5b + c$ ------------ (6)

(4) − (3): $28 = 37a + 7b + c$ ------------ (7)

(6) − (5): $10 = 12a + 2b$ ------------------ (8)

(7) − (6): $15 = 18a + 2b$ ------------------ (9)

(9) − (8): $5 = 6a$

Therefore: $a = \dfrac{5}{6}$

Substituting $a = \dfrac{5}{6}$ in (8), we get $b = 0$

Substituting $a = \dfrac{5}{6}$ and $b = 0$ in (5), we get: $c = 3 - \dfrac{35}{6} = \dfrac{17}{6}$

Substituting the above values for a, b and c in (4): $45 = \dfrac{320}{6} - \dfrac{68}{6} + d$

$45 = 42 + d$

$d = 3$

Therefore: $T_n = \dfrac{5}{6}n^3 - \dfrac{17}{6}n + 3$

B1. (a) $T_{10} = a + 9d = 4 + 9 \times 3 = 31$, $S_{10} = \dfrac{10(4 + 31)}{2} = 175$

(b) $T_{10} = a + 9d = 3 + 9 \times 4 = 39$, $S_{10} = \dfrac{10(3 + 39)}{2} = 210$

(c) $T_{10} = a + 9d = 25 - 9 \times 5 = -20$, $S_{10} = \dfrac{10(25 - 20)}{2} = 25$

(d) $T_{10} = -6 + 9(-3) = -33$, $S_{10} = \dfrac{10(-6 - 33)}{2} = -195$

(e) $T_{10} = 3 + 9(5) = 48$, $S_{10} = \dfrac{10(3 + 48)}{2} = 255$

(f) $T_{10} = \dfrac{1}{2} + 9(\dfrac{1}{2}) = 0.5 + 4.5 = 5$, $S_{10} = \dfrac{10(0.5 + 5)}{2} = 5 \times 5.5 = 27.5$

(g) $T_{10} = 1 + 9(\dfrac{2}{3}) = 1 + 6 = 7$, $S_{10} = \dfrac{10(1 + 7)}{2} = 5 \times 8 = 40$

(h) $T_{10} = 4 + 9(-\dfrac{1}{4}) = 4 - 2.25 = 1.75 = 1\dfrac{3}{4}$

$S_{10} = \dfrac{10(4 + 1.75)}{2} = 5 \times 5.75 = 28.75 = 28\dfrac{3}{4}$

B2.(a) AM $= \dfrac{8 + 20}{2} = 14$

(b) AM $= \dfrac{-3 + 15}{2} = 6$

(c) $T_7 = 39$

$3 + 6d = 39$

$6d = 36$

$d = 6$; The 5 means are: 9, 15, 21, 27, 33

(d) $T_9 = 44$

$12 + 8d = 44$

$8d = 32$

$d = 4$; The 7 means are: 16, 20, 24, 28, 32, 36, 40

(e) $T_{11} = 54$

$4 + 10d = 54$

$10d = 50$

$d = 5$; The 9 means are: 9, 14, 19, 24, 29, 34, 39, 44, 49

(f) $T_8 = 11$

$6\dfrac{1}{3} + 7d = 11$

$7d = 4\dfrac{2}{3}$

$d = \dfrac{2}{3}$; The 6 means are: $7, 7\dfrac{2}{3}, 8\dfrac{1}{3}, 9, 9\dfrac{2}{3}, 10\dfrac{1}{3},$

(g) $T_7 = 21$

$7.8 + 6d = 21$

$6d = 13.2$

$d = 2.2$; The 5 means are: 10, 12.2, 14.4, 16.6, 8.8

(h) $T_{10} = -17.8$

$-5.65 + 9d = -17.8$

$9d = -12.15$

$d = -1.35$; The 8 means are: -7, -8.35, -9.7, -1.05, -12.4, -13.75, -15.1, -16.45

B3. (a) $T_n = ar^{(n-1)}$

$T_8 = ar^7 = 1 \times 2^7 = 128$

$S_8 = \dfrac{1(2^8 - 1)}{2 - 1} = 255$

(b) $T_n = ar^{(n-1)}$

$T_8 = ar^7 = 3 \times 2^7 = 384$

$S_8 = \dfrac{3(2^8 - 1)}{2 - 1} = 3 \times 255 = 765$

(c) $T_n = ar^{(n-1)}$

$T_8 = ar^7 = 2 \times 3^7 = 2 \times 2187 = 4374$

$S_8 = \dfrac{2(3^8 - 1)}{3 - 1} = 6560$

(d) $T_n = ar^{(n-1)}$

$T_8 = ar^7 = 9 \times (\frac{1}{3})^7 = \dfrac{9}{2187}$

$S_8 = \dfrac{9((\frac{1}{3})^8 - 1)}{\frac{1}{3} - 1} = \dfrac{9(\frac{1}{6561} - 1)}{-\frac{2}{3}} = 13.50$

(e) $T_n = ar^{(n-1)}$

$T_8 = ar^7 = 2 \times (\frac{1}{2})^7 = \dfrac{1}{64}$

$S_8 = \dfrac{2((\frac{1}{2})^8 - 1)}{\frac{1}{2} - 1} = \dfrac{2(\frac{1}{256} - 1)}{\frac{1}{2}} = \dfrac{255}{64} = 3\dfrac{63}{64}$

(f) $T_n = ar^{(n-1)}$

$T_8 = ar^7 = 5 \times (-2)^7 = -640$

$S_8 = \dfrac{5(1 - 2^8)}{1 - (-2)} = \dfrac{5(1 - 256)}{3} = -425$

(g) $T_n = ar^{(n-1)}$

$T_8 = ar^7 = \dfrac{1}{6} \times (\frac{3}{4})^7 = \dfrac{729}{32768}$

$S_8 = \dfrac{\frac{1}{6}(1 - (\frac{3}{4})^8)}{1 - \frac{3}{4}} = \dfrac{\frac{1}{6}(1 - \frac{6561}{65536})}{\frac{1}{4}} = \dfrac{58975}{98304}$

(h) $T_n = ar^{(n-1)}$

$T_8 = ar^7 = 0.2 \times (4)^7 = 3276.8$

$S_8 = \dfrac{0.2(4^8 - 1)}{4 - 1} = \dfrac{0.2(65535)}{3} = 4369$

B4. (a) $GM = \sqrt{4 \times 16} = 8$

(b) $T_5 = ar^4$

$162 = 2r^4$

$r^4 = 81$

$r = 3$; The 3 means are: 6, 18, 54

(c) $T_6 = ar^5$

$-96 = 3r^5$

$r^5 = -32$

$r = -2$; The 4 means are: -6, 12, -24, 48

B4.(d) $T_7 = ar^6$

$\dfrac{5}{64} = 5r^6$

$r^6 = \dfrac{1}{64}$

$r = \dfrac{1}{2}$; The 5 means are: $\dfrac{5}{2}, \dfrac{5}{4}, \dfrac{5}{8}, \dfrac{5}{16}, \dfrac{5}{32}$

(e) $T_6 = ar^5$

$6144 = 6r^5$

$r^5 = 1024$

$r = 4$; The 4 means are: 24, 96, 384, 1536

(f) $T_5 = \dfrac{1}{2}r^4$

$\dfrac{1}{162} = \dfrac{1}{2}r^4$

$r^4 = \dfrac{1}{81}$

$r = \dfrac{1}{3}$; The 3 means are: $\dfrac{1}{6}, \dfrac{1}{18}, \dfrac{1}{54}$

(g) $T_5 = 7r^4$

$112 = 7r^4$

$r^4 = 16$

$r = 2$; The 3 means are: 14, 28, 56

(h) $T_8 = -4r^7$

$\dfrac{1}{32} = -4r^7$

$r^7 = \dfrac{-1}{128}$

$r = \dfrac{-1}{2}$; The 6 means are: 2, -1, $\dfrac{1}{2}, \dfrac{-1}{4}, \dfrac{1}{8}, \dfrac{-1}{16}$

B5. (a) $S_{10} = 5(4 + 9 \times 5) = 245$

(b) $S_{12} = 6(12 + 11 \times 2) = 204$

(c) $S_{20} = 10(6 + 19 \times 2) = 440$

(d) $S_{14} = 7(16 + 13 \times 1.5) = 248.5$

(e) $S_9 = 4.5(-16 + 8 \times -3) = -180$

B5.(f) $S_8 = 4(2\frac{1}{3} + 7 \times \frac{5}{6}) = 4(\frac{7}{3} + \frac{35}{6}) = 4 \times \frac{49}{6} = 32\frac{2}{3}$

(g) $S_{18} = 9(8 + 17 \times (2.5)) = 9 \times 50.5 = 454.5$

(h) $S_{16} = 8(-8.8 + 15 \times 2.1) = 8 \times 22.7 = 181.6$

B6. (a) $T_{12} = a + 11d$

$38 = a + 11 \times 3$

$a = 5$

First term $= 5$

(b) $a + 3d = 21$

$a + 8d = 56$

$5d = 35$

$d = 7$

$a = 0$

$T_{15} = 0 + 14 \times 7 = 98$

(c) $-7 + 13d = 58$

$13d = 65$

$d = 5$

$S_{12} = 6(-14 + 11 \times 5) = 6 \times 41 = 246$

(d) $S_1 = a = -6$

$S_2 = a + d = -9$

$d = -3$

The first 4 terms are: -6, -9, -12, -15

(e) $a + 8d = 1$ -------- (1)

$S_5 = S_{11}$

$2.5(2a + 4d) = 5.5(2a + 10d)$

$5a + 10d = 11a + 55d$

$-6a - 45d = 0$ --------- (2)

$(1) \times 6$: $6a + 48d = 6$ -------- (3)

$3d = 6$

$d = 2$

$a = -15$

$T_{17} = a + 16d = -15 + 32 = 17$

(f) $S_n = \dfrac{n(2a + (n - 1)d)}{2}$

$255 = \dfrac{n(6 + (n - 1)5)}{2}$

$510 = n(5n + 1)$

That is: $5n^2 + n - 510 = 0$

$(5n + 51)(n - 10) = 0$

Therefore: $n = 10$

That is, 10 terms will add up to 255.

(g) $a = 7, d = 7, l = 98$

$T_n = a + (n - 1)d$

$98 = 7 + (n - 1) \times 7$

$7n = 98$

$n = 14$

$S_{14} = \dfrac{n(a + l)}{2} = \dfrac{14(7 + 98)}{2} = 7 \times 105 = 735$

(h) $S_8 = 4(3 \times 8 + 7)\ 4 \times 31 = 124$

$S_7 = 3.5(3 \times 7 + 7) = 3.5 \times 28 = 98$

$T_8 = 124 - 98 = 26$

B7.(a) $T_n = ar^{(n-1)}$

$729 = 1 \times 3^{(n-1)}$

$3^6 = 3^{(n-1)}$

$n - 1 = 6$

$n = 7$

$S_7 = \dfrac{1(3^7 - 1)}{3 - 1} = \dfrac{2186}{21093}$

(b) $T_n = ar^{(n-1)}$

$2048 = 2 \times 2^{(n-1)}$

$1024 = 2^{(n-1)}$

$3^{10} = 3^{(n-1)}$

$n - 1 = 10$

$n = 11$

$S_{11} = \dfrac{2(2^{11} - 1)}{2 - 1} = 2 \times 2047 = 4094$

(c) $T_n = ar^{(n-1)}$

$0.125 = 8 \times (\tfrac{1}{2})^{(n-1)}$

$\dfrac{1}{8} = 8 \times (\tfrac{1}{2})^{(n-1)}$

$\dfrac{1}{64} = (\tfrac{1}{2})^{(n-1)}$

$(\tfrac{1}{2})^6 = (\tfrac{1}{2})^{(n-1)}$

$n - 1 = 6$

$n = 7$

$S_7 = \dfrac{8(1 - \tfrac{1}{2}^7)}{1 - \tfrac{1}{2}} = \dfrac{8(1 - \tfrac{1}{128})}{\tfrac{1}{2}} = 8 \times \dfrac{127}{128} \times 2 = \dfrac{127}{8}$ or $15\tfrac{7}{8}$

B7.(d) $T_n = ar^{(n-1)}$

$\frac{1}{256} = \frac{1}{2} \times (\frac{1}{2})^{(n-1)}$

$\frac{1}{256} = (\frac{1}{2})^n$

$(\frac{1}{2})^8 = (\frac{1}{2})^n$

$n = 8$

$S_8 = \frac{0.5(1 - \frac{1}{2}^8)}{1 - \frac{1}{2}} = \frac{0.5(1 - \frac{1}{256})}{\frac{1}{2}} = \frac{1}{2} \times \frac{255}{256} \times 2 = \frac{255}{256}$

(e) $T_n = ar^{(n-1)}$

$3280\frac{1}{2} = 1\frac{1}{2}(3)^{(n-1)}$

$2187 = (3)^{(n-1)}$

$3^7 = (3)^{(n-1)}$

$n - 1 = 7$

$n = 8$

$S_8 = \frac{1.5(3^8 - 1)}{3 - 1} = 1.5 \times \frac{6560}{2} = 4920$

(f) $T_n = ar^{(n-1)}$

$0.00486 = 2(0.3)^{(n-1)}$

$0.00243 = (0.3)^{(n-1)}$

$(0.3)^5 = (0.3)^{(n-1)}$

$n - 1 = 5$

$n = 6$

$S_6 = \frac{2(1 - (0.3)^6)}{1 - 0.3} = \frac{2(1 - 0.000729)}{0.7} = \frac{2 \times 0.999271}{0.7} = 2.855$

B7.(g) $T_n = ar^{(n-1)}$

$31250 = 2(5)^{(n-1)}$

$15625 = (5)^{(n-1)}$

$5^6 = (5)^{(n-1)}$

$n - 1 = 6$

$n = 7$

$S_7 = \dfrac{2(5^7 - 1)}{5 - 1} = 2 \times \dfrac{78124}{4} = 39062$

(h) $T_n = ar^{(n-1)}$

$-64 = \dfrac{1}{8}(-2)^{(n-1)}$

$-512 = (-2)^{(n-1)}$

$(-2)^9 = (-2)^{(n-1)}$

$n - 1 = 9$

$n = 10$

$S_{10} = \dfrac{\frac{1}{8}(1 - (-2)^{10})}{1 + 2} = \dfrac{\frac{1}{8}(1 - 1024)}{3} = \dfrac{1}{8} \times \dfrac{-1023}{3} = \dfrac{-1023}{24} = -42.625$

B8.(a) $ar^4 = \dfrac{64}{81}$

$ar^6 = \dfrac{256}{729}$

$r^2 = \dfrac{256}{729} \div \dfrac{64}{81} = \dfrac{4}{9}$

$r = \pm\dfrac{2}{3}$

When $r = \dfrac{2}{3}$, $a = \dfrac{64}{81} \times \dfrac{81}{16} = 4$

When $r = -\dfrac{2}{3}$, $a = 4$

Therefore, the first term $= 4$ and the common ratio $= \pm\dfrac{2}{3}$

(b) Sum to infinity $= \dfrac{a}{1-r} = \dfrac{8}{1-r} = 12$

$1 - r = \dfrac{8}{12} = \dfrac{2}{3}$

$r = \dfrac{1}{3}$

The common ratio $= \dfrac{1}{3}$

C1.(a) $(1 + x)^3 = {}^3c_01^3 + {}^3c_11^2x + {}^3c_21x^2 + {}^3c_3x^3 = 1 + 3x + 3x^2 + x^3$

(b) $(2 + x)^4 = {}^4c_02^4 + {}^4c_12^3x + {}^4c_22^2x^2 + {}^4c_32x^3 + {}^4c_4x^4 = 16 + 32x + 24x^2 + 8x^3 + x^4$

(c) $(m - n)^5 = m^5 - 5m^4n + 10m^3n^2 - 10m^2n^3 + 5mn^4 - n^5$

(d) $(a + 2)^6 = a^6 + 12a^5 + 60a^4 + 160a^3 + 240a^4 + 192a^5 + 64$

(e) $(2a - 3b)^7 = 128a^7 - 192a^6b + 6048a^5b^2 - 15120a^4b^3 + 22680a^3b^4 - 20412a^2b^5$
$\quad\quad\quad\quad\quad + 10206ab^6 - 2187b^7$

(f) $(1 + 0.2)^4 = 1 + 0.8 + 0.24 + 0.032 + 0.0016$

(g) $(2 + 0.05)^3 = 8 + 0.6 + 0.015 + 0.000125$

(h) $(3p + 1)^6 = 729p^6 + 1458p^5 + 1215p^4 + 540p^3 + 135p^2 + 18p + 1$

C2. The fourth term in the expansion of $(2x + 3y)^7$ is:

$T_4 = {}^7C_3(2x)^4(3y)^3 = \dfrac{7 \times 6 \times 5}{3 \times 2 \times 1} \times 16x^4 \times 27y = 15120x^4y^3$

C3. $(1.02)^{1/2}$

$= (1 + 0.02)^{1/2} = {}^{1/2}C_{0(1)}1^{1/2} + {}^{1/2}C_{1(1)}{}^{-1/2}(0.02) + {}^{1/2}C_{2(1)}{}^{-3/2}(0.02)^2 + {}^{1/2}C_{3(1)}{}^{-5/2}(0.02)^3 + \ldots\ldots$

$= 1 + 0.5(0.02) + 0.5 \times (-\frac{1}{2}) \times \dfrac{(0.02)^2}{2} + 0.5 \times (-\frac{1}{2})(-\frac{3}{2}) \times \dfrac{(0.02)^3}{6} + \ldots\ldots$

$= 1 + 0.01 - 0.00005 + 0.0000005 + \ldots\ldots\ldots = 1.00995$

C4. The fifth term in the expansion of $(1 + 0.04)^{-3}$

$= {}^{-3}C_4(1)^{-7}(0.04)^4 = \dfrac{-3 \times -4 \times -5 \times -6}{4 \times 3 \times 2 \times 1} \times (0.04)^4 = 0.0000384$

C5. The fourth term in the expansion of $(1 + x^2)^{1/2}$

$T_4 = {}^{1/2}nC_3x_{(1)}{}^{-5/2} \times (x^2)^3 = \dfrac{0.5(-0.5 \times -1.5)}{6}x^6 = \dfrac{3}{16}x^6$

C6. The probability of success $p = \dfrac{1}{6}$ (in one throw) $q = \dfrac{5}{6}$

The third term in the expansion $(\dfrac{5}{6} + \dfrac{1}{6})^5$ gives the required probability

Therefore, the probability that in five throws of a die 3 appears twice:

$= {}^5C_2 \times (\dfrac{5}{6})^3 \times (\dfrac{1}{6})^2 = \dfrac{5 \times 4}{2} \times 1 \times \dfrac{126}{216} \times \dfrac{1}{36} = \dfrac{1250}{7776} = \dfrac{625}{3888}$

C7. Let $P(n) = 1^3 + 2^3 + 3^3 + \ldots + n^3 = \frac{1}{4}n^2(n + 1)^2$

<u>STEP 1:</u> We first show that p (1) is true.

When n = 1, Left Hand Side = 1

Right Hand Side, $\frac{1}{4}(1)(4) = 1$

Therefore, P (1) is true.

<u>STEP 2:</u> We assume that P(k) is true

That is: $P(k) = 1^3 + 2^3 + 3^3 + \ldots + k^3 = \frac{1}{4}k^2(k + 1)^2$

Add $(k + 1)^3$ to both sides:

$1^3 + 2^3 + 3^3 + \ldots + k^3 + (k + 1)^3 = \frac{1}{4}k^2(k + 1)^2 + (k + 1)^3$

$= (k + 1)^2[\frac{k^2}{4} + (k + 1)] = \frac{1}{4}(k + 1)^2[k^2 + 4k + 4] = \frac{1}{4}(k + 1)^2[(k + 2)^2]$

That is, $P(k + 1) = \frac{1}{4}(k + 1)^2[(k + 2)^2]$ | k replaced by k + 1 in P(k)

That is, on assuming that P(n) is true for n = k, it is also true for n = k + 1.

Therefore, P(n) is true for all positive integer values of n.

C8. To prove that $17^n - 12^n$ is divisible by 5:

Let $P(n) = 17^n - 12^n$

When $n = 17^n - 12^n = 17 - 12 = 5$

Therefore, the statement is true when n = 1

We assume that it is true for n = k

That is: $P(k) = 17^k - 12^k = 5D$ | i.e. 5 times some value

$17^k = 5D + 12^k$

Now: $P(k + 1) = 17^{(k + 1)} - 12^{(k + 1)} = 17 \times 17^k - 12 \times 12^k = 17(5D + 12^k) - 12 \times 12^k$

$= 85D + 17 \times 12^k - 12 \times 12^k = 85D + 5 \times 12^k = 5(17D + 12^k)$

The statement is true also for n = k + 1

Therefore, the statement is true for all positive integer n.

Find the sum of the following series to the number of terms indicated.

1. (a) $6 + 3 + 0 - 3$ .... to 12 terms

(b) $\dfrac{1}{4} + \dfrac{1}{2} + 1 + $ ..... to 10 terms

(c) $\dfrac{1}{2} + \dfrac{1}{6} + \dfrac{1}{18} + $ .... to infinity

(d) $3 + 4 + 5\dfrac{1}{3} + $ .... to 7 terms

(e) $1.2 + 1.8 + 2.7 + $ ..... to 6 terms

---

2. (a) The first term of a geometric sequence is 6 and the fourth term is -162, find the common ratio.

(b) Find the 11th term of a GP whose third term is 16 and the 7th term is 1.

(c) Find the first term of a geometric progression whose third term is $2\dfrac{1}{4}$ and sixth term is $\dfrac{16}{81}$.

---

3. A binomial experiment consists of four independent trials. The probability of success in each trial is 0.2. Find the probability of obtaining exactly 0, 1, 2, 3 and 4 successes, respectively, in this experiment.

---

4. Prove that for all $n \geq 1$:

$$1 \times 2 + 2 \times 3 + 3 \times 4 + 4 \times 5 + \ldots\ldots\ldots\ldots n(n + 1) = \frac{1}{3}n(n + 1)(n + 2)$$

---

5. (a) Find the sum of all numbers from 1 to 100 both inclusive.

(b) Find the sum of the first 20 terms of an arithmetic progression whose first term is 2 and common difference 5.

---

6. (a) Find the tenth term of a geometric progression whose third term is 16 and whose seventh term is 1.

(b) For the above GP, find the sum of the first 15 terms.

---

7. A fair die is rolled five times. Find the probability of obtaining:
   (a) exactly four 5's
   (b) exactly two even numbers
   (c) all results greater than 3
   (d) a 5 on the first roll only

---

8. Use mathematical induction to prove that $3^{3n} + 2^{(n + 2)}$ is divisible by 5 for all positive integers n greater than or equal to 1.

1. (a) $S_{12} = 6[12 + 11(-3)] = 6[12 - 33] = -126$

(b) $S_n = \dfrac{a(r^n - 1)}{r - 1}$

$S_{10} = \dfrac{0.25(2^{10} - 1)}{2 - 1} = 0.25(1023) = 255\dfrac{3}{4}$

(c) $S_\infty = \dfrac{a}{1 - r} = \dfrac{0.5}{1 - \frac{1}{3}} = \dfrac{0.5}{\frac{2}{3}} = \dfrac{3}{4}$

(d) $S_n = \dfrac{a(r^n - 1)}{r - 1}$

$S_7 = \dfrac{3\left(\left(\frac{4}{3}\right)^7 - 1\right)}{\frac{1}{3}} = 9\left(\dfrac{16384}{2187} - 1\right) = 58.424$

(e) $S_n = \dfrac{a(r^n - 1)}{r - 1}$

$S_6 = \dfrac{1.2\left(\left(\frac{3}{2}\right)^6 - 1\right)}{\frac{1}{2}} = \dfrac{1.2\left(\frac{729}{64} - 1\right)}{\frac{1}{2}} = 2.4\left(\dfrac{665}{64}\right) = \dfrac{399}{16} = 24\dfrac{15}{16}$

2. (a) $T_4 = 6r^3 = -162$

$r^3 = -27$

$r = -3$

(b) $ar^2 = 16$

$ar^6 = 1$

$r^4 = \dfrac{1}{16}$

$r = \dfrac{1}{2}$

$a = \dfrac{16}{\frac{1}{4}} = 64$

$T_{11} = ar^{10} = 64 \times \left(\dfrac{1}{2}\right)^{10} = \dfrac{64}{1024} = \dfrac{1}{16}$

2.(c) $ar^2 = \dfrac{9}{4}$

$ar^5 = \dfrac{16}{81}$

$r^3 = \dfrac{64}{729}$

$r = \dfrac{4}{9}$

$a = \dfrac{9}{4r^2} = \dfrac{9 \times 81}{4 \times 16} = \dfrac{729}{64} = 11\dfrac{25}{64}$

---

3. $p = 0.2$; $q = 0.8$

$(0.8 + 0.2)^4 = (0.8)^4 + 4 \times (0.8)^3(0.2) + 6 \times (0.8)^2(0.2)^2 + 4(0.8)(0.2)^3 + (0.2)$

$= 0.4096 + 0.4096 + 0.1536 + 0.0256 + 0.0016$

Probability of no success = 0.4096

Probability of one successes = 0.4096

Probability of two successes = 0.1536

Probability of three successes = 0.0256

Probability of four successes = 0.0016

---

4. Let $P(n) = 1 \times 2 + 2 \times 3 + 3 \times 4 + 4 \times 5 + \ldots\ldots\ldots\ n(n + 1) = \dfrac{1}{3}n(n + 1)(n + 2)$

When $n = 1$; LHS $= 1 \times 2 = 2$; RHS $= \dfrac{1}{3}1(1 + 1)(1 + 2) = 2$

Assume that the proposition is true for $n = k$

Therefore, $P(k) = 1 \times 2 + 2 \times 3 + 3 \times 4 + \ldots\ldots\ k(k + 1) = \dfrac{1}{3}k(k + 1)(n + 2)$

Now add $(k + 1)(k + 2)$ to both sides of the equation:

$1 \times 2 + 2 \times 3 + 3 \times 4 + \ldots k(k + 1) + (k + 1)(k + 2) = \dfrac{1}{3}k(k + 1)(k + 2) + (k + 1)(k + 2)$

$= (k + 1)(k + 2)[\dfrac{1}{3}k + 1] = \dfrac{1}{3}(k + 1)(k + 2)(k + 3) = P(k + 1)$

Thus, the proposition is true for all $n \geq 1$

---

5. (a) $S_n = \dfrac{n}{2}(a + l)$

$S_{100} = \dfrac{100}{2}(1 + 100) = 50 \times 101 = 5050$

(b) $S_{20} = \dfrac{20}{2}(4 + 19 \times 5) = 10 \times 99 = 990$

6. (a) $ar^2 = 16$

$ar^6 = 1$

$r^4 = \dfrac{1}{16}$

$r = \dfrac{1}{2}$

$a = \dfrac{16}{\left(\frac{1}{2}\right)^2} = 64$

$T_{10} = ar^9 = 64 \times \left(\dfrac{1}{2}\right)^9 = \dfrac{64}{512} = \dfrac{1}{8}$

(b) $S_{15} = \dfrac{64\left(\left(\frac{1}{2}\right)^{15} - 1\right)}{\frac{1}{2}} = \dfrac{64\left(\frac{1}{32768} - 1\right)}{-\frac{1}{2}} = 128\left(\dfrac{32767}{32768}\right) = \dfrac{32767}{256} = 127\dfrac{255}{256}$

---

7. (a) $p = \dfrac{1}{6}$; $q = \dfrac{5}{6}$

From the expansion of $\left(\dfrac{5}{6} + \dfrac{1}{6}\right)^5$

Probability exactly four 5's $= {}^5C_4\left(\dfrac{5}{6}\right)^1\left(\dfrac{1}{6}\right)^4 = 5 \times \dfrac{5}{6} \times \dfrac{1}{1296} = \dfrac{25}{7776}$

(b) The probability of getting an even number $= \dfrac{3}{6} = \dfrac{1}{2}$

That is, $p = \dfrac{1}{2}$; $q = \dfrac{1}{2}$

From the expansion of $\left(\dfrac{1}{2} + \dfrac{1}{2}\right)^5$

Probability exactly 2 even numbers $= {}^5C_2\left(\dfrac{1}{2}\right)^3\left(\dfrac{1}{2}\right)^2 = 10 \times \dfrac{1}{8} \times \dfrac{1}{4} = \dfrac{10}{32} = \dfrac{5}{16}$

(c) The probability of obtaining a number greater than 3 $= \dfrac{3}{6} = \dfrac{1}{2}$

That is, $p = \dfrac{1}{2}$; $q = \dfrac{1}{2}$

From the expansion of $\left(\dfrac{1}{2} + \dfrac{1}{2}\right)^5$

Probability all results greater than 3 $= {}^5C_5\left(\dfrac{1}{2}\right)^0\left(\dfrac{1}{2}\right)^5 = \left(\dfrac{1}{2}\right)^5 = \dfrac{1}{32}$

(d) The Probability of obtaining 5 on the first roll only $= \dfrac{1}{6} \times \dfrac{5}{6} \times \dfrac{5}{6} \times \dfrac{5}{6} \times \dfrac{5}{6} = \dfrac{625}{7776}$

259

8. Let $P(n) = 3^{3n} + 2^{(n+2)}$

When $n = 1$; $P(1) = 3 + 2 = 35$

35 is a multiple of 5 and so the proposition is true for $n = 1$

Assume true for $n = k$

Therefore, $P(k) = 3^{3k} + 2^{(k+2)} = 5D$

$3^{3k} = 5D - 2^{(k+2)}$

$3^{3k} = 5D - 4 \times 2^k$

If $n = k + 1$

$P(k+1) = 3^{3(3k+3)} + 2^{(k+3)} = 27 \times 3^{3k} + 8 \times 2^k = 27(5D - 4 \times 2^k) + 8 \times 2^k$

$= 135D - 108 \times 2^k + 8 \times 2^k = 135D - 100 \times 8 \times 2^k = 5(27D - 20 \times 8 \times 2^k) = $ multiple of 5

Therefore, $3^{3n} + 2^{(n+2)}$ is divisible by 5 for all positive integers n greater than or equal to 1.

11. GEOMETRY

Geometry is the study of shapes and their properties. Geometry is divided into Plain Geometry and Solid Geometry.

- **Plain Geometry** deals with lines, triangles, quadrilaterals, polygons and circles which are two dimensional. Solid geometry deals with three dimensional objects like cubes, prisms, cylinders and spheres.

- **A Straight Line** is the shortest path from a point A to point B. Euclid defined a line as a "breathless length," and a straight line as a line that "lies evenly with the points on itself".

- **An angle** is the space between two lines that meet each other. The size of an angle is measured in degrees or radians. An angle in a straight line is 180 degrees or π radians.

- **A reflex angle** is an angle between 180^0 and 360^0

TRIANGLES

A triangle has three sides and three angles. All three angles add up to **180** degrees. A triangle with unequal angles and unequal sides is called a **scalene triangle**.

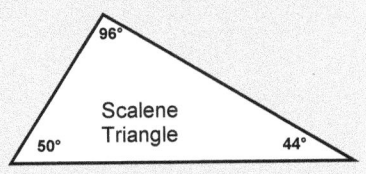

When all the sides of a triangle are equal in length, the angles are also equal. That is, each angle is **60** degrees.
Such a triangle is called an **equilateral triangle**.

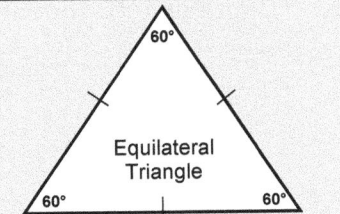

When only two sides of a triangle are equal, it is called an **isosceles triangle**. The angles opposite to the equal sides of an isosceles triangle are equal.

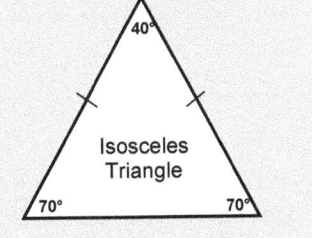

If an isosceles triangle has **90** degrees as one of its angles, then it is referred to as a **right-angled** isosceles triangle.

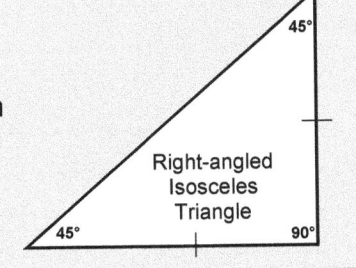

When a triangle has angles less than 90 degrees, it is referred to as an **acute angled** triangle

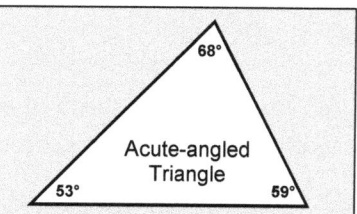

Acute-angled Triangle

If one of the angles of a triangle is more than 90 degrees, it is referred to as an **obtuse angled** triangle

Obtuse Angled Triangle

Any triangle with one of the angles equal to 90 degrees is a **right-angled triangle**.

Hypotenuse   Opposite side

Right-angled Triangle

θ   90°

Adjacent side

The side opposite to the 90-degree angle is called the **Hypotenuse**. If we take one of the other two angles and call it θ (theta), the side opposite to it is called the **opposite side** and the other one, the **adjacent side**.

FEATURES OF STRAIGHT LINES AND TRIANGLES

Two intersecting lines contain two pairs of vertically opposite angles. In each pair, the vertically opposite angles are equal.

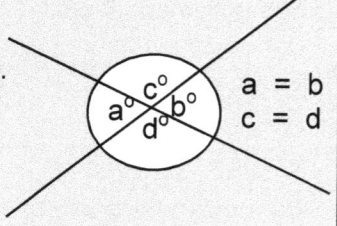

a = b
c = d

When two lines do not intersect, they are called **parallel lines**.

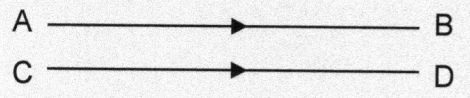

When a line is drawn from a point to intersect another line at 90 degrees, they are said to be **perpendicular** to each other.

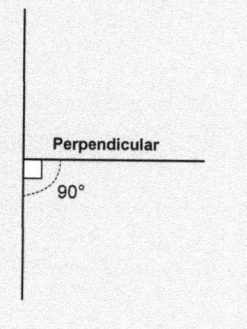

Perpendicular

90°

A line that cuts two parallel lines is called a **transversal**. The angles formed that are in corresponding positions are **corresponding angles** and those in alternate positions are **alternate angles**.

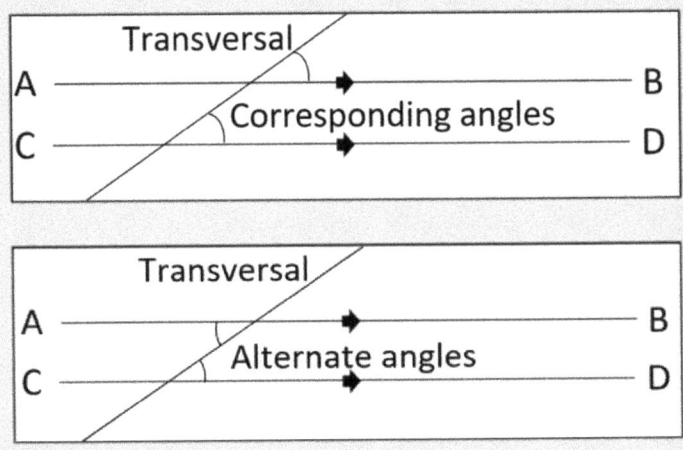

Co- interior angles add up to 180. That is, they are supplementary.

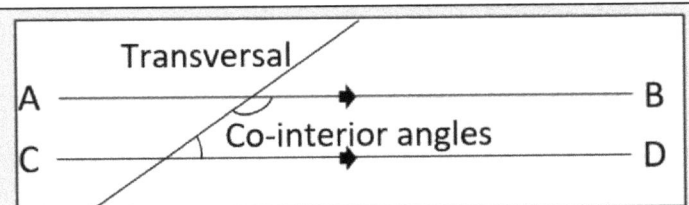

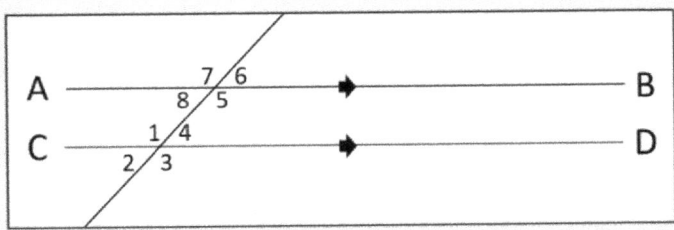

Referring to the above diagram, name the pair or pairs of numbers for each of the following:

(i) Alternate angles

(ii) Corresponding angles

(iii) Co-interior angles

(iv) Vertically opposite angles

Solution:

(i) Alternate angles: 1 and 5, 4 and 8

(ii) Corresponding angles: 1 and 7, 2 and 8, 4 and 6, 3 and 5

(iii) Co-interior angles: 1 and 8, 4 and 5

(iv) Vertically opposite angles: 5 and 7, 6 and 8, 1 and 3, 2 and 4

RIGHT ANGLED TRIANGLES

Angles and sides of any triangle are connected by the Sine rule and Cosine rule. (See section on Trigonometry in Book 2 for details). In a right-angled triangle, the square on the hypotenuse is equal to the sum of the squares on the other two sides.

$$c^2 = a^2 + b^2$$

Where, 'c' is the length of the hypotenuse and 'a' and 'b' are the lengths of the other two sides.

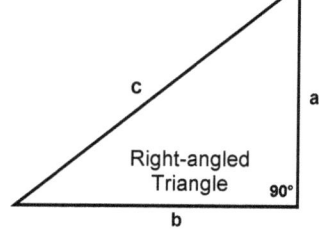

Right-angled Triangle

Pythagoras' Theorem: The square of the length of the hypotenuse of a right-angled triangle equals the sum of the squares of the lengths of the other two sides.

Three numbers that satisfy the Pythagorean theorem are called the **Triads.**

Examples:

- 3, 4, 5
- 5, 12, 13
- 7, 24, 25
- 9, 40, 41
- 11, 60, 61

Multiples of these are also triads, e.g.
- 6, 8, 10
- 9, 12, 15

Example:

In a right-angled triangle, the hypotenuse is 39 cm and one side is 15 cm. What is the length of the other side?

Let the length of the side be x.

Therefore, $x^2 + 15^2 = 39^2$ | Pythagoras' Theorem |

$x^2 = 39^2 - 15^2 = 1521 - 225 = 1296$

$x = \sqrt{1296} = 36$

CONGRUENT TRIANGLES

Two triangles are congruent if they are the same in every respect. One should be able to be superimposed on the other.

Rules for congruency:

Two triangles are congruent if one of the following four rules is satisfied:
1. Three sides of one triangle are equal to three sides of the other (SSS).
2. Two sides and the angle included between them of one triangle are equal to two sides and the angle included between them of the other (SAS).
3. Two angles and a side of one triangle are equal to two angles and a **corresponding side** of one of the equal angles of the other are equal (AAS).
4. The hypotenuse and one side of one right angled triangle are equal to the hypotenuse and one side of the other (RHS).

Example:

Two lines AB and CD bisect at X. Prove that ΔAXC and ΔBXD are congruent. Hence deduce that AC and BD are equal and parallel.

<u>Data:</u> AX = BX and CX = DX

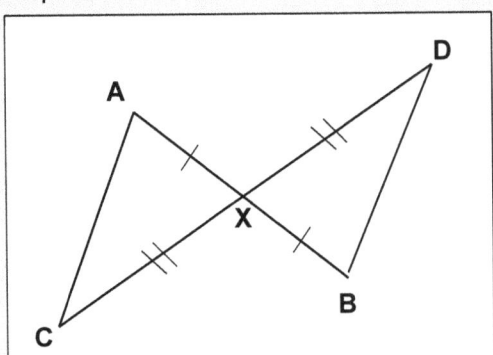

<u>Prove:</u> (i) ΔAXC ≅ ΔBXD
       (ii) AC = BD and AC∥BD

<u>Construction:</u> Join AC and BD

<u>Proof:</u> In the two triangles AXC and BXD

AX = BX (given)

CX = DX (given)

Incl. ∠AXC = Incl. ∠BXD | Vertically opposite angles |

Therefore, ΔAXC ≅ ΔBXD | SAS rule satisfied |

Hence, AC = BD | Sides opposite to equal angles |

∠ACX = ∠BDX | Angles opposite to equal sides |

Symbol	Meaning
≅	'is congruent to'
∥	'is parallel to'

But these are alternate angles in relation to AC and BD. Therefore: AC∥BD.
Similar steps are followed in other problems to show that one of the 4 conditions for congruency is satisfied.

PERIMETER OF A TRIANGLE

A line drawn from a vertex of a triangle perpendicular to the side opposite to it (called the base) is the **perpendicular height of the triangle**. If the three sides of a triangle are a, b, c and its perimeter, 2s then:

$$2s = a + b + c \quad \text{or} \quad s = \frac{a + b + c}{2}$$

Example:

For a triangle with sides a = 7, b = 6 and c = 5, calculate its semi-perimeter.

$$s = \frac{7 + 6 + 5}{2} = \frac{18}{2} = 9$$

Therefore: semi-perimeter = 9

Area of a triangle

If the length of the base and the height of a triangle are known, then its area is calculated as:

$\frac{1}{2} \times$ Base × Height

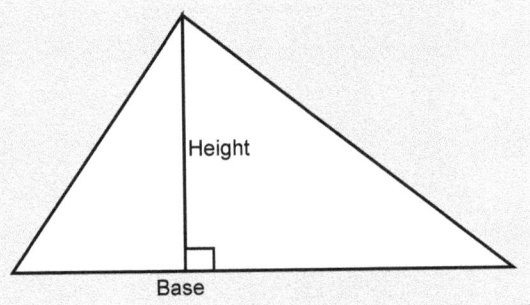

Example:

What is the area of a triangle with a base of 8cm and a height of 6cm?

Area $= \frac{1}{2} \times 8 \times 6 = 24cm^2$

Heron's formula

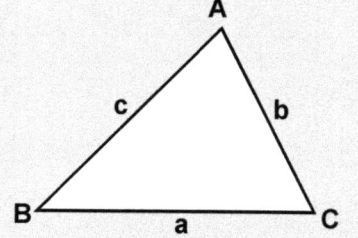

If the lengths of the sides of a triangle are known,
then its semi perimeter and area are calculated as follows:

Semi Perimeter: $s = \dfrac{a+b+c}{2}$

Area: $A = \sqrt{s(s-a)(s-b)(s-c)}$

Example:

A triangle has sides 9cm, 6cm and 5cm. Calculate is semi perimeter and area.

$2s = 9 + 6 + 5 = 20$

Semi perimeter $= 10cm$

Area $= \sqrt{10(10-9)(10-6)(10-5)} = \sqrt{200} = 10\sqrt{2}cm^2$

An **exterior angle of a triangle** is an angle formed by one side of the triangle and the extension of one of its adjacent sides. The exterior angle of a triangle is equal to the sum of the interior opposite angles (i.e. In the diagram below, 159 = 108 + 51).

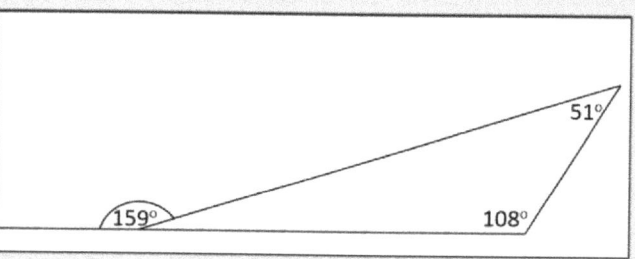

In the diagram below, the perpendicular from the vertex formed by the two equal sides of an isosceles to the side opposite to it **bisects that side and the angle** included by the two equal sides (the same is true for an equilateral triangle also).

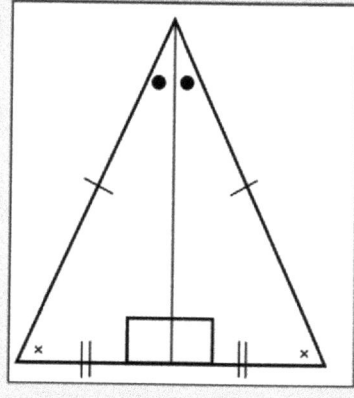

266

Similar triangles

If two triangles are of different sizes but have the same angles, then the two triangles are said to be similar. If two triangles are similar then their sides are **proportional**.

The two triangles are similar with:

Angle A = Angle X

Angle B = Angle Y

Angle C = Angle Z

Therefore: $\dfrac{BC}{ZY} = \dfrac{AB}{XY} = \dfrac{AC}{XZ}$

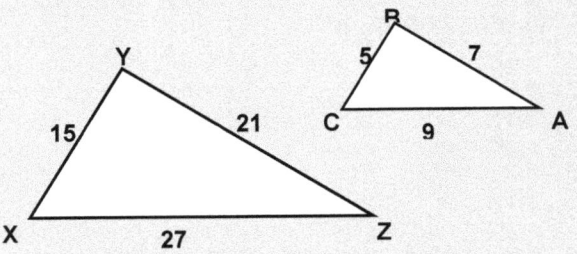

Areas of similar triangles

If two triangles are similar, then the **ratio of their areas are equal to the ratio of the squares** of the corresponding sides.

Example 1:

The two similar triangles ABC and XYZ have angle C equal to angle Z, with the sides opposite to them of 3.7 and 11.1 units respectively. Calculate the ratio:

(i) XY:AB

(ii) Area of ΔXYZ:Area of ΔABC

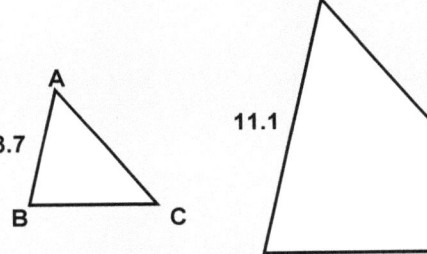

$XY:AB = \dfrac{11.1}{3.7} = 3:1$

Area of ΔXYZ:Area ofΔ ABC $= \dfrac{11.1^2}{3.7^2} = 9:1$

Example 2:

ABC is a triangle. DE is parallel to BC. If BC = 8cm and DE = 5cm, calculate the following:

(i) the ratio AD:DB

(ii) the ratio of the areas of ΔADE and ΔABC

(iii) the ratio of the area of the figure DBCE and ΔABC

(i) AD:AB = DE:BC (since triangles ADE and ABC are similar)

$AD:DB = \dfrac{AD}{DB} = \dfrac{AD}{AB - AD} = \dfrac{5}{8-5} = \dfrac{5}{3} = 5:3$

(ii) Area of ΔADE:Area of ΔABC $= \dfrac{DE^2}{BC^2} = 25:64$

(iii) $\dfrac{\Delta ADE}{\Delta ABC} = \dfrac{25}{64}$

$\dfrac{\Delta ABC - \Delta ADE}{\Delta ABC} = \dfrac{64 - 25}{64}$

$\dfrac{\text{Area of Figure DBCE}}{\Delta ABC} = \dfrac{64 - 25}{64} = \dfrac{39}{64}$

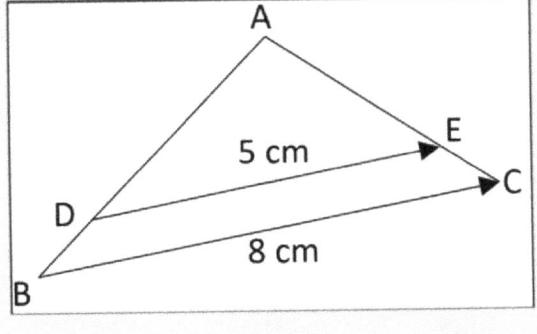

Example 3:

In a triangle ABC, D and E are any points on AB and AC respectively and DE is parallel to BC. If AD = 2cm, AB = x, DE = 4cm and BC = 7cm, Calculate x.

If D and E are **any points**, then:

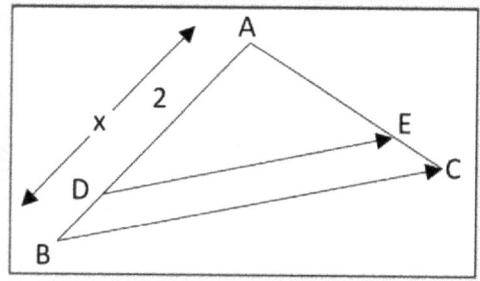

$$\frac{AD}{AB} = \frac{AE}{AC} = \frac{DE}{BC}$$

That is: $\dfrac{2}{x} = \dfrac{4}{7}$

4x = 14

Therefore: x = 3.5 cm

The Midpoint Theorem

The line connecting the midpoints of two sides of a triangle is **parallel to and equal to one half** of the third side.

D is the mid-point of AC and E is the mid-point of BC

That is, DE is Parallel to AB, DE = $\dfrac{1}{2}$AB

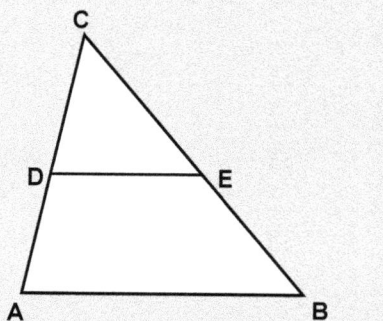

Example:

In relation to the above diagram, if AB = 8cm, calculate the value of DE.

DE = $\dfrac{1}{2}$ AB = $\dfrac{1}{2}$ × 8 = 4cm

QUADRILATERALS

A quadrilateral is any four-sided figure. It can be convex or concave.

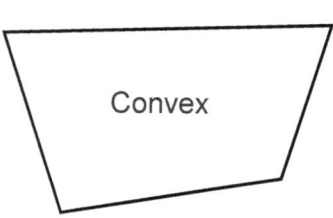

Convex

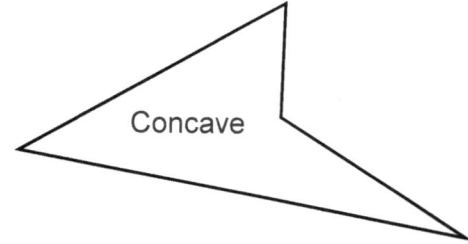

Concave

There are six basic types of quadrilaterals:

- Rectangle
- Square
- Parallelogram
- Rhombus
- Trapezium
- Kite

A **Rectangle** is a quadrilateral with two pairs of equal and parallel sides and all four angles are right angles. The diagonals are equal and bisect each other.

Perimeter = 2a + 2b units

Area = a × b = ab square units

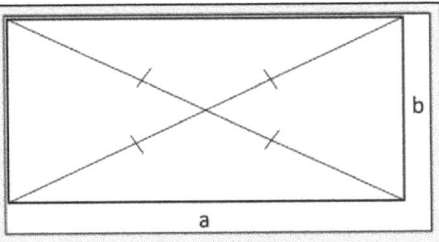

A **Square** is a rectangle but all sides are equal.
The diagonals are equal and bisect each other at 90 degrees.

Perimeter = 4a units

Area = a × a = a^2 square units

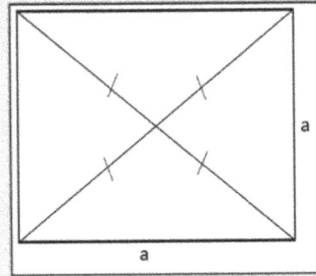

A **parallelogram** is a rectangle except that the opposite sides and angles are equal and no angle is 90 degrees. The diagonals bisect each other.

Perimeter = 2a + 2b units

Area = b × h = bh square units

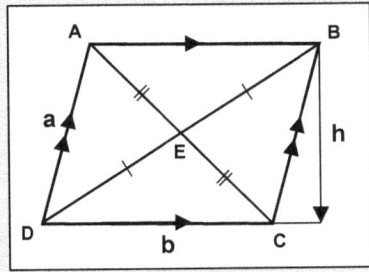

A **Rhombus** is a square but angles are not 90 degrees. The opposite angles are equal and the diagonals bisect each other at right angles and bisect the angles.

Perimeter = 4a

Area = $\frac{1}{2}$pq where p and q are the lengths of the diagonals.

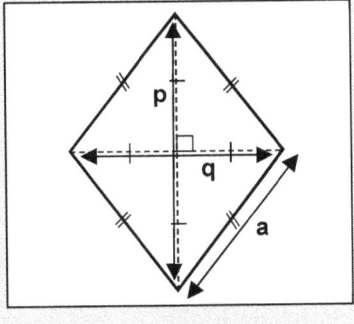

A **Trapezium** is a quadrilateral with one pair of opposite sides parallel.

Area of a trapezium = $\frac{1}{2}$(a + b) × h

Where a and b are the parallel side lengths and h = height

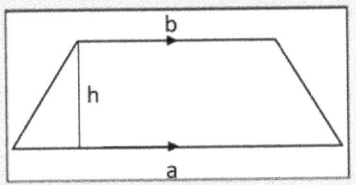

A **Kite** is a quadrilateral with two pairs of equal sides. There are two unequal diagonals, the larger one bisects the smaller one at right angles.

Perimeter = 2a + 2b units

Area = $\frac{1}{2}$pq, where p and q are the lengths of the diagonals.

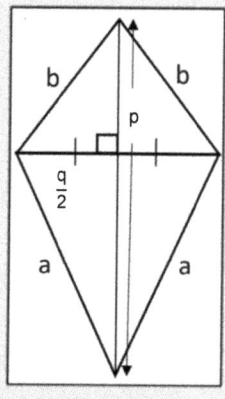

A polygon is a closed plane figure with three or more sides that are all straight. However, the ones with **five** or more sides are specifically regarded as polygons. The sides of a polygon may or may not be all equal. When equal, they are referred to as regular polygons. Otherwise they are irregular polygons.

The sum of all the interior angles of a polygon with n sides is **(2n − 4) × 90 degrees**. In order to obtain one interior angle of a regular polygon, we divide the sum by n. A polygon is given a name according to the number of sides it has as shown below:

Number of sides	Name of Polygon	Sum of interior angles	Value of one Interior angle
5	Pentagon	540 degrees	108 degrees
6	Hexagon	720 degrees	120 degrees
7	Heptagon	900 degrees	128.57 degrees
8	Octagon	1080 degrees	135 degrees
9	Nonagon	1260 degrees	140 degrees
10	Decagon	1440 degrees	144 degrees

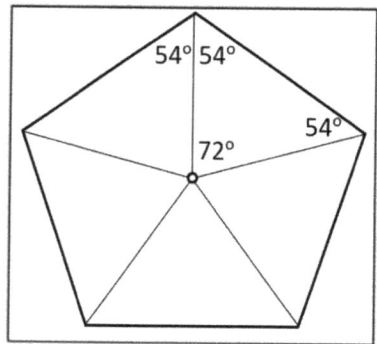

Regular Pentagon

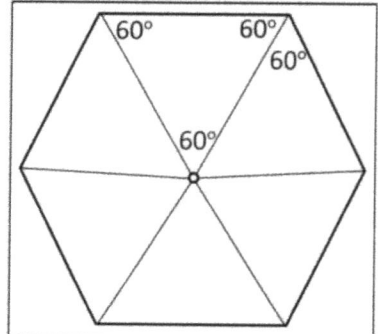

Regular Hexagon

The **Area of a regular polygon** is half the product of its perimeter and **apothem.** That is:

$$\text{Area} = \frac{1}{2} \times \text{perimeter} \times \text{apothem}$$

Apothem is the length of the perpendicular from the centre of a regular polygon to one of its sides.

Example:

Calculate the area of a **regular pentagon** if one side is 3cm and the apothem is 2cm.

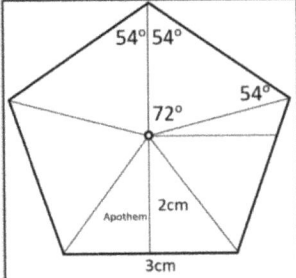

Area $= \dfrac{1}{2} \times 15 \times 2 = 15\text{cm}^2$

Alternatively, we obtain five equal triangles by joining the centre of the regular pentagon to the vertices. The area of one triangle is: $\dfrac{1}{2} \times 3 \times 2 = 3\text{cm}^2$. Therefore, the area of the pentagon is $5 \times 3 = 15\text{cm}^2$.

If the apothem is not given, it can be calculated using trigonometry.

Example:

Calculate the area of a regular hexagon if one side is 3cm and the apothem is h.

Apothem $h = (9 - \dfrac{9}{4})^{1/2} = (\dfrac{27}{4})^{1/2} = \dfrac{1}{2} \times 3\sqrt{3}$ (using Pythagoras' Theorem)

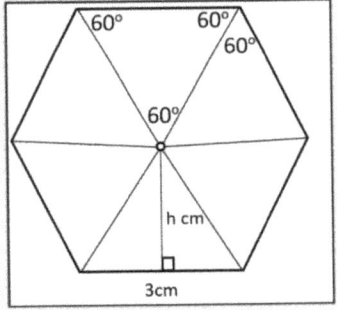

Area $= \dfrac{1}{2} \times$ perimeter $\times$ apothem $= \dfrac{1}{2} \times 18 \times h = 9h\text{cm}^2$

$= 9 \times \dfrac{1}{2} \times 3\sqrt{3} = \dfrac{1}{2} \times 27\sqrt{3}\text{cm}^2 = 23.38\text{cm}^2$

CIRCLE

A circle is the path of a point that moves so that its distance from a fixed point is a constant. The fixed point is called the **centre** of the circle. The line connecting two points on the circle and passing through the centre Is called the **diameter** of the circle. Half the length of a diameter is called the **radius** of the circle. The line joining any two points on the circle but not passing through the centre is called a **chord.**

The **circumference of a circle** is the linear distance around it. It is equal to $3\dfrac{1}{7} \times D$.

That is, the circumference **C**, of any circle is $3\dfrac{1}{7}$ times its diameter D.

The constant $3\dfrac{1}{7}$ or $\dfrac{22}{7}$ is represented by the Greek alphabet pi (π). Therefore:

$$\mathbf{C = \pi D = 2\pi r} \quad \text{(since D = 2r)}$$

A portion of the circumference of a circle is called an **arc.** Its length (L) is caculated as the product of the radius of the circle and the angle (in radians) subtended by the arc at the centre (i.e. L = rθ). **A segment** of a circle is the area beween a chord and and an arc. The portion of the circle between two radii and an arc is a **sector.** The **perimeter of a sector** is equal to L + 2r units. The **area of a sector** of a circle is $\frac{1}{2}r^2\theta$ where θ is in radians. The **Area** of a circle is the space inside a circle and is measured in square units.

> ## The **Area, A $= \pi r^2$**

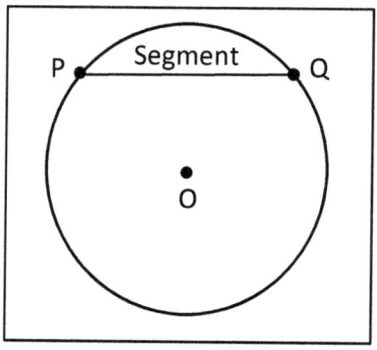
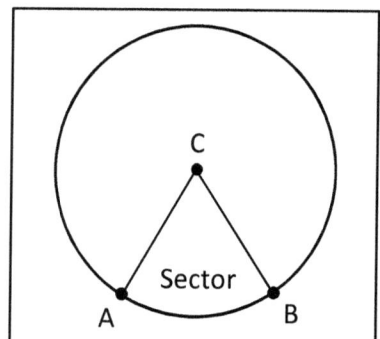

- A **tangent** to a circle from an external point is a straight line that **touches** the circle.
- A **secant** to a circle from an external point is a line that **cuts** the circle.

> # CIRCLE THEOREMS

1. A perpendicular from the centre of a circle to a chord bisects the chord.

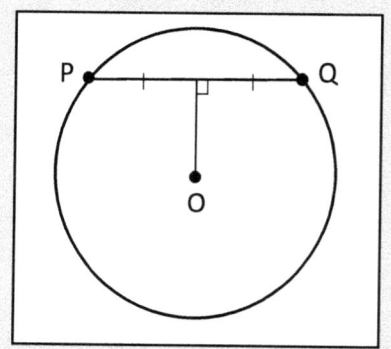

2. Equal chords of a circle are equidistant from the centre.

   OP = OQ

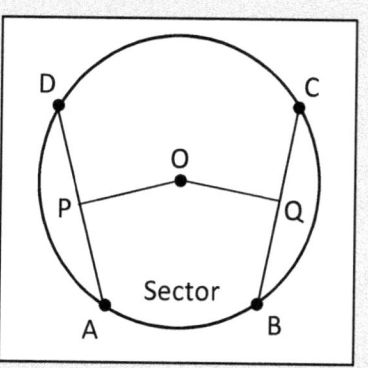

3. The products of the lengths of the line segments
   on each chord are equal.

   AD = BC

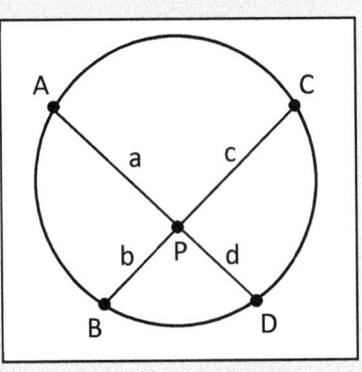

4. Angle in a semi-circle is a right angle.
   An angle subtended by a diameter
   at a point in a circle is a right angle.

   Angle XYZ = 90^0

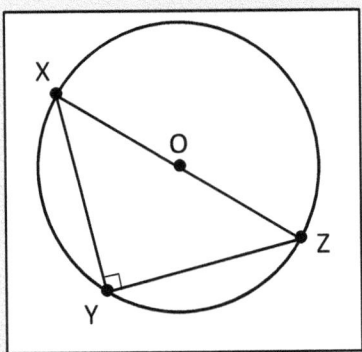

5. Angles in the same segment are equal.
   Angles subtended by the same arc
   at the circumference are equal.

   θ = 40

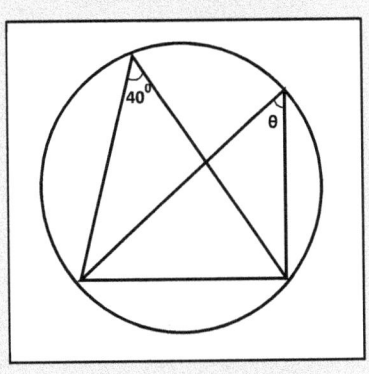

6. Angle subtended by an arc at the centre of a circle
   is twice that subtended at the circumference.

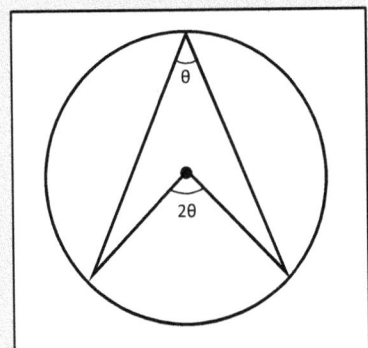

7. The opposite angles of a cyclic quadrilateral (a quadrilateral inscribed in a circle) add up to 180 degrees (i.e. they are supplementary).

a + c = 180 degrees

b + d = 180 degrees

e = a

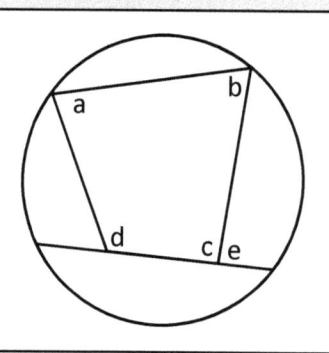

8. The two tangents from an external point to a circle are equal in length.

BA = BC (OB bisects angle ABC)

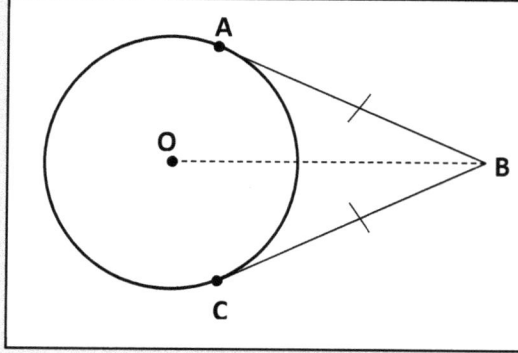

9. The angle between a tangent and a chord is equal to the angle in the alternate segment. The chord AB makes 45^0 with the tangent at A. x^0 is the angle in the alternate segment.

x = 45^0

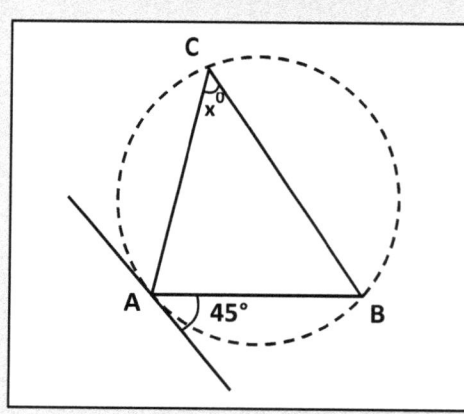

11. The square of the length of the tangent to a circle is equal to the product of the lengths of the external secant segment and the secant segment.

$UV^2 = UX \times UY$

- UV is the external secant segment
- UY is the secant Segment

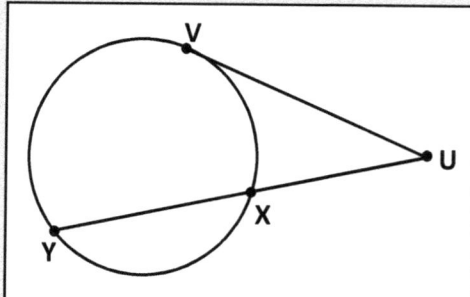

Example:

In the circle above, if UX = 4cm and XY = 5cm, find the length of UV.

UV^2 = UX × UY = 4 × 9 = 36

UV = 6cm

THREE DIMENSIONAL SHAPES

Unlike two-dimensional shapes, three-dimensional shapes have thickness or depth. They have faces, edges and vertices. **They have surface area and volume.**

A **cube** has 6 square faces, 12 edges, and 8 vertices.

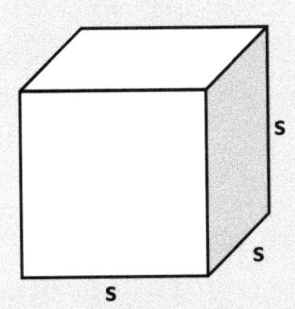

Surface area of a cube = $6s^2$ square units

Volume of a cube = s^3 cubic units

(s is the length of an edge)

A **cuboid** differs from a cube in its shape only. While each face of a cube is a square, each face of a cuboid is a rectangle. A cuboid's length (l), width (w) and height (h) are different.

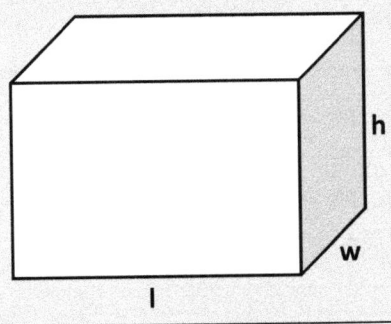

Surface area of a cuboid:

= 2[(l × w) + (l × h) + (w × h)] square units

Volume of a cube:

= l × w × h cubic units

A right circular solid **cylinder** has two circular bases of radii r connected by a curved surface of height, h which when opened up is rectangular in shape with dimensions 2πr and h.

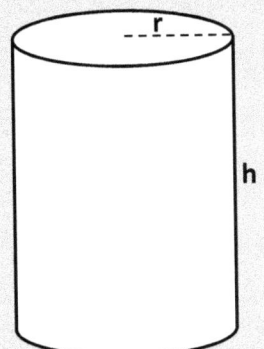

Surface area of a solid cylinder = $2\pi r^2 + 2\pi rh$ square units

Volume of a cylinder = $\pi r^2 h$ cubic units

A right circular **cone** is a three-dimensional geometric shape with a curved surface that tapers smoothly from a flat base (usually circular) to a point called the vertex.
It has a vertical height (h) as well as a slant height (s).

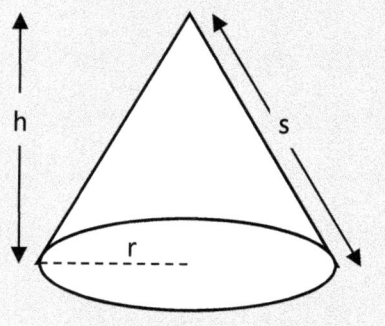

Surface area of a right cone $= \pi r^2 + \pi r s$

Volume of a cone $= \frac{1}{3}\pi r^2 h$

A **sphere** is a three-dimensional ball formed by rotating a circle about one of its diameters. All points on it are equal distance from the centre.

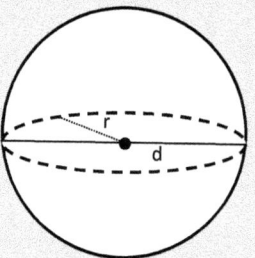

Surface area of a sphere $= 4\pi r^2$

Volume of a sphere $= \frac{4}{3}\pi r^3$

Any solid with polygonal side is a **polyhedron**. Thus cones, spheres, and cylinders are not polyhedrons. The common polyhedrons are prisms, pyramids and Tetrahedrons.

PRISM

A prism is a polyhedron, with two parallel faces called bases. The other faces are always rectangles. The prism is named by the shape of its base. Thus, there are triangular and rectangular prisms.

A regular right **triangular prism** has 5 faces, 6 vertices and 9 edges.
It has two triangular shapes and three rectangular shapes.

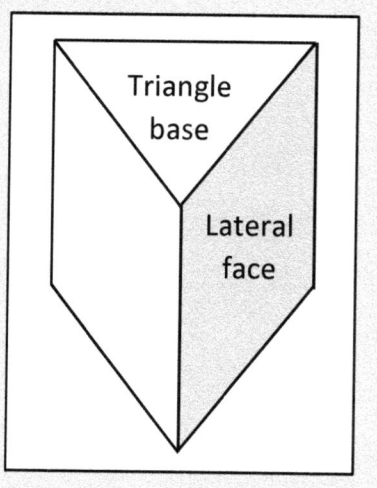

Total surface area:

= height × (a + b + c) + (2 × base area)

- a, b, c are sides of the base triangle

- base area is the triangular base area

Volume = area of base × height

A solid 3-dimensional object with 6 rectangular faces is a **rectangular prism**.
A cuboid is also a rectangular prism.

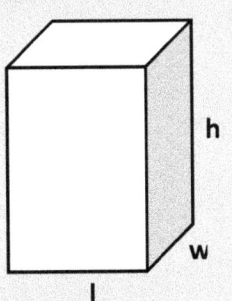

Surface area of a cuboid:

= $2[(l \times w) + (l \times h) + (w \times h)]$ square units

Volume of a cube:

= $l \times w \times h$ cubic units

A **pyramid** is a polyhedron that has a base, which can be any polygon, and three or more triangular faces that meet at a point called the apex.

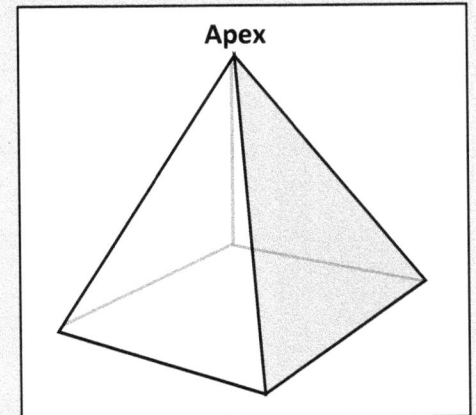

Apex

Total Surface Area:

= Area of base + 4 × area of a triangle

Volume of a regular rectangular pyramid:

= Area of base × $\dfrac{h}{3}$ (where h is the vertical height)

A **tetrahedron** also known as a triangular pyramid, is a polyhedron composed of four triangular faces, six straight edges, and four vertex corners. Each side is an equilateral triangle, with side length of 'a' units.

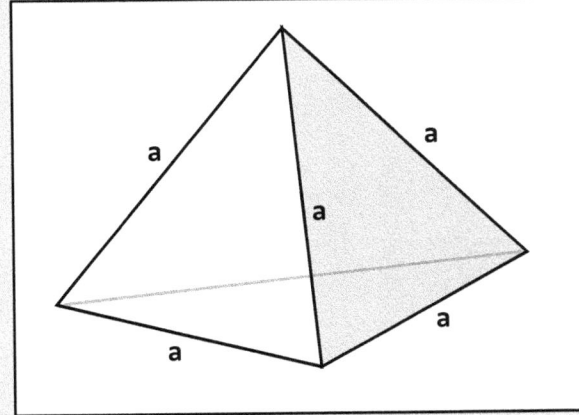

Area of one side = $\sqrt{3}a^2$

Total Surface Area of a regular tetrahedron:

= $4\sqrt{3}a^2$ square units

The volume of a regular tetrahedron:

V = $a^3\dfrac{\sqrt{2}}{12}$

MISCELLANEOUS PROBLEMS

A1. Find the value of the pronumerals in the following:

(a)

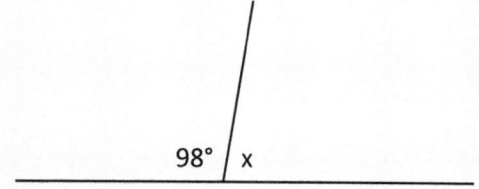

98° x

(b)

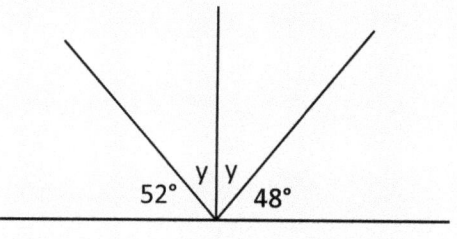

52° y y 48°

A2. (a) Find the supplements of: 45^0, 82^0 and 144^0

(b) Find the complements of: 28^0, 56^0 and 69^0

A3. Find the value of the pronumerals in the following:

(a)

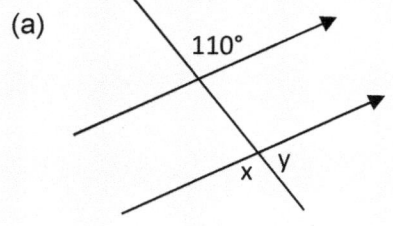

110°

x y

(b)

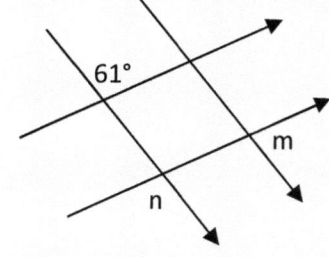

61°

m

n

A4. Find the value of x in each of the following using the exterior angle properties.

(a)

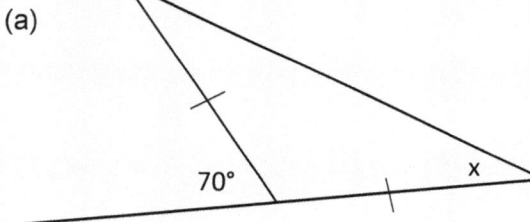

70° x

(b)

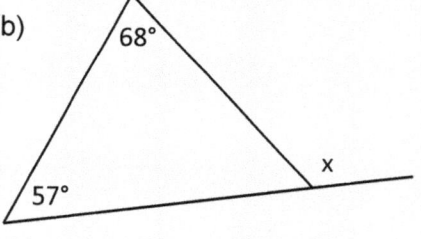

68°

57° x

A5. (a) In a right-angled triangle, if the hypotenuse is 4.5 cm and one of the other two sides is 3.6cm. What is the length of the third side?

(b) What is the length of the hypotenuse, if the lengths of the other two sides of a right-angled triangle are 15cm and 36cm?

A6. In a triangle PQR, S and T are points on PR and QR respectively. PT bisects angle QPR and ∠PQS = ∠PRQ. PT and QS intersect at U. Prove using the exterior angle property that QU = QT

A7. ABC is a triangle. D and E are points on AC and BC respectively such that DE is parallel to AB. If AD = x, CD = 8cm, BE = 3cm and CE = (x + 2), find the value of x using similar triangle ratio.

A8. ABC is a triangle. P and Q are the mid-points of AB and AC respectively. R is the mid-point of QC. PQ and BR are produced to meet at S. Prove the following:
(a) Triangles BCR and SQR are congruent
(b) R is the mid-point of SB
(b) PQ:QS = 1:2

B1. The angles of a quadrilateral are in the ratio 1:2:3:4.
What are the angles of the quadrilateral?

B2. The sum of the interior angles of a regular polygon is 1260. How many sides has the polygon. What is its name?

B3. PQRS is a Rhombus. T is a point on PS such that RT bisects angle PRS.
Prove that angle STR is three times angle PRT.

B4. ABCD is a parallelogram. The bisectors of angles A and B meet on CD at E. Prove:
(i) E is the midpoint of CD
(ii) Angle AEB is 90^0

B5. What is the area of a trapezium whose parallel sides are of lengths 4cm and 6cm and its height is 5cm?

B6. The diagonals of a Rhombus measure 8cm and 18 cm. What is its perimeter?
What is its area?

B7. What is the area of a triangle whose sides are 4cm, 8cm and 10cm?

B8. What is the size of each interior angle of the following regular polygons:
(a) 8 sided
(b) 10 sided
(c) 14 sided

C1. A circle has a diameter 7cm long. Calculate its:
(a) circumference
(b) area

C2. An arc of a circle of radius 6.3 cm subtends an angle of 60^0 at the centre. Calculate:
(a) the length of the arc
(b) the area of the sector formed by joining the ends of the arc to the centre of the circle

C3. The opposite angles of a cyclic quadrilateral are $(x + 30)^0$ and $(x - 18)^0$.
Find the value of x.

C4. Two chords of a circle AB and CD intersect at X. If AX = 3cm, BX = 4cm and CX = 2.5cm, calculate the length of DX.

C5. Two points X and Y on the circumference of a circle are subtended by an arc AB. If angle AXB is $(x + 15)^0$ and angle AYB is $(4x - 21)^0$ find the value of x.

C6. Two circles meet at points X and Y. AXB and CYD are two lines which meet one circle at A and C and the other at B and D. Prove that AC is parallel to BD.

C7. PA is a tangent to a circle and PBC a secant. If PA = (x + 5), PB = x and BC = 13cm, find the value of x.

C8. OA and OB are radii of a circle centre O. DAE is a tangent to the circle at A. If angle OBA is 30^0, calculate the value of angle ACB where C is a point on the circumference in the larger segment AB (Give two methods).

D1. A cube has a side length of 10cm. Calculate its:
(a) total surface area
(b) volume

D2. A cuboid has dimensions 8cm × 6cm × 4cm. Calculate its:
(a) total surface area
(b) volume

D3. A cone and a cylinder have the same volume of 210cm^3 and the same height of 12cm. Which of these two solids has a larger surface area?

D4. Calculate the volume of a sphere with a radius of 14cm.

D5. Calculate the total surface area of a right triangular prism given that its height is 9 cm, the triangular base area is 24cm^2 and the sides a, b, c of the triangular base 6cm, 8cm and 10cm respectively.

D6. Find the surface area and volume of a square pyramid with a base edge of 16 cm and height 8 cm.

D7. Calculate the area of a Tetrahedron with side 6cm. What is its volume?

D8. Find the volume of a rectangular pyramid with base dimensions 14cm × 8cm and vertical height 12cm.

ANSWERS TO MISCELLANEOUS PROBLEMS

A1. (a) $98 + x = 180$

$x = 180 - 98 = 82$

(b) $52 + 2y + 48 = 180$

$2y + 100 = 180$

$2y = 80$

$y = 40$

A2. (a) $135^0, 98^0, 36^0$ (b) $62^0, 34^0, 21^0$

A3. (a) $110 + y = 180$

$y = 70$

$x + y = 180$

$x = 180 - 70 = 110$

(b) $m = 61, n = 180 - 61 = 119$

A4. (a) $2x = 70, x = 35$

(b) $x = 57 + 68 = 125^0$

A5. (a) Length of third side $= \sqrt{4.5^2 - 3.6^2} = \sqrt{8.1 \times 0.9} = 2.7\text{cm}$

(b) Hypotenuse $= \sqrt{15^2 + 36^2} = \sqrt{225 + 1296} = \sqrt{1521} = 39\text{cm}$

A6. Prove: QU = QT

Proof: $\angle QTU = x + y$

$\angle QUT = x + y$ Since $\angle PQS = \angle PRQ$

$\therefore \angle QTU = \angle QUT$ $\triangle$ QUT is isosceles

$\therefore$ QU = QT

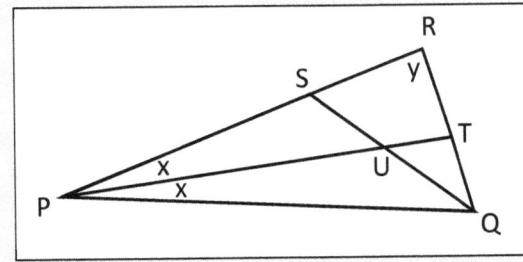

A7. $\dfrac{8}{x+8} = \dfrac{x+2}{x+5}$

$8x + 40 = x^2 + 10x + 16$

$x^2 + 2x - 24 = 0$

$(x+6)(x-4) = 0$

$x = 4$

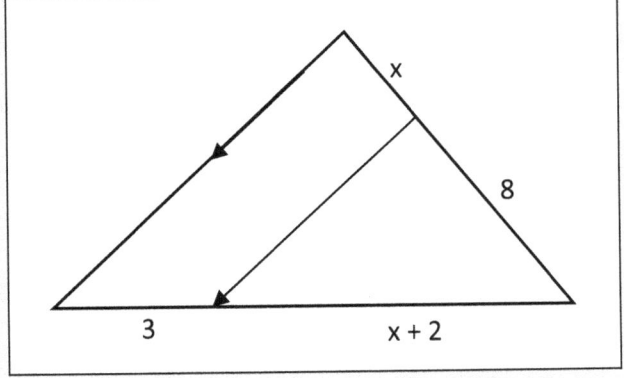

A8. Prove: (a) ΔBCR ≅ ΔSQR

           (b) R is the mid-point of BS

           (c) PQ:QS = 1:2

∠AQP = ∠BCR | Corresponding angles since PQ∥BC |

∠SQR = ∠AQP | Vertically opposite angles |

∴ ∠SQR = ∠BCR

Now, In the two triangles BCR and SQR:

∠BCR = ∠SQR | Proved above |

∠BRC = ∠SRQ | Vertically opposite angles |

CR = QR | Given |

∴ ΔBCR ≅ ΔSQR | AAS |

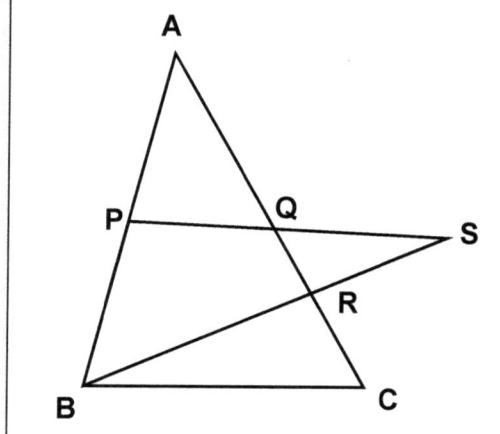

Hence, BR = SR and BC = QS

Therefore, R is the mid-point of BS

(c) PQ = $\frac{1}{2}$BC | Since P and Q are midpoints of AB and AC |

But, BC = QS

∴ PQ = $\frac{1}{2}$QS

That is, PQ:QS = 1:2

B1. Let the angles of the quadrilateral be x, 2x, 3x and 4x.

Therefore, x + 2x + 3x + 4x = 360

10x = 360

x = 36

The angles of the quadrilateral are: 360, 720, 1080 and 1440

B2. Let the number of sides of the polygon be n.

Therefore: (2n − 4) × 90 = 1260

2n × 4 = 14

2n = 18

n = 9

The polygon is a nonagon.

B3. Prove: ∠STR = 3 × ∠PRT

Proof: Let ∠PRT = x

Therefore: ∠SRT = x

Hence: ∠PRS = 2x

But: ∠RPS = ∠PRS = 2x | PSR is an isosceles triangle

Now, ∠STR = 3x | exterior angle of triangle PTR

Therefore: ∠STR = 3 × ∠PRT

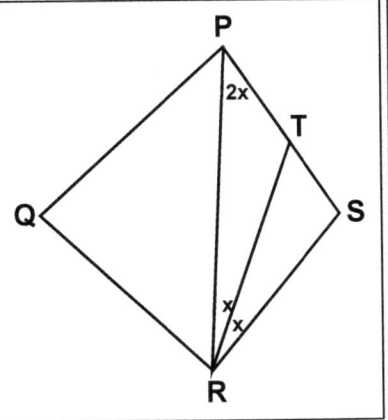

B4. Prove: (a) DE = CE
            (b) ∠AEB = 90°

Proof: Let ∠ABC = 2x and ∠DAB = 2y

ΔADE and ΔBCE are isosceles.

∴ AD = DE and BC = CE

But AD = BC

∴ DE = CE | opposite sides of parallelogram

Now, 2x + 2y = 180°

x + y = 90 | co-interior angles since AD∥BC

∴ ∠AEB = 90° [180 − (x + y)]

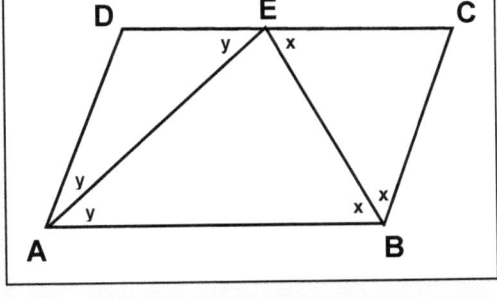

B5. Area of Trapezium = $\frac{1}{2}$(a + b) × h

= $\frac{1}{2}$(6 + 4) × 5 = 25cm^2

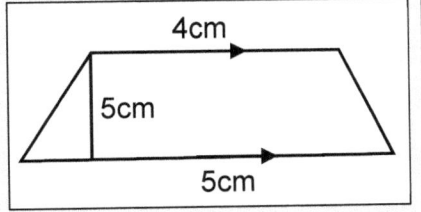

4cm

5cm

5cm

B6. Perimeter of Rhombus = 4a | a = side of the Rhombus

= 4 × $\sqrt{16 + 81}$ = 4 × $\sqrt{97}$ = 4 × 9.85 = 39.4cm

Area of Rhombus = $\frac{1}{2}$pq | p and q are lengths of diagonals

= $\frac{1}{2}$ × 8 × 18 = 72cm^2

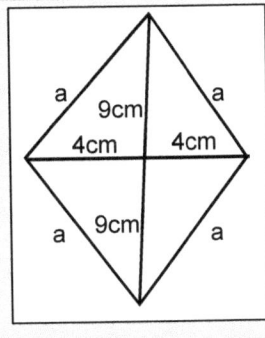

B7. 2s = 4 + 8 + 10 = 22

s = 11

Area of triangle = $\sqrt{s(s-a)(s-b)(s-c)}$ = $\sqrt{11(11-4)(11-8)(11-10)}$

= $\sqrt{11(7)(3)(1)}$ = $\sqrt{231}$ = 15.2cm^2

B8. An interior angle of:

(a) 8-sided polygon $= \dfrac{2 \times 8 - 4 \times 90}{8} = 1350$

(b) 10-sided polygon $= \dfrac{2 \times 10 - 4 \times 90}{10} = 1440$

(c) 14-sided polygon $= \dfrac{2 \times 14 - 4 \times 90}{14} = 154.290$

C1. (a) Circumference of a circle $= 2\pi r = 2 \times \dfrac{22}{7} \times \dfrac{7}{2} = 22$cm

(b) Area of a circle $= \pi r^2 = \dfrac{22}{7} \times \dfrac{7}{2} \times \dfrac{7}{2} = 38\dfrac{1}{2}$cm^2

C2. (a) Length of an arc of a circle $= r\theta = 6.3 \times \dfrac{60}{180}\,\pi$ (θ is in radians)

$= 6.3 \times \dfrac{1}{3} \times \dfrac{22}{7} = 6.6$cm

(b) Area of a sector of a circle $= \dfrac{1}{2}r^2\theta = \dfrac{1}{2} \times 6.3 \times 6.3 \times \dfrac{1}{3} \times \dfrac{22}{7} = 20.79$cm^2

C3. The opposite angles of a cyclic quadrilateral add up to 180^0.

$\therefore x + 30 + x - 18 = 180$

$2x = 180 - 12 = 168$

$x = 84^0$

C4. $DX \times 2.5 = 3 \times 4$

$DX = \dfrac{12}{2.5} = 4.8$ cm

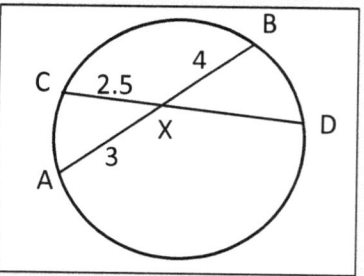

C5. Angles subtended at the circumference by the same arc are equal.

$\therefore x + 15 = 4x - 21$

$3x = 36$

$x = 12$

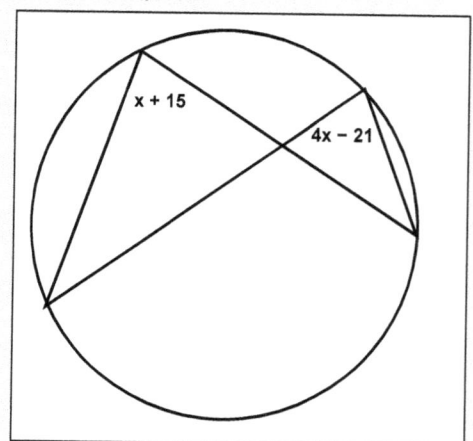

C6. Let ∠DBX = x and ∠CAX = y

Therefore: ∠CYX = x and ∠DYX = y | Ext. angle = interior opp. angle

But: ∠CYX + ∠DYX = 180⁰ | Angle in a straight line

∴ x + y = 180⁰

But x and y are co-interior angles of ACDB

∴ AC is parallel to BD

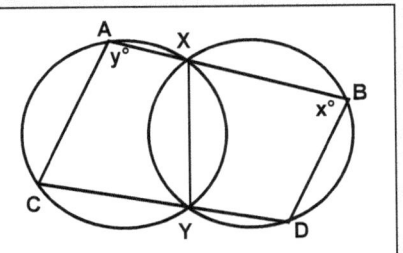

C7. PB × PC = PA²

$x(x + 13) = (x + 5)^2$

$x^2 + 13x = x^2 + 10x + 25$

$3x = 25$

$x = 8\frac{1}{3}$cm

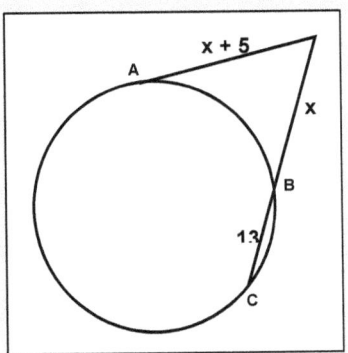

C8. Method 1: ∠OAB = ∠OBA = 30⁰ | Triangle OAB is isosceles

∴ ∠AOB = 120⁰

∠ACB = 60⁰ | Angle subtended by an arc at the centre is twice angle subtended at the circumference

Method 2: ∠OAB = 30⁰ | Triangle OAB is isosceles

∠OAE = 90⁰ | Angle between tangent and radius

∴ ∠BAE = 60⁰

But: ∠BAE = ∠ACB | Angle between tangent and chord is equal to angle in the alternate segment

∴ ∠ACB = 60⁰

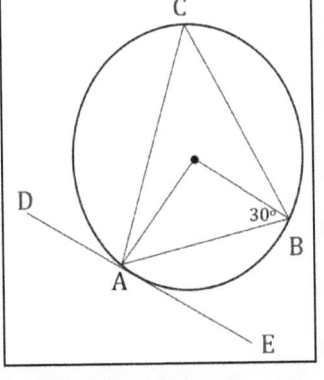

D1. A cube has 6 equal square faces.

Area of one face = 10 × 10 = 100cm²

Total surface area = 6 × 100 = 600cm²

Volume of cube = $L^3 = 10^3 = 1000$cm³

D2. (a) Area of cuboid = 2(8 × 6) + 2(6 × 4) + 2 (8 × 4) = 96 + 48 + 64 = 208cm²

(b) Volume of cuboid = 8 × 6 × 4 = 112cm³

D3. Volume of cone $= \frac{1}{3}\pi r^2 h = \frac{1}{3} \times \frac{22}{7} \times (r_1)^2 \times 12$

$\therefore \frac{264}{21} \times (r_1)^2 = 210$

$(r_1)^2 = \frac{21 \times 210}{264} = 12.115$

$r_1 = 3.48\text{cm}$

Volume of cylinder $= \pi r^2 h = \frac{22}{7} \times (r_2)^2 \times 12$

$\therefore \frac{264}{7} (r_2)^2 = 210$

$(r_2)^2 = \frac{210 \times 7}{264} = 5.568$

$r_2 = 2.36\text{cm}$

Surface area of cone $= \pi (r_1)^2 + \pi r_1 L = \frac{22}{7} \times 12.115 + \frac{22}{7} \times 3.48 \times \sqrt{12^2 + 12.115}$

$= 38.08 + \frac{22}{7} \times 3.48 \times 12.495 = 38.08 + 136.66 = 174.74\text{cm}^2$

Surface area of cylinder $= \pi (r_2)^2 + 2\pi r^2 h = \frac{22}{7} \times 5.568 + 2 \times \frac{22}{7} \times 2.36 \times 12$

$= 17.499 + 178.01 = 195.51\text{cm}^2$

Therefore, the cylinder has a larger surface area

D4. Volume of a sphere $= \frac{4}{3}\pi r^3 = \frac{4}{3} \times \frac{22}{7} \times 14 \times 14 \times 14 = 11498.67\text{cm}^3$

D5. Total surface area of a right triangular prism $=$ height $\times$ base perimeter $+ 2 \times$ base area
$= h(a + b + c) + 2 \text{ (base area)} = 9(6 + 8 + 10) + (2 \times 24)$
$= 9 \times 24 + 2 \times 24 = 216 + 48 = 264\text{cm}^2$

D6. Total surface area of a square pyramid $=$ Area of square base $+ 4 \times$ area of a triangle
$= 16 \times 16 + 4 \left(\frac{1}{3} \times 16 \times 8\right) = 256 + 256 = 512\text{cm}^2$
Volume of a square pyramid $= l \times b \times h = 16 \times 16 \times 8 = 2048\text{cm}^3$

D7. Area of a tetrahedron $= 4\sqrt{3}a^2$ | a = length of a side of triangle
$= 4\sqrt{3} \times 6 \times 6 = 144\sqrt{3}\text{cm}^2$

Volume of a tetrahedron $= \frac{\sqrt{2}}{12}a^3 = \frac{\sqrt{2}}{12} \times 6 \times 6 \times 6 = 18\sqrt{2}\text{cm}^3$

D8. Area of a rectangular pyramid $= \frac{\text{Area of base} \times \text{height}}{3} = \frac{14 \times 8 \times 12}{3} = 448\text{cm}^3$

1. Find the values of the pronumerals in each of the following:

(a)

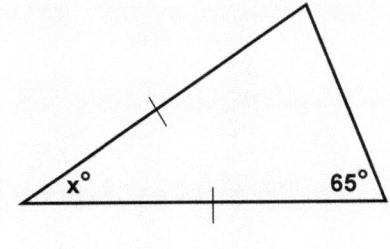

(b)

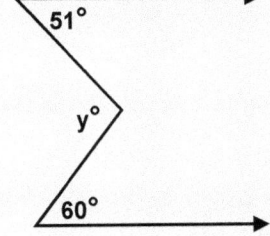

(c)

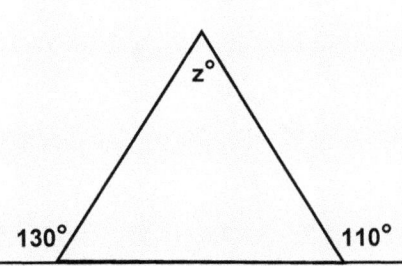

(d)

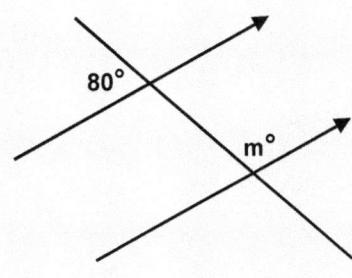

2. (a) Prove that: $s = p + q$

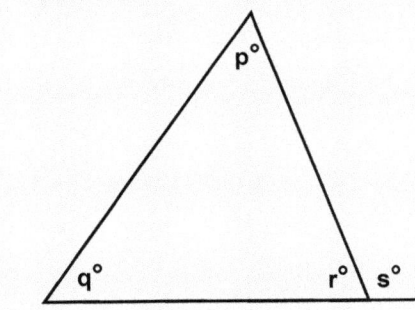

(b) Find the value of y.

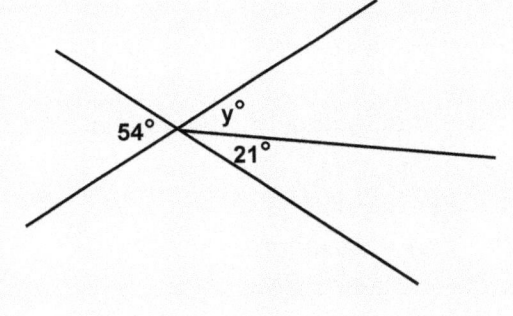

3. In the diagram, PQ = 5cm, QS = 22cm, ST = 9cm.
    Calculate the length of PT correct to 2 decimal places.
    (Hint: Draw a line from T perpendicular to PQ produced)

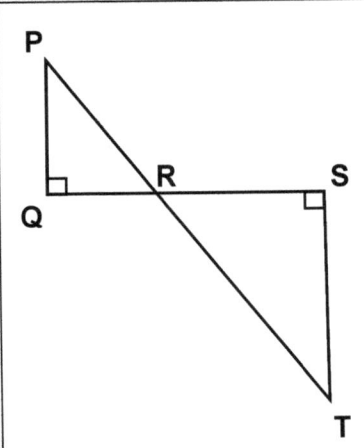

4. Calculate the perimeter and area of the following:

(a)

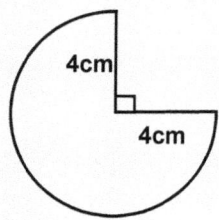

4cm

4cm

(b)

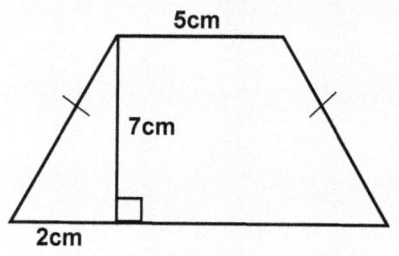

5cm

7cm

2cm

5. One of the conditions for a quadrilateral to be a parallelogram is that its opposite sides must be equal in length. PQRS is a parallelogram. X and Y are points on PR such that PX = RY. Prove that SXQY is a parallelogram.

6. Calculate the value of the pronumerals in the following diagrams:

(a)

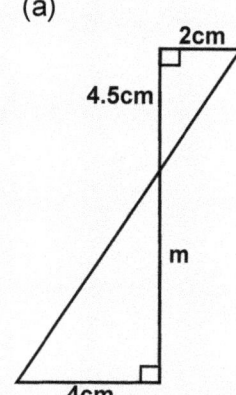

2cm

4.5cm

m

4cm

(b) AB is the diameter

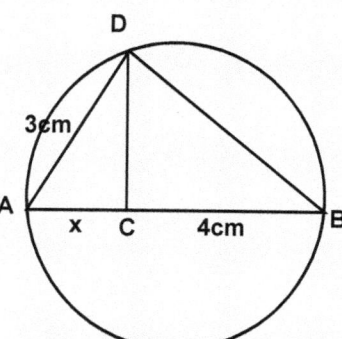

D

3cm

A

x C

4cm

B

(c)

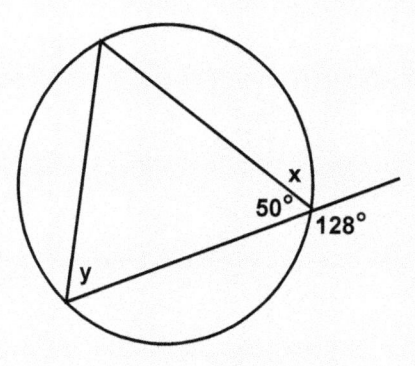

x

50°

128°

y

7. (a) The number of diagonals of an n-sided polygon is $\dfrac{n(n-3)}{2}$.

Calculate the number of diagonals of:
   (i) a pentagon
   (ii) a hexagon
   (iii) a decagon.

(b) Calculate the volume of a hexagonal prism of height 6.5cm with a base edge of 4cm.

8. (a) The volume of the solid shown below is 1386mm^3. Calculate its length.

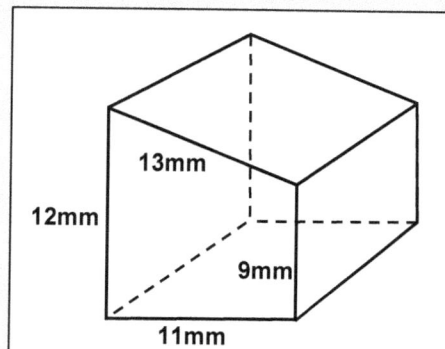

13mm

12mm

9mm

11mm

(b) Find the area of the annulus formed by two concentric circles of radii 8cm and 6cm (leave the answer in π).

1. What is the area of the cloth required (including that for the ground) to make a tent in the shape and dimensions shown below?

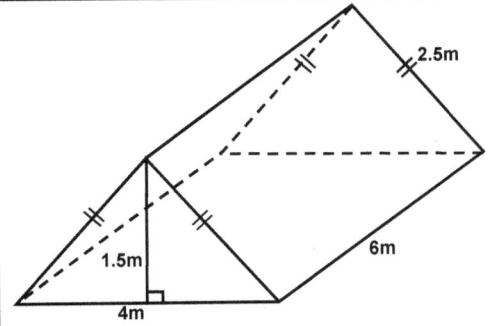

Area of the ground $= 6 \times 9 = 54m^2$

Area of the two triangular shapes $= 2 \times \dfrac{1}{2} \times 6 \times 2.25 = 13.5m^2$

Area of the two rectangular shaped sides $= 2 \times 9 \times 3.75 = 67.5m^2$

Area of cloth required $= 54 + 13.5 + 67.5 = 135m^2$

2. You want to build a fence around your rectangular swimming pool. The dimensions of the pool are 6.6m by 5.4m. You want the border around the pool to be of uniform width. If you have 28 metres of fencing, find the width of the border.

Let the width of the border be x metres.

Length of fence $= 6.6 + 2x$

Width of fence $= 5.4 + 2x$

Perimeter of fence $= 2 \times (6.6 + 2x + 5.4 + 2x) = 2(12 + 4x) = 24 + 8x$

Therefore, $24 + 8x = 28$

$8x = 4$

$x = \dfrac{1}{2}$ metre $= 50cm$

Width of border $= 50cm$

3. A cylindrical lead pipe is 8cm long. Its internal and external diameters are 3.15cm and 4.65 cm respectively. It is melted and cast into a solid cylinder 7cm long. Find the diameter of the solid cylinder correct to two decimal places.

Volume of metal in the pipe $= \pi(4.65^2 - 3.15^2) \times 8 = 3.14 \times 7.8 \times 1.5 \times 8 = 293.90cm^3$

Let r be the radius of the solid cylinder.

Therefore: $\pi \times r^2 \times 7 = 293.90$

$r^2 = \dfrac{293.90}{3.14 \times 7} = 13.37$

$r = 3.656$

Diameter of the solid cylinder $= 7.31cm$

1. (a) $x + 65 + 65 = 180$

   $x + 130 = 180$

   $x = 50^0$

   (b) $y = 51 + 60 = 111^0$

   (c) $z + 50 = 110$

   $z = 60^0$

   (d) $m + 80 = 180$

   $m = 100^0$

2. (a) $p + q + r = 180$ Angles of a triangle

   $r + s = 180$ Angle in a straight line

   That is: $p + q + 180 - s = 180$

   $p + q - s = 0$

   $s = p + q$

   (b) $y + 21 = 54$

   $y = 33^0$

3. $PT^2 = 22^2 + 14^2 = 484 + 196 = 680$

   $PT = 26.08$

4. (a) Perimeter $= 4 + 4 + 4 \times \dfrac{270}{180} \times \pi = 8 + 18.84 = 26.84$cm

   Area $= \dfrac{3}{4}\pi r^2 = \dfrac{3}{4}\pi \times 4 \times 4 = \dfrac{3}{4} \times 3.14 \times 16 = 37.68$cm^2

   (b) Let the length of equal sides $= x$cm

   Therefore, $x^2 = 7^2 + 2^2 = 49 + 4 = 53$

   $x = 7.28$cm

   Perimeter $= 2 \times 7.28 + 5 + 9 = 14.56 + 14 = 28.58$cm

   Area $= \dfrac{1}{2} \times (5 + 9) \times 7 = 7 \times 7 = 79$cm^2

5. Prove: SXQY is a parallelogram

   Proof: In the two triangles SXP and RYQ:

   SP = RQ   Opposite sides of parallelogram

   PX = RY   Given

   Incl. $\angle$SPX = Incl. $\angle$QRY

   Therefore, the triangles SXP and RYQ are congruent.

   Hence: SX = QY

   Similarly, the two triangles PXQ and SYR are congruent.

   Hence: SY = QX

   Therefore, SXQY is a parallelogram

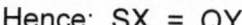

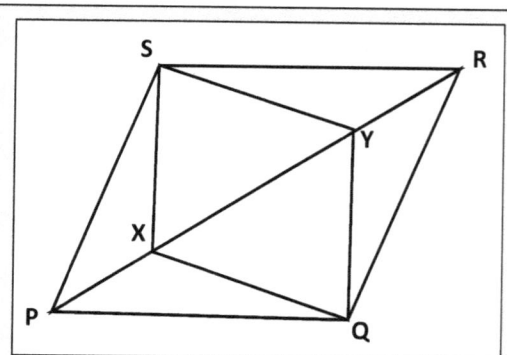

6.(a) The two triangles in the diagram are similar.

Therefore: $\dfrac{2}{4} = \dfrac{4.5}{m}$

$2m = 18$

$m = 9$

(b) $\angle ADB = 90^0$ $\boxed{\text{Angle in a semi-circle}}$

The two triangles ACD and ABD are similar.

Therefore: $\dfrac{3}{x+4} = \dfrac{x}{3}$

i.e. $x^2 + 4x = 9$

$x^2 + 4x + 9 = 0$

$x = \dfrac{4 \pm \sqrt{16 + 36}}{2} = \dfrac{4 \pm \sqrt{52}}{2} = \dfrac{4 \pm 2\sqrt{13}}{2} = \sqrt{13} - 2$

(c) $50 + x = 128$ $\boxed{\text{Vertically opposite angles}}$

$x = 78^0$

$y = x = 78$ $\boxed{\text{Angle between tangent and chord equals angle in the alternate segment}}$

7. (a) (i) Number of diagonals of a pentagon $= \dfrac{5(5-3)}{2} = 5$

(ii) Number of diagonals of a hexagon $= \dfrac{6(6-3)}{2} = 9$

(iii) Number of diagonals of a decagon $= \dfrac{10(10-3)}{2} = 35$

(b) Volume of a hexagonal prism $= \dfrac{3}{2}\sqrt{3}a^2h = \dfrac{3}{2}\sqrt{3} \times 4 \times 4 \times 6.5 = 270.2\text{cm}^3$

---

8. Area of Trapezium $= \dfrac{1}{2}(12 + 9) \times 11 = 115.5\text{mm}^2$

Let the length of the solid be xmm

Therefore, the volume of solid $= 115.5x\text{mm}^3$

That is, $115.5x = 1386$

$x = \dfrac{1386}{115.5} = 12$

Length of solid $= 12\text{mm}$

(b) Area of annulus $= \pi(8^2 - 6^2)$

$= \pi(64 - 36) = 28\pi\text{cm}^2$

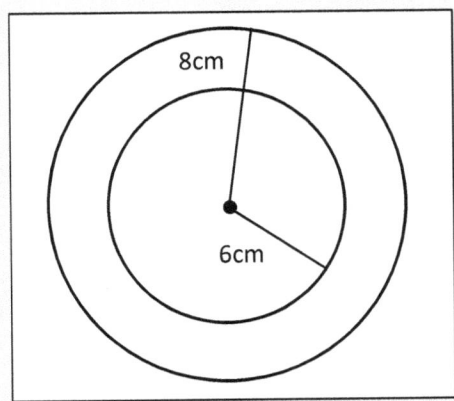

12. STATISTICS – DATA ANALYSIS

Statistics is the science of collecting numerical facts (or data), studying and analysing them, and drawing conclusions. Data may relate to number of births, deaths, production, sales, imports, exports, salaries and wages, profits and losses, employment, etc. Data also refers to actual observations relating to certain measurements that result from an investigation. Since these measurements take varying values, they are called **variables**.

Statistics can be divided into two basic areas:

1. **Descriptive** statistics involves arranging, summarising and presenting data so as to be meaningful.

2. **Inferential** statistics is a body of methods which is used for drawing conclusions about a population based on a sample taken from the population.

Data falls into two main types:

1. **Numerical** data can be **discrete** or **continuous.**

- **Discrete** refers to a set of values which are integers that correspond with a count of some sort e.g. number of children in a family, number of houses in a street

- **Continuous** data are associated with measuring. They take any value within a range e.g. temperature, height of an individual

2. **Categorical** data can be **nominal** or **ordinal**.

- **Nominal** data are those that are divided into sub groups. They are data that cannot be ordered or measured e.g. eye colour, hair colour, a person's gender.

- **Ordinal** data are those that are put in a ranked order. They are data placed into some kind of order or scale e.g. age, movie ratings.

A useful method of **arranging data** is to group it into intervals called **"classes"** and to record the number of observations in each class. This arrangement is called **frequency distribution** (or frequency table). An example of a class interval is shown below:

Wages: $20 and Under $30
        $30 and Under $40 etc.

The size of the class interval (or class width) is $10

- The number of classes to be used depends on the number of measurements.

- The difference between the highest and lowest measurements is called the **Range**.

- The number of classes is obtained by using the formula:

$$\text{Number of classes} = \frac{\text{Range}}{\text{Size of class interval}}$$

In order to maintain a certain amount of accuracy, it is preferable to use between 8 and 12 classes (the formula is valid only when all the class intervals are equal).

An example of a frequency distribution with three classes is shown below:

Wages (class)	Employees (frequency)
$20 to $29	8
$30 to $39	15
$40 to $49	10

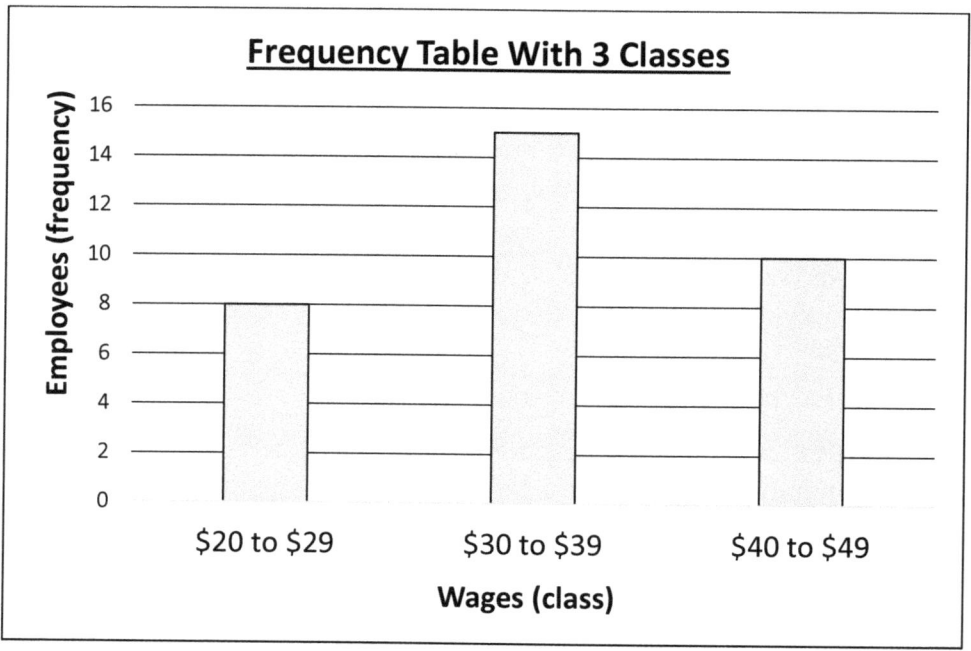

Each class has a lower number and an upper number. The lower number is called the **lower-class limit** and the upper number is called the **upper-class limit.** The difference between the upper-class limit and the lower-class limit of a class is its **width.** The sum of the two class limits of each class divided by two is called its **mid-point.**

For example, the mid-point of the first class is: $\dfrac{\$20 + \$29}{2}$ = $24.50

The **class boundary** is the midpoint of the upper-class limit of one class and the lower-class limit of the subsequent class. The upper-class boundary of one class and the lower-class boundary of the subsequent class are the same. The upper-class boundary of the first class and the lower-class boundary of the second class in the above example are the same and are equal to $29.50.

- The number of items falling in each class is called the class **frequency.**
- The sum of the frequency of a class and those of all other classes above it is called its **cumulative frequency.**
- The ratio of a class's frequency to total frequency is called its **relative frequency.**

The following table illustrates the terminology encountered previously:

Lower Class Limit ($)	Upper Class Limit ($)	Mid-point ($)	Class Frequency	Class Cumulative Frequency	Class Relative Frequency
101	200	150.5	5	5	$\frac{5}{40} = 0.125$
201	300	250.5	8	13	$\frac{8}{40} = 0.2$
301	400	350.5	10	23	$\frac{10}{40} = 0.25$
401	500	450.5	12	35	$\frac{12}{40} = 0.3$
501	600	550.5	5	40	$\frac{5}{40} = 0.125$

FREQUENCY TABLES

Example:

Arrange the weights (in kilograms) of 40 students given below in a frequency distribution table using appropriate number of classes and class intervals:

50	54	60	63	66	68	72	80	55	75
52	48	58	62	67	45	61	68	44	59
47	55	71	64	66	79	48	41	61	48
56	75	43	70	57	62	50	55	40	43

Solution:

Class	Mid-point (x)	Tally	Frequency (f)
40 – 44	42	卌	5
45 – 49	47	卌	5
50 – 54	52	IIII	4
55 – 59	57	卌 II	7
60 – 64	62	卌 II	7
65 – 69	67	卌	5
70 – 74	72	III	3
75 – 79	77	III	3
80 – 84	82	I	1
			40

SOURCES OF DATA

There are several publications in statistics which fall under the following headings:

1. General statistical journals

2. Specific journals

Data is collected and published by both the government and private organisations.

- **Primary data** refers to quantitative information collected for the primary purposes of a statistical work. It is data collected through questionnaires, interviews and so on.

- **Secondary data** refers to information already published by specialist organisations but used in a current statistical work.

VISUAL PRESENTATION OF DATA

Statistical information is grasped easily if presented using some sort of visual aid. The visual aids used are as follows:

Bar Charts

Simple Bar Charts: A series of rectangular bars of the same width which are separated, where each rectangular bar represents a single quantity which varies. These charts show changes over a period of time very clearly by means of different heights of the charts.

Multiple or Compound Bar Charts: Similar data relating to two or more periods are displayed by drawing adjacently jointed bars for each period.

Component Bar Chart: Different components in a particular data are shown using a single partitioned bar. The component bar charts show the relationship of the whole to the separate parts making the whole.

A **pie chart** takes the shape of a circle divided into various sectors, each sector subtending a percentage of 360^0 at the centre of the circle. The different sectors represent the components, the areas of which are proportional to the amount of each component.

Like component bar charts, the pie charts enable the reader to compare the relative sizes easily. As the name suggests, **line graphs** show the data by means of connecting lines. They are useful for showing the upward or downward trend.

Pictograms are a visual display of data using a preferred picture. By using one's imagination the data is presented in an informative and interesting manner through the picture.

Summarising large masses of raw data using the above charts and graphs make it easier for the reader to understand them better as eyes and brain detect and act on visual patterns faster.

Example:

The following data is in relation to the number of cars sold in 20XX by XYZ Company which deals in three models of a particular make. Represent the data by a simple **bar chart**.

XYZ Company — Sale of cars in 20XX	
Make of car	Cars sold
Model A	10 000
Model B	15 000

Solution:

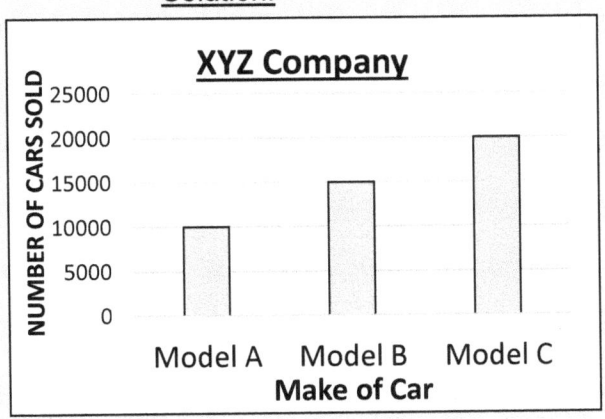

Example:

The following data is in relation to the number of cars sold in 3 successive years by XYZ Company which deals in three models of a particular make. Represent the data by means of **multiple bar charts** and **component bar charts**.

XYZ Company — Sale of cars over 3 years			
Make of car	Year 1	Year 2	Year 3
Model A	10,000	15,000	20,000
Model B	15,000	20,000	25,000
Model C	20,000	10,000	15,000

Solution:

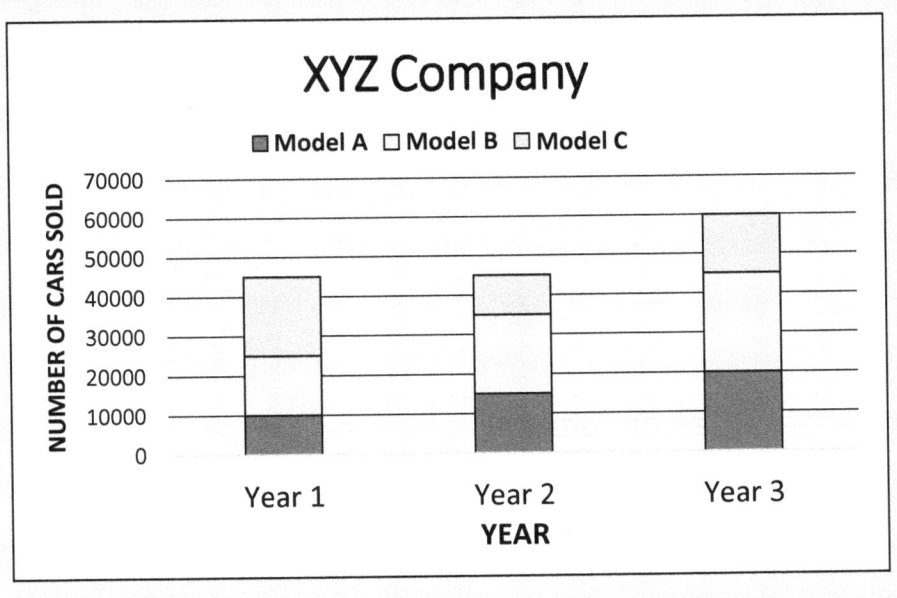

ABC Ltd with three Sales Divisions had the following sales for January and February. Represent these in a **Pie Chart**.

ABC Ltd — Divisional Sales		
Sales Division	January	February
1	50k	80k
2	30k	60k
3	40k	40k
	120k	**180k**

Solution:

Step 1: Express each division's sales as a percentage of its total sales for each month.

Division	January	February
1	$\frac{50}{120} \times 100 = 41.67\%$	$\frac{80}{180} \times 100 = 44.45\%$
2	$\frac{30}{120} \times 100 = 25\%$	$\frac{60}{180} \times 100 = 33.33\%$
3	$\frac{40}{120} \times 100 = 33.33\%$	$\frac{40}{180} \times 100 = 22.22\%$
	100%	**100%**

Step 2: Calculate the equivalent number of degrees for each division for each month (100% represent 360^0 i.e. 1% = 3.6^0).

Division	January	February
1	$41.67\% = 41.67 \times 3.6 = 150^0$	$44.45\% = 44.45 \times 3.6 = 160^0$
2	$25\% = 25 \times 3.6 = 90^0$	$33.33\% = 33.33 \times 3.6 = 120^0$
3	$33.33\% = 33.33 \times 3.6 = 120^0$	$22.22\% = 22.22 \times 3.6 = 80^0$
	360^0	**360^0**

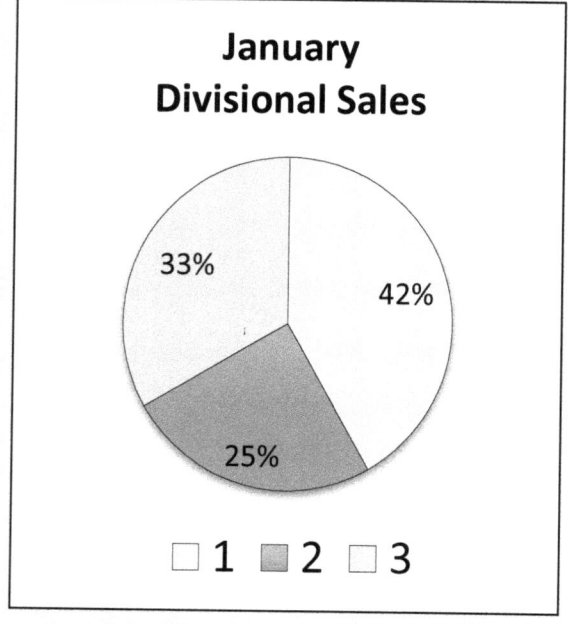

January Divisional Sales

☐ 1 ◼ 2 ☐ 3

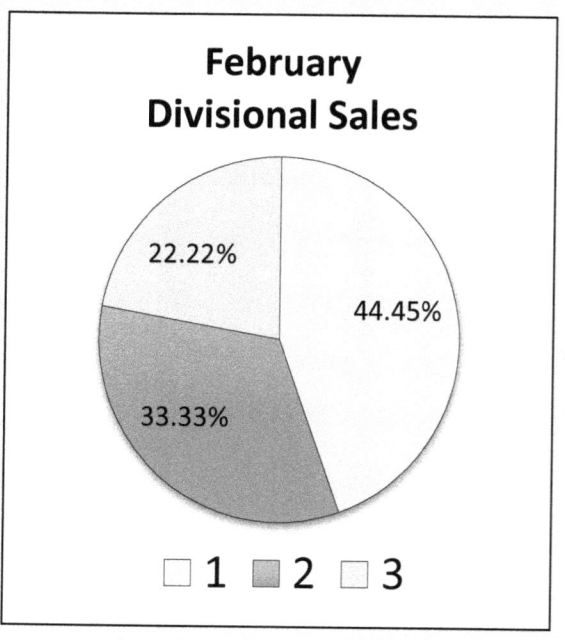

February Divisional Sales

☐ 1 ◼ 2 ☐ 3

298

Example:

The amount of sales recorded in a company for 12 months is given below.
Represent these sales by a **line graph**.

Month	Amount	Month	Amount
January	57k	July	188k
February	84k	August	139k
March	44k	September	146k
April	136k	October	75k
May	185k	November	71k
June	209k	December	47k

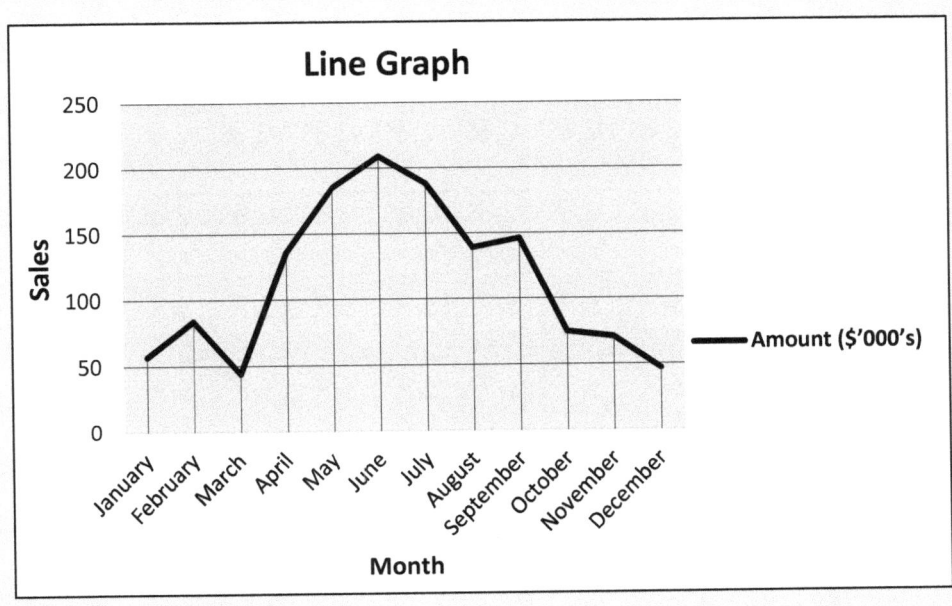

Example:

Represent the sales of 40 units, 55 units and 60 units of a product by a company for the first three months of a year by a **pictogram** using the picture of a "heart" to represent 10 units.

Solution:

Key: ♥ = 10 units

MEASURES OF CENTRAL TENDENCY

The **average** of a set of data is the sum of all the data in the set divided by the number of values in the set. Another name for average is **Mean** (or Arithmetic mean). It is considered as the representative value or the central value. Apart from the mean, there are two other measures of central tendency. These are:

- **The median**: the value separating the higher half from the lower half of a data set.
- **The mode**: the number that occurs most frequently in the set.

A **raw score** is an unaltered measurement. A **raw data** set is a collection **of raw scores. Ungrouped data** is data given as individual data points. **Grouped data** is data given in various class intervals. The number of times each score occurs is called the frequency. A table constructed showing all the scores and their frequencies is called **a frequency table** (or frequency distribution).

MEAN OF UNGROUPED DATA

If the variable X has four values X_1, X_2, X_3 and X_4, then their **mean** (denoted by $\bar{X}$) is:

$$\bar{X} = \frac{X_1 + X_2 + X_3 + X_4}{4}$$

This can be written in a simple form by using the summation notation Σ (pronounced sigma).

$$\bar{X} = \frac{\Sigma X_i}{n}$$

X_1, X_2, X_3 and X_4 are the individual values of X_i when i = 1, 2, 3 and 4 respectively, and n = 4.

The disadvantage of a mean as a measure of central tendency is that it is seriously affected by extreme values (**or outliers**) of X_i. It is the best to leave out the extreme values before calculating the mean.

Example 1:

  Calculate the mean of the following observations: 34, 64, 68 70, 71, 74.

Solution:

34 is an outlier and so we leave it out of the calculation.

$$\text{Mean} = \frac{64 + 68 + 70 + 71 + 74}{5} = \frac{347}{5} = 69.4$$

If the values of the variable X occur with frequency (more than once), then all the values could be added together, and the total divided by the total number of items. Alternatively, it is convenient (and quicker) at times to use the following formula:

$$\bar{X} = \frac{\Sigma fx}{\Sigma f}$$

- Σfx is the sum of the product of each x value and its corresponding f value.
- The number of items n is Σf.

Example 2:

Calculate the mean of 64, 68 70, 71, 74 where the observations occur with frequency 3, 2, 4, 1 and 2 respectively.

Solution:

x	f	fx
64	3	192
68	2	136
70	4	280
71	1	71
74	2	148
Total	12	827

$$\text{Mean} = \overline{x} = \frac{\Sigma fx}{\Sigma f} = \frac{827}{12} = 68.92$$

A **weighted mean** or weighted average is calculated when some data values are more important than the others.

Example:

A teacher considers the marks awarded to the students in an examination in the subject he taught are three times more important than the marks awarded for the assignment given to them. What is the weighted mean mark of a student who obtained 60% for the examination and 90% for the assignment?

Solution:

$$\text{Weighted mean} = \frac{(60 \times 3) + (90 \times 1)}{3 + 1} = \frac{270}{4} = 67.5\%$$

The numbers 3 and 1 are called the weights

The **Median** of an ungrouped data is the middle item when the data is arranged in the ascending or descending order. If there are two middle items as would be the case when there area even number of items, the median is the sum of the two items divided by two.

Example 1:

Determine the median of the following 7 items: 3, 13, 15, 10, 26, 36, 65.

Solution:

There are an odd number of items. If we arrange them in ascending order, the items will be written: 3, 10, 13, **15**, 26, 36 65, and the median is the middle item which is the fourth item.

Therefore: Median = 15

Example 2:

Determine the median of the following 8 items: 3, 13, 15, 10, 18, 26, 36, 65.

There are even number of items. If we arrange them in ascending order, the items will be written: 3, 10, 13, **15, 18,** 26, 36, 65. The median is the average of the middle two items which are the fourth and the fifth items.

Therefore: Median = $\dfrac{15 + 18}{2}$ = 16.5

Mode is the most frequently occurring score. If all items have the same frequency, then no mode exists. A distribution of data can have more than one mode. Depending on the number of modes, the data is described as unimodal, bimodal, trimodal etc.

Example 1:

Determine the mode of the set: 1, 2, 3, 3, 3, 4, 4, 5, 6

3 occurs the greatest number of times. Therefore the mode is 3.

Example 2:

Determine the mode of the set: 2,3, 4, 4, 4, 5, 5, 6, 6, 6, 7, 8

There are two modes here; 4 and 6 occur the same number of times. Therefore, the set is bimodal with modes 4 and 6.

MEAN, MEDIAN AND MODE OF GROUPED DATA

The formulae used and calculation of the mean, median and mode when we deal with grouped data are Illustrated by the examples in the next page. The formula for the **mean** of the grouped data occurring with frequency is the same as that used for the ungrouped data except that the x values represent the midpoints of the different classes.

Example 1:

Calculate the **mean** hourly wages of the grouped distribution of employees given below:

Hourly wages	Number of Employees
$10 up to $14	20
$15 up to $19	12
$20 up to $24	10

Solution:

Class	Midpoint (x)	f	fx
$10 up to $14	12	20	240
$15 up to $19	17	12	204
$20 up to $24	22	10	220
Total		**42**	**664**

Mean = $\overline{x}$ = $\dfrac{\Sigma fx}{\Sigma f}$ = $\dfrac{664}{42}$ = $15.81

Example 2:

Calculate the **median** hourly wages of the following grouped distribution:

Hourly wages	Number of Employees
$10 up to $14	20
$15 up to $19	12
$20 up to $24	10

Solution:

Class	f	Cumulative f	
$10 up to $14	20	20	
$15 up to $19	12	32	←
$20 up to $24	10	42	
	42		

Firstly, we have to identify the class in which the median lies. This is the class in which the middle value of the distribution lies.

In this example, this is the class where the 21st item [i.e. $(\frac{42}{2})^{th}$ item] lies.

The median class is $15 up to $19.

The formula for calculating the median of a grouped data is:

$$\text{Median} = L_{me} + \frac{\frac{\Sigma f}{2} - C}{f(me)} \times \text{class interval}$$

L_{me} = Lower class limit of the median class

C = The cumulative frequency of the class lower than the median class.

$f(me)$ = The frequency of the median class.

$$\text{Median} = 15 + \frac{\frac{42}{2} - 20}{12} \times 5 = 15 + \frac{1}{12} \times 5 = 15 + 0.42 = \$15.42$$

Example 3:

Calculate the **modal** hourly wages of the following grouped distribution:

Hourly wages	Number of Employees
$10 up to $14	20
$15 up to $19	12
$20 up to $24	10

Solution:

Class	f
$10 up to $14	20
$15 up to $19	12
$20 up to $24	10
	42

Firstly, we have to identify the class in which the mode lies. This is the class in which the most occurring value of the distribution lies. The modal class is $10 up to $14. The formula for calculating the mode of a grouped data is:

$$\text{Mode} = L_{mo} + \frac{d_1}{d_1 + d_2} \times \text{class interval}$$

L_{mo} = Lower class limit of the modal class

d_1 = difference between modal class frequency and that of the next lower class.

d_2 = difference between modal class frequency and of the next higher class.

$$\text{Mode} = L_{mo} + \frac{d_1}{d_1 + d_2} \times \text{class interval} = 10 + \frac{20 - 0}{(20 - 0) + (20 - 12)} \times 5$$

$$= 10 + \frac{20}{28} \times 5 = \$13.57$$

MEASURES OF SPREAD OF DATA

When data is arranged in an ascending order, the score that is one quarter of the way through the scores is called the **Lower Quartile (Q1)** and the score that is three quarters of the way through is called the **Upper Quartile (Q3)**.

Q1 is the middle value in the first half of the data set. Q3 is the middle value in the second half of the data set. In other words, Q1 is the median of the lower half and Q3 is the median of the upper half of the data arranged in an ascending order. The mean is denoted by **Q2**.

- The term **Range** refers to the difference between the highest and lowest score.
- The difference between the upper and lower quartiles is called the **Interquartile range** which shows the spread of the middle half of the data.

While the mean, median and mode measure the central tendency, Range and Interquartile range measure the spread of data.

Example 1:

Find the lower quartile (Q1), median and upper quartile (Q3) of the following:

2, 6, 8, 9, 10, 12, 16 | Arranged in ascending order |

Lower quartile = Median of the lower half = 6 | $(\dfrac{n+1}{4})$th item = 2nd |

Median = middle number = 9

Upper quartile (Q3) = Median of the upper half = 12 | $3(\dfrac{n+1}{4})$th item = 6th item |

Example 2:

Determine the mean, median, mode, range, lower quartile, upper quartile and the interquartile range of the following ungrouped frequency distribution.

Score	1	2	3	4	5	6	7	8	9
Frequency	3	4	6	5	7	4	3	5	2

Solution:

Score (x)	f	fx	Cumulative frequency
1	3	3	3
2	4	8	7
3	6	18	13
4	5	20	18
5	7	35	25
6	4	24	29
7	3	21	32
8	5	40	37
9	2	18	39
Total	39	187	

Mean = $\bar{x}$ = $\dfrac{\Sigma fx}{\Sigma f}$ = $\dfrac{187}{39}$ = 4.795 = 4.8

Median = 19.5^{th} item = 5

Mode = 5

Range = 9 − 1 = 8

Lower Quartile (Q1) = 9.75^{th} item = 3

Upper Quartile (Q3) = 29.25^{th} item = 7

Interquartile range = 7 − 3 = 4

Example 3:

Determine the mean, median, mode, lower quartile, upper quartile and quartile deviation of the following grouped frequency distribution.

Score	10–14	15–19	20–24	25–29	30–34	35–39	40–44	45–49
Frequency	4	20	16	12	14	10	8	2

Solution:

Score	Midpoint (x)	f	fx	Cumulative frequency
9.5 – 14.5	12	4	48	4
14.5 – 19.5	17	20	340	24
19.5 – 24.5	22	16	352	40
24.5 – 29.5	27	12	324	52
29.5 – 34.5	32	14	448	66
34.5 – 39.5	37	10	370	76
39.5 – 44.5	42	8	336	84
44.5 – 49.5	47	2	94	86
	Total	**86**	**2312**	

$$\text{Mean} = \bar{x} = \frac{\Sigma fx}{\Sigma f} = \frac{2312}{86} = 26.884 = 26.9$$

$$\text{Median} = L_{me} + \frac{\frac{\Sigma f}{2} - C}{f(me)} \times \text{class interval} = 24.5 + \frac{43 - 40}{12} \times 5 = 24.5 + 1.25 = 25.75$$

$$\text{Mode} = L_{mo} + \frac{d_1}{d_1 + d_2} \times \text{class interval} = 14.5 + \frac{20 - 4}{(20 - 4) + (20 - 16)} \times 5$$

$$= 14.5 + \frac{16}{20} \times 5 = 18.5$$

$$\text{Lower quartile (Q1)} = 21.5^{th} \text{ item} = 14.5 + \frac{17.5}{20} \times 5 = 18.87$$

$$\text{Upper quartile (Q3)} = 64.5^{th} \text{ item} = 29.5 + \frac{12.5}{14} \times 5 = 33.96$$

$$\text{Quartile deviation} = \frac{Q3 - Q1}{2} = \frac{33.964 - 18.875}{2} = 7.54$$

GRAPHICAL REPRESENTATION OF FREQUENCY DISTRIBUTION

The data in a frequency table is usually presented as a **histogram.** A histogram is a diagram of a series of connected rectangles using class width on the horizontal axis as the width of each rectangle. The area of each rectangle is proportional to the frequency of the variable which is shown on the vertical axis.

Example:

Use the following frequency table to construct a histogram:

Class Interval	Frequency
0 to 4	5
5 to 9	10
10 to 14	20
15 to 19	15

Solution:

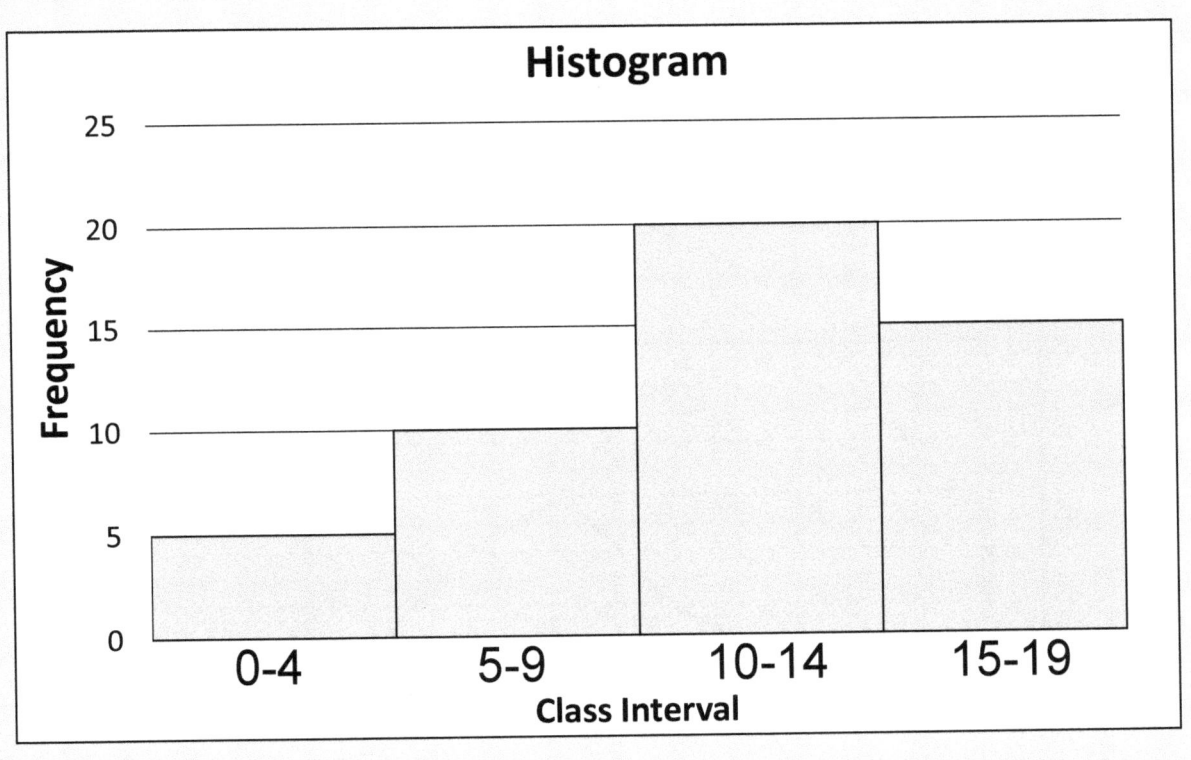

Frequency Polygon

When the midpoints of the tops of the rectangles of a histogram are joined, a polygon is obtained which reveals the continuous changes across the score range.

It is really a line graph of class frequency plotted against the class mid-points. The polygon can be shown along with the histogram or separately.

Example:

Use the following frequency table, construct both a histogram and a frequency polygon.

60 – 69	5
70 – 79	10
80 – 89	20
90 – 99	15
100 – 109	5
110 – 119	3

Solution:

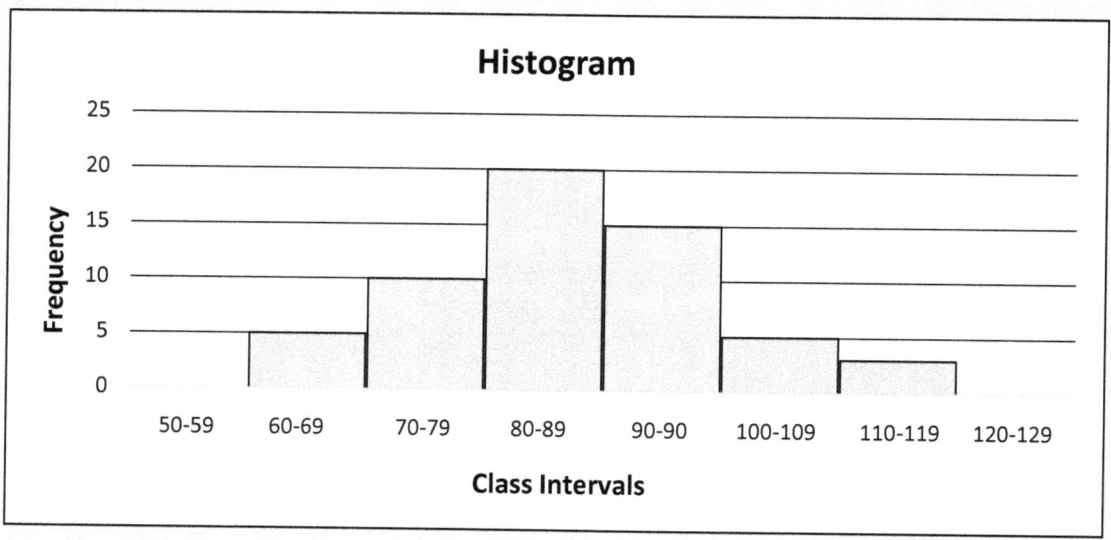

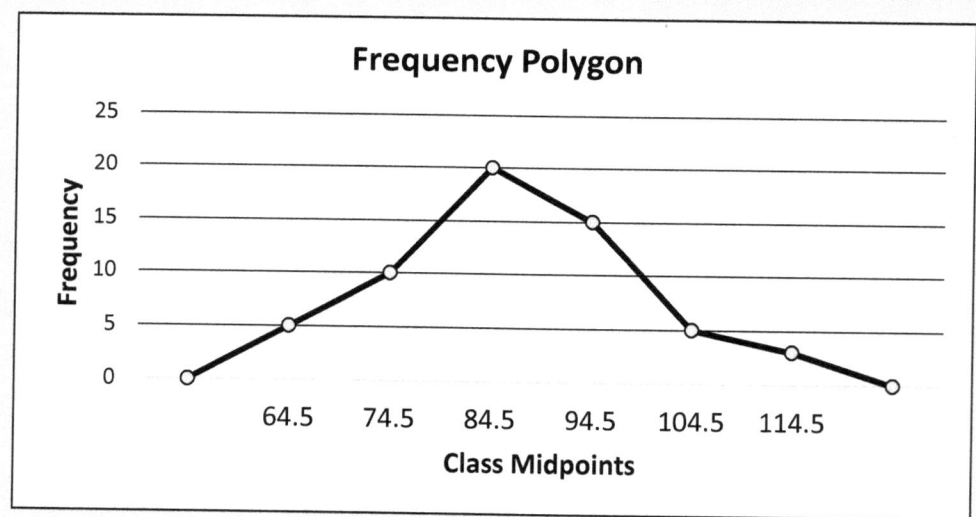

CUMULATIVE FREQUENCY CURVE (OGIVE)

When the cumulative frequencies (on the vertical axis) are plotted against the mid-points of the classes (on the horizontal axis), an elongated S-shaped curve called the Ogive is obtained. Sometimes, it is more meaningful to use lower class limits rather than the mid points.

- When the lower-class limits are used against the cumulative frequencies more than lower class limits, the Ogive is referred to as "**More than**" Ogive.
- When the lower-class limit is used against cumulative frequencies less than lower class limits, it is called the "**Less than**" Ogive.

Example:

Use the following frequency distribution to draw Ogives:

Class	Frequency
1 – 20	10
21 – 40	20
41 – 60	70
61 – 80	40
81 – 100	10
101 – 120	–

Solution:

Class	Mid-point	Frequency (f)	Cumulative frequencies more than lower class limit	Cumulative frequencies less than lower class limit
1 - 20	10.5	10	150	0
21 - 40	30.5	20	140	10
41 - 60	50.5	70	120	30
61 - 80	70.5	40	50	100
81 - 100	90.5	10	10	140
101 - 120	110.5	0	0	150

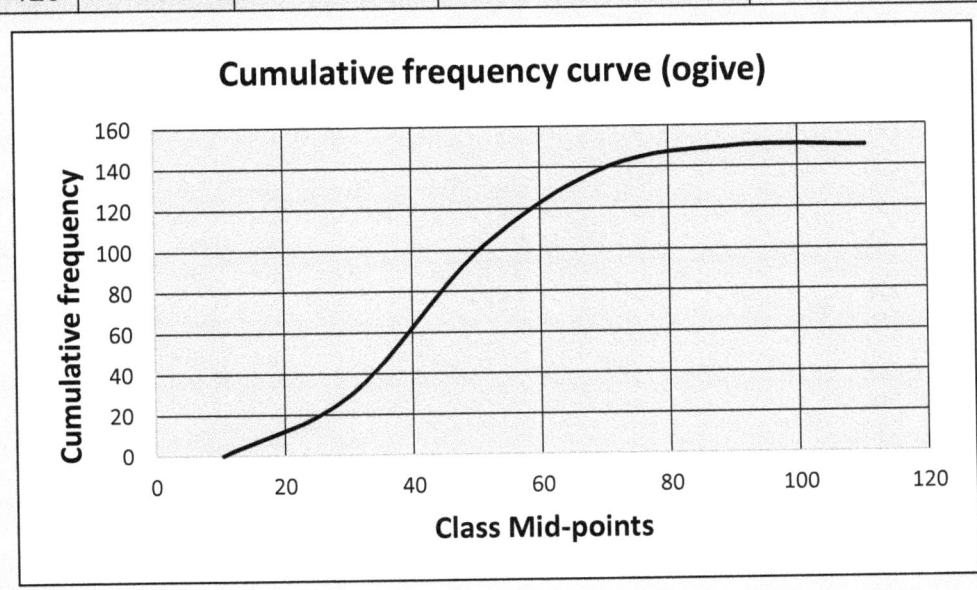

309

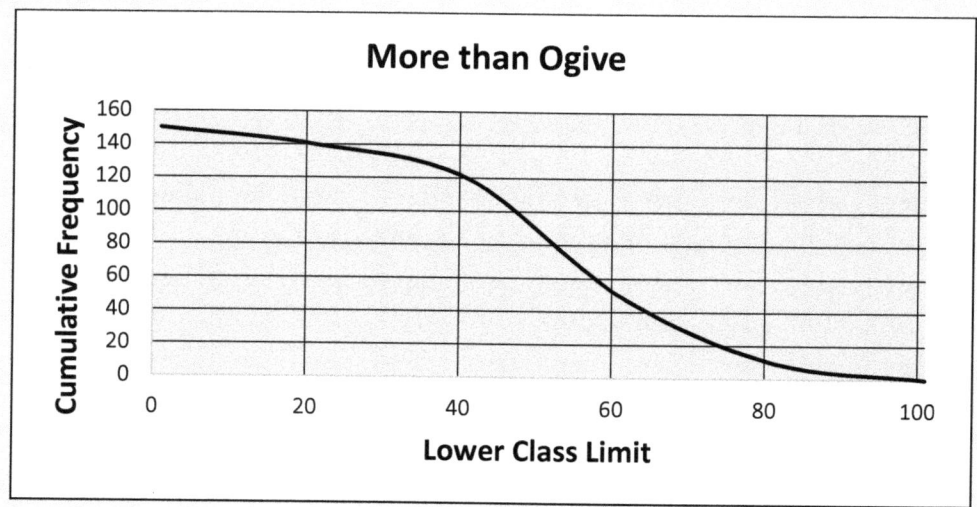

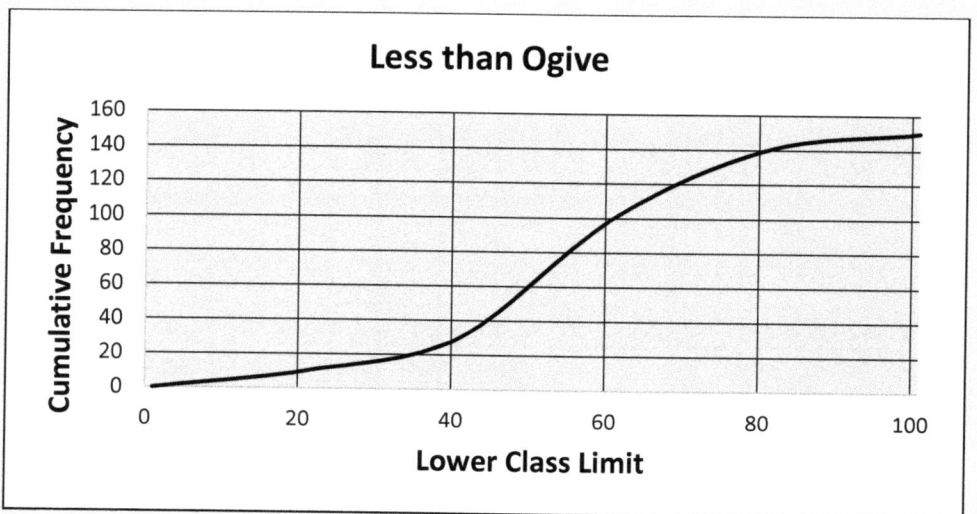

If the "more than" and "less than" Ogives are drawn on the same graph, the value on the horizontal axis corresponding to the **point at which they intersect**, represents the **Median** of the given data set.

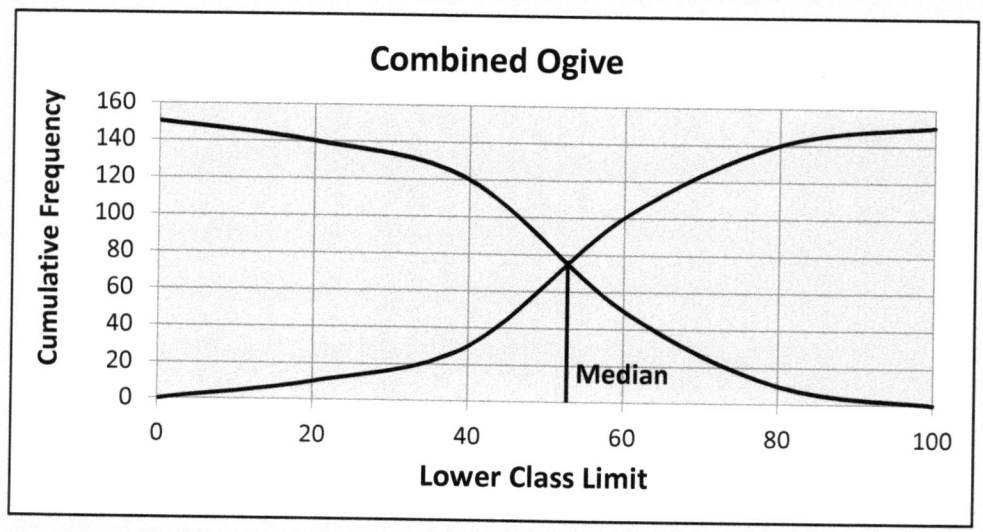

OTHER DATA ANALYSIS TOOLS

A **dot plot** displays data using **dots.** It is similar to histogram and is used for relatively small data sets. The height of the column of **dots represents** the frequency for a value.

Example:

Draw dot plot for numbers 0, 1, 2, 3, 4, 5, 6, 7, 8, 9, 10 with frequencies 3, 4, 1, 5, 2, 6, 3, 3, 4, 2, 3 respectively

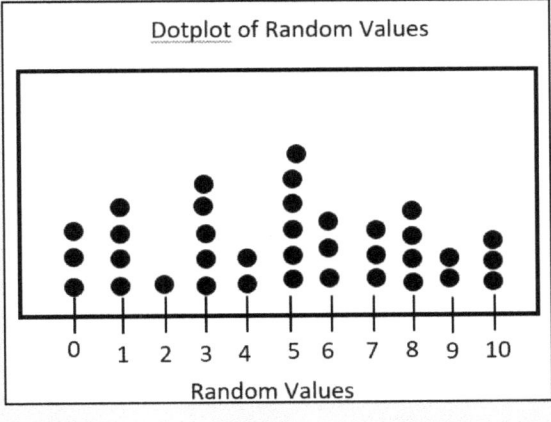

A **stem-and-leaf plot** is a device for presenting data in a graphical format, similar to a histogram, to assist in visualizing the shape of a distribution. It uses a special table where each data value is split into a "*stem*" (the first digit or digits) and a "*leaf*" (usually the last digit). Stem and leaf displays are not suitable for large data sets, they are often useful for data sets with up to 200. These are usually used to represent discrete numerical data.

Example:

The following illustrates the Stem and Leaf plot of ages of 30 people who attended a function.

Key: 5 | 4 = 54 years old

Stem	Leaf
1	6, 8
2	2, 3, 4, 4, 6, 8, 9
3	0, 3, 3, 6, 8, 9, 9
4	0, 1, 2, 2, 3, 5, 7
5	2, 3, 4, 4
6	0, 2, 3,

A **box-and-whisker plot** is constructed to display a distribution of data based on a five-number summary namely, "minimum", first quartile (Q1), median (Q2), third quartile (Q3), and "maximum". The data to be represented is first arranged in an ascending order and the quartiles are identified. A box is then drawn from the first quartile to the third quartile. Also, a vertical line is drawn through the box at the median. Finally, a **whisker** is drawn from lower quartile to the minimum and another is drawn from upper quartile to the maximum.

Example:

Construct a Box and whisker plot to display the five-number summary by using the data below:

1, 12, 15, 19, 22, 22, 26, 28, 29, 45

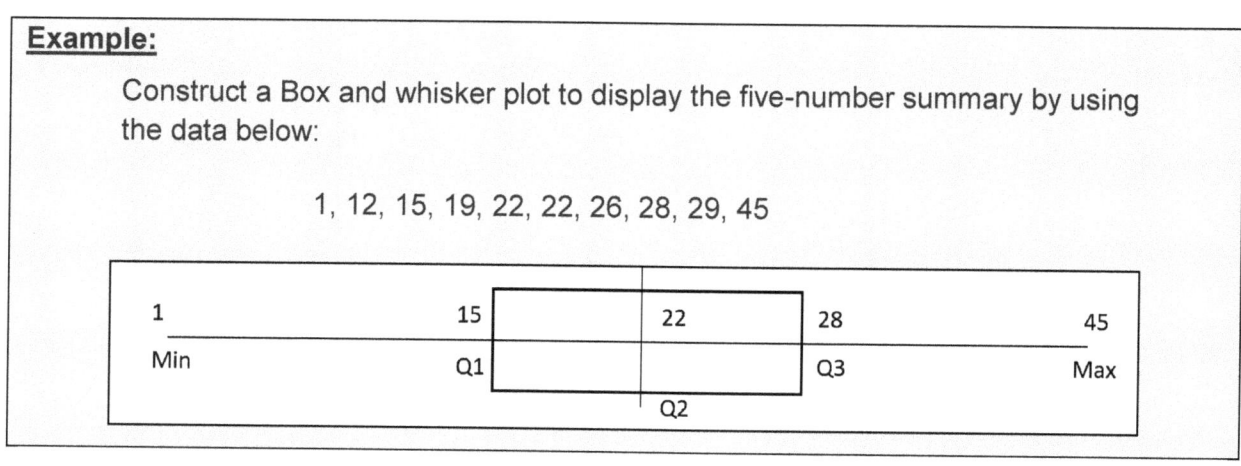

A distribution of data that lacks symmetry is said to be **skewed**. A frequency polygon with a **long left tail is negatively skewed** e.g. household incomes, ages of people at a retirement home. A frequency polygon with a **long right tail is positively skewed** e.g. ages of patrons at a night club, mileage on used cars.

Examples:

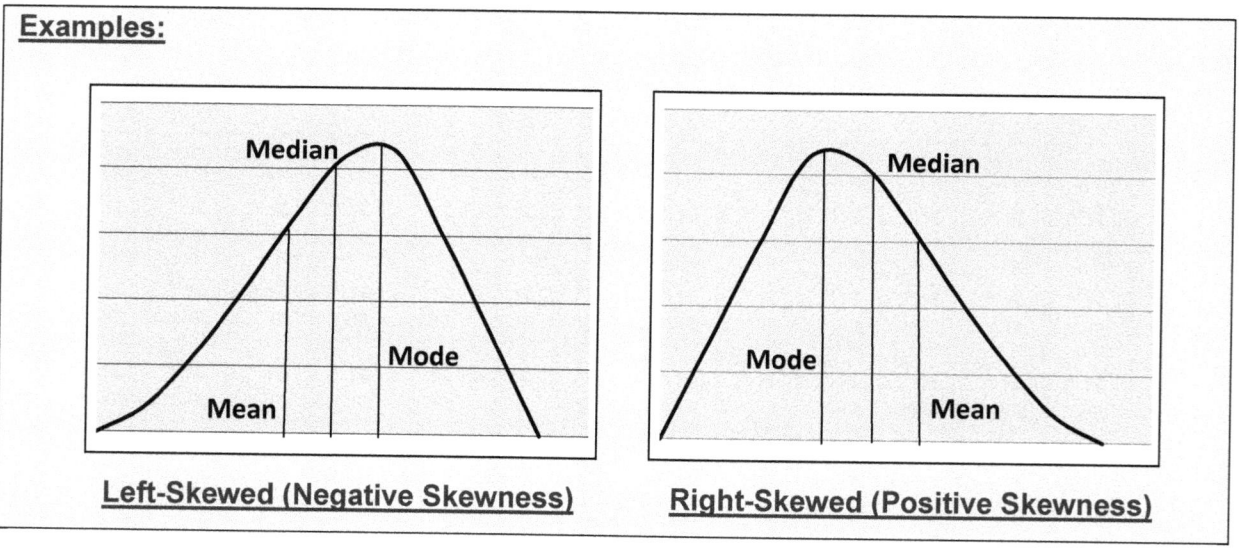

Observe that the mean is **less** than the median and both the mean and the median are less than the mode of a negatively skewed data. In the case of a positively skewed data, the mean is **greater** than the median and both the mean and median are greater than the mode.

The extent of skewness is called the coefficient of skewness and is measured as:

$$\text{Coefficient of Skewness} = \frac{3(\text{Mean} - \text{Median})}{\text{Standard deviation}}$$

The Coefficient of Skewness will be negative for negatively skewed data, because the mean of such a distribution is lower than its median. Standard Deviation is explained below under the heading **'Dispersion of Data'**.

The coefficient of skewness lies between -3 and 3

A distribution that is not skewed is called a normal distribution. The mean, median and mode are of the same value and hence the coefficient of skewness is zero.

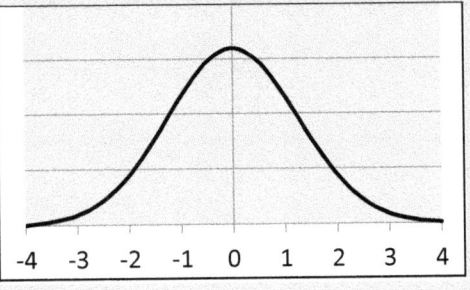

DISPERSION OF DATA

The spread of data about the mean is called dispersion. The various measures are:

- **Range**
- **Quartile Deviation**
- **Mean Deviation**
- **Variance**

Range is the difference between the smallest and largest values of a given set of data. It gives a rough idea of the extent of dispersion.

Example:

Calculate the range of the following data:

7, 3, 9, 20, 13, 15, 22, 11

Solution:

Smallest value = 3;   Largest value = 22;   Range = 22 – 3 = 19

Quartile Deviation:

If a set of values is arranged in an ascending order, 25% of them will lie below a certain value. This value is called the **Lower Quartile, Q1** (also called the 25th percentile). Similarly, 25% of the values will lie above a certain value. This value is called the **Upper Quartile, Q3** (also called the 75th percentile). **The median is the Middle Quartile, Q2**. The difference between Q3 and Q1 is called the **Inter quartile range** and represents 50% of the data.

The **Semi Interquartile range** is half the interquartile range or $(\frac{Q3 - Q1}{2})$

It is little affected by extreme values and hence considered as a more suitable measure of dispersion for skewed distribution. The semi interquartile range is often referred to as **Quartile deviation**. A relative measure of dispersion based on the quartile deviation is known as the coefficient of quartile deviation.

$$\boxed{\textbf{Coefficient of Quartile deviation} \ = \ \frac{\textbf{Q3} - \textbf{Q1}}{\textbf{Q3} + \textbf{Q2}}}$$

This coefficient can be used for comparing the dispersion of two or more sets of data.

Example:

Calculate the quartile deviation (i.e. semi inter quartile range) and the coefficient of quartile deviation of the following set of data.

16, 20, 22, 30, 35, 40, 45, 50, 60, 70 ,80, 85

Solution:

$$Q1 \ = \ \frac{22 + 30}{2} \ = \ 26$$

$$Q3 \ = \ \frac{60 + 70}{2} \ = \ 65$$

$$\text{Quartile Deviation} \ = \ \frac{Q3 - Q1}{2} \ = \ \frac{Q3 - Q1}{2} \ = \ \frac{65 - 26}{2} \ = \ 19.5$$

$$\text{Coefficient of quartile deviation} \ = \ \frac{Q3 - Q1}{Q3 + Q2} \ = \ \frac{65 - 26}{65 + 26} \ = \ \frac{39}{91} \ = \ 0.43$$

Mean Deviation (ungrouped data)

Mean Deviation (MD) measures the dispersion as the average of the deviations of each item of a set of data from their mean value. The deviations are absolute values.

$$\textbf{MD} \ = \ \frac{\sum |\textbf{x} - \bar{\textbf{x}}|}{\textbf{n}}$$

Example:

Calculate the mean deviation of the following ungrouped data:

2, 5, 6, 8, 10, 11

Solution:

$$\text{Mean} \ = \ \frac{2 + 5 + 6 + 8 + 10 + 11}{6} \ = \ \frac{42}{6} \ = \ 7$$

The absolute values of the differences of each number from the mean are:

5, 2, 1, 1, 3, 4

Sum of the deviations = 16

$$\text{Mean deviation} \ = \ \frac{16}{6} \ = \ 2\frac{2}{3} \ = \ 2.67$$

Mean Deviation (grouped data)

The formula for calculating the mean deviation of a grouped frequency distribution is:

$$\textbf{MD} \ = \ \frac{\sum \textbf{f} |\textbf{x} - \bar{\textbf{x}}|}{\textbf{n}}$$

Example:

Calculate the mean deviation of the following grouped frequency distribution:

Height	Number of students
150 – 154	6
155 – 159	10
160 – 164	16
165 – 169	18

Solution:

Mid-Point (x)	f	fx	$x - \bar{x}$	$f(x - \bar{x})$
152	6	912	-9.6	57.6
157	10	1570	-4.6	46.0
162	16	2592	0.4	6.4
167	18	3006	5.4	97.2
Total	**50**	**8080**		**207.2**

$$x = \frac{8080}{50} = 161.6$$

$$\text{Mean Deviation} = \frac{\sum f|x - \bar{x}|}{n} = \frac{2072}{50} = 4.14$$

Standard deviation is another method for finding the spread of data about the mean. It is widely used for the reason that it takes into account every score in the data to calculate its distance from the mean.

Example 1:

Calculate the standard deviation (SD) of the following **ungrouped data**.

$$2, 5, 6, 8\ 10, 11$$

Solution:

The formula to calculate the standard deviation is:

$$SD = \sqrt{\frac{\sum|x - \bar{x}|^2}{n}}$$

x	$x - \bar{x}$	$x - \bar{x}^2$
2	-5	25
5	-2	4
6	-1	1
8	1	1
10	3	9
11	4	16
Total: 42		**56**

Mean $= x = \dfrac{42}{6} = 7$; Standard deviation $= \sqrt{56/6} = 3.055$

The square of the standard deviation is called the **Variance.**

Variance $= (3.055)^2 = 9.33$

Example 2:

Calculate the standard deviation (SD) of the following **grouped data**.
What is the variance?

Height	Number of students
150 – 154	6
155 – 159	10
160 – 164	16
165 – 169	18

Solution:

The formula to calculate the standard deviation is:

$$SD = \sqrt{\frac{\sum f|x - \bar{x}|^2}{n}}$$

Mid-Point (x)	f	fx	x – x̄	(x – x̄)²	f(x – x̄)²
152	6	912	-9.6	92.16	552.96
157	10	1570	-4.6	21.16	211.60
162	16	2592	0.4	0.16	2.56
167	18	3006	5.4	29.16	524.88
Total	**50**	**8080**			**1292.00**

$$\text{Mean} = x = \frac{8080}{50} = 161.6$$

$$SD = \sqrt{\frac{\sum f|x - \bar{x}|^2}{n}} = \sqrt{\frac{1292}{50}} = 5.083$$

$$\text{Variance} = (5.083)^2 = 25.84$$

DIFFERENTIATING POPULATION AND SAMPLE STATISTICS

The standard deviation formula seen above applies to a population. In the case of standard deviation for a sample drawn from a population, we use **n − 1** in the denominator of the formula instead of **n**. The symbols used for mean and standard deviation are also different.

- **Mean of a sample** is represented by $\bar{x}$ and **that of a population** by **μ** (pronounced mew)
- **Standard deviation of a sample** is represented by "s" and **that of the population** by "σ"

In order to compare two sets of similar data (e.g. the salaries of two professions) to determine the extent of relative dispersion of data about the mean, a measure called the **coefficient of variation** is used. It is obtained by dividing the standard deviation by the mean. That is:

$$\text{Coefficient of variation} = \frac{\sigma}{\mu} \times 100$$

i.e. Standard deviation as a percentage of the mean

MISCELLANEOUS PROBLEMS

1. A frequency distribution is divided into six classes as follows:

    $20 – 24; $25 – 29; $30 – 34; $35 – 39; $40 – 44; $45 – 49

State:
(a) the class boundaries
(b) the class interval
(c) the class marks (i.e. midpoints)

2.(a) How many of the numbers given below fall into each of the classes:

    40 – 44; 45 – 49; 50 – 54; 55 – 59?

    53, 42, 48, 40, 41, 50, 49, 52, 57, 59, 45, 44, 43, 47, 59, 42, 51, 50

(b) The class marks of a frequency distribution are: 3, 8, 13, 18 and 23.
    What are the class limits of this distribution?

3.(a) For each class of the frequency distribution given below, what is:
   (i) the cumulative frequency
   (ii) the relative frequency?

Class	Frequency	Cumulative frequency	Relative frequency
0 - 9	15		
10 - 19	22		
20 - 29	38		
30 - 39	16		
40 - 49	9		

(b)(i) What percentage of the items are above 19?
  (ii) What percentage of the items are below 40?
  (iii) What percentage of the items are above 9 and below 40?

---

4. Illustrate by means of a component bar chart and a pie chart, the following data relating
   to the cost incurred in making a product by a company.

            Raw material supplies — 55%

            Salaries and wages — 30%

            Overheads — 15%

---

5. Group the following 50 numbers into a table showing the frequency in each of the
   classes: 2 – 4; 5 – 7; 8 – 10; .... 20 – 22.

            13, 9, 5, 11, 14, 6, 5, 8, 11, 13, 10, 16, 15, 3, 19, 18, 9,

            9, 5, 12, 13, 12, 15, 9, 18, 12, 16, 7, 12, 13, 11, 18, 15,

            9, 21, 9, 11, 6, 2, 12, 10, 16, 2, 14, 14, 17, 8, 15, 11, 12

6. Determine the median and mode of the following grouped distribution:

Fortnightly wages	Number of employees
$400 – $499	15
$500 – $599	12
$600 – $699	16
$700 – $799	17
$800 – $899	4
$900 – $999	3

7. Use the following table and draw a "less than" Ogive and a "more than" Ogive In the same diagram.

Class	Frequency	Frequency more than lower class limit	Frequency less than lower class limit
1 – 5	10	60	0
6 – 10	14	50	10
11 – 15	12	36	24
16 – 20	10	24	36
21 – 25	8	14	46
26 – 30	6	6	54
31 – 35	–	0	60

Calculate the median using the formula and compare the result with that obtained from the graph.

8. (a) Represent the numbers given below on a stem and leaf plot:

18, 26, 32, 59, 27, 61, 75, 45, 34, 35, 80, 28, 51, 64, 24,
82, 17, 46, 20, 69, 21, 19, 73, 12, 29, 48, 62, 67, 23

(b) In a class of 30 students, the marks obtained in a mathematics test were recorded as follows:

A+	4
A	7
A–	6
B+	8
B	2
C+	3

Represent this data using a dot plot.

(c) Represent the following set of data using a boxplot.

5, 6, 6, 7, 10, 11 13, 15, 16

State the range, lower Quartile, Upper Quartile and the Interquartile Range.

1.

Class limits	Class boundaries	Class interval	Class mark
20 – 24	19.5 – 24.5	5	22
25 – 29	24.5 – 29.5	5	27
30 – 34	29.5 – 34.5	5	32
35 – 39	34.5 – 39.5	5	37
40 – 44	39.5 – 44.5	5	42
45 – 49	44.5 – 49.5	5	47

2.(a)

Class Limits	40 – 44	45 – 49	50 – 54	55 – 59
Tally	︳︳︳︳ ︳	︳︳︳︳	︳︳︳︳	︳︳︳
Frequency	6	4	5	3

(b)

Class mark	Class limits
3	1 – 5
8	6 – 10
13	11 – 15
18	16 – 20
23	21 – 25

3.(a)

Class	Frequency	Cumulative frequency	Relative frequency
0 – 9	15	15	0.15
10 – 19	22	37	0.22
20 – 29	38	75	0.38
30 – 39	16	91	0.16
40 – 49	9	100	0.09

(b)(i) Percentage of items above 19 = 38 + 16 + 9 = 63

(ii) Percentage of items below 40 = 15 + 22 + 38 + 16 = 91

(iii) Percentage of items above 9 and below 40 = 22 + 38 + 16 = 76

4. Calculation of angles:

Raw material supplies = 0.55 × 360 = 1980

Salaries and wages = 0.3 × 360 = 1080

Overheads = 0.15 × 360 = 540

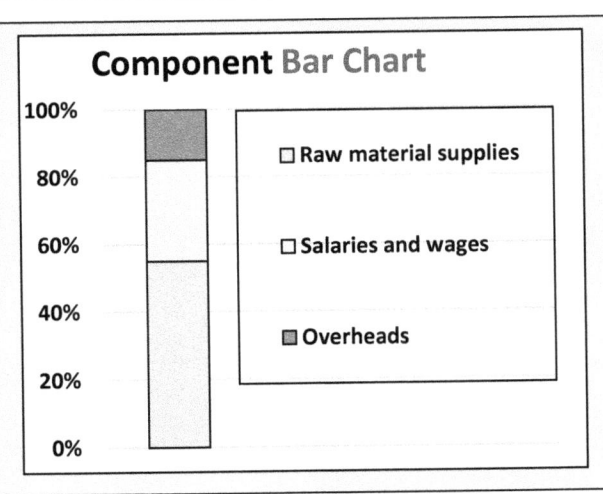

319

4.(Continued)

PIE CHART

☐ Raw material supplies ☐ Salaries and wages ☐ Overheads

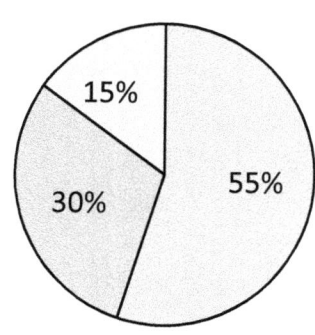

5.

Class	Tally	Frequency
2 – 4	‖	2
5 – 7	﷼﷼﷼﷼ ‖	6
8 – 10	﷼﷼﷼﷼ ﷼﷼﷼﷼	10
11 – 13	﷼﷼﷼﷼ ﷼﷼﷼﷼ ﷼﷼﷼﷼ ‖	16
14 –16	﷼﷼﷼﷼ ﷼﷼﷼﷼	10
17 –19	﷼﷼﷼﷼	5
20 – 22	‖	1

6. Median: $L_{me} + \dfrac{\dfrac{\Sigma f}{2} - C}{f(me)} \times$ class interval $= 600 + \dfrac{33.5 - 27}{16} \times 100$

$= 600 + 40.625 = \$640.63$

Mode $= L_{mo} + \dfrac{d_1}{d_1 + d_2} \times$ class interval $= 700 + \dfrac{17 - 16}{(17 - 16) + (17 - 4)} \times 100$

$= 700 + \dfrac{1}{14} \times 100 = \$707.14$

7.

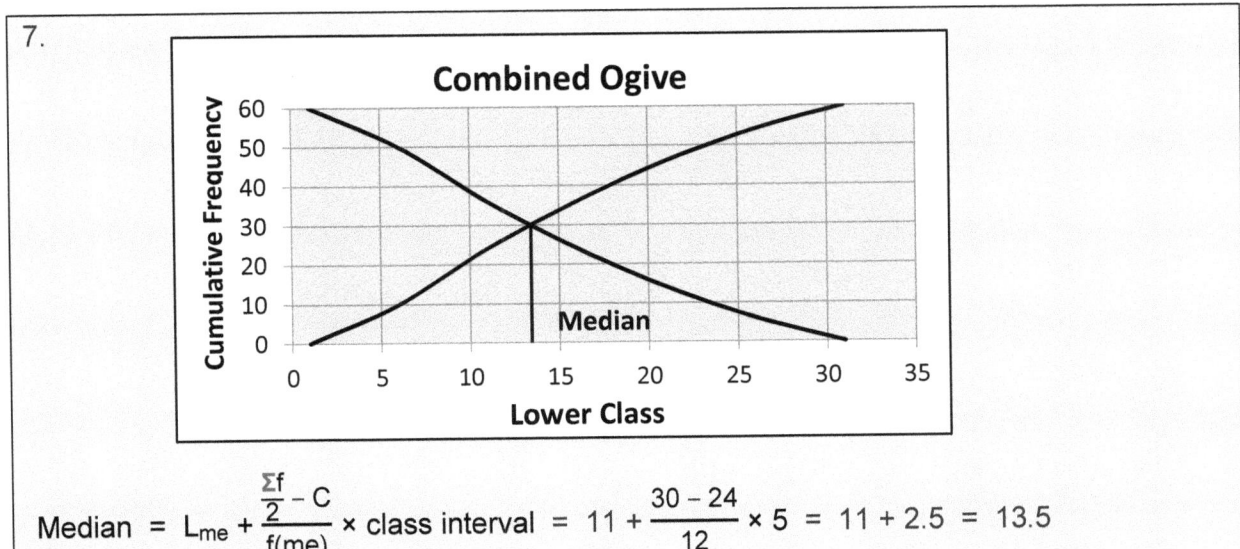

$$\text{Median} = L_{me} + \frac{\frac{\Sigma f}{2} - C}{f(me)} \times \text{class interval} = 11 + \frac{30 - 24}{12} \times 5 = 11 + 2.5 = 13.5$$

8.(a)   Stem and Leaf plot

Stem	Leaf
1	2, 7, 8, 9
2	0, 1, 3, 4, 6, 7, 8, 9
3	2, 4, 5
4	5, 6, 8
5	1, 9
6	1, 2, 4, 7, 9
7	3, 5
8	0, 2

(b)

Dot plot of grades

Grades

(c)   Boxplot

5	6	10	14	16
Min	Q1		Q3	Max

Q2

Range $= 16 - 5 = 11$

Lower Quartile (Q1) $= 6$

Upper Quartile (Q3) $= 14$

Interquartile range $= Q3 - Q1 = 8$

PRACTICAL APPLICATIONS

1. A person's monthly expenses (in dollars) on petrol for nine months are as follows:

$$120, 70, 65, 73, 70, 70, 110, 95, 87$$

Calculate: (a) the mean monthly expense
(b) the median expense
(c) the modal expense

What is the best value to use for budget purposes?

Solution:

Arranging the data in ascending order, we have:

$$65, 70, 70, 70, 73, 87, 95, 110, 120$$

(a) Mean monthly expense $= \dfrac{760}{9} = \$84.44$

(b) Median monthly expense $= \$73$

(c) Modal expense $= \$70$

(d) Mean is the best value to use for budget purposes.

---

2. By calculating the coefficient of variation of the data given below, state whether the doctors' salaries or accountants' salaries are more variable.

Salary	Mean	Standard deviation
Doctors	$200,000	$20,000
Accountants	$120,000	$15,000

Solution:

Coefficient of variation (doctors) $= \dfrac{\sigma}{\mu} \times 100 = \dfrac{20,000}{200,000} \times 100 = 10\%$

Coefficient of variation (accountants) $= \dfrac{\sigma}{\mu} \times 100 = \dfrac{15,000}{120,000} \times 100 = 12.5\%$

Though the standard deviation for doctors' salaries is greater than the standard deviation for accountants' salaries, the coefficient of variation for accountants' salaries is greater than that for the doctors signifying that there is a greater dispersion from the mean salaries in the case of accountants.

322

3. The rates paid by the house owners in two new small suburbs A and B are as follows:

Rates ($)	Number of house owners	
	Suburb A	Suburb B
180 – 199	50	40
200 – 219	100	80
220 – 239	120	100
240 – 259	80	60
260 – 279	10	8
280 – 299	6	6

For the rates in each suburb, calculate:

(a) mean

(b) standard deviation

(c) median

(d) mode

What is the coefficient of skewness in each case?

Solution:

Suburb A:

Rates	Midpoint (x)	f	fx	$(x - \mu)$	$(x - \mu)^2$	$f(x - \mu)^2$
180 – 199	189.5	50	9,475	35.52	1,261.67	63,083.50
200 – 219	209.5	100	20,950	15.52	240.87	24,087.00
220 – 239	229.5	120	27,540	4.48	20.07	2,408.40
240 – 259	249.5	80	19,960	24.48	599.27	47,941.60
260 – 279	269.5	10	2,695	44.48	1,978.47	19,784.70
280 – 299	289.5	6	1,737	64.48	4,157.67	24,946.02
		366	**82,357**			**115,231.55**

$$\text{Mean} = \mu = \frac{82,357}{366} = \$225.02$$

$$\text{Standard deviation} = \sqrt{\frac{\sum|x - \bar{x}|^2}{n}} = \sqrt{\frac{115,231.55}{366}} = \$17.74$$

$$\text{Median} = L_{me} + \frac{\frac{\sum f}{2} - C}{f(me)} \times \text{class interval} = 220 + \frac{183 - 150}{120} \times 20 = \$225.50$$

$$\text{Mode} = L_{mo} + \frac{d_1}{d_1 + d_2} \times \text{class interval} = 220 + \frac{120 - 100}{(120 - 100) + (120 - 80)} \times 20$$

$$= 220 + \frac{20}{20 + 40} \times 20 = \$226.67$$

$$\text{Coefficient of Skewness} = \frac{3(\text{Mean} - \text{Median})}{\text{Standard deviation}} = \frac{3(225.02 - 225.50)}{17.74} = \frac{-1.44}{17.74} = -0.081$$

3.(Continued)

Suburb B:

Rates	Midpoint (x)	f	fx	$(x - \mu)$	$(x - \mu)^2$	$f(x - \mu)^2$
180 – 199	189.5	40	7,580	35.51	1,260.96	50 438.40
200 – 219	209.5	80	16,760	15.51	240.56	19 244.81
220 – 239	229,5	100	22,950	4.49	20.16	2 016.01
240 – 259	249.5	60	14,970	24.49	599.76	35 985.61
260 – 279	269.5	8	2,156	44.49	1,979.36	15 834.88
280 – 299	289.5	6	1,737	64.49	4,158.96	24 953.76
		294	**66 153**			**148 473.47**

$$\text{Mean} = \mu = \frac{66,153}{294} = \$225.01$$

$$\text{Standard deviation} = \sqrt{\frac{\sum |x - \bar{x}|^2}{n}} = \sqrt{\frac{148,473}{294}} = \$22.47$$

$$\text{Median} = L_{me} + \frac{\frac{\sum f}{2} - C}{f(me)} \times \text{class interval} = 220 + \frac{147 - 120}{100} \times 20 = \$225.40$$

$$\text{Mode} = L_{mo} + \frac{d_1}{d_1 + d_2} \times \text{class interval} = 220 + \frac{100 - 80}{(100 - 80) + (100 - 60)} \times 20$$

$$= 220 + \frac{20}{20 + 40} \times 20 = \$226.67$$

$$\text{Coefficient of Skewness} = \frac{3(\text{Mean} - \text{Median})}{\text{Standard deviation}} = \frac{3(225.01 - 225.40)}{22.47} = \frac{-1.17}{22.47} = -0.052$$

324

1. The weights of 40 male students (rounded to the nearest kilogram) is given below. Construct a frequency distribution using six classes: 54 – 58, 59 – 63, etc.

$$63, 75, 68, 60, 65, 57, 68, 72$$
$$66, 72, 64, 67, 62, 67, 69, 65$$
$$76, 57, 63, 80, 74, 54, 70, 75$$
$$66, 79, 65, 67, 66, 70, 64, 61$$
$$73, 66, 61, 65, 68, 71, 66, 58$$

2. Using the following data relating to rainfall in a number of centres during a given period, prepare a histogram and then a frequency polygon by joining the midpoints of the tops of the rectangles.

Rainfall (cm)	Number of centres
26 – 50	5
51 – 75	26
76 – 100	10
101 – 125	9
126 – 150	8
151 – 175	3
176 – 200	1
201 – 225	0

3. Arrange the following (population) numbers in a frequency distribution and then calculate:
   (a) Mean
   (b) Standard deviation
   (c) Coefficient of variation

$$9, 5, 8, 9, 10, 4, 6, 4, 7, 9, 8, 5, 7, 3, 5, 3, 8, 9, 4, 3, 8, 5, 10, 3$$

4.(a) Calculate the interquartile range and quartile deviation of the following set of data:

$$39, 32, 34, 30, 45, 48, 38, 50, 62, 39 \ 59, 52$$

(b) Illustrate the data using a boxplot.

5. Calculate the variance and standard deviation of the following data assuming that the data is:
   (a) population data
   (b) sample data

$$575, 577, 578, 579, 581$$

6. Calculate the variance and standard deviation of the following data assuming that it relates to:
   (a) a population
   (b) a sample

$$10, 16, 18, 20, 22, 24$$

7. Arrange the population figures given below in a frequency distribution and then calculate:
   (a) The mean
   (b) The standard deviation
   (c) The coefficient of variation

$$8, 3, 6, 9, 11, 3, 5, 6, 5, 4, 6, 7$$
$$8, 3, 5, 6, 11, 2, 2, 3, 4, 7, 8, 9$$

8. The table below shows the distribution of the scores obtained by 200 students in an examination:

Score	Number of students
76 – 80	2
71 – 75	5
66 – 70	9
61 – 65	19
56 – 60	32
51 – 55	55
46 – 50	38
41 – 45	21
36 – 40	10
31 – 35	6
26 – 30	3

Construct a "less than" Ogive and use it to estimate:

(a) the median score

(b) the interquartile range

(c) the number of students scoring more than 42

(d) the 60th percentile

(e) the percentile corresponding to a score of 60

ANSWERS TO PRACTICE SET 12

1. <u>Frequency Distribution Table</u>

Class	Tally	Frequency
54 – 58	IIII	4
59 – 63	IIIII I	6
64 – 68	IIIII IIIII IIIII II	17
69 – 73	IIIII II	7
74 – 78	IIII	4
79 – 83	II	2

2. <u>Histogram and frequency polygon</u>

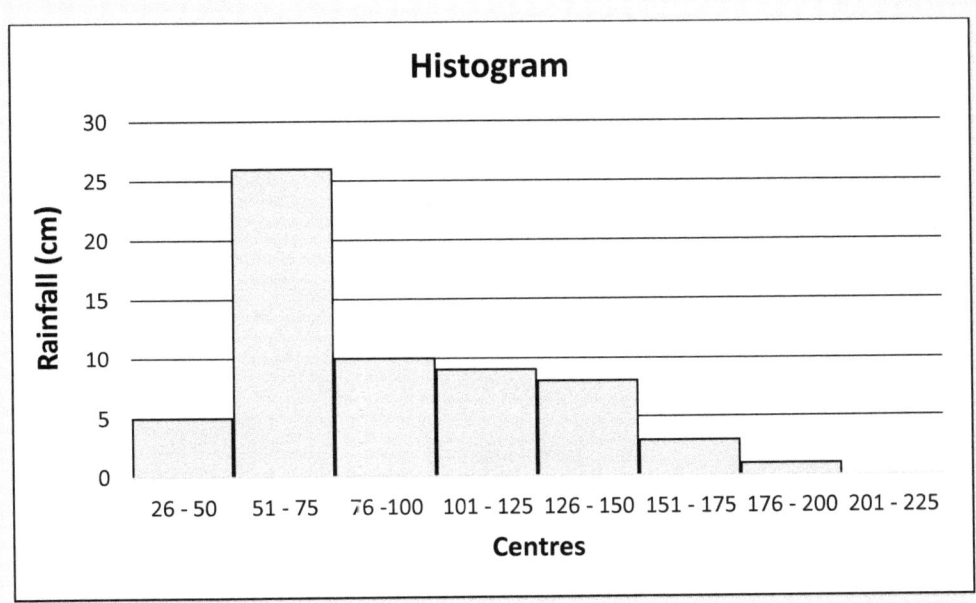

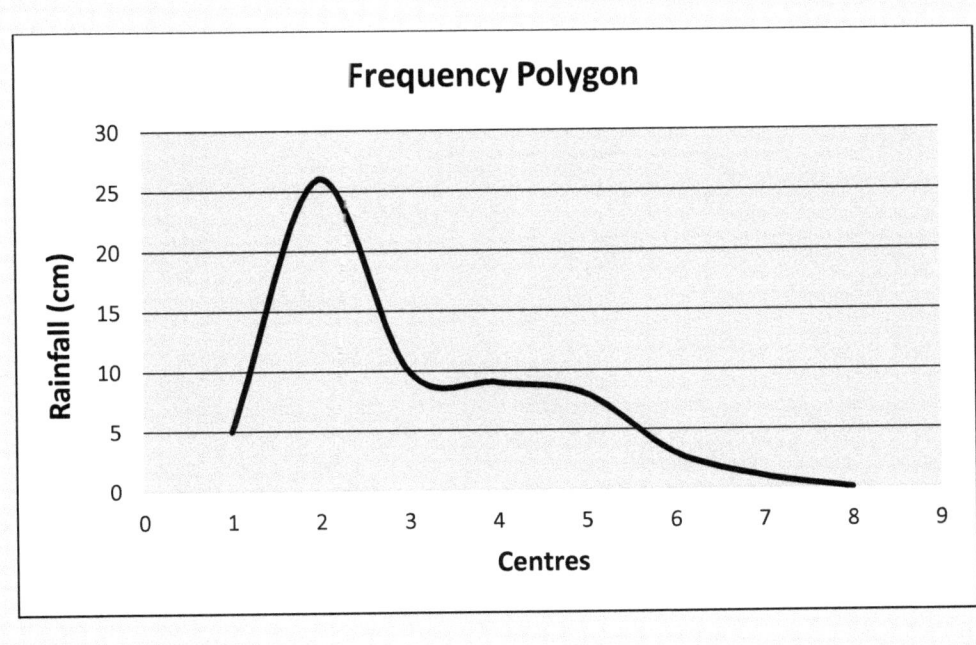

3.   9, 5, 8, 9, 10, 4, 6, 4, 7, 9, 8, 5, 7, 3, 5, 3, 8, 9, 4, 3, 8, 5, 10, 3

x	f	fx	$x - \mu$	$(x - \mu)^2$	$f(x - \mu)^2$
3	4	12	-3.33	11.09	44.36
4	3	12	-2.33	5.42	16.26
5	4	20	-1.33	1.77	7.08
6	1	6	-0.33	0.11	0.11
7	2	14	0.67	0.45	0.9
8	4	32	1.67	2.79	11.16
9	4	36	2.67	7.13	28.52
10	2	20	3.67	13.47	26.94
	24	**152**			**135.33**

Mean $= \mu = \dfrac{152}{24} = 6.33$

Standard deviation $= \sqrt{\dfrac{135.33}{24}} = 2.38$

Coefficient of variation $= \dfrac{2.38}{6.33} \times 100 = 37.6\%$

4.(a)   39, 32, 34, 30, 45, 48, 38, 50, 62, 39, 59, 52

Arranging the numbers in an ascending order:

   30, 32, 34, 38, 39, 39, 45, 48, 50, 52, 59, 62

Lower Quartile $= \dfrac{(n + 1)\text{th}}{4}$ item $= 3\dfrac{1}{4}\text{th}$ item $= 35$

Upper Quartile $= \dfrac{3(n + 1)\text{th}}{4}$ item $= 9\dfrac{1}{4}\text{th}$ item $= 51.5$

Interquartile range = Upper Quartile – Lower Quartile = 16.5

Quartile deviation = Semi-interquartile range $= \dfrac{\text{Upper Quartile – Lower Quartile}}{2}$

(b)   **Boxplot**

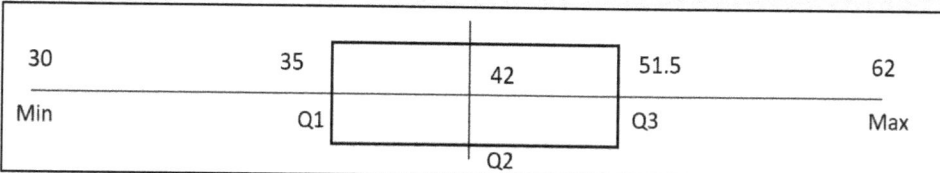

30	35	42	51.5	62
Min	Q1	Q2	Q3	Max

5.   575, 577, 578, 579, 581

Subtract the lowest number 575 from each of the numbers and get:

0, 2, 3, 4, 6   Shortcut

Population Mean $= \mu = \dfrac{15}{5} = 3$

Population Variance $= \sigma^2 = \dfrac{\Sigma(x-\mu)^2}{n} = \dfrac{20}{5} = 4$

Population Standard Deviation $= \sqrt{4} = 2$

Sample Mean $= x = \dfrac{15}{5} = 3$

Sample Variance $= S^2 = \dfrac{\Sigma(x-\bar{x})^2}{n-1} = \dfrac{20}{4} = 5$

Sample Standard Deviation $= \sqrt{5} = 2.24$

x	$x-\mu$	$(x-\mu)^2$
0	-3	9
2	-1	1
3	0	0
4	1	1
6	3	9
15		**20**

6.   10, 14, 18, 20, 22, 24

Population Mean $= \mu = \dfrac{108}{6} = 18$

Population Variance $= \sigma^2 = \dfrac{\Sigma(x-\mu)^2}{n} = \dfrac{136}{6} = 22.67$

Population Standard Deviation $= \sqrt{22.67} = 4.76$

Sample Mean $= x = \dfrac{108}{6} = 3$

Sample Variance $= S^2 = \dfrac{\Sigma(x-\bar{x})^2}{n-1} = \dfrac{136}{5} = 27.2$

Sample Standard Deviation $= \sqrt{27.2} = 5.22$

x	$x-\mu$	$(x-\mu)^2$
10	-8	64
14	-4	16
18	0	0
20	2	4
22	4	16
24	6	36
108		**136**

7.   8, 3, 6, 9, 11, 3, 5, 6, 5, 4, 6, 7, 8, 3, 5, 6, 11, 2, 2, 3, 4, 7, 8, 9

x	f	fx	$x-\mu$	$(x-\mu)^2$	$f(x-\mu)^2$
2	2	4	-3.875	15.015	30.03
3	4	12	-2.875	8.266	33.06
4	2	8	-1.875	3.516	7.03
5	3	15	-0.875	0.766	2.30
6	4	24	0.125	0.016	0.06
7	2	14	1.125	1.266	2.53
8	3	24	2.125	4.516	13.55
9	2	18	3.125	9.766	19.53
11	2	22	4.125	17.015	34.03
	24	**141**			**142.13**

7.(Continued)

(a) Mean = 5.875

(b) Standard deviation = $\sqrt{\dfrac{142.13}{24}}$ = 2.43

(c) Coefficient of variation = $\dfrac{2.43}{5.875}$ × 100 = 41.4%

8.

Score	Number of students	Cumulative frequency	Frequency more than lower limit	Frequency less than lower limit
76 – 80	2	200	2	198
71 – 75	5	198	7	193
66 – 70	9	193	16	184
61 – 65	19	184	35	165
56 – 60	32	165	67	133
51 – 55	55	133	122	78
46 – 50	38	78	160	40
41 – 45	21	40	181	19
36 – 40	10	19	191	9
31 – 35	6	9	197	3
26 – 30	3	3	200	0

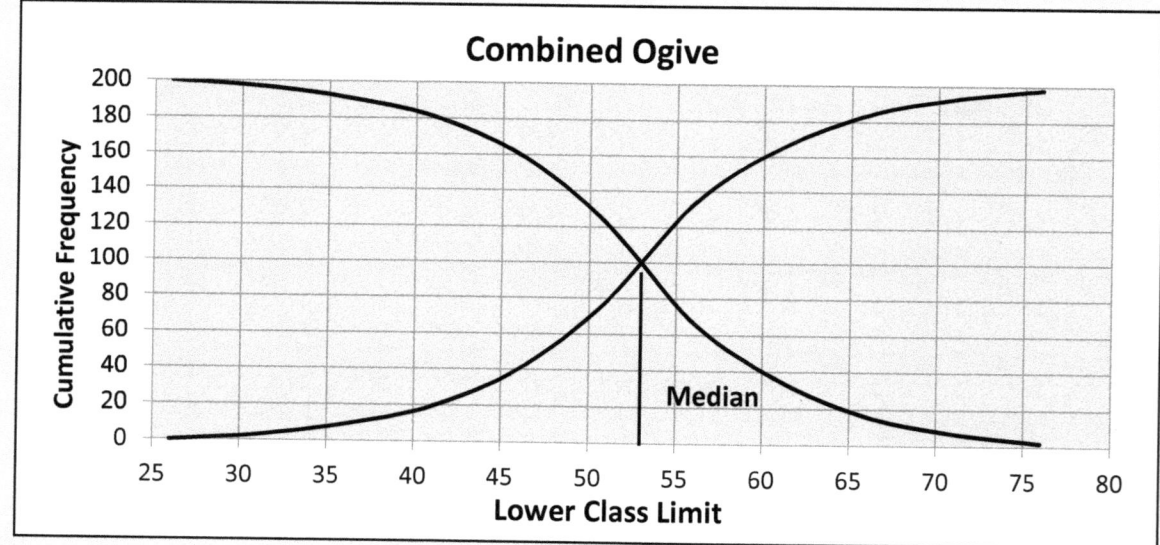

(a) Median score = $L_{me} + \dfrac{\frac{\Sigma f}{2} - C}{f(me)}$ × class interval = $51 + \dfrac{100 - 78}{55}$ × 5 = 53

(b) Interquartile range = Q3 – Q1 = (75th percentile – 25th percentile) = 10

(c) Number of students scoring more than 42 = 177

(d) 60th percentile = 47

(e) Percentile corresponding to the score 60 = 20

Note: Percentile shows the value below which a given percentage of observations falls.

www.ingramcontent.com/pod-product-compliance
Lightning Source LLC
Chambersburg PA
CBHW041508120626
46551CB00018B/2347